ANCIENT ISRAEL

VOLUME ONE

LILITH AND THE ANGELS
From an original painting by F. H. Amshewitz, R.B.A.

Page 78

Frontispiece, Vol. I

ANCIENT ISRAEL

VOLUME ONE

ANGELO S. RAPPOPORT

SENATE

Ancient Israel Volume One

Previously published by
The Gresham Publishing Company, London

This edition published in 1995 by Senate, an imprint of
Studio Editions Ltd, Princess House, 50 Eastcastle Street,
London W1N 7AP, England

ISBN 1 85958 170 6

Printed and bound in Guernsey by
The Guernsey Press Co. Ltd

FOREWORD

To the average person myth and legend are things from the distant past, a time when people still believed that day and night were the result of the sun being pulled across the sky by a chariot, that if you sailed too close to the edge of the world you might fall off into the jaws of hungry serpents, and that with the help of the philosopher's stone it was possible to turn lead into gold.

Yet whether or not we wish to acknowledge them, myths and legends still abound today. Maybe not in the classical form of gods who pull the strings of the universe—although the Allah of the Moslem religion or the figurehead of Buddhism are myths to worshipers of the Judeo-Christian God, and vice versa—but certainly in the stereotypes, beliefs, and apocryphal wisdom to which all societies cling that set them apart from other cultures and give them identity within the history of their people.

The impulse to create myths has never been extinguished and no doubt never will be. Dictionaries tell us that a myth is a historical story that embodies a cultural or world view, and that a legend is a more secular expression of a myth, a historical tale that cannot be substantiated. But these definitions fail to emphasize that both are a natural expression of the human need to put the unknowable or inexplicable into some kind of easily recognizable order. To the Greeks and Romans, that might have meant anthropomorphizing the unpredictability of natural disasters by endowing these events with the same personalities they saw bringing about the orderly and regular change of seasons. From our twentieth-century perspective, that may seem like a rather primitive way of looking at the natural world. Yet in modern science, nuclear physicists are postulating the existence of sub-atomic particles that defy all natural laws as we know them, that are unobservable, and yet must be present from the effect they appear to have on observable phenomena. Who is to say that centuries from now, this will seem any less absurd than a religious culture that attributed the coming of winter to Persephone's unwilling return to the underworld? The history of knowledge is the history of discarded myths.

The myths and legends of a particular culture usually provide more of an insight into that culture than standard history texts. They express matters larger than everyday life—what a society most fears, most reveres, most hopes for and most wants to believe—but which significantly affect everyday life. The myths and legends of ancient Israel are no exception. The Hebrew culture, whose identity is more bound up with its religion (a sort of intermediary between myth and history) than most, is an example. Reading the numerous legends and variants that Angelo S. Rappoport has gathered in *Ancient Israel: Myths and Legends*, one cannot help but ask questions about the people that produced them. What kind of authority did they seek in a divinity who would smite cedars for their pride and make them weep? Presumably the same unquestionable kind of authority which God would later use to discipline man for the same offense. Who can leave the heroic treatments of David, Moses, and Isaac without coming to the conclusion that these men were role models for their culture.

Rappoport reminds us that the myths and legends of ancient Israel were always concerned with the manifestation of divine will and that they had a moral purpose. That these allegories had a didactic function is undeniable, but it should also be kept in mind that, even in their "un-reality," they are admirably practical. When one wants to know why something is, and how it came to be that way, one has only to turn to myth to find the shortest distance

between the two points. To note that after the divine will created
the earth—but before it created man—it "called into being the
Divine Throne, the Holy Law, Repentance, Paradise, Hell, the
Holy Temple, and the name of the Messiah; in a word, all the
conditions which represent Divine Providence, Law and Order,
Good Deeds, Reward and Punishment, Prayer and Redemption,"
is to learn that man came into a world of predetermined rules that
were subject neither to interpretation nor abrogation. Why must
man follow these rules? Because they were ordained before his
creation. In a world where the black and white of moral and
ethical values constantly threatens to turn gray, myth provides a
spiritual compass with which the individual can always find true
north.

A serious discussion of a society's myths risks giving them
more weight than even their creators would. No group fashions its
culture from myths; rather, myth, like any other art, is an artifact
of the culture. (It should be remembered that myths and legends
spring from the same oral tradition that eventually gave rise to
literature.) Readers should come to *Ancient Israel: Myths and
Legends* to find out something more about the ancient Hebrew
culture than he already knows, perhaps by comparing its myths
with the myths of his own nationality, or balancing different
myths that have arisen over the same theme within the Hebrew
culture. That these stories sometimes clash with each other in no
way diminishes their value. Myths are not right or wrong. They
simply are there, because mankind needs them and has the imagination to create them.

—Richard Michaels

Contents

CONTENTS

CONTENTS

CONTENTS

Plates

VOLUME ONE

xiii

PREFACE

The times when the myths and legends, fables and parables contained in Jewish post-Biblical literature, in the *Talmud* and in the *Midrashim*, were taken literally and quoted for the purpose of throwing ridicule upon the people of Israel are behind us. The science of folk-lore now looks upon myths and legends as congenial products of the popular mind and of the soul of the people. Such products Jewish mythical and legendary lore may claim to be. All myths and legends owe their origin and existence to the conceptions of the people and their traditions. They are manifesting the characteristics of each race, mirroring its soul, its dreams and hopes, its joys and sorrows.

Jewish myths and legends are therefore of interest to us because they reveal the soul of a people, of a peculiar people. All through Jewish myth and legend there is an echo of sadness, but also of hope. The present may be gloomy, but the Lord never forsakes those who put their trust in Him. Jewish myths and legends also possess a particular attraction for us, be we Christians or Jews, because they all centre round Biblical personages and the episodes related in the Bible, which is the book *par excellence*, and which for centuries has exercised a cultural influence upon humanity. They cluster round personages with whom we have been familiar since our earliest childhood.

In Western modern prose and poetry Biblical personages are usually depicted and represented in such a way as to convey

to us a wrong impression. They often strike us as caricatures,
so strange as to offend our religious and æsthetic feelings.
Such is not the case in the legendary lore of the Hebrews,
which is an eastern product. Here the personages with whom
we are familiar are painted in their original and natural colours.
However much they may be surrounded by imaginary descriptions, it is always done in a Biblical spirit, in a spirit congenial
to that of the Testament. Monologues and dialogues taking
place in heaven or upon earth, angels descending at the express
command of God and taking part in the actions of men, do not
at all shock us. The Rabbis and mythographers of Judaism
gave a full expression to the beliefs and traditions of the people,
to the floating myths and legends, but they invested this
legendary lore with a beautiful symbolism.[1] They made use
of this branch of post-Biblical lore as a means of expression
for speculative thought and profound spiritual teaching.

A study of Jewish myth and legend is almost necessary if
one wishes to understand and appreciate the ethical background of Jewish life and literature, of the people who were
the first to fuse life, literature, economics, and politics into one
with ethics and religion (as has been done by the Prophets
and continued by the gentle Rabbi of Nazareth). More than
any other branch of Jewish literature, perhaps, the legendary
lore shows us the outlook of the Jews upon life and the world.
In order, however, to appreciate these myths and legends, fables,
tales, and parables, at their full value, the reader should bear
in mind the social surroundings under which they developed.
He should read these myths and legends without European
prejudices, and not look at them with European eyes.

> " Wer den Dichter will verstehen,
>   Muss in des Dichters Lande gehen,"

says Heine.

---

[1] That dealer in curiosities, Isaac D'Israeli, entirely misunderstood the symbolism of
Jewish legendary lore (see *Curiosities of Literature*, 1835, Vol. I, pp. 100–5).

The myths and legends of Israel deal with the creation of the world, the mysteries of creation, angels and demons, Paradise and Hell, with the creation of Man, with Patriarchs, Prophets, and Priests, with kings and popular heroes. Their origin lies not so much in a desire to invent as in that of explaining Holy Writ and human destiny. Long after the Biblical canon had been closed and Israel had left its national soil, the Jews continued to weave legends round Biblical personages and Biblical episodes, and this poetic activity extended over ten centuries. Its tendency was to supplement by phantasy, imagination, legend, and exposition, what appeared incomprehensible in Holy Scripture. In our opinion Jewish myths and legends are *not* the " first and primitive material out of which evolved and developed the Bible ". We are not looking for myth and legend in the Bible.

We deal in the Introduction with the influence which India, Egypt, Babylonia, and Persia have exercised upon Jewish myth and legend, and also with the influence which Jewish legendary lore has, in its turn, exercised upon mediæval folk-lore. Throughout this volume (and the following) we have also referred to Mohammedan tradition, and the reader is offered a survey of the legends of Islam clustering round Biblical characters.

This work is intended for the general reader who may have heard of the myths and legends clustering round Biblical characters and episodes, but who has no opportunity of reading them, the sources being inaccessible to him. We hope, however, that even the scholar will peruse these volumes with interest and to some advantage, whilst the Biblical student may find therein points to interest him. We have read almost all the sources available and referred to them in our notes and in the appended bibliography. Not only Hebrew and Aramaic sources, but also Hellenistic have been consulted, and we have made an effort to bring together as many myths and legends

as time and space would permit us. The scattered threads
of all these myths, and especially legends, we have woven
together in such a way as to form a continuous narrative.
We hope, therefore, that our readers will peruse with interest
and enjoyment the myths, legends, and tales contained in the
following chapters.

ANGELO S. RAPPOPORT.

INTRODUCTION

I

The Characteristics of Jewish Myth and Legend

Jewish myths have this in common with the myths of other nations, that they are the offspring of phantasy and imagination, without any basis of reality. All the powers of nature are placed under the control and rule of a higher will. Like the myths of other nations, the myths of Israel, too, are mostly allegories describing the origin and development of some power of nature.

Jewish myths, however, differ considerably in many of their characteristics from the myths of other peoples. The nations of antiquity looked upon the personified powers and manifestations of nature as upon so many independent and self-sufficing beings. For them, nature was a conglomeration of numerous manifestations of wills. Jewish myths differ in this respect, for Jewish thought is based upon the idea of *one* unique will, manifesting itself in the Universe. The invisible rulers of all natural manifestations are therefore the servants and representatives of this one and unique power ruling the Universe.

Another characteristic trait distinguishing Jewish myths from the myths of other nations is the following: The higher beings manifesting themselves in corporeal shape and form, and who, in the mythologies of other nations, take an interest and a part in human actions, do so *without any moral purpose*. Jewish myths, on the contrary, are always based upon a moral and ethical idea. The Most High, the Supreme Ruler of the Universe, is the source of moral perfection and the moral being *par excellence*, His sole aim and constant desire being the happiness, prosperity, and welfare of His creatures. He vouchsafes unto men as unto all the creatures His benevolence and mercy. Only when the latter abandon the right path and act contrary to morality, does He wax wroth with them, often punishing them severely. His punishment, however, is not the result of revenge, but serves a moral purpose, for His punishment and His chastisements are intended to make the sinners repent, turn back, and mend their ways. He is thus once more acting in accordance with the principles of morality. And just as the Supreme Being, the Most High, so all His representatives, the superior beings who serve to execute His commands, are highly moral beings, their slightest transgressions being punished severely. In the mythologies of other nations myth and religion are closely interwoven. Among the Greeks, for instance, the numerous gods and semigods, and even the heroes, had their separate cults and enjoyed divine worship and honour. Not so among the Jews. Myth among the Jews is only in so far related to religion as it endeavours to proclaim and to lay stress upon the omnipotence of the Creator, one and unique, and to glorify the Lord of the Universe, all His representatives serving to increase His power. They enjoy no divine worship whatever, they themselves, on the contrary, being engaged in proclaiming the power and majesty of the One God, glorifying His name and singing hymns in His praise.

A further characteristic trait which distinguishes Jewish myths from the myths of other nations concerns the plastic arts. Among the nations of antiquity, and particularly among the Greeks, myths were from the very beginning closely related to and interwoven with the plastic arts. Every product of imagination and phantasy, however grotesque and bizarre, was made manifest to the people and was impressed upon their minds by an artistic representation in colour and line, painted on canvas or carved in marble and stone. Wherever the eye turned, in temples, upon public places, and in private houses, it met the artistic representation of some national myth which thus impressed itself upon the mind of the nation and became part of the national spirit.

Not so among the Jews. The Mosaic Code rigorously forbids the plastic imitation of all natural phenomena and of the manifestations of the powers of nature. Myths, therefore, could not for long take root in the popular mind of the Jews, and only remained the patrimony of the cultured and educated, of the scribes, the scholars and teachers. According to their own conceptions and philosophies, their *Weltanschauungen* and the schools of thought to which they belonged, these learned men extended and elaborated the myths, but always with a view to ethical teachings and moral lessons to be drawn from the respective myths. Thus Jewish myth does not always remain in a sphere accessible to the uncultured mind, but lives and moves and has its being on the Pisgah heights of thought which are only attained by a developed intellectuality. From the domain of popular imagination Jewish myth has, therefore, for the most part, passed into the realm of metaphysics.

Jewish myths may be lacking the attractiveness and *joie de vivre* of Greece, but they are distinguished by their innate moral basis.

The majority of Jewish myths and legends came into existence towards the end of the Jewish national life, and bear the traces of Persian or Græco-Roman influence. But everywhere these influences were adapted to Jewish monotheistic conceptions and were modified accordingly. Persian dualism, the struggle between Ormuzd and Ahriman, did not suit Jewish monotheism, and the principle of evil and darkness was imagined not as an equal power with the principle of good, and as an independent creator, but as a rebel against his master, as the winged Seraph Sammael, who, as a punishment for his arrogance, was hurled from regions celestial into those of darkness. Jewish myth further shows another characteristic distinguishing it from the myths of Greece. Both sexes, masculine and feminine, are admitted into the heaven of Greece. Both males and females exercise with equal arbitrariness their unlimited powers, benevolent or pernicious, controlling the destinies of man. Gods and goddesses in the Greek Pantheon have their serving spirits representing both sexes. In Jewish myths, on the contrary, the feminine sex is entirely excluded from celestial regions, to which women, in a truly Oriental way, are not admitted. On the other hand, the female beings abound in the realm of darkness. There are no female angels but numerous female demons in Jewish myths, a circumstance due to Oriental influences.

And yet, man and woman are equally admitted into Paradise. Serah, the daughter of Asher, entered Paradise alive, and there were prophetesses in Israel upon whom the Divine Spirit descended.

Jewish myths deal with all parts of the Universe. They extend to heaven and to earth, water and air, angels and demons, Paradise and Hell.

Just as the myths of other nations, the myth of ancient Israel is the graceful, light-winged child of phantasy, the foster-child of the two wonderful twin sisters Religion and Language which, from the very beginning of civilization, have raised savage man from the depths of animal instinct to a higher spiritual level. The ethical purpose of Jewish myths and legends is to explain the course of the Universe and the destinies of man. They endeavour to show that all creatures are guilty and should strive to expiate their guilt. Whilst, however, the mythographers of other nations turned to nature, the Jews turned to the Bible, and the majority of their myths and legends are based upon passages of the Holy Writ, endeavouring to explain them so as to appeal to the people. Jewish myths and legends, therefore, mostly deal with Old Testament history, and with Old Testament characters, and it was in the direction of the Bible that Jewish imagination, the imagination of the mythographers of Judaism, took its flight. These myths and legends were based upon and woven round the Biblical episodes of the Creation of World and Man, of the Garden of Eden, the Creation and Fall of Adam, the Fallen Angels, the stories about the Patriarchs, Prophets, and Priests, of the Kings and Heroes.

It was natural, however, that pagan elements should penetrate into these myths and legends. Round the Biblical stories were woven legends and myths not only about the Only God, but about a host of angels, demons, and spirits who are the mediators between Jehovah and Israel. The Jews are a wandernation, and so is their lore. In the course of their peregrinations the Jews adopted many ideas and conceptions from their neighbours with whom they came into contact. The Jewish lore, which originated in the ruins of Palestine, was carried to and continued in Babylonia and Africa, and the river which issued forth from the Holy Land was later on swelled by the stream of mysticism which discharged its waters upon the intellectual productions of the Jews and fertilized the field of their imagination.

II

Foreign Influence upon Jewish Myth and Legend

Jewish myths and legends, although a product of the national Jewish spirit, are subject to many foreign influences. Palestine was from the beginning a thoroughfare where East and West met and mingled, and, from a political point of view, it was, perhaps, unfortunate that Moses should have chosen a spot where the eastern and western legions were destined constantly to meet. From an intellectual point of view, however, the Promised Land had the advantage of becoming, to a certain extent, the melting-pot of different civilizations and *Weltanschauungen*. Foreign civilizations, Egyptian, Persian, Babylonian, and Indian, have left their traces upon Judaism, and especially upon the Jewish myths and legends which, side by side with the Law, were developed among the nation, handed down from generation to generation, and penetrated into the oral law and its Haggadic portions.

Both the *Talmud* and the *Midrashim* distinctly show traces of foreign influence in their Haggadic portions, i.e. in the myths, legends, tales, and parables. Often these influences are diametrically opposed to the spirit of Judaism, whilst on other occasions they are changed and adapted so as to suit the ethical exigencies of Judaism.

It was especially during the Hellenistic period that foreign myths and legends penetrated into Judaism and gained citizen rights. The Hellenistic Jews, who wrote in Greek, were not eclectic, but thoroughly syncretistic and easily accessible to foreign influences. The description of the death of Adam and of Eve, where angels came to bury them, the description of the death of Moses, where we read that the Creator Himself came to take his soul and that the three ministering angels, Michael, Gabriel, and Zagsagel were present, preparing the Prophet's couch and spreading out a sheet of fine linen, are reminiscent of Egyptian mythology. Amsath, Huphy, Daumatuf, and Quabah Sanuf, the four Egyptian geniuses of death, are supposed to remain near the soulless body, and separate gods watch over every limb.[1] Egyptian and Phœnician myths and legends of gods and heroes are introduced into Jewish popular lore. They are changed, altered, and adapted, so as to suit the spirit of monotheism, but never can they deny their foreign origin. Myths and legends relating to the mysteries of creation, of life and death, to the birth of the child, to the cradle and the death-bed, to the domains of theogony and apotheosis, enter *en masse* from Egypt, Phœnicia, and Greece, and later on from Babylonia, Persia, and India, and are re-echoed in Talmud and Midrash. Thus, in the pages of this volume, we have told many legends relating to the angels, the creation of the world, the death of Adam and Abraham, and generally the angel of death.

From the Jews this conception of the four angels being present at the death of man was taken over by Christianity and gnosticism.

The legends relating to Eve often remind us of the Egyptian goddess Isis, those relating to Adam of Yima or Yemshid, whilst the legends about Joseph (as related in the second volume of this work) distinctly resemble those of Osiris and the Egyptian myths about this divinity. The death of Joseph and the finding of his coffin by Moses, as related in Jewish legend, bear a striking resemblance to the myth about Osiris. Typhon, we read in Plutarch,[2] had once, by a ruse, prevailed upon his brother Osiris to lie down in a box. Thereupon Typhon closed the box, nailed it up, poured molten lead over

---

[1] See Güdemann, in *Monatsschrift*, Vol. XXV, p. 227.
[2] Plutarch, *De Is. et Os.*, 22, 13.

it, and threw it into the Nile. Isis, informed of this deed, wandered about, searching for the body of her son. She was at last informed by children, to whom the gift of prophecy had been vouchsafed, in which direction the coffin had been carried away by the waters of the Nile. She found the coffin and buried it. It is Isis in Egyptian mythology who finds the coffin, whilst it is Serah in the Jewish legend. Güdemann[1] rightly remarks that the name of Serah's father, Asser or Asher, may have some connection with the Egyptian name of Osiris, which is Assar. It has also been pointed out that the legends relating to Crœsus and his wealth had penetrated into the Talmud, where they centre round the name of Eliezer ben Charsum, who was immensely wealthy, and on the day of whose death Belshazzar was born.[2]

Of the Greek legend of Ariadne and her thread, we are reminded by a legend in *Midrash Shir-Hashirim*[3] and in *Midrash Koheleth*.[4] There was once a vast palace with numerous entrance doors, and whoever entered the palace lost his way therein. A wise man, one day, fastened a reel of reed at the entrance, and the people were thus able to find their way in the labyrinth without losing themselves. That the *Haggadah*, which contains the essential parts of Jewish myths and legends, has borrowed from Hellenism, is undeniable, although it is not always easy to trace the sources. The story of the bed of Procrustes is found in *Sanhedrin*,[5] where it is told of the Sodomites.

Not only Greece, Egypt, and Phœnicia, but Persia, Babylonia, and even distant India exercised their influence upon the myths and legends of Israel as they have come down to us in Talmud and Midrash. The Indian work *Pantshatantra*, which was destined to be translated during the later Middle Ages by a Jew, was, no doubt, known to the Rabbis of the

---

[1] *Monatsschrift*, Vol. XXV. p. 231.
[2] *Yoma*, 9a; 35b; *Midrash Koheleth*, 4 8; see also Perles, in *Monatsschrift*, Vol. XXI. pp. 268-70.   [3] I. 1.   [4] 2, 12.   [5] 109b.

Talmud and the Haggadists of the Midrash. The story of Nahum Ish Gimso [1] reminds us of an Indian story in the *Pantshatantra*.[2]

The legend about the creation of Eve which explains the reasons why woman was created from the rib of man is explained as follows in the Midrash. Eve was not created from the head of Adam, lest she should be vain, nor from his eyes, lest she should be wanton, nor from his mouth, lest she should be given to gossiping, nor from his ears, lest she should be an eavesdropper, nor from his hands, lest she should be meddlesome, nor from his feet, lest she should be a gadabout, nor from his heart, lest she should be jealous. She was drawn from man's rib, which is a hidden part, so that she might be modest and retiring. And yet, notwithstanding all the precautions taken by the Creator, woman has all the faults God wished to guard her against.[3]

This passage finds a parallel in the following Indian legend:

When the Creator had made up His mind to fashion woman, He suddenly noticed that the matter at His disposal had already been entirely used up in the creation of Adam. What did He do? He took the undulations of the serpent, the clinging faculty of the creepers, the trembling of the blade of grass, the erect stature of the reed, the velvet of the flower, the lightness of the leaf, the look of the gazelle, the cheerfulness of the sun-ray, the tears of the clouds, the inconstancy of the wind, the softness of down, the sweetness of honey, the cruelty of the tiger, the burning heat of fire, the freezing effect of ice, and the chattering of the magpie, mixed all these elements together and created woman.[4]

The legends and myths about Adam, as contained in Jewish sources, in Talmud and Midrash, also bear traces of Persian influence. The influence of Parsism, if not upon

---

[1] *Taanit*, 21a.   [2] Th. Benfey, *Pantshatantra*, I, 129.   [3] *Genesis Rabba*, 18.
[4] Cf. August Wunsche, in *Wissenschaftliche Beilage der Leipziger Zeitung*, 1905, No. 67; see also Daehnhardt, *Natursagen*, Vol. I, p. 123, note.

the Bible, as some scholars pretend,[1] is paramount when we come to Jewish myths as contained in the Midrashim and the Haggadic portions of the Talmud. The majority of legends relating to Adam which we have told in the pages of this book bear a striking resemblance to the stories of Yima or Yemshid and of Meshia, although, of course, it is difficult to draw the line and to prove to what an extent the Jews influenced their Persian neighbours, and to what an extent they were influenced by the latter.

Jewish demonology has also been influenced by the Persians, although some scholars are of opinion that it is un-wise to draw hasty comparisons between Jewish and Persian demonology.[2] It must, however, be admitted that the Adam legends and those of Yima and Meshia have much in common. The reader will find many of the legends of Adam from Talmud and Midrash quoted in the following pages.

Jewish mythographers drew largely and borrowed from their Persian neighbours not only because the latter were already a highly civilized nation, but also because the Persians were opposed to the image cult. Persian was also the vernacular of the Jews dwelling in the country, as we are informed in the Talmud.[3] In the *Vendidad* we read that Yima is called the Brilliant One, because (as explained by a commentator) light emanated from him. He was destined to live eternally, but, in consequence of his sin, he was condemned to death. Like Adam, who fasted 130 years and kept away from Eve,[4] Yima, too, after his fault, repented.[5]

Of Indian origin may be the story of King Solomon and Asmodeus who usurped the King's place, whilst the King was wandering about in distant lands, begging from door to door. The legend was taken over by the Mohammedans and brought to

---

[1] Erik Stave, *Ueber den Einfluss des Parsismus auf das Judentum*, Haarlem, 1898.
[2] See *Revue des Etudes Juives*, Vol. VIII, p. 202.
[3] *Sotah*, 49b.   [4] *Erubin*, 18b.
[5] Kohut, in *Z.D.M.G.*, Vol. XXV, pp. 59-94.

Europe, where it appeared at first in the *Gesta Romanorum*, and was told of the Emperor Jovinianus.[1]

Of Indian origin may also be the legend of Abraham and Nimrod. Terah, the father of Abraham, had handed over his son to the terrible Nimrod that he might punish him for his iconoclasm.

" If," said Nimrod, " thou wilt not worship the God of thy father, then worship at least fire."

" Why," said Abraham, " should we worship fire rather than water? Is not water stronger than fire which it has the power to quench?"

" Well then," replied Nimrod, " prostrate thyself before water and worship it."

" Clouds," said Abraham, " are greater than water, for they contain in themselves this element."

" Well then, adore the clouds," said Nimrod.

" The wind," again said Abraham, " is more powerful than the clouds, for it disperses them. Why should we not worship the wind?"

" Then, worship the wind," replied Nimrod, growing impatient.

" Man," said Abraham imperturbably, " is even stronger than wind, for he can fight against it. Why should we not worship man?"

Nimrod's patience was now at an end, and he gave orders that Abraham be thrown into the fiery furnace.[2]

Jewish legend also relates that when the Egyptians were about to seize the new-born Jewish babes with the intention of killing them, the earth opened her mouth and swallowed them up, thus protecting them until they had grown up, when

[1] See, however, against Varnhagen, *Ein indisches Märchen auf seiner Wanderung*, Berlin, 1882, the refutation in *Revue des Etudes Juives*, Vol. XVII, pp. 58–65.

[2] See *Genesis Rabba*, 38; Benfey, *loc. cit.*, 376–7; see also Koehler, *Germania*, Vol. II, pp. 481–5, where several mediæval fables containing the same idea are mentioned; see also A. C. M. Robert, *Fables Inédites*, Paris, 1825, Vol. I, p. ccxvii, and compare the fable by La Fontaine, *La Souris métamorphosée en Fille*.

they returned to their respective homes.[1] In the same tractate of the Talmud it is also related that when Moses was born, the house was filled with light, and parallels to this legend are found not only in the life of Buddha, who cast a light upon his surroundings when he was still in his mother's womb,[2] but also in those of Aesculapius and Servius Tullius. It is further related[3] that, when the Israelites had passed the Red Sea, the sucklings began to sing hymns in praise of the Lord. The Indian Prithu, Buddha, the Greek Apollo, all spoke immediately after their birth, whilst Bacchus sang in his mother's womb.[4]

III

Jewish Influence upon Mediæval Folk-lore

If Jewish myths and legends bear the traces of Egyptian, Indian, Persian, Babylonian, or Greek influence, Jewish legendary lore has, on the other hand, penetrated into European literature and affected the fables, parables, and heroic tales of other nations. To a great extent the folk-literature of the Middle Ages owes its dissemination to the Jews. They carried the precious merchandise from East to West and back again from West to East. The Jews have ever been famous as commercial travellers, but they have not always limited their sphere of action to material goods. They have also hawked about the intellectual and poetical wares and products of humanity: Religion, Philosophy, Poetry, and Folk-lore. St. Paul may be said to have been the first and most famous traveller of this kind. He introduced to the Aryan world the best products of Judea: The Prophets and Christianity. Medi-

---

[1] *Sotah*, 12b.
[2] P. Toldo in *Studien zur vergleichenden Litteraturgeschichte*, 1901, p. 339.
[3] *Sotah*, 30b.   [4] Toldo, *loc. cit.*, p. 340.

ators of the spiritual and intellectual life of distant lands and of a remote past, the Jews brought to Europe intellectual treasures and enriched mediæval literature with the wealth of an apocryphal and legendary lore. Hellenistic and Roman, French and German, Italian, or English culture has affected the Jews, but they, too, have influenced the peoples among whom it has been their destiny to dwell. Although not all popular tales, myths, or legends mentioned also in Jewish sources can be directly attributed to the Jews—for they may have been derived from third and earlier sources—a good many myths, legends, tales, and fables were brought to Europe by the Jews and found citizen rights in European literature. It would, for instance, be going too far to ascribe all beast-fables to the Talmud, for a good many of them may owe their origin to India and Egypt, but there is no doubt that they were brought to Europe by the Jews. It is, however, no exaggeration to say that most myths and legends about Creation and the Old Testament characters found in mediæval and modern literature may directly be traced to the Talmud and the Midrashim. The Jews transmitted these legends and tales to their neighbours. During the Middle Ages they were, perhaps, the best translators;[1] they took up the spade and dug the gold from the rich mines, bringing it speedily into circulation. Through their translations they acquainted Europe with the mythical and legendary lore of the East. Three converted Jews produced the most favourite popular works during the Middle Ages. They were: Petrus Alphonsus, author of the *Disciplina Clericalis*; John of Capua, who translated into Latin *Kalila and Dimna*, or the *Fables of Bidpai*, from the Hebrew of a certain Rabbi Joel;[2] and finally Pauli, author of *Schimpf and Ernst*. We must further mention the *Mishle Sendebar*, and Ibn Chisdai's *Prince and Dervish* (*Barlaam and Josaphat*). The latter work was not translated from Hebrew into any

---

[1] See M. Steinschneider, *Die Hebräischen Uebersetzungen des Mittelalters und die Juden als Dolmetscher*, 2 Vols., Berlin, 1893.

[2] See M. Gaster, in *Monatsschrift*, 1880, p. 36.

other language till the end of last century, but it may still have influenced European literature.

Jewish influence upon Christianity and Christian legends has been admitted by many Christian scholars.[1]   Several legends contained in the little book *Hibbur Yafeh*, written by Rabbi Nissim,[2] have evidently been translated or utilized by Rudolf von Ems (*Der gute Gerhard*).[3]   The legends about Adam, Joseph, and Moses in Christian sources may be traced to Jewish influences.

Unfortunately, many tales of which no trace is to be found in either Talmud or Midrash are attributed to the Jews, the Talmud being given as their source.   During the sixteenth century, when Reuchlin and Pfefferkorn waged their famous war for and against the Talmud, many pamphlets appeared wherein, as is usually the case, passages from the Talmud were consciously and purposely represented in an unfavourable light.   Comparative mythology was yet unknown in those days, and what now appears merely an allegory or a legend was taken literally.

Thus it is interesting to notice that, in a poem dating from the year 1557, Hans Sachs[4] relates the following story.

The Creator had taken a rib from Adam, intending to shape woman out of it.   He put it aside and was busy removing the blood from His hands, when a dog, passing by, caught up the rib and ran off with it.   An angel caught the dog by his tail and tore it off.   Out of the dog's tail the Lord made woman, long-haired, and beautiful of figure.   Woman possesses now two qualities which are due to her dog-tail origin.   Like the dog, who wags his tail when he is anxious to get something, woman flatters and caresses man when she wishes to get something

---

[1] H. Gunter, *Die christliche Legende des Abendlandes*, Heidelberg, 1910.
[2] See Zunz, *Gottesdienstliche Vorträge*, p. 133.
[3] See Gaster, *Germania*, Vol. XXV, pp. 274–84.
[4] *Fabeln und Schwänke*, ed. Gotze, I, 522, No. 182; see also Daehnhardt, *loc. cit.*, pp. 19–20.   Of Jewish origin are also the two poems by Hans Sachs, *The Monk with the Capon*, and *The Gold in the Stick of Cydias* (Cf., however, *Zeitschrift für vergl. Litteraturgesch.*, Vol. XI, pp. 38–59).

out of him. She barks like a dog when she does not get her will. Now this legend is found in the folk-lore of the Bulgarians, Hungarians, Lettonians, Ukrainians, &c.[1] Hans Sachs, however, attributed this story to the Talmud, just as another story in Hermann Schraders' *Bilder-Schmuck der deutschen Sprache* is attributed to the Talmud. There is, of course, nothing of the kind either in the Talmud or in the Midrashim.

A similar error was made by Thomas Moore, who wrote a poem based on the legend that Adam was created with a tail and that out of this tail God made Eve, giving as its origin Rabbinic Lore. It is entitled: *The Rabbinical Origin of Woman*, and was printed in the edition of 1826 on page 467. It runs as follows:

> They tell us that woman was made of a rib
> Just picked from a corner so snug in the side;
> But the Rabbins swear to you that this is a fib,
> And 't was not so at all that the sex was supplied.
>
> And old Adam was fashioned, the first of his kind,
> With a tail like a monkey, full yard and a span,
> And when nature cut off this appendage behind,
> Why, then woman was made of the tail of the man.
>
> If such is the tie between women and men,
> The ninny who weds is a pitiful elf,
> For he takes to his tail, like an idiot, again,
> And makes a most damnable ape of himself.
>
> Yet, if we may judge, as the fashion prevails,
> Every husband remembers the original plan,
> And knowing his wife is no more than his tail,
> Why, he leaves her behind him as much as he can.

The legend, however, that Adam was created as an androgyne, and that Eve had been cut off from his body, is of

---

[1] See Daehnhardt, *Natursagen*, Vol. I, pp. 115–24.

rabbinic origin, and has found its way into Arabic and Christian literature.

The Jewish legend according to which God took for the creation of Adam dust from the four corners of the world, red, black, white, and brown,[1] is not only found in Arabic and Syriac literature, but has also a parallel in Slavonic literature.[2]

In the *Dialogue between Saturn and Solomon* it is stated that Adam's body was made from earth, his red blood out of fire, his breath out of the wind, his inconstancy of mind from the clouds, his eyes out of flowers, his sweat out of dew, and his tears out of salt.[3] This legend is also found in a different version in Russian folk-lore.[4]

We are referring in this volume to Lilith, who, according to rabbinic legend, was the first wife of Adam. The influence of this legend may be traced, as it seems to us, in Russian folk-lore, where it is said that woman had been made out of a dough and placed in the sun to dry. A dog swallowed her up, and the Lord created another woman out of Adam's rib.[5]

The story of Noah, Satan, and the planting of the vine, related in the pages of this volume from the *Midrash Tanchuma* (*Gen.* 9, 20), may be of Indian origin, as the four qualities of the vine are described in a collection of anecdotes and sayings of Indian sages. Wine has four qualities which it communicates to those who drink it; they are the qualities and characteristics of the peacock, the ape, the lion, and the pig.[6] Anyhow, this legend, which, in a different version, is also related in *Genesis Rabba*, 36, and is referred to in *Yalkut* I, § 61, not only occurs in Arabic but has penetrated into European literature. Damiri tells this story of Adam.[7] It is found in the

---

[1] See Ch. 13.   [2] Daehnhardt, *loc. cit.*, p. 112.
[3] See R. Koehler, *Kleinere Schriften*, Berlin, 1900, Vol. II, p. 2.
[4] Daehnhardt, *loc. cit.*, p. 111.   [5] *Ibid.*, p. 116.
[6] See *Z.D.M.G.*, Vol. XL, pp. 412, 425; Daehnhardt, *loc. cit.*, p. 308.
[7] See Goldziher in *Z.D.M.G.*, Vol. XXIV, p. 209, note 2; Grünbaum, *Neue Beiträge zur semitischen Sagenkunde*, p. 435.

Gesta Romanorum,[1] is mentioned by Pauli in his *Schimpf and Ernst*,[2] in a German poem of the fourteenth century, and in a poem by Hans Sachs.[3]

A modern Greek legend (where Satan is not one of the dramatis personæ), which reminds us of the journey of Dionysius to Naxos, relates the following story. When Saint Dionysius (who takes the place of the pagan God) was still young, he travelled through Hellas to Naxia. He saw a small plant which was very beautiful and took it with him. Afraid lest it would dry up under the scorching sun before he reached Naxia, he found the bone of a bird and stuck the plant into it. It grew, however, so fast that its roots soon traversed the bone. The Saint, therefore, stuck the bone of the bird into the bone of a lion, and this again, when the plant still continued to grow, into the bone of an ass. When he arrived at Naxia and found that the roots of the plant were entangled with the bones of the bird, of the lion, and of the ass, he planted it just as it was. Wonderful grapes grew up, out of which Dionysius pressed wine. And lo! when men drank of it they acquired all the characteristic traits of birds, lions, and asses. When a man drinks one cup he sings like a bird, he is as strong as a lion when he drinks more, and makes an ass of himself when he has had too much wine.[4]

The story of Noah and the planting of the vine, and especially the four qualities of wine, is also found in various Slavonic tales and legends, in a German poem by Joh. Martin Usteri, and in Victor Hugo's *Les Misérables*.[5] Daehnhardt also mentions an Indian tale which relates how opium came into existence, and this story bears a striking resemblance, if not to the part

---

[1] Ed. Oesterley, p. 539.   [2] Ed. Oesterley, p. 161.
[3] See Daehnhardt, *loc. cit.*, p. 303; *Revue des Traditions Populaires*, IV, p. 411; R. Koehler, Vol. I, p. 577; Tendlau, *Das Buch der Sagen*, p. 181; see also Grünbaum, *Jüdisch-Deutsche Chrestomathie*, p. 184.
[4] See Hahn, *Griechische und albanische Maerchen*, II, 76; Daehnhardt. *loc. cit.*, p. 308; Grünbaum, *Neue Beiträge zur semitischen Sagenkunde*, p. 440.
[5] Book VI, Ch. 9; cf. Koehler, *loc. cit.*, Vol. I, p. 577.

which Satan is supposed to have taken in the planting of the vine, at least to the qualities wine is said to possess.

A Rishi once changed a mouse into a cat, a dog, an ape, a pig, an elephant, and a maiden. The maiden becomes queen, but one day falls into a well and is drowned. At the advice of the Rishi she is left there, and the well is stopped. From her body grows the plant out of which opium is made. The smoker of opium acquires all the characteristic traits of the animals into which the mouse had been changed. He is frolicsome like the mouse, loves milk like the cat, is quarrelsome like the dog, dirty like the ape, wild like the wild pig, and proud like a queen.[1]

The Midrash relates that Abraham, after imagining that either the moon or the sun had created the world and were the rulers of the Universe, came to the conclusion, when he saw them disappear from the sky, that they were only servants of the Creator and dependent upon a higher will. He broke the idols of his father, and was brought before Nimrod and thrown into a burning furnace, but, whilst the servants of Nimrod who approached the fire were immediately consumed, Abraham walked about unmolested in the midst of the flames.[2] The entire legend from the Midrash is found (as Mr. Israel Levi has already discovered before us) in the works of St. Athanasius,[3] where it is told of Melchizedec, a brother of Melchi, and a son of Queen Salem and of her husband, an infidel Greek whose name was also Melchi. The Christian author bases his story upon a passage in the *Epistle to the Hebrews*, 7, 3, where it is said: " He is without father or mother. . . ."

Many stories found in the Midrash about the cruelty of Sodom and the sentences of its judges we have related in the pages of this volume. The story about the long and short beds reminds us of the bed of Procrustes, whilst Benfey[4] calls

---

[1] Daehnhardt, *loc. cit.*, pp. 299–300.   [2] See Ch. 19.
[3] Migne, *Patrologia Graeca*, Vol. XXVIII, col. 523–9.   [4] *Loc. cit.*, p. 402

attention to a tale by Lutfullah in which the judge follows the method of the judges of Sodom.

In the third century of the Hegira there lived in Cairo a judge of the name of Mansur ben Musia. A soldier had borrowed money from a Jew and given the latter a bill wherein he promised him a pound of his flesh, should he be unable to pay. When the day of payment arrived, the soldier found himself unable to pay his debt; the Jew wanted to drag him before the judge, and the soldier escaped. In his flight he jostles a pregnant woman whom he knocks down so that she miscarries, runs against a rider, gives his horse a blow and knocks out the latter's eye. He runs on, climbs up upon a hut, falls through the roof and kills a man. The Jew, the cousin of the pregnant woman, the rider, and the son of the man who had been killed, catch the soldier and bring him before the judge. In front of the latter's house they see a drunken man, whilst another man, still alive, is being buried. The judge now pronounces the following sentences: With regard to the Jew, he decides in the Shakespearian fashion, namely:

Therefore prepare thee to cut off the flesh.
Shed thou no blood, nor cut thou less nor more,
But just a pound of flesh; if thou cut'st more

. . . .

Thou diest, and all thy goods are confiscate.[1]

As for the rider, who was asking half the price of his horse which he valued at 200 gold pieces, the judge decrees that the horse be cut lengthwise into two equal halves, the undamaged half being kept by the owner, whilst the damaged be given to the soldier, who, however, should pay 100 gold pieces to the rider. With regard to the woman, the soldier is to live so long with her until she has another child. As for the son whose father the soldier had killed, the son is to get upon the roof of the hut, fall down upon the soldier and thus

[1] *The Merchant of Venice*, Act IV, Scene I.

kill him. Naturally, all the plaintiffs withdraw their claims.
When the judge is asked who the drunken man is, he replies
that he is the taster, drinks being often mixed with poison.
As for the man who was being buried alive, two witnesses had
testified that he had died, but he had now returned. As the
two witnesses confirmed their statement that the man had
really died, it could not be his real self but a ghost, and in order
to put an end to the discussion, the judge had ordered the man
to be buried.[1]

Numerous stories about demons and devils in mediæval
literature are traceable to the East, and especially to Jewish
literature. They have been imported into Europe by the
Crusaders, the Moors of Spain, and especially by the Jews.
The story of the wood-cutter and the Spirit in *Thousand and
One Nights* reminds us of the famous tale of Belfegor as related
by Machiavel, where a certain peasant makes his fortune by
curing noble persons possessed by Belfegor. Belfegor had
been sent down to earth to find out whether there was any
truth in the complaints of many souls brought to hell that
their predicament was due to their wives. Belfegor, in order
to find out the truth, married a lady of birth, and settled in
Florence under the name of Roderic de Castile. His wife
being somewhat of a scold, he was glad to escape from her
and to keep in hiding by possessing certain noble ladies. In
the case of the daughter of the King of France, he refused to
leave her, in spite of the entreaties of the peasant to whom he
owed a debt of gratitude. The peasant at last used a stratagem
and approaching the possessed princess exclaimed: " Roderic,
your wife is coming in search of you." Scarcely had Belfegor
heard these words than he leaped out of the princess and
descended straight to hell, where he confirmed the statement
the truth of which he had been commissioned to find out.[2]

---

[1] See Benfey, *loc. cit.*, pp. 402–3; see also Gaster, in *Monatsschrift*, 1880, pp. 115–17.
[2] See Dunlop, *History of Prose Fiction*, Vol. I, pp. 186–8; Benfey, *loc. cit.*, pp. 525–6.

Now this tale, which also spread in various Slavonic countries, may be traced in the Talmud,[1] where it is told of the demon Ben-Temalion who entered the daughter of the Emperor of Rome and was expelled by Rabbi Simon ben Yohai. One day the Rabbi and several other men went as a deputation to Rome with a view to asking the Emperor to revoke certain edicts against the Jews. Ben-Temalion meeting them on the way, offered them his services. He would enter the royal princess and consent to leave her only when the Rabbi was asked to cure her of her madness. Ben-Temalion kept his word. As the princess was constantly calling for Rabbi Simon, he was summoned into the Imperial presence and undertook to cure the princess. He whispered into her ear the name of Ben-Temalion, and the demon immediately left the possessed maiden. As a reward for his cure, Rabbi Simon obtained from the Emperor the repeal of the laws hostile to the Jews. Such is the Jewish legend as given in the Talmud, in Rashi, and in the *Tefillat R. Simon ben Yohai*.[2]

It has, however, been pointed out by some scholars that during the first centuries of our era the legends about holy men and saints exorcising devils and curing possessed men and women were particular only to the Christian literature. Some have, therefore, seen in the story of Ben-Temalion an historical background, referring to a Roman Senator who was friendly disposed to the Jews,[3] whilst Mr. Israel Levi[4] maintains that the story of Ben-Temalion (or Ben Talmion) is a Christian legend about the apostle Bartholomew which found entrance into the Talmud.[5] We see, however, no reason for these theories. The Jewish legend may be traced to an Indian source[6] and the Christian legend is based upon the Talmud. It

---

[1] *Meilah*, 17b.
[2] Jellinek, *Beth-Hamidrash*, Vol. IV, pp. 117–8; see also *ibid.*, Vol. VI, pp. 128–30.
[3] See Geiger's *Zeitschrift*, Vol. II, pp. 273–8.
[4] *Revue des Etudes Juives*, Vol. VIII, pp. 200–2; Vol. X, pp. 68–93.
[5] See Fabricius, *Codex Novi Test.*, p. 674; Migne, *Dictionnaire des Apocryphes*, II, col. 153–7. [6] See Benfey, *loc. cit.*, I, p. 520.

is more probable that the friendly demon is turned into a Saint than vice versa.

In the *Çuka Saptati* the following story is told.

In the town of Vatsaman there once lived a Brahman who was wise but very poor. His wife, Karagara, was such a shrew that a friendly demon, dwelling in a tree near the house, escaped to the desert on account of her bad temper. Soon afterwards the Brahman himself, unable to stand any longer the temper of his wife, left his house. He met the demon who thus addressed him: " Fear not, O Brahman, I was an inmate of thy house and I will do thee a good turn. Go thou to the town of Mrigavati where the King of Madana lives. I will enter the body of his daughter and only consent to leave her at thy command. The Brahman went to Mrigavati and everything happened as the demon had arranged. Thereupon the demon entered the body of another princess, but when the Brahman was called and asked to cure her, the demon refused to leave his new abode, in spite of the Brahman's adjurations. When, however, the latter suddenly exclaimed: " Here cometh my wife Karagara," the demon took fright and fled.[1]

The story of King Solomon and the finding of the Shamir finds parallels in Arabic and European literature. An Arabic tale based upon the Talmud story[2] runs as follows. One day King Solomon summoned the Ifrits or Afrits, demons and jinns, and commanded them to bring before him the demon Sahr. " O Prophet of God," said the Ifrits, " Allah has given unto this Sahr so much strength that all the demons together are unable to do anything against him. There is only *one* way by which this Sahr may be brought into our power. Every month he visits a source situated upon an island where he drinks his fill. It is now our advice to empty this source and

---

[1] See *Çuka Saptati*, transl. by R. Schmidt, Kiel, 1894, pp. 66-7 (46th night); Benfey, *loc. cit.*, I, pp. 519-20; *Revue des Etudes Juives*, Vol. X, pp. 68-9; *Z.D.M.G.*, Vol. XXXI, p. 332.   [2] *Gittin*, 68b.

fill it with wine. When Sahr comes to visit the source and does not find any water, he will drink the wine, get intoxicated, and fall asleep. We shall then be able to seize him and bring him before thee." Solomon commanded them to act accordingly. The jinns emptied the source of water, filled it with wine, and hid themselves near by behind trees. Soon Sahr appeared, and smelling the wine, exclaimed: " O wine, thou art delicious, but thou dost deprive one of intelligence, makest stupid the wise, and causest regret." He left the source without having drunk out of it. On the third day, being tormented by thirst, he returned. " I cannot escape," he exclaimed, " the fate which God has decided to bring upon me." He drank his fill, made a few steps, but fell down. From all sides the Ifrits hurried to the spot and carried him away, whilst flames were issuing forth from his mouth and nostrils. When Sahr appeared before Solomon and beheld his signet ring, his strength left him, and humbly prostrating himself before the king, he called out: " How great is thy power, O Prophet of God, but it will leave thee one day and nothing but remembrance will remain!" " Thou speakest the truth," said Solomon.[1]

That Solomon required the Shamir wherewith to cut the stones for the Temple is also related by Kazwini. The diamond is a stone which cuts all other stones. Now when King Solomon began to build the Temple, he commanded the demons to hew stones. They caused such a noise that the people complained. The king thereupon summoned the most wily among the jinns into his presence and asked them whether there existed a means how to hew the stones without making any noise. " We, O Prophet," replied the Ifrits, " know not of such a means, but there is a demon named Sahr who is not in thy service; he may know of it." Solomon commanded the Ifrits to bring this demon into his presence, and when he

---

[1] Alkisai, quoted by Grünbaum, in *Neue Beiträge zur semitischen Sagenkunde*, pp. 227–8.

came he put the same question to him. " I know of a stone, O Prophet of God," replied Sahr, " with which thou mayest cut stones without causing any noise, but I know not where the stone may be found. I will tell thee, however, how to find out where this stone is. Visit an eagle's nest." Solomon commanded the Ifrits to find an eagle's nest. The eagle was just away, and they placed a glass globe over his young. When the eagle came and saw his young imprisoned under the glass globe, he flew away. He returned on the following morning holding a stone in his beak, and with this stone he cut the glass. When Solomon heard this, he summoned the eagle into his presence. " Tell me, where didst thou find the stone with which thou didst cut the glass globe?" " The stone, O Prophet of God," replied the eagle, " I found upon a mountain in the west, the *Samur* mountain." When Solomon heard this, he had stones brought from the Samur mountain with which the stones for the Temple were cut.[1]

The story of King Solomon and the finding of the Shamir is mentioned not only by Petrus Comestor in his famous work (*Historia Scholastica*), but also by Garnerius, bishop of Langres (1195), and is related in the poem *Das Lob Salomons*, a German epic dating from the eighth century.[2] The author of this poem has evidently borrowed from the Babylonian Talmud his reference to the " Worm on the Lebanon ".

" King Solomon," says the author, " made up his mind to catch a dragon (Ashmedai), and in order to do so, he emptied all the water wells of Jerusalem, and filled one of them with wine and hydromel. The dragon drank and, being intoxicated, was easily caught and sent to King Solomon. Thereupon the dragon thus addressed the king: ' Sire, if thou releasest me I will teach thee how to build the Temple in one year.' Thereupon the dragon told the king of a worm on the Lebanon

---

[1] Grünbaum, *loc. cit.*, pp. 229–30.
[2] See K. Mullenhoff und Scherer, *Denkmäler deutscher Poesie und Prosa aus dem 8-12 Jahrhundert*, 3rd ed., Berlin, 1892, I, pp. 124–41.

out of the sinews of which he advised him to make a cord wherewith to saw stones. King Solomon gave orders for the worm to be caught on the Lebanon, and out of its sinews a cord was made, so that the king could build the Temple without making use of any iron tools, in accordance with the instructions he had received." [1]

The Shamir is mentioned by Grimm in his *Deutsche Mythologie*, and by A. Kuhn, in his *Herabholung des Feuers*.

" The spring wurzel," writes Grimm, " is a herb that can be procured in the following manner: The nest of a green or black woodpecker, while she has chicks, is closed tight with a wooden bung; the bird, on becoming aware of this, flies away, knowing where to find a wonderful root which men would seek in vain. She comes carrying it in her bill and holds it before the bung, which immediately flies out as if driven by a powerful blow. Now, if you are in hiding and raise a great clamour on the woodpecker's arrival, she is frightened and lets the root fall."[2] Grimm then relates the story of the rock-splitting Shamir as found in the Talmud.[3]

The Shamir is either a worm or a stone, and was one of the ten marvels created in the evening twilight of the sixth day or the first Friday.[4]

In Jewish tradition, the Shamir is an insect rather than a stone. In some non-Jewish works, on the other hand, a plant is described to which the power of splitting stone is attributed. This reminds us of the story of Rabbi Simon, who had nailed up the nest of the hoopæ (the bird Dukhiphath). The latter brought a plant and placed it upon the nail which was at once destroyed. This story has passed to the Greeks,[5] and is incorporated in the *Gesta Romanorum* where it is told of the Emperor Diocletianus.

---

[1] *Kings*, 6, 7; see Leo Landau, *Hebrew-German Romances, Teutonia*, Leipzig, 1912, XXI, p. 16.
[2] Grimm, *Teutonic Mythology*, London, 1883, Vol. III, p. 973.
[3] See *ibid.*, Vol. IV, p. 1598, note. [4] *Abot*, V, 6.
[5] See Aelian., *Histor. animal.*, III, 26.

In a learned article, Israel Levi pointed out the resemblance of the story of Ashmedai, especially in the first part where the demon is performing certain actions which strike Benajah as strange, with the story of the *Hermit and the Angel*.[1] We are referring to this comparison in Vol. II, where we venture to differ from the eminent authority. The story of Asmodeus and Benajah only in so far resembles that of the Angel and the Hermit that in both we see a being endowed with supernatural powers, committing certain acts which strike his companion as strange, but which are justified by deeper reasons known to him alone. Here, however, it is the question of the Shamir that interests us, and no mention whatever of this worm or stone is made in the story of the Angel and the Hermit. The story of the Shamir is also found in the *Historical Mirror* by Vincent de Beauvais, and is related by Gervasius of Tilbury.[2] As for the tale relating Solomon's exile and return, we again find parallels not only in the *Gesta Romanorum*, but also in English and German mediæval poetry. (*Robert of Cysilie*, and *Der nackte König*).[3]

The story of the fox and the weasel,[4] which we have related in this volume and which is taken from the *Alphabetam Siracidis*, finds a parallel in *Yalkut* I, § 182, and in Berechya Ha-Nakdan's *Fox-fables*, No. 105. An exactly similar story is found in Benfey's *Pantshatantra*, and in the Syr. translation of Bickell (Leipzig, 1876), where it is related of the turtle.[5]

Rabbinic myths, legends, and tales have entered Moslem literature, and Mohammed and his commentators have largely drawn from Jewish sources, especially from the Haggadah, as the pages of this volume will show. Such, for instance, is

---

[1] See *Revue des Etudes Juives*, Vol. VIII, pp. 64–73; Gaston Paris, *La Poésie du Moyen Age*, pp. 151–87.

[2] *Otia Imperialia*; see also Cassel, in *Denkschriften der Königl. Akad. der Wissenschaften*, Erfurt, 1854.

[3] See F. H. von der Hagen, *Gesammtabenteuer*, 1850, Vol. III, p. cxv and p. 409.

[4] See Ch. 14.

[5] See Benfey, *loc. cit.*, I, pp. 475–8; Gaster, in *Monatsschrift*, 1880, pp. 475–8.

the myth of Shemhazai and Azael, a tale of Jewish origin which, in Mohammedan literature, is told of Harut and Marut.[1] The Jews themselves, however, may have borrowed this myth from Babylonia. Estira, who rejected the advances of the fallen angel, is Ishtar, or Istahar, goddess of love and passion, worshipped in Syria and Palestine under the name of Ashtoreth, who played an important part in the mythology of the Assyrians and Babylonians. She is supposed to have fallen in love with the hero named Gilgamesh who, however, refused to yield to her charms and rejected her advances. When Istahar asked him to kiss her and be her bridegroom, Gilgamesh reminded her of the sad fate incurred by her previous lovers who were driven forth from her embrace and encountered many misfortunes. Enraged at such an insult, Istahar, who was the daughter of the god Anu, went up to heaven and asked her father to avenge her.[2]

The story of Sunda and Upasunda in the *Mahabharata* also bears a striking resemblance to the myth of Shemhazai and Azael and of Harut and Marut. Sunda and Upasunda were so austere that they acquired much merit for themselves and ultimately sovereignty over heaven and earth. Brahma, jealous of them, created a lovely maiden named Tilottamâ whom he sent as a gift to the brothers. Both brothers desiring to have her as wife, hate sprang up in their hearts, and they slew each other. The maiden returned to Brahma, who was delighted at her achievement. He blessed her and said: " Thou shalt circle all over the world where the sun shines, and no one shall be able to gaze at thee on account of thy brilliancy."[3] The Jews may have borrowed the tale of Shemhazai and Azael from Babylonia, but there is no doubt that Mohammed derived it from a Jewish source.

[1] See Ch. 6.
[2] See M. Jastrow, *Religion of Babylonia and Assyria*, 1898; P. Haupt, *Das babylonische Nimrodepos*, Leipzig, 1884-91; see also Tisdal, *The Original Sources of the Quran*, 1905, pp. 101-2.   [3] See Tisdal, *loc. cit.*, p. 103

Jewish legends and tales have also penetrated into *Thousand and One Nights*. Although according to Benfey, " the substance of all the fables may be entirely traced to India," [1] the Talmud may also be considered as one of the sources of *Thousand and One Nights*.

The story of the pious man who refused to commit the sin of adultery, and to whom a ruby, taken from the throne he was to occupy in Paradise, was sent down from heaven, is to be found literally in the Talmud (*Taanith*, 24b–25a), where it is told of the pious Rabbi Chanina ben Dosa whose poverty was proverbial. The tale of the Sultan of Yemen and his three sons, who were exceedingly sharp and intelligent, and could guess the truth from the most insignificant details which would escape the eye of the ordinary observer, is to be found literally in the Talmud[2] and in *Midrash Echa*, where the stories are told of the inhabitants of Jerusalem, renowned for their cleverness and logical deductions of which a modern Sherlock Holmes might have been proud. Not only into *Thousand and One Nights* but also into European literature have these tales found entrance, and some are mentioned in the collection *Cento novelle antiche* (thirteenth century) and in Voltaire's *Zadig*. The story of the *Wandering Jew* seems to us to be a development of the legends clustering round the Prophet Elijah, and Chidhr of the Moslems, whilst the Faust legend has many analogies with the story of Solomon and Ashmedai.[3]

The story of the blind and the lame joint-gardeners of a rich man who stole the fruit of the garden, the lame getting upon the shoulders of the blind man, is based upon the conversation between the Emperor Antonine and Rabbi Jehuda. This tale has been incorporated in the *Gesta Romanorum*.[4]

---

[1] *Loc. cit.*, I, p. 117.   [2] *Sanhedrin*, 104.
[3] See for reference notes, Vols. II and III of this work.
[4] Cf. Perles, in *Monatsschrift*, 1873, p. 14 ff.

IV

The Sources of Jewish Myth and Legend

Jewish myths and legends have come down to us in the rich and abundant storehouse of post-Biblical literature. They are scattered all over the *Talmud*, " the vast sea of the Talmud ", and over the *Midrashim*, or the so-called expository literature. Much material is also found in the *Targumim*, or Biblical translations and paraphrases, in the *Apocrypha* and in the *Apocalypses*, and above all in the *Pseudoepigraphical* literature. The works of Philo and Josephus, of Demetrius and Artapanus, the commentaries of the Pentateuch and the works of the later mystics, are also sources which we have consulted for the present and the following volumes. In the Talmud the myths and legends are to be found in the *Haggadah* (*Agada*), that is, in the Haggadic portions of the Talmud. And here it will be necessary, for the benefit of the general reader, to explain the meaning and nature of the Haggadah.

Originally Haggadah meant recitation of the teaching of Scripture, and, in a narrower sense, the exegetic amplification of Biblical passages, especially of the non-legal portions. Gradually the word was applied to Biblical exegesis and interpretation in general. It explained the Law from both the religious and the ethical standpoints, expressing religious and philosophical, ethical, and mystical thoughts, but always with a view to bringing near to man Him at whose word the world came into being. Its purpose was that of inducing man to walk in the ways of the Lord.[1]

The Haggadah, or narrative, was the popular branch of the expository literature, for, instead of dealing with ritual

---

[1] See Sifri, *Deuteron.*, 11, 22.

and legal matters, as does the *Halachah*, it concerned itself
with old traditions, customs, and beliefs, myths and legends,
parables and allegories, in a word, with all that enters not
only into the domain of mythology but also into that of folk-
lore. Whilst the Halachah concerned itself with the legal
portions of the Bible, the Haggadah drew its material from the
narrative portions and the poetical passages of the Old Testament. The Haggadah is thus the more cheerful sister of the
serious Halachah. Her office is to *say* and to relate, and, in
order to be able to do so effectively, one of the characteristics
of the Haggadah had to be freedom. It had its origin in human
reflection, but also in freedom of thought and in subjective
conceptions, and it is therefore a product of the times and of
the ideas prevalent, subject to the social surroundings under
which the Haggadists lived and moved. Foreign influences,
Indian, Egyptian, Babylonian, Persian, and Hellenistic, left
their traces upon the Haggadah which did not come to an
end with the conclusion of the Talmud towards the close of
the fifth century (A.D.), but continued for many centuries.
Anthropomorphism and superstitions, which are foreign to the
spirit of Judaism, thus crept in and gained citizen rights in
the Haggadah.[1]

Zunz has defined the Haggadah as follows.

" It is intended both to bring heaven down to the com-
munity and to lift man up to heaven. Its aim is both to glorify
God and to comfort Israel. The Haggadah, therefore, contains not only myths, legends, fables, and tales, but also religious truths and moral maxims, legends from Jewish history
which attest Israel's past greatness and its nationality, and
comforting reflections which are calculated to give new courage
to the people in exile. It kept aloof, at first, from mysticism,
and refrained from entering the domain of metaphysics, but
following the example of the East, the Haggadah, where it

[1] See E. Schürer, *Geschichte der jüd. Litteratur*, Vol. II, pp. 349-50.

treats of the creation of the world and the hosts of angels, often allowed itself to indulge in an even exaggerated anthropomorphism." [1] The Haggadah is thus a sister of the Halachah, or the legal post-Biblical literature, and, like the latter, it bases itself on Holy Scripture, confining itself only to the historical and ethical parts. Often, however, it not only draws ideas from the text, but also tries to introduce new ideas into the text, endeavouring to justify such ideas by Biblical quotations, so as to impress the people.[2]

Some scholars, however, reject this division of post-Biblical lore, especially Talmudic, into Halachah and Haggadah. They define Haggadah as the " primitive literature of Israel, out of which issued the collection of the myths and legends of the Bible ", and which also contains those myths and legends which had been eliminated from the Biblical canon.[3] But even Goldziher, who sees in the Bible the principal source of Jewish myth, admits the importance and value of the Haggadah as a source of Jewish mythology.[4]

During centuries the Haggadah or Haggadic lore, as contained in the sources enumerated above, flourished and developed as a branch of popular poetry, but the Rabbis and teachers in the schoolhouses took hold of the popular traditions and made use of them for their own ethical purposes. The Haggadah thus became an enchanted realm of poetry upon whose flower-gardens generations laboured with loving care. These flower-gardens open before the student's gaze, every flower wafting to him the perfume of the East.[5]

Heine compared the Haggadah to the mild light of the moon, and the hanging gardens of Babylonia.[6] Mild and dreamy, peaceful and soothing indeed is the Haggadah, pro-

---

[1] Zunz, *Gottesdienstliche Vorträge*, 1892, pp. 362–3.
[2] See Hamburger, *Real-Encyclopædie*, s.v. *Agada* and *Agadisches Schrifttum*.
[3] See Ch. Harari, *La Tradition littéraire Hébraïque*, Genève, 1918, pp. 170 and 280.
[4] J. Goldziher, *Der Mythos bei den Hebräern*, 1876, p. 35; see also Schürer, *loc. cit.*; Güdemann in *Revue des Etudes Juives*, Vol. IX.
[5] See Karpeles, *Geschichte der jüd. Litteratur*, p. 127.
[6] *Romanzero, Rabbi Jehuda ben Halevi.*

ducing the effect of the poetic twilight, and like the gardens
of Babylonia which are said to have been laid out by the king
of Babylon in order to remind Semiramis, his queen, of the
hills in her native land, so the Haggadah wafts to Israel in
exile the perfume of its native soil.[1]

The Haggadah has also been compared to those angels
whose existence is a fleeting one. They emerge from the fiery
river, *Nehar di Nur*, sing a hymn of praise in honour of the
Creator, and disappear.[2] Its purpose was to attract the hearers
and to cheer them up. The Haggadah is a mosaic in both
senses of the word. It is *mosaic*, because it is based upon the
Books of Moses, and it is mosaic because its construction
resembles that oriental invention which is called *mosaic*.[3]

It contains the elements of the myths and legends of other
nations, it deals with solar myths and lunar myths, with cosmic
myths and zoological myths, with the attributes of God, with
angels and demons and all creation, but everything is derived
from and substantiated by the Bible. Angels and demons
people and poetically personify nature, yet it is not the nature
of the Aryans and of the Slavs, but that of the monotheistic
Semites and of the Bible-respecting Hebrews.

To a certain extent we may apply to the Haggadah the
words by which Matthew Arnold defined poetry, namely,
" a criticism of life ". The Haggadah invented new tales and
legends, adjusted old ones, but infused them with an ethical,
philosophical, and even political purpose. The floating myths
of the Jews were collected by the Rabbis of the Talmud and
by the Haggadists of post-Talmudic times. They made a
critical selection of existing material and systematized it so
as to suit the needs of the people, but always for the purpose
of explaining and *criticizing* life and human actions.

[1] See Grünbaum, *Neue Beiträge zur semitischen Sagenkunde*, p. 3; see also Josephus, *Contra Ap.*, I, 19, 20.
[2] See De Rossi, *Meor Enaim*, ed. Mantua, p. 77.
[3] See Grünbaum, *Gesammelte Aufsätze*, p. 4.

MYTH AND LEGEND OF ANCIENT ISRAEL

VOLUME I

CHAPTER I

Mysteries of Creation

The God of Israel—Difference between Indian, Persian, Egyptian, Greek, and Jewish myths—Manifestation of the God of Israel—He manifests Himself unto Moses—The High-Priest Ishmael ben Elisha blesses the Lord—The abode of God—He fills the whole universe—Clad in clouds, He visits His worlds—The daily occupations of the Creator—Certain missions are not entrusted to angels—God Himself changes the flames into a garden of roses and saves Abraham—Creation of the world—God produces a fine subtle matter, the *Hylé* of the Greeks—Tohu and Bohu—The four elements— Premundane Creation—The Torah, or Divine Wisdom—The counsel of the Torah—The Throne of Glory—The heavenly court of justice—The cosmos an animated being—The plurality of the worlds—Many worlds created and destroyed—Nine hundred and seventy-four generations existed before the creation of the world.

UNLIKE the myths of other nations — the myths of India, Egypt, Persia, and Greece—Jewish myth deals but little with the origin of God. He was there before the mountains were born, before the world was created, and from the beginning of time to the end of days He exists and is God.[1] Since time immemorial His throne is established.[2] Jewish myth-makers, according to the advice of Ben Sira, refrain from inquiring into the mysteries of Divinity. " So far thou hast permission to speak; thenceforward thou hast not permission to speak. For thus it is written in the Book of Ben Sira: Seek not out

[1] *Ps.* 90, 2.　　　　[2] *Ibid.*, 93, 2.

1

the things that are too hard for thee, and into the things that are hidden from thee inquire thou not. In what is permitted to thee instruct thyself; thou hast no business with secret things."[1] God was, has been, and is, and that was sufficient even for those who indulged in creating and fashioning the myths of Israel. Therein consists the difference between the myths of Israel and those of other nations who relate the birth of their respective Gods.

If, however, Jewish myth is silent as to the origin of God, it dwells frequently upon the fantastic descriptions of His essence, His abode, His actions, and His daily occupations. Like the myths of other nations, Jewish myth, too, imagines the Creator of the Universe as a perfect being resembling man, who was created in His image. His attributes are omnipotence, omniscience, benevolence, and loving-kindness.

On certain, although rare, occasions, this ruler of the Universe takes the shape of man in order to manifest Himself to His creatures. Thus Jewish myth relates that one of the three strangers, whom Abraham so hospitably received in his tent in the plain of Mamre, was God Himself who had appeared in human shape to His perfect servant, the son of Terah.[2] It was God Himself who frequently manifested Himself to Moses, and in the shape of an old man He appeared to Sennacherib, King of Assyria.[3]

One day, Jewish myth relates, the High-Priest Ishmael, the son of Elisha, upon entering the Holy of Holies, perceived the Almighty sitting upon a throne and asking the priest for a blessing. " Mayest Thou," promptly said the High-Priest, " never be swayed by wrath against Thy creatures, and may it be Thy will to treat them with mercy and loving-kindness."[4] The Almighty nodded His head in approval. We find a parallel in Greek myth, when we read of Jupiter

[1] *Hagigah*, 13a.　　[2] *Pirke de Rabbi Eliezer*, Ch. 29.　　[3] *Sanhedrin*, 95b.　　[4] *Berachoth*, 7a.

who nodded his head when Thetis interceded for her son Achilles.[1]

The abode of God is frequently dealt with in Jewish myth. The wonderful starlit vault above us is the seat of the Almighty. Here He dwells surrounded by His heavenly hosts. The myth makers of post-exilic Judaism were, however, not satisfied with *one* Heaven and imagined seven, placing the seat of the Creator in the seventh or the highest. But this abode, the seventh Heaven, is only the preferred and favourite dwelling place of the God of Jewish myth. He is everywhere and fills the whole universe. Basing themselves upon the words of the Psalmist, Jewish mythographers imagine the omnipresence of the Creator.[2]

The soul fills the body, just as the Divine presence fills the Universe.[3] Frequently, the God of Jewish myth leaves this abode in Heaven and descends upon earth to pay a visit to His creatures. Herein, however, Jewish myth once more differs considerably from the myths of other nations. Jupiter harnesses his iron-shod, golden-maned horses, and, arrayed in golden garments, seated in his chariot, visits the world.[4] The God of Jewish myth is clad in clouds and visits His worlds upon the wings of the wind. He is seated upon the Throne of Glory and His chariots are upon the Ophanim. He rideth upon a swift cloud and upon the wings of the wind, for it is said: " And he rode upon a cherub, and did fly; yea, he flew upon the wings of the wind." [5]

Whilst the Gods of pagan antiquity are like ordinary mortals, sharing their passions and even their vices, the God of Israel, even of Jewish myth, where anthropomorphistic conceptions play such an important rôle, is a perfect ethical being, whose superiority and Divine attributes are manifested even in moments of wrath and anger.[6] His Divine attributes

---

[1] *Iliad* I, 524.   [2] *Ps.* 139, 8–10; *Is.* 6, 3.   [3] *Berachoth,* 10a.   [4] *Iliad* VIII, 41.
[5] *Ps.* 18, 10; *Pirke de Rabbi Eliezer,* Ch. 4.   [6] *Pesachim,* 87b.

describe His high perfection, for which human language can find no adequate description.[1]

Largely does Jewish myth dwell upon the minute description of the daily occupations of Divinity. The day consists of twelve hours, and during the first four hours the Creator explains to His heavenly hosts the precepts of the Divine law. During the next four hours He is seated on the throne of judgment, judging the actions of his creatures. During the last four hours He is again busy ordaining the sustenance and protection of his creatures.[2] But whilst the God of Jewish myth usually commissions His ministering angels to execute His commands, He often reserves unto Himself certain missions which He, in His loving-kindness and mercy, executes Himself. Such are the birth of the child, the distribution of rain, and the resuscitation of the dead.[3] These missions are not entrusted to any angel, but are directly executed by the God of Jewish myth Himself. Marriages, too, are, according to Jewish myth, concluded in Heaven under the direction of God Himself.[4]

Very frequently, according to Jewish myth, God refuses to allow one of His ministering angels to interfere in the affairs of man, but Himself condescends to vouchsafe His assistance and His help to His beloved creatures, and especially to His faithful and perfect servants. Thus, when Abraham was thrown into the furnace, by order of the terrible Nimrod, the angel Gabriel was ready to hasten to Abraham's assistance, but the Creator waved him back, and Himself changed the flames into a bed of roses upon which the son of Terah went to sleep, to the amazement of the servants of Nimrod.[5]

The angel of death is also never allowed to take the souls of perfect men and to separate them from their bodies. It is God Himself, according to Jewish myth, who bids the souls

---

[1] *Berachoth*, 33b.　　　[2] *Abodah Zarah*. 3b.　　　[3] *Taanith*, 2a.
[4] *Moed Katon*, 18b; *Leviticus Rabba*, 8.　　　[5] *Pesachim*, 118a.

of these perfect favourites of Divinity to leave their earthly prison-houses, sparing them the agonies of death.[1]

THE CREATION OF THE WORLD

God and the world are, according to Jewish myth, two inseparable conceptions, standing to each other in the relation of cause and effect. The world came into existence by the will of God, because He wished creation and especially man to glorify and sanctify His name, and to proclaim His glory.[2] The world and man were created for the purpose of giving God an opportunity to manifest His glory, His omnipotence and His benevolence.[3] He created the world by the word of His mouth. In Indian myth we read that Brahma, by the word of His mouth, called into being all the creatures of the visible world. But Jewish myth differs from the myth of India, for none of the Jewish myths in either pre-talmudic or post-talmudic times speak of any pre-existing matter out of which the world was called into being. It was created out of nothing, and thus Jewish myth is in strict accordance with Holy Writ.

From absolute nothingness All-Father, the Creator, first produced a fine subtle matter, which had no consistence whatever, but possessed the potential power to receive the imprint of form. This was the first matter, or what the Greeks called *Hylé*.

From this first matter, which was *Tohu*, the Creator produced all things. He then clothed it in form which is *Bohu*. First matter, which the Creator extracted from nothing, at first resembled one point, which was the stone of foundation of creation. This stone of foundation God shaped in four different forms which are fire, water, earth, and air. These four elements envelop each other. Water surrounds earth; air surrounds water; fire surrounds air. When this point or

---

[1] *Baba Batra*, 17a.   [2] *Pirke de Rabbi Eliezer*, Ch. 3.   [3] *Genesis Rabba*, 1.

stone of foundation had taken these four forms, it became luminous, " and it was light ". The world was created.[1]

At the moment of creation, say other mythographers, the four cardinal points were united to the four elements: fire, air, water, and earth. Out of the amalgamation of these God fashioned Adam. His body was the union of two worlds, the world above and the world below. The four elements are the first mystery of everything, for they are the progenitors and the fathers of all the worlds. From them issued gold, silver, iron, and copper, and from the mixture of these four other metals issue. Fire, water, air, and earth are the first roots of the worlds above and of the worlds below, for all the created worlds are based upon them.

But before creating the Universe, relates Jewish myth, before God called into being the visible world, He established the conditions under which the world He had decided to create could endure for ever. The world could not exist, said the Almighty, if there were not first laws and conditions necessary for its continued existence. Such conditions were, according to Jewish myth, Divine Providence, the Law, Repentance, Punishment and Reward, Prayer and Freewill.

God, therefore, before fashioning Heaven and Earth, and the whole visible world, man and the other creatures, called into being the Divine Throne, the Holy Law, Repentance, Paradise, Hell, the Holy Temple, and the name of the Messiah; in a word, all the conditions which represent Divine Providence, Law and Order, Good Deeds, Reward and Punishment, Prayer and Redemption.[2]

Thus, before the world was created, the Maker of the Universe existed alone with His name. It entered His mind to create the world, and he drew the plan of the world, but it would not stand. He traced the foundations of the world,

---

[1] Nachmanides, *Commentary to the Pentateuch*.
[2] *Pirke de Rabbi Eliezer*, Ch. 3; *Nedarim*, 39b; *Pesachim*, 54a.

that is He drew its plans, after which the world was to be created. He is likened unto an architect who draws the plans before building a palace.

The *Torah*, which is wisdom, was with the Creator prior to Creation, and He took counsel with her concerning the creation of the world. The Torah, or wisdom, advised Him to create the world and she said: " Lord and Sovereign of the Universe! Thou art the Sovereign and the King, but there is no host over whom Thou canst rule; there is also no people who could pay honour unto Thee and glorify Thy name." And the Creator listened unto the counsel of the Torah, which is wisdom, for it pleased Him greatly.[1] The pre-existent emanation of the Torah, or the Law, from God, thus occupies the place of the *Logos*.

As for the Throne of Glory, it is suspended in the air high above, and the Divine Glory hath the appearance of the colour of amber. One half is fire and the other is hail, being the two attributes of love and justice. Life is at His right hand and death at His left.[2] A sceptre of fire is in His hand and a veil separates the Divine Glory from the ministering angels, only seven angels being allowed to minister within the veil which is called *Pargod*.[3]

The footstool of the Creator is like unto fire and hail, and represents Justice and Love. And the foundations of the throne, round which fire is continually flashing, are righteousness and justice by which He rules the world.

But none of the ministering angels, neither the *Chajjoth*, nor the *Ophanim* know the place of His Glory. All stand in awe and dread, in trembling and fear. And although standing near the place of Glory, *at* the side of the throne, the ministering angels know not the place of His Glory. Therefore, they only respond: " Blessed be the Glory of the Lord from His place." [4]

[1] *Pirke de Rabbi Eliezer*, Ch. 3.
[2] *Ibid*, ch. 4; see also Jellinek, *Beth-Hamidrash*, Vol. II, p. 41.
[3] *Hagigah*, 5a, 15a; *Yoma*, 77; *Berachoth*, 18b.   [4] *Ezek.* 3, 17.

Throughout Jewish myth, dealing with cosmogony and creation, there also runs the old Oriental idea that everything that exists upon earth has its counterpart in heaven.

This idea is even older than the Platonic doctrine of Ideas. The Rabbis of the Talmud teach that the realm of earth corresponds to the celestial realm. Rabbi Abahu, who lived in the third century of our era, says that all that is above exists also below. You will find that everything that the Eternal created above He also created below.[1]

But in retaining the old Oriental conception Jewish myths and legends always presuppose the idea of an omniscient, all-wise Creator who created everything according to a wise plan.

Herein lies the whole conception of Jewish myth with regard to cosmogony.[2]

Thus, the prototype of the earthly garden of Eden is the celestial Eden or Paradise. The prototype of the earthly court of justice is the celestial one, presided over by the Creator himself. This heavenly court holds its sittings in the highest heaven, in the vicinity of the Throne of Glory. The secret scribe and vice-president of this celestial court of justice is Metatron. He is assisted by the angels Jophiel and Suriel, whilst the angel Enphiel is the keeper of the seal, and the angels Achseriel and Rasiel are the heralds. The archangels Michael, Gabriel, Raphael and Uriel (also Nuriel) are the assessors. In this celestial court two seats of glory exist, one for justice and the other for mercy. The Jewish legends speak not only of the celestial court of justice but also of a heavenly academy, and relate that many of the just and pious Rabbis were allowed to be present in this heavenly academy whither they were carried up and down in their chairs by ministering angels.[3]

The Rabbis of the Talmud also go so far as to imagine

[1] *Exodus Rabba*, 33.   [2] E. Bischoff, *Babylonisch-Astrales*, p. 21.   [3] *Baba Mezia*, 85b.

the cosmos as an animated being. And just as man is endowed with a living soul, so the whole universe is singing the praises of and is rendering homage to the living Creator. The sun, the moon and the stars, in a word, the entire cosmos is a living being endowed with a soul. The entire visible world is a being endowed with life. Man is the crown of creation, and everything that God created in man He also created in the cosmos.[1]

This conception of the cosmos as a living being is also met with in the Babylonian myth, where Marduk, after his victory over the goddess Tiamat, creates the world out of her body. Here, as Bischoff rightly remarks,[2] we have the doctrine of modern philosophers who teach a psycho-physical monism. The soul of the world is an idea common to Plato, the Neoplatonists, Paracelsus, and others.[3]

The present world, however, is neither the first nor the only world in existence. Before the world was created there existed already many others. The Eternal created many worlds and destroyed them until He produced the present cosmos. And He spake: "The other worlds did not please me, but this one does please me."[4] The pre-existing worlds were preparations for the present one. In this mythical conception lies the idea of an organic progress. When the pre-existing worlds had fulfilled their purpose they disappeared. Not only the worlds, however, but also all their inhabitants had been created and destroyed; they came and went.[5] Nine hundred and seventy-four generations had existed before the creation of this world, but they were swept away because they were wicked and did not please the Lord of the Universe.[6]

Thus many worlds preceded the creation of the present

Abot de Rabbi Nathan, Ed. Schechter, p. 46a; W. Bacher, Die Agada der Tanaiten, Vol. I, p. 365; Midrash Tehillim, Ps. 19, 2.   [2] Loc. cit., p. 108.
[3] Paulsen, Einleitung in die Philosophie, 1893, pp. 91–116, 239–251; Midrash Tehillim, Ps. 19, 2; Koheleth Rabba, 1, 4.
[4] Genesis Rabba, 3; see also W. Bacher Die Agada der Palästinensischen Amoräer, Vol. II, p. 138.   [5] Midrash Tehillim, Ps. 90, 5.   [6] Hagigah, 13b–14a.

one, worlds came and disappeared. In this mythical conception one may already trace the modern evolutionary idea. Jewish myth and legend further speak of a plurality of worlds. Apart from our own cosmos, there are numerous other cosmic systems. God, teach the Rabbis, has many cosmic worlds, and, carried upon the wings of the Cherubim, He manifests His presence in all of them.[1]

----

[1] *Abodah Zarah, 3b.*

CHAPTER II

The Story of Creation

The six days of creation—The lump of snow—The stone of foundation
—The arrogant waters—The trees of Bashan and the mountain of iron—
The light of the Divine garment—The four corners of the world—The
incompleted corner facing north—The waters and the sand—The creation
of Light—The two luminaries—Sun and moon—Two Kings with one crown
—The complaint of the moon and its punishment—The chariot of the sun
—The habitation of the moon—Worship of the moon—Astarte, Urania,
and Isis—Leviathan and Behemoth—The story of creation in the Slavonic
Book of Enoch—The stone Advel—The substance called Arkas—Things
created on eve of Sabbath.

THE story of the six days of creation is related differently
in various sources. On the first day the Creator took a lump
of snow from underneath the throne of His Glory and threw
it upon the surface of the waters, and it became earth. And
then He took a stone of foundation and threw it upon the
place where once the Temple was to stand, and the world was
founded upon it. And He called to the earth and commanded
it to stand still and not to toss about like a ship upon the waves
of the sea.

On the second day the Creator said there should be a dam
or *rakia* in the midst of the waters, that is the waters were
commanded to divide themselves, one portion ascending
and the other descending. But the waters were arrogant and
rebelled against the command of the Creator, and all ascended.
And the Creator said: " I commanded you to divide, one portion to ascend and the other to descend," but the waters were

obstinate and refused to obey the command of the Creator of the Universe. Then the Creator stretched out His little finger and tore the waters into twain, and the lower portion descended suddenly.

And on the third day all the trees and timber in the garden of Eden were created, and all the trees and fruit trees upon earth. And when the cedars of Lebanon and the trees of Bashan saw that they had been created first, they raised their heads and were proud. But the Creator said: " I hate pride and arrogance," and He forthwith created iron to cut down the proud trees. When the trees saw that the Lord of the Universe had created a mountain of iron, they wept bitterly, and some of them are known as weeping trees. When the Creator heard them weeping, He asked them why they cried. " We thought," replied the trees, " that no one is like unto us in the world, who are the tallest in creation; but now Thou hast created iron to destroy us." " You will furnish the handle for the axe, and you will rule over the iron as the iron will rule over you," replied the Creator, and thus He made peace between them.[1]

On the fourth day He took fire and sealed it, and fashioned the sun out of it. It is called *Shamesh*,[2] because it serves the world. And He took light and sealed it and fashioned the moon out of it. And both luminaries were alike. But the moon grew jealous and complained to the Creator. It was punished and its light was diminished. Thereupon the moon pleaded and said: " Lord of the Universe, I have only spoken one word and so great is my punishment." But the Creator replied: " In days to come thy light will once more be as the light of the sun."[3]

On the fifth day He created out of light and water the Leviathan and all the fishes in the sea. On the sixth day He

---

[1] *Genesis Rabba*, 5.
[2] *Shamesh*, to minister, wait upon; see Jastrow, *Dictionary of the Targumim, s.v.*
[3] *Hullin*, 60b; *Genesis Rabba*, 6; *Midrash Agadah*, ed. Buber, p. 3.

took water and dust and light and created all the animals, and the wild beasts and the domestic animals, and the birds and the creeping worms.[1]

The book called *Pirke de Rabbi Eliezer* describes the story of the creation as follows: The heavens He created from the light of His garment. He took His garment and stretched it out and the heavens extended farther and farther, until the Creator cried unto them to stop. " Be stayed," He said, " it is sufficient," and they stopped. And then the Creator took the snow from beneath His throne of glory and scattered it upon the waters, and the waters became congealed and the earth was formed. And thus the snow became earth. The hooks of the heavens He fixed in the waters of the ocean which flow between the ends of the heavens and the ends of the earth. He created four corners or directions in the world, facing east, south, west, and north. From the corner facing east there goeth forth to the world light, whilst the dews and rains of blessing descend upon the world from the corner facing south. The treasuries of snow and hail are stored up in the corner facing west, and from there cold and rain and heat descend upon the world. But the corner facing north was not completed, for the Creator said: " Let anyone come and finish this corner and then the world will know that he is a God." This corner is the abode of lightning and thunder, of winds and of earthquakes; here also dwell the demons and spirits, for it is from the northern corner that evil breaks forth and comes upon the world.[2]

On the second day the Creator of the Universe called into existence the firmament, the angels, and the fire of Gehenna, for on the second day the Creator did not say " and it was good ". The firmament which He created on the second day divides the waters above from the waters below, and

---

[1] *Midrash Konen*, Jellinek, *Beth-Hamidrash*, Vol. II, pp. 24–27.
[2] *Jeremiah*, i, 14; *Pirke de Rabbi Eliezer*, Ch. 3.

were it not for that firmament the world would be engulfed by the waters above it and below it.

On the third day the earth was as flat as a plain, the waters covering the entire surface of the whole earth. At the word of the Creator the waters gathered and were rolled into the valleys, and the hills and mountains appeared. The waters then became proud and arrogant, rose tumultuously to a great height, covered the face of the earth, and threatened to over-run and drown the whole earth. But the Creator rebuked them, subduing them and placing them beneath the hollow of His feet, making the sand the boundary and fence of the sea. And when the mighty waters saw the sand-grains, how small and insignificant they were, they laughed at them and mocked them. "We are not afraid of you," they said, "for the smallest wave will destroy you and swallow you up." The sand-grains appointed to fight against the waves of the sea were frightened, but the biggest of the sand-grains said: "My brothers, do not be afraid. We are powerless and in-significant as long as we are separate, and the slightest breeze can blow us away. If, however, we stick together we are a great power, and able to oppose the inrush of the arrogant waters." And from all corners of the earth the sand-grains came and united into one compact mass, so that the arrogant waters were frightened and drew back. And when the waters rise and see the sand, they recede and return to their place. They neither diminish nor increase because God has measured them in the palm of his hand.[1]

On the fourth day He created the sun and the moon. And the two luminaries were created both equal, one was not greater than the other, for they were both equal in shape and form and height, and they illumined the world equally. But soon rivalry arose between them, and they quarrelled.

[1] *Midrash Tehillim, Ps.* 93; *Pirke de Rabbi Eliezer,* Ch. 3; *Baba Batra,* 74*b.* See also *Monatsschrift für Geschichte und Wissenschaft d. Judent.,* 1912, p. 148.

The moon was not satisfied, for she envied the illuminating powers of the sun. And she appeared before the Father of All, and thus she spake: " Thou didst create the heavens and the earth, but the heavens are greater than the earth; Thou also didst create fire and water, but water is stronger than fire, for it has the power to extinguish fire. Now Thou didst create the sun and the moon who are both equal and are alike unto two kings with one crown." And the Father of All rebuked the moon and thus He spake: " As thou didst obstinately refuse to do my will, and didst harbour evil intentions against thy colleague the sun, thou shalt be made smaller. Sixty times will I diminish thy size, and thy brightness shall be sixty times smaller than the brightness of the sun." And thus the greater light was set to rule the day, and the lesser light, that is the moon, to rule the night.[1]

The sun is led and accompanied by ministering angels both during the day and during the night. Crowned as a bridegroom, the sun rides forth every day in a chariot. In summer his rays look down upon the earth and would consume it with fire, but every night he takes a cooling bath in the ice above so as to temper the inner heat.[2] The Divine Glory resides in the west, and the sun, having risen in the east and set in the west, enters in the presence of Divine Glory, and bowing low thus he speaks: " Lord of the Universe! I have fulfilled all Thy commands." [3]

The moon inhabits a place between the clouds and the thick darkness, which are like two dishes one above the other. These clouds form the clothing or covering of the moon who travels between them, peeping out from between the two in the form of a little horn until the middle of the month, when it is full moon. From the middle to the end of the month, the moon is being gradually covered by the clouds between which she travels,

---

[1] *Hullin*, 60b.   [2] *Genesis Rabba*, 6.
[3] M. Gaster, *The Chronicles of Jerahmeel*, p. 11 (3, 5).

until the end of the month when she is entirely covered.[1]

The worship of the moon was very extensive among the Orientals, and Holy Scripture bids the Israelites to be very careful when they see the sun, the moon, the stars, and the entire host of heaven and not to pay them worship, for they are only creations of the only God and appointed for the service of the nations on earth.[2] " If I beheld the sun when it shined," says Job, " or the moon walking in brightness, and my heart has been secretly enticed, or my mouth hath kissed my hand." [3] The moon was worshipped in Asia under the name of Meni, of Astarte, the Goddess of the Groves, the Queen of Heaven. She is Urania and Coelestis in Syria, the Isis of Egypt, and Alilat of Arabia. She is the Diana, Bellona, Minerva of the Greeks; sacrifices were offered unto her, in the highways and upon roofs of houses. Even human sacrifices were offered unto the moon according to Strabo and Lucian. The Jewish myth-makers, among whom monotheism always struggled against Asiatic heathen polytheism, have therefore woven many myths and legends about the moon. All these myths, however, have, as has been pointed out, an ethical setting.

On the fifth day the waters, at the command of the Creator, brought forth all kinds of animals, and Leviathan, the flying-serpent whose dwelling is in the deepest waters.

On the sixth day the Creator brought forth all kinds of animals from the earth. And He also called forth from the earth the Behemoth which stretches its limbs upon a thousand hills and seeks its daily food upon a thousand hills.[4] It drinks the waters of the Jordan which encompass the land of Israel, half of them flowing above the earth and half below the earth. And the day of the great Messianic banquet prepared for the righteous, this beast will be sacrificed and served.[5]

---

[1] M. Gaster, *The Chronicles of Jerahmeel*, p. 11 (3, 5).
[2] *Deuteron.* 4, 19; 17, 3.   [3] *Job*, 31, 26, 27.   [4] *Ps.* 1, 10; *Job*, 40, 15.
[5] *Pirke de Rabbi Eliezer*, Ch. 11; see also *Baba Batra*, 75a; *Genesis Rabba*, 7; *Midrash Agadah*, edit. Buber, p. 3.

The Slavonic *Book of Enoch* describes the story of creation as follows: Before everything visible was, the All-Father wandered about among the invisible like the sun which is wandering from east to west and from west to east. But whilst the sun has rest in itself, He, the Creator, had none, because He was the All-Father and Creator. And He decided to lay the foundations and to produce the visible Creation. And he commanded that the visible issue and descend from the invisible.

And there came forth a very big stone called *Advel*, and He, the Creator, saw it and lo, Advel had in its body a big light. And He said: " Burst asunder, Advel, thou fiery stone, and let the visible issue forth from thee." And Advel, the fiery stone, burst asunder and out of it broke forth an immense light and forth came an immense æon which revealed the whole creation as it had been conceived and designed by the Creator, the All-Father. And out of it He made His own throne and sat upon it.

And He said unto the light: " Rise higher and be fixed above the throne and become the foundation of all celestial things." And for the second time All-Father called to the invisible deep and caused to come forth a substance called *Arkas*, firm and heavy and red. And He spoke unto Arkas, the substance heavy and very red: " Burst asunder, Arkas, and let issue forth out of thee the creation of all things below." And when Arkas was divided there issued forth from it an æon, dark and immense, bearing in itself the creation of all things below. And the Creator spake unto it: " Go down and be fixed below and become the foundation of the creation of all things below and there should be nothing beneath the darkness." And there is nothing beneath the darkness, as there is nothing above the light which is the foundation of all celestial things. And He commanded that a portion of the light and of the darkness should mix, and out of this

mixture of light and darkness issued forth a thick substance
which was firm. This was water. And the Creator spread it
out above the darkness which is below and underneath the
light which is above, and thus the waters were spread out in
both directions. And He surrounded the waters with light
and made seven circles within, fashioning them like crystal,
moist and dry, that is like glass, and having the appearance
of ice. And these were the seven heavens, and He showed
unto each its place and its way. And thus He made firm
the circle of heaven and He also made firm the great stone
of foundation. Thereupon He commanded the waters under
the heavens to assemble. And the waves of the waters below
the heavens were turned into stone, firm and immense,
out of which stones earth was fashioned, which was called
dry land. In the midst of the earth He placed the abyss.[1]
And He gathered the sea in one place and bound it as with
a yoke, and thus He spake unto the sea: " I set a limit unto
thee and thou wilt not trespass and separate from thy elements."

On the eve of the Sabbath, that is in the twilight of the
sixth day, ten things were created, and these were: the mouth
of the earth,[2] the mouth of the well;[3] the mouth of the ass;[4]
the rainbow;[5] the Manna;[6] the Shamir;[7] the shape of the
alphabet, the writing, the tables of the Law, and the ram
which Abraham sacrificed in the place of Isaac.[8]

[1] R. H. Charles and Morfill, *The Secrets of Enoch.*   [2] *Numbers*, 16, 32.
[3] Well of Hagar, *Gen.* 21, 19; and *Numbers*, 21, 16.   [4] *Numbers*, 22, 28.
[5] *Genesis*, 9, 13.   [6] *Exodus*, 16, 15.   [7] *I Kings*, 6, 7.
[8] *Pesachim*, 54a; *Pirke de Rabbi Eliezer*, Ch. 19; see also *Palest. Targum* to *Numbers*,
22, 28.

CHAPTER III

The Seven Heavens or Firmaments
and the Seven Underworlds

Description of the seven heavens—Villon, Rekia, Shekhakim, Szebhul, Maon, Makhon, and Araboth—The unborn souls—Enoch visits the seven heavens—The rebellious angels—Paradise—The gates of the sun—The watchers—The seven underworlds—Eretz hatachtonah—Adamah, Arka, Ge, Neshia, Zija, Tebel—The two rulers of Arka—Ephrira and Kastimon—The ten unholy, gruesome spheres—Thomiel, Goiel, Sairiel—The hurling raven—The sphere of Sammael.

THE SEVEN HEAVENS

THE number of firmaments is already discussed in Talmudic myth. One Rabbi is of opinion that there are two firmaments, but others maintain that there are seven. It has been rightly pointed out that this number seven is due to Babylonian influences, where we read of a sevenfold division of the Lower World. When *Ishtar* descends to Hades she has to pass through seven gateways in order to reach the interior of the infernal city.[1] The doctrine of the seven heavens is also found among the Parsees. The Slavonic *Enoch* and the *Testament of the Twelve Patriarchs* [2] also speak of the seven heavens.

In the *Testament of Levi*,[3] the third son of Jacob, we read of a vision which Levi had, beholding the seven heavens.

The *Chronicles of Jerahmeel* also speak of the seven heavens. The Lord then opened the seven doors of the seven

---

[1] R. H. Charles, *Expository Times*, Nov.–Dec., 1895.
[2] See R. H. Charles, *The Testament of the Twelve Patriarchs*, 1917, and article in Hastings' *Dict. of the Bible*.   [3] *Ibid*, pp. 36–37.

heavens, and revealed himself unto Israel, face to face in His
glory and with His crown.[1]

According to Jewish myth, both in the Talmud, the Midrashim, the *Pseudapigraphia* and later sources, there are thus
seven heavens: the *Villon* (Vellum), in which there is the
sun; the *Rekia*, in which the sun shines, and the moon,
stars, and planets are fixed; the *Shekhakim*, in which the
millstones are kept to make the *manna* for the pious; *Szebhul*,
in which are the upper Jerusalem and the Temple and the
Altar, and in which Michael, the chief angel-prince, offers
sacrifices; the *Maon*, in which the angels of the Ministry
dwell, they sing by night and are silent by day (for the sake
of the honour of Israel); *Makhon*, in which are the treasures
of snow and hail, the chambers of noxious dews, the recep-
tacles of water, the chambers of wind, and the cave of mist;
their doors are of fire.

The last heaven is *Araboth*. Here justice, judgment,
and righteousness dwell. Here also are the treasures of life,
peace and blessing; here the souls of the just and righteous
dwell together with the souls of those who are to be born in
future; here also is the dew by which the dead are once to
be raised. In Araboth also are the *Ophanim* and *Seraphim*,
and living creatures and ministering angels, and the Throne
of Glory, and over it is enthroned the Great King.[2]

With regard to the souls yet unborn, Jewish myth places
them in the seventh heaven.

In the beginning of things God the All-Father also created
a great number of souls destined one day to inhabit a human
body. There is a treasure or storehouse in Heaven where
these souls are kept until the moment arrives for each of them
to descend upon earth and be united to " mortal coil ". According to some myths these souls are hidden beneath the

---

[1] Gaster, *The Chronicles of Jerahmeel*, p. 148 (52, 11).
[2] *Hagigah*, 12b; *Pirke de Rabbi Eliezer*, Ch. 4.

throne of All-Father, whilst in other places it is maintained that the souls yet unborn walk freely in the celestial fields in company of the souls of the pious who have already passed through a body.[1] All these souls inhabit the seventh heaven where all the treasures of life and blessing are kept. The Redeemer will only come when all these souls created at the beginning of things will have sojourned upon earth and " shuffled off mortal coil ".[2]

Some souls are spirits sent down upon earth and ordered to inhabit a human body as a punishment for faults committed. For others it is a test and an opportunity to show their strength. In the struggle of the soul, the celestial inmate, against the passions and instincts inherent in matter, the soul has an opportunity to show its worth and remain faithful to its celestial origin or to betray it.[3]

The *Midrash of the Ten Commandments* gives the following description of the seven heavens: He further created the seven heavens or *rakiim*. The lowest of the seven heavens is called *Villon* and is like a curtain drawn before the houses, so that those who are inside can see all that happens outside, but those who are outside cannot perceive those who are within. And there are windows in the Villon, through which the ministering angels can see the children of men and all the mortals and their doings, whether they are walking on the path of righteousness or not. And above the Villon is the second heaven called *Rakia*. In it are fixed the stars and planets and constellations, and in it there are twelve windows corresponding to the twelve hours of day and night. And three hundred and sixty-five angels minister and are set to serve the sun and to lead it from window to window whilst it turns round the world. In the night they lead the moon before these windows.

And above the Rakia is the third heaven called *Shekhakim*,

---

[1] *Hagigah*, 12b.   [2] *Niddah*, 13b; *Yebamoth*, 62a.   [3] *Genesis Rabba*, 9.

or clouds. Above the Shekhakim is the Szebhul, and above the Szebhul is the *Makhon* or the fifth heaven. It contains the treasuries of snow and hail, and the apartments of dew, and the chambers of storm and wind. And all are closed behind doors of fire. And above the Makhon is the sixth heaven which is *Maon*, and where dwell hosts of angels who sing hymns of praise during the night. It also contains the treasuries of blessing. Above Maon is *Araboth*, which is the abode of right and justice, and of the dew of life and of blessing. It is the abode of the souls of the just and the pious, and here is the Throne of Glory and here dwell the holy Seraphim and Cherubim, who glorify and sanctify the Creator.[1]

The seven heavens are also described in the Slavonic *Enoch*: The angels thereupon carried Enoch to Heaven. In the first heaven he saw a great sea, which was greater than the earthly sea and where the rulers of the stars were dwelling. There were also the treasuries of snow and ice, and dread angels were guarding them. In the second heaven Enoch saw prisoners suspended and awaiting eternal judgment. They were the angels who had rebelled against God, and they begged Enoch to intercede for them and obtain the mercy of the Most High. But Enoch replied: " I am but a mortal man who knoweth not whither he goeth or what awaiteth him, and I am not worthy to pray for angels." In the third heaven Enoch saw a garden, full of trees of beautiful colour, bearing fruit, ripe and fragrant. There was also the tree of life on which rests the glory of God, when the Lord of the Universe comes to visit Paradise. This place, said the angels accompanying Enoch, is prepared for those who feed the hungry, clothe the naked, and raise the fallen; who accomplish righteous judgment and walk without blame before the Lord. In the northern region of this third heaven Enoch further saw a place very terrible to behold. It was full of gloom and

---

[1] *Midrash of the Ten Commandments,* Jellinek, *Beth-Hamidrash,* Vol. I, p. 64.

impenetrable darkness, surrounded on all sides by fire, cold and ice. " This place," said the angels accompanying Enoch, " is prepared for those who commit deeds of wickedness on earth; who are guilty of lying and stealing, of murder and theft, of envy and calumny; who oppress the poor and harbour evil thoughts."

From the third heaven Enoch was conducted to the fourth, and here he was shown the courses of the sun and of the moon.

He also witnessed the phœnixes and the *chalkadri* who had heads of crocodiles and feet and tails of lions. Nine hundred measures was their size, and their appearance of purple colour like the rainbow. They attended the chariot of the sun upon which it rides forth to shine upon the world, and each had twelve wings. There he also saw the eastern and western gates of the sun. In the fifth heaven Enoch saw the watchers who had rebelled against God, and whose brethren had already been confined in torment in the second heaven. Thereupon Enoch was carried to the sixth heaven, and here he saw the angels who record the deeds of man, regulate the courses of the stars and all the powers of nature. At last he was raised to the seventh heaven. And there he saw the Throne of Glory and hosts of angels sitting on the steps of the Throne. And Enoch fell down and worshipped. Thereupon the archangel Michael divested him of his earthly robes, and anointed him with the oil from the tree of mercy, and clothed him in the raiment of God's glory, and he became like one of the glorious inhabitants of the celestial regions.[1]

THE SEVEN UNDERWORLDS

And just as there are seven heavens so there are also seven planets of the earth; surrounded, like seven globes, by heavens. The seven earths are one beneath the other, and counting

[1] Charles and Morfill, *The Secrets of Enoch.*

upwards their names are as follows: the nethermost world (*Eretz hatachtonah*), *Adamah*, *Arka*, *Ge*, *Neshia*, *Zija*, and *Tebel*. The last is the uppermost of the worlds or earths, and is situated under the source of life.

It is related that when Adam was expelled from the Garden of Eden, he was sent to the nethermost earth, that is the *Eretz hatachtonah* which is a place of perdition, where nothing grows, and where there is no light, but utter darkness, for the heaven which is called Villon is dark. And when Adam entered this place a great fear seized him, and the flaming sword was turning round in the utter darkness and he knew not where to hide himself. And thus he remained for twenty-four hours and repented of his sins. The Creator had mercy upon him, and brought him to the second earth called Adamah. On this earth there is light from the stars and planets, and it is inhabited by demons and spirits.

Upon Arka there is a light shed by the sun, and it is inhabited by men, some of whom are giants, whilst others belong to a race of pigmies, and they are not endowed with reason such as the inhabitants of the earth planet called Tebel.

Sometimes they are just, but sometimes they are wicked and evil, endeavouring to cause harm to those who inhabit the upper earth which is Tebel, that is our own planet.

In Arka, which is the land of light and darkness, two rulers reign, one over light and the other over darkness.

And there was strife between them. They made peace only when Cain, who had slain his brother Abel, came down to them. They are named Ephrira and Kastimon. One of them has the face of a bull, and the other that of an eagle, but when they are in darkness they change into serpents and creep on their bellies. And when they pass the place where Aza and Azael are chained, the two chained demons awake and cry aloud and begin to rove about between the mountains of darkness, in their fear that the Creator will now call them to judgment. Ephrira and Kastimon swim over the seas and rove about in the world, and when they perceive Naamah [1] they follow her and endeavour to seize her, but she leaps sixty thousand miles and appears to men in different shapes, trying to seduce the race of men. Ephrira and Kastimon return once more to Arka, their abode in the netherworlds.

Gia or Ge is a vast place and is the length of the Gehinnom, or hell. Gia is near the element of fire, and its inmates possess wealth and precious stones. They make gifts to all those who come down to them either in consequence of the transmigration of souls, or driven by avarice and cupidity. Gia is situated in the midst of the seven worlds, and its inhabitants are well versed in witchcraft, but they also possess other wisdom.

And the fifth world is called *Neshia* (which is derived from the word *Neshia*, forgetfulness) and it is inhabited by a race of pigmies who have no memory whatever.

The sixth world is called *Zija*, and it is very dry and peopled by a race of very handsome men. They are always searching after sources or streams and often enter the waters and thus swim up to Tebel, the planet which is inhabited by the race of men. There is more faith in them than among other men.

Zones resembling in their nature the seven different worlds are to be found upon the earth which we inhabit, namely Tebel, containing races of men resembling in their appearance and nature those mentioned above.[2]

There are also ten unholy dark and gruesome spheres, spheres of darkness as counterparts to the spheres of light.

The first sphere of darkness is called *Thomiel*, derived from the word *Thomim* which means twins, for this dark sphere is the twin sister of the highest celestial region.

---

[1] Naamah, the sister of Tubal Cain, who is supposed to have been the wife of Shamdon and the mother of Asmodeus.

[2] *Emek hamelekh*, fol. 179, col. 4; 180, col. 1; *Yalkut Rubeni, Genesis*; see also Eisenmenger, *Entdecktes Judenthum*, Vol. I, p. 459; M. Bin Gorion, *Die Sagen der Juden*, Vol. I, pp. 330–334.

And, just as there is a ruler in the region of light, there is one also in the region of darkness. (Here again we evidently have the influence of Persian dualism.)

The second sphere is called *Goiel*—derived from the word *goah*, to bleat—for from that sphere there continually issues forth a bleating intended to disturb the Divine harmony and radiance and the order reigning in the Universe.

The third sphere is named *Sairiel*—derived from *sair*, hairy—which is the mother of everything wicked and evil. All evil deeds and wicked unholy powers, also venomous speech issue forth from this unholy sphere.

The fourth sphere makes the world tremble, and is constantly endeavouring to annihilate and destroy it. It drives out peace from the Garden of Eden and from the world, and is anxious to rout out all lovely plants.

The fifth sphere is the beginning of a tangible world, but still invisible to the human eye. The throne of the ruler of this sphere is made of living flame. And were it not for the mercy and loving-kindness of the Creator, the evil hosts and inmates of this sphere would have long ago destroyed all living creatures in one instant. From this terrible and unholy sphere issue forth sin and evil inclinations and spread in the world. It is also the abode of the angel of death who dwells in this unholy sphere.

The sixth sphere is constantly at war with omnipotent Providence. At certain moments it rebels against and declares war to the Ruler of the Universe. And then the world trembles in its foundations, harmony is disturbed, and terrible events occur and weigh heavily upon the upper and netherworlds.

The seventh sphere is called the hurling raven. For, as the cruel raven throws away its brat, so the ruler of this unholy sphere is constantly endeavouring to throw away and scatter the holy seed guarded in the treasury of the world's foundation.

The eighth sphere is the sphere of *Sammael*. It is responsible for strife and discomfort which exist in the world. For the ruler of this sphere roves all over the world and destroys the treasures of all other spheres. The inhabitants of this sphere know not the truth, and appear in different shapes. But they are always *red*. Their banner is red, their armies are red, their clothes are red, and the ground beneath them is *red*. The prince of the ninth sphere is called Gamliel. His servants change into serpents and spread horror among all those who behold them. The tenth sphere is called Lilith, and its prince is called Sariel; he is the great king of the demons who rule over the air.[1]

[1] *Yalkut Rubeni, Genesis*; Bin Gorion, *loc. cit.*, pp. 335–337.

CHAPTER IV

The Heavenly Hosts

Difference between Jewish and other myths—Divine messengers—Belief in higher beings—Angelology of the Old Testament—Jewish folklore—Conflict between monotheism and polytheism—The angelology of the Talmud—Persian and Babylonian influence—The hierarchy of the angels—The Ascension of Moses—He meets numerous angels—The Erelim—Nogah and Maadim—The Ishim—The angel Dinah or Jephephiah—The functions of the angels—Akatriel and Sandalphon—Rahab, prince of the sea—Ridja, lord of rain—Ben Nez, prince of storm—Tutelary angels—The creation of the angels—Created on second or fifth day—Creation of angels discussed by Fathers of Christian Church—St. Augustine, and Origen—Dionysius the Areopagite.

The Angels

With regard to angels Jewish myth differs considerably from the myths of other nations.

In the various mythologies of both eastern and western nations all the phenomena of nature, all universal and local occurrences are looked upon as the manifestations of separate independent divinities. The gods of Greece and India are many and various. They recognize, it is true, a superior God, a chief, but they, too, enjoy divine honours and dignities.

Jewish myth differs in this respect as in many others from such conceptions. Here, all natural manifestations, all universal and local events are the result of the will of *one* perfect Being, the Eternal and Creator, from whom everything emanates and to whom everything is subject.

Even Jewish myth, steeped as it was in monotheism, would not tolerate an idea bordering on duality or plurality of gods.

The ministering angels, therefore, peopling the Pantheon created by Jewish myth, are not at all independent agents with Divine power, independence, and free will. They enjoy no will of their own, but are the obedient and willing messengers and agents of a Divine Providence whose bidding they are bound to do. God Himself being often too exalted and too high to interfere in the affairs of the world, excepting certain rare occasions, charges these angels to execute His decrees.

The Rabbis of the Talmud, and the exponents of pretalmudic and post-talmudic Jewish myth and legend, were so anxious to avoid any idea that could give rise to the conception of duality and, above all, plurality, that they distinctly repeated the teaching that the angels were created either on the second or on the fifth day. Premundane creation was limited to abstract ideas, to wisdom, reward, and punishment.

The belief in higher beings, more perfect than man, is common to antiquity and especially to the Orient. Not only were the heavens and the whole universe peopled with angels and demons, that is to say, with good and evil spirits, but primitive man, and especially the Orientals, believed in the influence which these higher and more perfect beings or spirits exercised upon the sublunar world. The angels also served as intermediaries between man and Divinity. The mythologies of antiquity are full of such spirits, partly good, partly evil, and arranged in a perfect hierarchy. The Old Testament knows almost nothing of such spirits, for whenever the mention of angels is made they are used in the sense of agencies of the Divine power. In the Old Testament, the appearance of angels is nothing else but the manifestation of the activity of Divinity in the world of the senses. They are messengers,[1] or the impersonal acts of Divine Providence.

---

[1] Malachim, ἄγγελοι.

Side by side, however, with the Old Testament, folklore
and popular imagination gave rise to a number of myths
and legends, which the Rabbis and masters of the Cabbala,
or Hebrew mysticism, subsequently utilized for allegorical
and ethical purposes. Jewish angelology and the myths and
legends about angels and demons passed through many
phases before they arrived to pure mysticism.

The angelology of the Jews has always been the result
of the conflict constantly waged between monotheism and
the polytheism of the Oriental past, which never ceased and
still lingered on in the imagination of the people. Before
the Babylonian captivity the struggle was one between the
One God—Unique and Universal, the God of the Hebrew
prophets—and the national, local Gods of Oriental antiquity.
Constantly the Jewish people showed a hankering for the
polytheism of Egypt and Canaan; constantly the people forgot
the worship of the One God and prostrated themselves before
the altars of the many gods of antiquity. Angelology became
a compromise between pure monotheism and polytheism.
Whilst, however, the Bible looks upon angels only as personi-
fications of the acts of the One God, the Babylonian captivity
was responsible for a considerable change. No angel is
mentioned by name in Holy Scripture. The Jews had no
angelology before the Babylonian captivity, and the Talmud
Jerushalmi remarks that the names of the angels were brought
from Babylon.[1] In Persia and Babylonia the Jews came
into contact with a new polytheism, and with an elaborate
angelology, rich and varied, the angelology of the Babylonians,
and especially of the Persians. The ancient Oriental polytheism
still lingered in the popular mind, and the people eagerly
grasped the ideas which gave such scope to their imagination
and satisfied their polytheistic inclinations. Monotheism, how-

---

[1] *Jer, Rosh-ha-Shanah*, I, 2; see Grünbaum in *Z.D.M.G.*, Vol. XXXI, p. 25*f*; *Genesis
Rabba*, 48; see also Bacher, *Die Agada der Palästinensischen Amoräer*, I, p. 412.

ever, was still deeply rooted in the Jewish mind, and the Unique and only God was often considered too sacred and too holy to weave myths and legends round Him.

Under the influence of Parsism and the teaching of Zarathustra, angels begin to appear in Jewish lore in human shape and form, receive separate names, and are arranged in an hierarchy like the servants and courtiers of a king. The heads and chiefs are called princes, and the Jewish myths know of six or seven such angel-princes. The influence of the teaching of Zarathustra upon the angel—and demon—myths of ancient Israel is quite comprehensible. The period during which the Jews lived in Persia and Media, whither they had been exiled by Nebuchadnezzar, coincides with the time of the highest development of the Zend cult. It was here in Persia that Israel acquired the popular Persian beliefs in Paradise and Hell, in angels, demons, and genii. But these myths and legends received at the hands of the Jewish nation a monotheistic colouring, and were made use of by the Rabbis of the Talmud and the masters of the Cabbala to teach monotheism, to extol the majesty, omnipresence and omnipotence of the Creator, and to draw moral and ethical lessons.

The first to mention an angel by name is *Tobit*, where we read that the angel Raphael conducted Tobias into Media.[1] Daniel, who lived at Babylon, already mentions the angels Michael and Gabriel.[2] The second book of *Esdras* mentions Uriel.[3]

Jewish angelology, however, was developed after the return of the Jews from Babylonian captivity, and the myths and legends gathering round the angels and demons are scattered through the Talmud, the Midrashim, and the works of the Cabbalists. Popular imagination ascribes to some of the angels the function of teaching Adam, Noah, the Patriarchs, Moses, and the later heroes of Jewish history. In fact, a whole

---

[1] *The Book of Tobit*, 3, 17; 11, 2.   [2] *Daniel*, 8, 16; 9, 21; 10, 21.   [3] 4, 36.

mass of myth and legend has been woven into the heroic history of Israel. The names of the angels are always a composition of the name of God and the special commission entrusted to them. And thus the name of each ministering angel depends upon his message and often varies with it.[1] On his breast each angel has a tablet, in which the name of God and that of the angel is combined.[2]

Numerous were the angels whom Moses beheld when he ascended to Heaven. This is described in the book called *The Ascension of Moses* (or *Gedullath Moshe*). Moses was carried up to Heaven by the angel Metatron, accompanied by fifteen thousand angels on the right hand and fifteen thousand angels on the left hand. In the first heaven he saw many windows at each of which stood an angel. And Metatron explained to him that these windows were the windows of life and of death, of prayers and supplication, of peace and war, of joy and tears, of sin and repentance, of life and death. In the second heaven he saw one angel three hundred parasangs long, accompanied by myriads of other angels who, as Metatron explained to him, were placed over the clouds and rain. In the third heaven Moses saw an angel whose length is a journey of five hundred years, accompanied by myriads of other ministering angels, placed over corn, trees, and fruits. They were called *Erelim*, and the angel presiding over them had seventy thousand heads and seventy thousand mouths in each head, and seventy thousand tongues in each mouth. In the fourth heaven he saw the Temple built of red, green, and white fire, of gems and carbuncle. And there he also saw the angels placed over the sun and the moon, over the stars and the planets. He further saw there the two stars called *Nogah* and *Maadim*, one standing above the sun to cool its intense heat in summer, and the other standing above the moon to protect the world against the cold of the moon.

---

[1] *Exodus Rabba*, 29; *Genesis Rabba*, 78.   [2] *Yalkut*, Vol. II, § 797; see W. Bacher, *loc. cit.*

In the fifth heaven Moses saw angels who were half of fire and half of snow, and although the snow was above the fire it did not extinguish it. They belonged to the angel-group called *Ishim*. In the sixth heaven Moses saw an angel whose length was a journey of five hundred years and who was entirely of ice, and myriads of angels belonging to the group of the *holy watchers* stood by his side and praised the Lord. And in the seventh heaven Moses saw the angel of wrath and the angel of anger, and also the angel of death. The angels of wrath and anger were wholly of fire and fastened with chains of dark and red fire. The angel of death was full of fiery eyes, so that anyone who looked at him fell down in dread. In this heaven, which is called *Araboth*, Moses also saw an angel called *Dina* who is teaching the souls created by God and placed in Paradise. His name is also Jephephiah.[1]

And thus, the heavenly hosts, the ministering angels, are represented in post - exilic Jewish myths and legends somewhat resembling the retinue of an Oriental ruler, whom even the foremost courtiers are not allowed to see in his secret and very private apartments. From behind a curtain (the *Pargod*) He issues His commands.[2] The ministering angels, or the *Malachei Hashareth*, are not only the agents of Providence, the messengers of Divine commissions, but they also have the function of singing hymns in praise of the Creator and of protecting mankind, in particular the virtuous and pious. The host of angels, whose function it is to sing hymns in praise of the Creator, are being daily created. They are called forth by the breath of Almighty from the rivers of liquid fire flowing under the throne of the Eternal. We thus find in Jewish literature, under the influence of the Persian religious system, a veritable Pantheon which could have easily become dangerous to Jewish monotheism. But Judaism

[1] *Gedullath Moshe*, Amsterdam, 1754; see also Gaster in *Journal of the Royal Asiatic Society*, 1893, pp. 572–620.
[2] *Berachoth*, 18b; *Sanhedrin*, 89b; *Yoma*, 77a. See also The Koran, *Sura*, 42, 50.

utilized these elements for the purpose of concentrating the plurality of Divine powers and manifestations in the power of the One God. There is no trace whatever in Jewish myth of any idea of either a plurality of Divinities or even of a dualism. Like the sun, the moon, and the stars, the angels are supernatural powers, obeying the command of the Creator and doing His bidding. They are all the servants of the Almighty, and even the angels of destruction only obey the command of God and execute His decrees.[1]

As the angels are vastly superior to men, in capacities and dignities, so popular imagination, in order to make them in some degree comprehensible to human understanding, invested them with a nature, offices, and occupations similar to those which occur among men. They are thus represented as servants and attendants of All-Father, the King of the Universe, who is surrounded by a court of angels like a great king. They are the courtiers and ministers, the attendants and councillors of the Divine King.

The Prophets had already spoken poetically of the angels as the host of heaven standing round the throne of the Lord of the Universe, and frequently sent to the lower world to execute His decrees. Thus we read in Job: " There was a day when the sons of God came to present themselves before the Lord." [2] " I saw the Lord sitting on His throne, and all the hosts of heaven standing by Him, on His right hand and on His left." [3]

The angels were thus supposed to be dwelling in Heaven, in the regions of light, and myth and legend became busy, describing how they are clothed in garments of light, radiance, and glory, standing before the throne of the Creator.

Innumerable are the functions of the angels. Some are appointed for celestial service, whilst others are attached to the earth and especially to man. Others again are continually

---

[1] E. Bischoff, *Babylonisch-Astrales*, p. 139. [2] *Job*, 1, 6. [3] *I Kings*, 22, 19.

travelling between Heaven and earth. To every thought and
to every action of man, either for good or for evil, there corresponds in Heaven or upon earth, in the netherworlds and
in space, a group of angels (or demons). The Jewish myths
and legends in the Talmud and in the Midrashim mention
the names of a number of such angels. *Akatriel* is specially
appointed to carry swiftly on his wings the words and innermost thoughts of man to the celestial regions and before the
throne of God, whilst *Sandalphon*, who surpasses in height
all his heavenly colleagues, passes his time in weaving crowns
of glory for his Creator.[1] There is another class of angels
whom the Creator calls into existence for a very short span
of time. They arise from the river of fire, sing a hymn to His
glory, and then disappear.[2]

Every day the angels pass before the throne of the Eternal,
and then take up their places and their functions.

Whenever a soul, after its sojourn upon earth, in the
prison house of the body, rejoins its heavenly abode, a joyous
tremor passes through the hosts of Heaven. The news is
passed on from one group of the celestials to another, and
all of them utter a shout of joy, giving thanks to the Master
who has brought back to them one of their companions.

And just as the planets influence the course of nature,
so the angels, too, preside over natural occurrences. Thus
Michael is the prince of snow, Gabriel the prince of fire,
Jorkami prince of hail, Rahab is the prince of the sea,[3] Ridja
the prince of rain.[4]

Rashi,[5] in his commentary to the passage in *Yoma*, 21*a*,
quotes *Taanith*, 25*b*, where it is said that Ridja resembles a calf
and stands midway between the upper and the nether waters.

It should be borne in mind that the planet of rain in the
Pleiades is in the sign of the bull.

---

[1] *Hagigah*, 13*b*.   [2] *Hagigah*, 14*a*; *Genesis Rabba*, 78.   [3] *Baba Batra*, 74*b*.   [4] *Taanith*, 25*b*.
[5] Solomon bar Isaac, French Commentator on Bible and Talmud (1040–1105).

Ben Nez is the prince of the storm.[1]   Numerous other
angels are mentioned in later Jewish Midrashic lore, such as
Galgaliel, Ophaniel, Barakiel (lightning), Lailahel (night),
Raashiel (earthquake), Shalgiel (snow), &c.

The choir of celestial singers consists of six hundred and
ninety-four myriads of angels, who daily pronounce and praise
the Holy name, saying: " Blessed be the name of Thy heavenly
glory from sunrise to sunset."[2]

The angels have another function and that is to accompany
man and watch over him. Every pious and virtuous act accomplished by man produces a tutelary angel. The tutelary angels
also have the function of pleading the cause of the just and
pious before the Throne of the Eternal. Whenever one of the
heroes or pious men of Israel meets with a calamity, or is in
great distress, they intercede before the Throne of Glory.
Thus, when Abraham raised his hand to sacrifice his son
Isaac, when Pharaoh intended to kill Moses, hosts of ministering angels prostrated themselves before the Throne of the
Eternal, and pleaded until the Creator saved them.[3]

With regard to the creation of the angels opinions differ.
Some say that the angels were created either on the second
or on the fifth day of Creation,[4] and that God consulted with
them when He said: " Let us make man in our image, after
our likeness."   Others, however, are of opinion that the
angels were created long before the world came into existence.

Apart, however, from the ministering angels created at
the beginning of the world, the creation of these winged
messengers is still being continued, for to execute every be-
hest of God a new angel is created who passeth away as soon
as he has executed the command of the Holy One.

---

[1] *Baba Batra*, 25a.
[2] *Pirke de Rabbi Eliezer*, Ch. 12; see also Kohut, in *Abhandlungen für die Kunde des Morgenlandes*, Vol. IV, p. 19
[3] *Genesis Rabba*, 65; *Pirke de Rabbi Eliezer*, Ch. 32; see also *Hagigah*, 5a.
[4] *Genesis Rabba* 1 and 3; see also G. Friedlaender's Transl. of *Pirke de Rabbi Eliezer*, p. 20, note 3.

Some of the ministering angels have only a very fleeting existence. They are created every day, and after having uttered the praises of the Eternal pass away into the river of fire, called Nehar di Nur, whence they issued. Companies of angels are thus being created daily, some of whom continue their existence, whilst others, issuing from the fiery river and created only for the daily service of the Eternal and for the purpose of executing His commands, pass away.[1]

Very frequently we also find in Rabbinic and Midrashic folklore, that the phenomena and powers of nature are hypostatized into angels. Sea and wind, hail and rain, life and death, health and disease, wealth and poverty are supposed to be presided over by a special angel.

The question of the creation of angels is discussed not only in Jewish lore but also in the works of the Christian Fathers of the Church. St. Augustine is of opinion that the angels were created on the first day and that they are included in the name of *Light*,[2] whilst Origen[3] writes that the angels were created long before the world. Some authors base themselves upon the passage in *Job*: " Where wast thou when I laid the foundation of the earth; and all the Sons of God shouted for joy?"[4]

Both the Rabbis of the Talmud and the Fathers of the Christian Church frequently refer to angels as appropriated to persons, nations, empires, countries, and cities. But already Daniel refers to Michael as the protector of Israel, and to the angel protector of Persia, when he makes the angel Gabriel say that " the prince of the kingdom of Persia withstood him one and twenty days ".[5] The idea of the tutelary angels of the various nations is supposed to have its foundation in the passage of the *Septuaginta*, " God had set the bounds of the peoples according to the number of the *angels* of Israel ".[6]

---

[1] *Hagigah*, 14a; *Book of Enoch*, 14, 19; 70, 1.
[2] St. Augustine, *Lib. I de Genesi ad litt.*, Cap. 9.   [3] Origen, *Hom. I in Genes.*
[4] *Job*, 38, 4, 7.   [5] *Daniel*, 10, 21.   [6] *Deuteron.* 32, 8.

This passage is supposed to mean the government of each particular country and nation with which God had entrusted His angels. The belief that guardian angels were commissioned to attend individuals, to take care of and to protect them, was shared by heathens and Jews alike, and is shared by the Fathers of the Church. Plato speaks of the two demons or genii who accompany every man, one prompting him to good, the other to evil, and Hesiod speaks of the aerial spirits designed to be the guardians of mankind.[1] In the *Vita Adami*, Adam refers to the guardian angels set to guard Eve and himself. It was during their absence that the enemy came to Eve and caused her to sin.

The celestial hierarchy is also the subject of many discussions in Jewish lore, parallels to which are found in the works of other nations. Many of the Fathers of the Church have discussed the question, and Dionysius the Areopagite, devotes an entire treatise to the question of the hierarchy of angels.

The precedence of the angels, their different names, according to their degrees of power and knowledge, all constitute so much material for numerous myths and legends. " We are not to be surprised," writes a Christian author, " at these visions fabricated by the Jews, for if they be compared with those of many Christian authors, who have settled a ceremonial and rules for precedency among angels, the Jews would appear not more blamable in this point than some Christians." [2]

---

[1] Hesiod, *Works and Days*, I, Vers. 121.
[2] Basnage, *Histoire des Juifs*, Vol. IV, Chap. 9; see also Calmet, *Dictionary of the Bible*, Vol. I, p. 128.

CHAPTER V

The Angel-Princes, or Archangels

The seven archangels: Michael, Gabriel, Uriel, Raphael, Metatron, Sandalphon, Rediyao (Ridia)—The four national angels of Israel—Uza the guardian angel of Egypt—The functions of the angels—The two angels of death, Gabriel and Sammael—The angel Rediyao—The story of Metatron —Metatron and Mithra—The Prince of the Presence—Sar Haolam—He teaches Moses—Elisha ben Abuyah meets Metatron—A Jewish Faust—The punishment of Metatron—The two Metatrons—Enoch-Metatron—Enoch is translated to Heaven where he becomes Metatron—Protest of the angels against Enoch-Metatron—Great honour shown to Enoch-Metatron—Thirty thousand gates of wisdom are opened to him—The mysteries of the Law and the secrets of Nature are revealed to Enoch-Metatron—He bears witness against the sinful generation of the Flood—The jealousy of the angels— Moses meets the angel Kemmuel, the guardian of Heaven, and Hadarniel —The fire of Sandalphon—The fiery river Rigyon—Gallizur, or Rasiel— The angels pay homage to Moses—Jephephiah hands over the Holy Law to Moses.

THE ANGEL-PRINCES

Apart from the ministering angels there are the angel-princes, four of whom surround the throne of the Creator. They are Michael, Raphael, Gabriel, and Uriel.

These angel-princes enjoy the privilege of being within the *Pargod*, or the veil, whilst all the others only hear Divine commands from behind the veil or curtain.[1]

The seven angel-princes, or archangels, in Jewish myth, correspond to the seven *Amshaspands* of Persia which are influenced by the seven Babylonian gods of the planets. The names of these angels are often changed in accordance with their particular functions,[2] and it is interesting to notice that

[1] *Hagigah, 5b; Pirke de Rabbi Eliezer, Ch. 4.*   [2] *Genesis Rabba, 78.*

when the star of Marduk is in the zenith, he is called Ninib.[1]

The seven angel - princes are: Michael, Gabriel, Uriel, Raphael, Metatron, Sandalphon, and Rediyao. They are above all others in rank and dignity, and are allowed in the vicinity of the Divine throne of light. Michael, which name means " Who is like God ", is to the right; Gabriel, which means " Strength of God ", is to the left; Uriel, which means " Splendour of God ", is in front of the Throne; and Raphael, which means " Healing from God ", is behind the Throne.[2] They are the four national angels, that is the angels of Israel, and hence their Hebrew names. They are the watchers of Israel. Michael's principal qualities are : mercy, loving-kindness, and peace.[3] He constantly pleads the cause of Israel and defends it before the Throne of the Eternal.

Thus, when the Almighty said to Michael, this tutelary angel of Israel: " Thy nation has sinned," the angel pleaded: " Lord of the Universe! There are many pious individuals who ought to outweigh the sin of the collectivity." [4] But all the other nations, too, have each their tutelary angels. The tutelary angel of Egypt is Uza, and when the children of Israel were led out of Egypt, Uza complained and clamoured for justice before the Throne of the Eternal. " The nation Thou art taking out of Egypt I have a right upon," argued Uza. But Michael, the defender of Israel, appeared and soon crushed all the arguments of Uza.[5]

Michael, the angel-prince, is the harbinger and messenger bringing and announcing good tidings. He is also the prince of peace, and as such is often called the high-priest, ministering in Heaven.[6]

In the *Book of Enoch* frequent mention is made of the angel of peace.

Gabriel, who is next to Michael, is the strength of the

[1] Jeremias, *Das alte Testament*, p. 78.   [2] *Numbers Rabba*, 2.   [3] *Yalkut*, § 186.
[4] *Yoma*, 77a.   [5] *Midrash Abkir*, quoted in *Yalkut*, § 241.   [6] *Hagigah*, 12b; *Zebachim*, 62a.

Lord. He manifests the Divine justice and punishment of the wicked, and only for the latter he is terrible, being mild with regard to the just. Divine justice is thus identified with Gabriel. He is to the left of the Creator, and represents not only the avenging and punishing power of the Almighty against Israel, but also against the hostile elements which arise in the midst of Israel or against other nations. He is the personification of justice and not, as imagined in the traditions of the Mohammedans, the enemy of Israel. Michael is made of snow, Gabriel of fire, but they live peacefully together without the fire of the one injuring the snow of the other.[1]

According to Moslem tradition, Gabriel is the national angel and the angel of revelation of the Moslems and is placed to the right of the Creator.

In Jewish legend, it was Gabriel who punished the Egyptian servant when she refused to fetch Moses out of the waters.[2] It was he who was busy in the destruction of Sodom,[3] but it was also Gabriel who marked the fronts of the wicked with a letter in blood, and those of the pious and just with a letter in ink, so that the angels of destruction should not harm them.[4]

Girt with his sword of justice ever since the six days of creation, Gabriel exercises justice in wars and on the battle-fields, punishing the traitors and helping the just.[5]

He also acts as angel of death. For there are two angels of death, one for the inhabitants of the Holy Land of Palestine, who is Gabriel, and the other, who is Sammael, for the rest of the world. Both Gabriel and Sammael receive their orders from Metatron who is the president of this triumvirate of death. Metatron issues his orders to Gabriel, Gabriel to Sammael, and the latter again to the ministering serving messengers of death who bring the departed souls to their senders.[6]

---

[1] *Debarim Rabba*, 5; see also *Shir-Hashirim Rabba*.   [2] *Sotah*, 12b; *Exodus Rabba*, 1.
[3] *Pirke de Rabbi Eliezer*, Ch. 25; *Genesis Rabba*, 50; *Baba Mezia*, 86b.
[4] *Sabbath*, 55a.   [5] *Sanhedrin*, 26a.   [6] *Yalkut Rubeni*, § 13; *Yalkut Chadash*, § 44.

Gabriel is fire, not only fire that consumes dry and even wet matter, but fire that drives away fire.[1]

Uriel personifies the radiance emanating from the Divine nature, and Raphael personifies the Divine power of healing. He heals and banishes disease, and is consequently known also under the name of Suriel, the angel who calls back or causes to disappear every disease.[2] He is mentioned in the *Book of Enoch* under the name of Surjan.

The angel Sandalphon stands upon the earth, whilst his head reaches the heavens. He is supposed to stand behind the chariot and to weave crowns for the Creator.[3]

The angel Rediyao, who has been compared to the Persian Ardvi-Cüra, is the angel of rain, the genius of water, both of the celestial and the earthly waters. His terrible voice resounds continually throughout the world. And some of the Rabbis relate in the folkloristic tales of the Talmud, that Rediyao resembles a calf. He stands midst between the upper and the lower water floods, or the *Tehomoth*. He cries unto the upper floods: " Let flow thy waters;" and unto the lower Tehomoth he commands: " Let arise thy floods." [4]

THE STORY OF METATRON

The myths and legends of ancient Jewish angelology are particularly busy with the angel-prince who is known as Metatron. It has been suggested that the idea of Metatron has been borrowed from the Persian Mithra, and that the very name of this angel, like all the other names of the angels, has come from Persia.[5] It seems to me that this is quite a plausible theory, although the majority of authors derive the name of Metatron from the Greek μεταδρόνος (or δρόνον) .[6]

Metatron is the prince of the Presence, the prince of the

---

[1] *Yoma,* 21b; see Kohut, *loc. cit.,* p. 33.   [3] *Berachoth,* 51a.
[3] *Hagigah,* 13b; *Exodus Rabba,* 21.   [4] *Taanith,* 25b.   [5] Kohut, *loc. cit.*
[6] A. Franck, *La Kabbale;* Graetz, *Gnosticismus;* Hirschfeld, *Frankels' Zeitschrift,* 1846, p. 353; Edersheim, *The Life and Times of Jesus the Messiah,* 1883, Vol. I, p. 47, note.

face, the prince of the world. Into the innermost chamber
of the Divine Presence he is allowed to penetrate, whilst
other angels only receive his commands from behind the
veil.[1]

He is the angel of God who spoke to Moses in the name
of the Lord of the Universe, and who received the mission
to lead the Children of Israel into the Holy Land. He is
severe and revengeful against all those who forsake the name
of the Lord.[2]

But Metatron is also the protector of the world, its super-
intendent into whose hands the world is given and who is
therefore called the *Sar ha-Olam*, the prince of the world.[3]

In early Jewish myth and legend Metatron is represented
as the vicegerent of the Creator. It is he who transmits the
orders of the Eternal to Moses. He also instructs infants who
have died without knowledge.[4] He is called the prince of the
universe, charged by God, the All-Father, to create the
world.

We thus find in the myth of Metatron the influence of the
idea of the demi-ourgos. Judaism, however, could not allow
this gnostic doctrine, and those who taught it were excom-
municated.

Metatron is also the preserver and guardian of the law
and of the Holy Writ, and it was he who afterwards became
the teacher and instructor of Moses. Kohut suggested that
Sagsagel, who is mentioned in Rabbinic legend as the teacher
of Moses and as being present at the latter's death, is only
another epithet for Metatron.[5] Metatron is thus the greatest
of all angels. He is the representative of God, the angel of
the face; he speaks in the name of God.

But Jewish monotheism strongly opposed the idea that
Metatron had either the power to forgive sins, or was to be

[1] *Hagigah*, 5a, 15a, 16a.   [2] *Sanhedrin*, 38b.
[3] *Hullin*, 66a; *Sanhedrin*, 94a; *Yebamot*, 16b.   [4] *Abodah Zarah*, 3b.
[5] Kohut, *loc. cit.*, p. 42.

adored or regarded as a mediator between man and his Maker.

Of Elisha ben Abuyah it is told that one day he saw Metatron sitting in Heaven and would have inferred that there were two supreme powers.

THE STORY OF ELISHA BEN ABUYAH AND METATRON

A Jewish Faust

And it came to pass that one day the Rabbi Elisha, the son of Abuyah, was allowed to pry into Paradise, and he perceived the angel Metatron, the recording angel, sitting on a seat, and registering the merits of the Children of Israel. At this sight the Rabbi was struck with astonishment, and would have inferred that there were two supreme powers in Heaven.

He exclaimed: " Is it not laid down that there is no sitting in Heaven and no shortsightedness?" And in order to prove the angel's inferiority, Metatron was ordered by the heavenly court to receive sixty fiery lashes from another angel. Metatron then asked and obtained leave to cancel all the past merits of the apostate Rabbi who was henceforth known by the name of *Akher* (another). And one day, which happened to be a Sabbath, and the day of atonement, the Rabbi was riding along when he heard from Heaven: " Return all the backsliding children, but Akher alone abide thou in thy sin." [1]

According to some sources, however, Metatron is supposed to be none other than Enoch, the son of Jared, after his translation to Heaven. The Enoch legend, in Jewish lore, gradually underwent a change. In the earlier Haggadah Enoch is not identical with Metatron.

In the Slavonic *Book of Enoch*, the son of Jared is described as a very wise man whom God loved and received, enabling

[1] *Hagigah*, 15a.

him to see the heavenly abodes, kingdoms of the wise, great, and never-changing God. Two angels, therefore, appeared to Enoch and bade him make ready to ascend to Heaven. Enoch thereupon admonished his sons to walk before the face of the Lord and to keep His judgments, and, furthermore, not to seek for him till he was brought back to them. Carried aloft through the air by the two angels he visited the seven heavens.

And when God had communicated to Enoch the secrets of Creation, and how he created the visible out of the invisible, he commanded him to return to earth for thirty days, there to teach his sons during that time. And Enoch did as the Lord had commanded him. He told his sons what he had seen, and admonished them and instructed them. He described unto them the courses of the sun and of the moon, thunder and lightning, Hell and Paradise, and impressed upon them the necessity of fearing God. But whilst fearing God they should never revile man, for man being made in the image of God, he who reviles man really reviles God. Enoch further admonished his sons not to swear, either by Heaven or by earth, to live in meekness, refrain from revenge, and to be open-handed and generous to the needy.

When the thirty days elapse, Enoch once more addresses his sons and the people who assemble at Achuzan to listen to his words and to take leave of him. He addresses them on various topics, bids them be faithful, and announces a time when there will be neither labour nor sickness, neither suffering nor sorrow, neither night nor darkness. He is then carried off to the highest heaven.

In the later Haggadah, however, Enoch, the son of Jared, becomes identical with Metatron.

He, Enoch, served before the Lord in truth, and was not among the inhabitants of the earth, for he was translated above into the firmament, through the word of the Lord;

and He called him by the name of Metatron, that is the great scribe.

Enoch himself related the story of his ascension to Heaven to Rabbi Ishmael, who spoke to him and asked him the reason of his great honour, and why he was greater than any prince, and higher than any angel.

And Enoch told the Rabbi as follows:

" I was in reality Enoch, the son of Jared. And when the generation of the Flood had sinned before the Lord and did not walk in the path of righteousness, the Lord took me from that sinful generation into the highest heaven, that I might be a witness against that generation. The Eternal, blessed be His name, removed me from earth, that I should stand before the Throne of Glory and the seat of His majesty, and before the wheels of His chariot, there to accomplish the requirements of the Most High. Thereupon my flesh became flame, and my arteries fire; my eyeballs became torches of fire, and the light of my eyes the flashing of lightning. My body became burning fire, my limbs fiery, burning wings, and the hair of my head was a flame. Flames were cleft asunder by my right hand. A wind, a storm and a tempest blew around me, and the voice of a mighty earthquake was before and behind me. I was carried to Heaven in a fiery chariot, by horses of fire. And when I entered into the presence of God, the sacred Chajjoth, Seraphim, Ophanim, Cherubim, all the fiery ministering angels recoiled five thousand three hundred and eighty miles at the smell of me, crying aloud: ' What a smell hath come among us from the son of woman. Why is he admitted into Heaven?' But the Almighty replied: ' Cherubim and Seraphim, ye, my servants all, know that I have exalted the son of Jared to be chief among the angels of Heaven. All my sons upon earth have rejected My sovereignty and are adoring idols, but the son of Jared alone hath remained faithful unto Me. In reward therefore for his virtue I exalt him.'" And the height of Enoch-Metatron is very great, for it would take a man five hundred years to walk from his heel to the crown of his head.[1]

Metatron is further described in Jewish myth as follows: Enoch-Metatron had seventy names, corresponding to the seventy languages of the world and to the seventy Kings of Kings. He was greater than all the princes of Heaven and earth, more beloved than all the ministering angels, and more powerful than all the mighty ones. He was Enoch the son of Jared. When the generation of the Flood walked in the path of evil and did evil deeds, the Creator took him, and he ascended to Heaven. And here he bore witness against the sinful generation of the Flood.

The Creator sent for him the heavenly prince Anphiel, and he took Enoch, he who was Metatron, before the very eyes of men and brought him in a fiery chariot, drawn by fiery horses up to Heaven. And ministering angels announced his ascent and brought him into the spheres of splendour. But the fiery Seraphim and Cherubim knew of his coming even when he was still sixty-five thousand three hundred miles away. And they murmured and said:

" What is the worth of this man born of woman, and who is he that he should come among us who are fashioned of liquid fire?" But the voice of the Creator resounded from one end of the world unto the other and proclaimed: " Do not murmur, ye my ministering angels, Cherubim and Seraphim. The race of men has become wicked, and the sons of men have done evil deeds. They have served and prostrated themselves before strange gods and idols. Enoch alone, the son of Jared, walked in the path of righteousness, and excelled in justice and virtue and faith. And this is his reward." And Enoch, the son of Jared, who was called henceforth Metatron,

---

[1] Menachem Recanati, *Commentary to the Five Books of Moses*; see also *Sepher Hekhalot*, in Jellinek, *Beth-Hamidrash*, Vol. V, pp. 172–175.

was carried upon the wings of splendour into the highest of
heavenly spheres, into the midst of a great palace in Araboth,
the seventh heaven.

And here, surrounded by fiery ministering angels, Cherubim
and Seraphim who do the bidding of the Creator of the Universe, between flaming Seraphim and radiant *Hashmalim*,
Enoch-Metatron became the chief of the hosts of ministering
angels.

And the Creator opened before Enoch-Metatron the
thirty thousand gates of wisdom, and the thirty thousand
gates of reason and intelligence. He also opened unto him
the gates of life and peace, of power and courage, of benevolence and generosity, of love and law, and of mercy, humility,
and fear of the Lord. And Enoch-Metatron received the
heavenly gifts of wisdom and knowledge, of reason and intelligence, of life and love, of mercy and courage, of power
and grace, of radiance, beauty and pride. And after he had
been endowed with these heavenly gifts, the Creator blessed
Enoch-Metatron with three hundred and sixty-five thousand
blessings, and he became great and glorified throughout the
Universe. And the Creator gave unto Enoch-Metatron seventy-
two wings, thirty-six to his right and thirty-six to his left.
And He also gave unto him three hundred and sixty-five
thousand eyes, and every eye is like unto the great heavenly
light.

He was endowed with all the splendour and beauty and
radiance that exist in the Universe. And Enoch-Metatron
is seated upon a throne of splendour, and a canopy of radiance,
light, and beauty is above him, for all the splendour and all
the light of the world are woven into it.

And a voice announced from Heaven to Heaven and all
over the earth, saying: " The Lord of the World, the Creator of
the Universe, has raised Enoch-Metatron, His faithful servant,
above all the princes in Heaven and upon earth, and made him

the mightiest angel of the Presence. And all supplications to
the Creator of the Universe are henceforth to be addressed
through Enoch-Metatron, for he is endowed with wisdom
and knowledge, with reason and understanding beyond all
other angels. And the mysteries of the upper worlds and of
the netherworlds are open unto Enoch-Metatron."

And all the mysteries of the law and the depths of piety
were revealed unto Enoch-Metatron. The innermost thoughts
of all the creatures are open to him, and all the riddles of the
Universe and the mysteries of creation are known to him.

Clad in a radiant garment of light, and wearing a crown
set with forty-nine precious stones that are more resplendent
than the sun, his radiance sheds its light in all the four corners
of Araboth and in the seven heavens, and in the four corners
of the earth.

And with a flaming finger the Creator of the Universe
engraved upon the crown of Enoch-Metatron all the signs
by which were created heaven and earth, the seas and rivers,
the mountains and the hills, the stars, planets, thunder and
lightning, snow and hail, storm and wind, all the elements of
the Universe, its harmony and order.

And when Enoch-Metatron placed the radiant crown
upon his head, all the princes and angels of the heavenly
host trembled and were filled with awe. And the angels of
fire and of lightning, of storm and wind, of wrath and fury,
of hail and snow and rain, of day and night, of the sun, the
moon, the stars, and planets, all those who are set over the
destinies of the world, they quaked and trembled before
Enoch-Metatron.

Blinded by the glory and radiance emanating from the
countenance of this prince of angels and leader of the heavenly
host, they fell upon their faces and did homage to him.

He bears witness against the sinful generation of men
who were destroyed in the great flood. For when men dare

to assail the benevolence and mercy of the Creator who wiped out the generation of the Flood and all their wives and children and their cattle and beasts, Enoch-Metatron, who was chosen from among them and ascended to Heaven, bears witness to the justice and mercy of All-Father who punishes the wicked and rewards the just and virtuous.[1]

THE JEALOUSY OF THE ANGELS

The angels are often supposed to be jealous of man and particularly of Israel, to whom the Eternal has vouchsafed His loving-kindness. Thus, when Moses ascended to Heaven to receive the Law, the angels raised a protest and plotted to destroy him. And it came to pass that when the son of Amram was carried in a cloud to the celestial regions he was met by the angel Kemuel, the gatekeeper of the abode of the angels, who commands the host of twelve thousand angels of destruction, keeping watch at the gates of *Rakia*. He barred the way to Moses and thus he spoke: " How darest thou approach the seat of the fiery inhabitants of Heaven, son of Amram? Return to earth, lest I destroy thee with my fiery breath." But the son of Amram boldly replied: " I come not of my own will, but with the permission of the Most High, blessed be His name, who commanded me, His servant, to appear before the Throne of Glory there to receive the Holy Law." And Moses wrestled with Kemuel and conquered him. Thereupon the son of Amram continued his way when he met the angel Hadarniel. This angel is taller and more terrible than the other celestial inhabitants, and at every word that he speaketh thousands of flashes of lightning issue from his mouth. Hadarniel raised his terrible voice which sent fear into the heart of Moses and caused him to quake. " How darest thou approach the seat of the Holy of Holies, O son of

---

[1] Jellinek, *Beth-Hamidrash*, Vol. V, pp. 172–176; see *ibid*, Vol. II, pp. 114–116; see also *The Book of Yashar*, Migne, *Dictionnaire des Apocryphes*, Vol. II.

Amram," he cried. But a voice from the Throne of Glory was heard which bade Hadarniel be silent. And thus spake the voice from the Throne of Glory. " Ever since you have been created by the word of My mouth, you have been jealous of man and have sought him quarrel. At the beginning of things, when it was My design to create man, many among you raised a protest and cried, ' What is man that Thou shouldst remember him.' [1] But I destroyed many hosts of these angels with My little finger,[2] and I created man in My own image. And now you seek quarrel with My faithful servant, the son of Amram, whom I have commanded to ascend to these heavenly regions to receive the Holy Law." Thus spake the voice from the Throne of Glory.

When Hadarniel heard these words he hastened before the throne of the Eternal, blessed be His name, and thus he pleaded: " Lord of the Universe! It is known unto Thee that I was unaware of Thy command to the son of Amram or that it was Thy sovereign will that he should appear in these celestial regions. And now I will be his guide and attendant, ministering unto him and obeying him even as a pupil does obey his master." Thereupon, Hadarniel, who is taller than his companions and from whose mouth issue forth flashes of lightning, bent low before the son of Amram and went before him, even as a pupil goes before his master. And when they reached the fire of Sandalphon, Hadarniel turned unto Moses and thus he spake: " O son of Amram! Turn back now, for I cannot bear the fire of Sandalphon, lest it will destroy me." When Moses perceived Sandalphon he was frightened in his heart, and prayed unto the Lord of the Universe to protect him from the fire of this mighty angel. The Lord had pity upon Moses and protected him with His boundless love, until he had passed the fire of Sandalphon. Of Sandalphon it is said that he is taller than his companions,

---

[1] *Ps.* 8, 6. [2] *Sanhedrin,* 38b.

and that his place is behind the celestial chariot (the Merkaba), weaving crowns of glory for the Creator.

When Moses had passed the fire of Sandalphon he met the angel Rigyon who is really a fiery river issuing forth from underneath the Throne of Glory.[1] In this fiery stream the angels bathe every morning. Whenever the ministering angels appear before the Throne of Glory to be judged by the Lord of the Universe, they plunge into the fiery river of Rigyon and are rejuvenated. When the son of Amram had passed the fiery river of Rigyon, he met the angel Gallizur, who is also called Rasiel. It is he who listens to what is being proclaimed behind the veil before the Throne of Glory, and makes it known unto the world. And the prophet Elijah, standing upon the mount of Horeb, hears the words proclaimed by the angel and announces the message to the world and to humanity.

Gallizur, he who is Rasiel, also stands before the Throne of Glory, and spreading out his wings intercepts the breath of the *Chajjoth*, for otherwise the ministering angels would all be burnt to death through the fiery breath of the Chajjoth. And when Moses, the son of Amram, perceived the angel Gallizur, he who is called Rasiel, he trembled mightily and quaked, but the Holy One, blessed be His name, protected him. Thereupon a host of angels of destruction who are hovering in the celestial regions, doing the bidding of the Lord of the Universe, met the son of Amram.

Jealous of the honour vouchsafed to the son of man, they made ready to destroy him with the fire of their breath, but the Holy One, blessed be His name, spread out over Moses the radiance from the Throne of Glory and saved him from the jealousy of the ministering angels.

And when the moment arrived for Moses to descend upon earth, trembling and terror seized him once more. But the Holy One, blessed be His name, called the angel Jephephiah,

---

[1] *Daniel*, 7, 10; *Threni*, 3, 23.

the prince of the law, of learning, and of knowledge, and commanded him to hand over the Holy Law to the son of Amram. When the ministering angels saw the honour done unto Moses, the faithful servant of the Lord of the Universe, they became his friends and taught him many secrets. And even the angel of death and Metatron, the prince of the Presence, taught him secrets.[1]

SANDALPHON

Have you read in the Talmud of old,
In the legends the Rabbins have told
    Of the limitless realms of the air,—
Have you read it—the marvellous story
Of Sandalphon, the angel of glory,
    Sandalphon, the angel of prayer?

How, erect, at the outermost gates
Of the City Celestial he waits,
    With his feet on the ladder of light,
That crowded with angels unnumbered,
By Jacob was seen, as he slumbered
    Alone in the desert at night.

The angels of wind and of fire
Chant only one hymn, and expire
    With the song's irresistible stress;
Expire in their rapture and wonder,
As harp-strings are broken asunder
    By music they throb to express.

But serene in the rapturous throng,
Unmoved by the rush of the song,
    With eyes unimpassioned and slow,
Among the dead angels, the deathless
Sandalphon stands listening breathless
    To the sounds that ascend from below,

---

[1] *Journal of Royal Asiatic Society*, 1893, pp. 588–590; see also Jellinek, *Beth-Hamidrash*, Vol. II, pp. 43–45; Wertheimer, *Batte Midrashot*, Vol. IV, pp. 22–30; Gaster, *The Chronicles of Jerahmeel*, pp. 144–146.

From the spirits on earth that adore,
From the souls that entreat and implore
  In the fervour and passion of prayer;
From the hearts that are broken with losses,
And weary with dragging the crosses
  Too heavy for mortals to bear.

And he gathers the prayers as he stands,
And they change into flowers in his hands,
  Into garlands of purple and red;
And beneath the great arch of the portal,
Through the streets of the City Immortal
  Is wafted the fragrance they shed.

It is but a legend, I know,
A fable, a phantom, a show,
  Of the ancient Rabbinical lore;
Yet the old mediæval tradition,
The beautiful strange superstition,
  But haunts me and holds me the more.

When I look from my window at night,
And the welkin above is all white,
  All throbbing and panting with stars,
Among them majestic is standing
Sandalphon, the angel, expanding
  His pinions in nebulous bars.

And the legend, I feel, is a part
Of the hunger and thirst of the heart,
  The frenzy and fire of the brain,
That grasps at the fruitage forbidden,
The golden pomegranates of Eden,
  To quiet its fever and pain.

H. W. Longfellow.

CHAPTER VI

The War in Heaven and the Fallen Angels

The revolt of the angels—Sammael, known also as Satan—His jealousy of first man—He struggles with the archangel Michael—Michael's song of triumph—Sammael is appointed angel of death—He often takes the shape of an angel of light—His function to tempt and accuse men—Sammael, called Iblis, in Mohammedan legend—The fallen angels, Shemhazai and Azael—The virtuous maiden—Shemhazai and Istahar or Estirah—The dream of Heyya and Aheyya—Shemhazai suspends himself between Heaven and earth—Istahar and Astarte—Aza and Azael—The pilgrimage of the magicians to the dark mountains, the abode of Aza and Azael—The fallen angels in the *Book of Enoch*—The plot of the angels on Mount Ardis—The fallen angels and the giants—The corruption of man—The story of Harut and Marut—Idris (Enoch) intercedes on their behalf—The punishment of Harut and Marut in Babylon—The angel of death—Moses and the angel of death—Michael refuses to take the soul of Abraham—The disappointment of the angel of death—He appears in his real, terrific form and frightens the servants of Abraham.

ALTHOUGH all the angels called into being by the Father of all were pure and holy, some of them allowed themselves to be swayed by pride. They dared to imagine themselves as powerful and as great as the Creator Himself, the Lord of the Universe. In their rebellion and subsequent fall, they dragged down with them a number of the celestial inmates. At the head of the rebels was he who is now known as Sammael or Satan. First of the Seraphim and the greatest of all created beings, he headed the rebels. He at first recognized only as his superior the Creator Himself, but soon a mad ambition entered his heart, and he wished to seat himself upon a throne as high as that of the Creator Himself. A terrible war was waged between the hosts headed by Sammael and those led by Michael, and Sammael was defeated.

Sammael, who is also known as Satan, was one of the Seraphim, with twelve wings, and a regent of the planet Mars, which, by the way, he still rules. Jealous of the Creator, he brooded rebellion. He desired to be as great as God and said in his heart: " I will ascend into Heaven, I will exalt my throne above the stars of God; I will sit also upon the mount of the Congregation in the sides of the North; I will ascend above the heights of the clouds; I will be like the Most High." [1] Sammael's jealousy knew no bounds, especially when he saw the favourite position of the first man. He refused to worship Adam and pay him homage, but, on the contrary, plotted with other angels to bring about the fall of man. Against the express command of the Creator he excited the passions of Adam and of Eve, who committed the first sin and were expelled from Eden. Sammael himself, however, after having led Adam and Eve into sin, had to suffer eternal punishment. Driven out of Heaven and from among his companions of light, the Seraphim, he and his hosts were precipitated out of the place of bliss, weighed down by the curse of the Creator. The Seraph did not submit without a struggle, and there was a war between Sammael and his hosts, on one side, and the angels who obeyed the will of God, on the other. It was the angel Michael especially who struggled with Sammael, the chief of the rebels. In his struggle the latter caught the wings of Michael and tried to drag him down with him in his fall, but the Eternal saved Michael, whence he has derived his name of the *Plethi*, or the Rescued. [2] Michael, on obtaining his great victory, sang a song of triumph to God.

" Glory to our God!" he sang; " praise to His Holy Name;

---

[1] *Isaiah*, 14, 13–14; *Yalkut Rubeni*, § 3.

[2] Rabbi Behai (Bahya), *Commentary on the Books of Moses*, section *Achare Moth*; see also Eisenmenger, *Entdecktes Judentum*, Vol. I, p. 831.

for He is our God, and glory be to Him. He is our Lord, and His be the triumph. His right hand He hath stretched forth and hath manifested His power. He hath cast down our adversary. Mad indeed are those who resist Him, and accursed are those who depart from His commandments! He knoweth all things and never can err! All that He wills is just and good, and His advice is holy. He is Supreme Intelligence and cannot be deceived, and His perfect being cannot will what is evil. Nothing is above that which is supreme, and nothing is better than that which is perfect. None is worthy beside Him, but those whom He hath made worthy. Above all things He must be loved, and adored as the Eternal King. Ye, who have abandoned your God, revolted against Him, and desired to be Gods yourselves, have now fallen from your high estates, and gone down like a fallen stone. Acknowledge now that God is great, that His works are perfect, and that His judgments are just. From eternity to eternity, through all the ages glory be to God, and praises of joy for all His works." [1]

And as it was Sammael who had been the cause of the penalty of death being decreed against the human race, for had Adam not sinned death would have been unknown, Sammael was appointed as the executioner of the human race, or the angel of death. He was cast down from Heaven as a punishment of his pride and jealousy, and fell down with all his company. By his envy and malice, death, with all other evils, came into the world. And by the permission of the Creator, Sammael still exercises an influence and has a government over his subordinates, who are fallen angels like himself. To test good men, and chastise bad ones, the Creator often makes use of Sammael or Satan. He seduces men and leads them upon the path of wickedness, for he or his subordinates often torment, obsess, or possess men and inspire them with wicked

---

[1] Fabricius, *Codex Pseudoepigraphus, Vet. Test.*, 1722, Vol. I, p. 21.

designs and evil intentions. Like a roaring lion he now roves about in the world, full of rage, intent upon destroying and betraying men and trying to involve them in guilt, wickedness and evil deeds.

His power and his malice, however, luckily for men, are restrained, and kept under control by the Creator, who has set a limit to Sammael's power.

Sometimes he can transform himself into an angel of light. He is the great enemy, the seducer, the slanderer, the accuser of man, the mischief-maker, and tempter. He is at once the evil instinct in man's heart and an evil agent external to man and real. He is the envious and malicious opponent of man. But he is not, as has been maintained,[1] a stupid hater, envious only of man and not a rebel, an enemy of God and of the principle of goodness. In Rabbinic demonology the spiritual element is not at all entirely eliminated. Very frequently Satan appears in Rabbinic literature as the personification of the principle of evil.

He is represented as the servant of God, whose function it is to tempt and accuse man, and often to punish. But he is also represented in Jewish legend as the rebel, not the equal and dual principle, but the unfaithful, disloyal, rebellious subject.

The apostate angel and chief of the rebels would have been condemned to utter destruction and consumed entirely by the little finger of the Almighty; but he was a necessary factor in the scheme of things.[2] In order that men may receive their reward or punishment for their actions, the Creator gave them freedom of will. By the exercise of their free will they either obey or transgress the commands of God. Men have the freedom to choose good or evil. Sammael's function is now to lead them astray and to induce them to commit sins. When he has succeeded he then appears as prosecutor

---

[1] Edersheim, *loc. cit.*, Vol. II, p. 753. [2] *Yoma*, 69b.

before the heavenly tribunal. He is thus, seducer, tempter, accuser, and executioner.[1] His name is Sammael, either from the word *simme*, meaning to deceive or to blind, or from *semol*, meaning left, because he stands on the left side of men. Others derive the name of Sammael from *sam*, poison, and *El*, God, or the venom of God, since he is also identical with the Angel of Death.[2]

And ever since his fall, Sammael, who is also known as Satan, the old Serpent, or the Unclean Spirit, endeavours to enlarge his kingdom of darkness and to increase his sway over man. Formerly chief among the angels of God, he is now the prince of the realm of darkness, and ruler of the devils. Cast out from Heaven, he still seeks to exalt himself into the place of the Creator, trying to lead men away from the worship of the true God, and then appearing before the throne of the Eternal to accuse them.

In Mohammedan tradition, the fall of the angels and the rebellion of Sammael, or of Iblis, is supposed to have taken place after the creation of man. When God made man, He thus addressed the angels: " Bow and adore him, for I have breathed a part of My spirit in him." And all the angels of Heaven, of every degree and form, adored man, and fell down before him. Iblis alone refused to obey. Out of pride and envy he refused to do the bidding of the Lord, and disobeyed Him. Thereupon he was cursed by the Creator, and cast out of Heaven and the realms of delight. The Koran also says that " all the angels adored Adam, but Satan or Iblis refused to do so ". " I will not adore Adam," he said, " for I am better than he. He is made of earth, but I am made of fire." God thereupon cursed Iblis, for his pride, vanity, and disobedience, and gave him the form of a devil. [3]

---

[1] *Baba Batra*, 16a.
[2] *Targum Jerushalmi, Genesis*, 3, 6; see also article *Sammael* in *Jewish Encyclopædia*.
[3] Zotenberg, *Chronique de Tabari*, 1867, I, Ch. 27.

The Story of Shemhazai and Azael

Among the followers of Sammael were other angels, and notably two known as Aza and Azael or Shemhazai and Azael, of whom the following myth is related.

When the generation of the Flood transgressed the commands of the Creator, sinned and served idols, the Lord of the Universe was greatly concerned, and grieved that He had created man. Then two angels, Shemhazai and Azael, appeared before the Lord, and thus they spake: " Lord of the Universe! When Thou didst create man did we not say: ' What is man that Thou shouldst remember him '. We would have taken the place of man to cultivate the earth, people and inhabit the world."

" Had you taken the place of man, and lived in the earthly world," replied the Creator, " you would have been worse than man, for swayed by passion you would have committed sins, more heinous sins than those committed by man. You would have been even more stubborn." " Give us Thy sanction, O Lord of the Universe, to dwell among the children of man and inhabit the earth, and we will sanctify Thy name." And the Creator gave sanction unto Shemhazai and Azael to descend upon earth and there to dwell. But the two angels, who had descended upon earth and mixed with the children of man, soon sinned and transgressed.

Shemhazai cast his eyes upon a handsome maid called Istahar or Estirah, and a mighty love for her was kindled in his heart. " Listen to my request," he pleaded, but she refused to lend an ear to his pleadings. " I will not lend an ear to thy pleadings until thou teachest me the name of the Creator by the mention of which thou art enabled to ascend to Heaven." And Shemhazai, swayed by his passion for Istahar, yielded to her request and taught her the secret name of the Creator. Istahar thereupon uttered the name, and in virtue of its power she ascended to Heaven and was saved from perdition. And because she had avoided sin and had remained pure, she was placed among the seven constellations or Pleiades where she shines brightly.[1] And when Shemhazai and Azael saw this they hardened their hearts, and chose wives from among the daughters of men, and married them and begat children. Shemhazai had two daughters whose names were Heyya and Aheyya, or Hiwwa and Hijja. And they led men into sin and transgression. Thereupon a messenger came from Heaven and announced unto Shemhazai and Azael that the world would soon be destroyed and the inhabitants all perish in a great flood. And Shemhazai was grieved in his heart and wept aloud. And Hiwwa and Hijja had a dream which greatly troubled them. For they saw angels with axes in their hands, cutting down all the trees in a great garden. And Shemhazai was sore troubled in his heart, and repented of his sins. He suspended himself between Heaven and earth, with head downwards, and thus he still remains, because he durst not appear before God. But Azael did not repent of his sins and continued to lead the children of men into transgression.[2]

In this legend we evidently have the influence of Chaldean mysticism, elaborated by the Jewish imagination in a Jewish spirit. Istahar is none other but Ishtar, or Astarte, the Venus of the Phœnicians, who alone fills the entire Phœnician Olympus. But in Jewish legend the Phœnician element is changed. Astarte is no longer the goddess of sin, but is rehabilitated by her contact with the angels. She resists temptation, pronounces the tetragrammaton by virtue of which she ascends to Heaven and receives an honourable place in the Pleiades.

[1] Istahar is evidently the Assyro-Babylonian goddess Ishtar, goddess of love and war.
[2] Jellinek, *Beth-Hamidrash*, Vol. IV, pp. 127–128; Gaster, *Chronicles of Jerahmeel*, p. 52; see also *Midrash Abkir*, quoted in *Yalkut*, § 44; Reymundus Martinus, *Pugio Fidei*, ed. Leipzig, p. 937; Geiger, *Was hat Mohammed aus dem Judentum genommen*, p. 107; Bartolocci, *Bibliotheca Magna Rabbinica*, I, p. 259; see for comparative literature, M. Grünbaum in *Z.D.M.G.*, Vol. XXXI, pp. 225–231.

Another version of this legend relates that Aza and Azael now live in the dark mountains, and that they are visited by the magicians who travel to them to learn wisdom. And as soon as the traveller is perceived by the two demons, they at once call aloud, and big and fiery serpents gather round and surround them. The travelling magician in the meantime waits at the entrance to the dark mountains. Then Aza and Azael send out to him a spirit or demon in the shape of a small animal resembling a cat. Its head is like the head of a serpent, and it has two tails. And when the magician perceives the little animal he covers his face. He holds in his hand a basin containing the ashes of a burnt white cock, which he throws into the face of the animal, that leads him to the place in the dark mountains where Aza and Azael are chained. Three times he steps upon the chain until he is addressed and spoken to by Aza and Azael. Closing his eyes he falls upon his knees and worships the fallen angels. And because he has burned incense before them, they teach him the art of magic and witchcraft. Thus he remains in the dark mountains for fifty days. And when the day arrives for his return into the world, he is led out of the dark mountains by the little animal which resembles a cat and by a fiery serpent.[1]

They are the self-same Aza and Azael who afterwards taught Solomon, the King of Israel, all secrets. Every day he mounted an eagle who bore him to the dark mountains where he learned wisdom from the mouth of Aza and Azael.[2]

The same legend is related in the *Book of Enoch*, although the tendency there is somewhat different. And in those days it happened that the sons of men had multiplied, and unto them were born daughters, both elegant and beautiful. And it came to pass that the sons of Heaven, that is the fallen angels, beheld the daughters of men and became enamoured of them.

---

[1] *Emek hamelekh*, p. 108b; Bin Gorion, *Die Sagen der Juden*, Vol. I, p. 319–321.
[2] *Emek hamelekh*, p. 5d; see also Jellinek, *Beth-Hamidrash*, Vol. II, p. 86.

And the sons of Heaven said to each other: " Come, let us select wives for ourselves from the offspring of men." But their leader named Samyaza (or Shemhaza) spoke unto them and said: " I fear that you will perhaps not be courageous enough to perform such an enterprise, and that I alone shall suffer for so grievous a crime." But all the sons of Heaven, when they heard the words of Shemhaza (Samyaza), swore and bound themselves by mutual execrations to execute the projected undertaking. Now their number was two hundred, and they all descended upon Ardis, which is the top of Mount Armon. The mountain they called Armon because they had sworn upon it, and had bound themselves by mutual execrations. And the names of the chiefs of the sons of Heaven who had thus sworn to take wives from among the daughters of man, were: Samyaza, Urakabarameel, Akibeel, Tamiel, Ramuel, Danel, Azkeel, Sarakuyal, Asael, Armers, Batraal, Anane, Zavebe, Samsaveel, Ertael, Turel, Yomyael, Azazyal, eighteen in all who were the prefects of the two hundred with Samyaza as their chief. And all these sons of Heaven took wives from among the daughters of men, and they taught their wives sorcery, incantations and the divining of roots. They begat children, and the women brought forth giants, whose stature was each three hundred cubits. These giants were a curse to men, for they devoured all that the labour of men had produced, until it became impossible to feed them. The giants injured beasts and birds, fishes and reptiles, ate their flesh and drank their blood.

And Azazyal taught men how to make swords, knives, shields, breastplates, the fabrication of mirrors, making them see that which was behind them. He also taught them the workmanship of bracelets and of ornaments, and also the use of paint, and how to beautify the eyebrows. He further taught them the use of valuable stones of all kinds, and the use of all sorts of dyes, and the world thus became greatly altered. It became corrupted in many ways. And the other sons of Heaven and the giants turned against men and destroyed them. And they cried out and their voice reached to Heaven. Then Michael, Gabriel, Raphael, Suryal, and Uriel, looking down from their celestial abode, saw the quantity of blood which was being shed upon earth and all the iniquity which was being done upon it, and said one to the other: " The earth deprived of her children has cried to God, and the cry has reached the gate of Heaven." And they turned to God, and thus they spake: " Thou art the Lord and King of all. Thou art the Lord of Lords, King of Kings and God of Gods. The throne of Thy glory is for ever and ever, and for ever and ever is Thy name sanctified and glorified. Thou possessest power over all things, and Thou hast seen what Azazyal hath done. Verily he hath taught every species of iniquity upon earth, and Samyaza hath taught sorcery, and the whole earth hath been filled with iniquity. And now the groaning of those who are dead is ascending to the gates of Heaven."

Thereupon the Creator of all sent out a messenger to the son of Lamech, commanding him to conceal himself, for all the earth would soon perish.[1]

A parallel to this legend is found in Moslem myth and legend, where it runs as follows: Harut and Marut were two angels who were chastised in Babylon. And it came to pass when Adam had been driven out of Paradise, that there were some among the angels who took pity upon him, and pleaded on his behalf before the throne of the Lord of the Universe.

But many more were those who hurled words of menace upon our first parent, because he had transgressed the command of the Eternal. And among those who heaped words of menace and insult upon Adam were the two angels Harut and Marut. But Adam thus addressed them: " O ministering angels of my Lord, have pity upon me and do not insult me

---

[1] *The Book of Enoch*, trans. by R. H. Charles, Chap. 6–7.

and hurl words of menace at me. For what has happened unto me was only by the will of the Lord of the Universe." And the Maker of the Universe tried the two angels, and they rebelled against Him and were expelled from Heaven. And it came to pass that in the days of Idris (Enoch) they approached the latter and begged him to intercede on their behalf before the King of the Universe, perchance He would forgive them. Said Idris (Enoch): " How am I to know that the Lord has forgiven you?" And they made answer: " Intercede on our behalf and pray for us to the Lord of the Universe, and if thou dost behold us and see us before thee, then thou wilt know that thy prayer has been heard and we have been forgiven. But if thou wilt not see us then surely it is a sign that we are doomed to perdition." And Idris listened to their words and prayed for them to the Eternal. But when he turned round he could nowhere behold them, and he knew that they were doomed. And it was given to Harut and Marut to choose between a punishment upon earth and a punishment in the world to come, but they preferred to suffer punishment upon earth. Thereupon they were exiled to Babylon, where they are tortured in a pit and will thus remain until the day of resurrection.

And Ibn Amr relates that when the ministering angels looked down from their celestial abode upon earth and saw how the sons of men were sinning and transgressing the commands of the Eternal, they accused them before the Creator. And the Father of the Universe said: " Had you been in man's place you would have been equally wicked."

But the angels exclaimed: " Lord of the Universe! Had we been in man's place we would have proclaimed Thy glory and praised Thee continually." And the Father of the Universe replied: "Choose among you two angels;" and they chose Harut and Marut who were sent down upon earth, and the desires and passions of man were put into them.

And very soon they sinned against the Lord of the Universe and transgressed his commands.

It was given to them to choose between punishment in this world and punishment in the next, but they preferred to suffer in this world, for it is only for a time, whilst suffering in the next is eternal. Such is the story of the two angels Harut and Marut who are punished at Babylon.[1]

THE ANGEL OF DEATH

The legends about the angel of death are to be found in the literature of many nations.

The angel of death, whom the Creator commissions to separate the soul from the body, is to be found in the myths and legends of the Arabians, Persians, Turks, and other nations.

He is called Azrael by the Arabians, and Mordad by the Persians. Popular imagination has woven many legends round the angel of death, and given rise to many superstitions.

When he has killed a man, we read in Jewish legendary lore, the angel of death washes his sword in the water of the house, thus communicating a mortal quality to it, and therefore the water is thrown away.[2]

Thus the angel of death is supposed to be seated on the grave of the person who dies, where he causes the wicked to suffer a second death. As soon as the dead is buried, the soul returns to the body and it becomes alive. Then the angel of death takes an iron chain, half of which is cold as ice and half burning hot. He strikes the body with it three times, separating its members, removing its bones, and reducing the whole to ashes. The good angels then come and gather and reunite all the parts, and re-

[1] Kazwini, *Cosmography*, Ethe's translation (1868), p. 126.
[2] See on angel of death *Abodah Zarah*, 20b.

place the body in the grave.   Such is the punishment of
those who have sinned; but the pious, especially those who
have liberally given alms, are exempt from such punishment.[1]

The legends in Talmud and Midrash of the angel of death
relate of his disappointments when coming to separate from
the body the soul of a pious man, one of the heroic and saintly
personages of Israel.

The Midrash *Petirat Moshe* (Death of Moses)[2] relates the
following legend:

When the day arrived for Moses to die, the Creator decided
not to allow the angel of death to interfere. He at first required
the angel Gabriel to command the soul of the son of Amram
out of the latter's body. But the angel Gabriel excused himself, whilst the angel Michael likewise desired to be dispensed
with in this particular case. The Creator then required the
angel Zagziel to fetch the soul of Moses, but this angel said
that having been the preceptor of Moses he could not take
away his life. The Creator then sent Sammael (who is at
once Satan and the angel of death). Sammael advanced to-
ward Moses, determined to force the soul out of the body
of the leader of the Children of Israel. Struck, however, with
the radiance of the countenance of Moses and by the virtue
of the name of God written on the rod with which Moses
performed his miracles, Sammael was compelled to retire.
It was the Creator Himself who subsequently condescended
to call forth the soul of Moses from his body.[3] A similar
disappointment had awaited Sammael when he came to take
the soul of Abraham. The angel Michael having replied that he
could not take the soul of Abraham, the Lord of the Universe
summoned Azazel (Sammael) the angel of death, the terrible

[1] Elia Levita, *Tishbi*; see also Eisenmenger, *loc. cit.*; Buxtorf, *Synagoga Judaica*, I, 35.

[2] See Jellinek, *Beth-Hamidrash*, Vol. I, p. 21; Zunz, *Gottesdienstliche Vorträge*, p. 146.

[3] Jellinek, *Beth-Hamidrash*, Vol. I, p. 129; see also *A Legend on the Death of Moses*, by
A. Löwy, in *Proceedings of the Society of Biblical Archæology*, Vol. IX (Dec., 1886), pp. 40–47.

and many eyed, he who carries the bitter cup of death, and who is therefore called Sammael, and bade him go and take the soul of Abraham.

" Cast aside," said the Lord of the Universe, to the angel of death, " cast aside thy terrific aspect and thy impurity and assume the radiant and lovely form of a shining angel. In the garb of a bright and beautiful angel of light, in the shape and form of a handsome youth, exhaling the beauty of regions celestial, go and appear to Abraham, and take away his soul with all gentleness." Thus spake the Ruler of the Universe, and Sammael gladly accepted the mission to take away the soul of Abraham. In the shape of a beautiful youth, radiant and sunlike in his splendour, he appeared before the son of Terah, in the plain of Mamre.

Abraham rose to meet his guest, and Sammael thus addressed the old man: " Peace unto thee, thou friend of the Most High." " And who art thou?" asked Abraham, " whence dost thou come and which is thy destination?" " I am the bitter cup of death," replied Sammael, " and I have come to take thy soul, for thy days have come to an end." " And dost thou appear to all men in such beautiful and radiant form?" asked Abraham. " No," said Sammael. " To the sinners and ungodly I appear in a terrible form. I am many eyed and serpent-headed, and I carry in my hand the bitter cup of poison, a drop of which I cast into the mouth of the sinner who is about to die. But to the just I appear with a crown of light upon my head, like a divine messenger of peace."

Thereupon Abraham, desirous of beholding the real shape of the angel of death, spoke the holy name of God and asked Sammael to appear in his true and terrific form. " Present to me," he said, " thy terrible and terrific form, and thy terror-inspiring shape that I may behold thee." And lo, the angel of death showed himself in all his ugliness, cruelty, and bitterness. He put on his most awful and terrible form, and appeared with seven dragon heads and fourteen faces.

Some of his heads had the face of serpents and others were breathing flames of fire, and the sight was so terrible that seven thousand servants, male and female, of Abraham's household died, and Abraham himself fainted. He soon, however, regained consciousness, interceded for his servants, and prayed for them who had died before their time, and the angel Michael brought them to life again.

" Resume now thy former beautiful form," said Abraham, " for I cannot bear thy terrible real shape." And Sammael resumed the shape of a beautiful angel, but refused to leave Abraham, following him wherever he went. Abraham, however, refused to give up his soul to Sammael.

At the command of the Almighty, the angel Michael came and lured away the soul of Abraham as if in a dream. A host of angels at once descended from Heaven, and taking the soul of the old man, received it in heaven-spun garments like snow, and bore it away on a fiery chariot.[1]

---

[1] *The Testament of Abraham*, published in Robinson's Texts and Studies, II, 2, Cambridge 1892.

CHAPTER VII

The Demons

The demonology of the Talmud—Rabbinic folklore—The devas of Ahriman—Shedim, Roukhin, Mazikin and Lilin—The functions and power of the demons—The theory of the microbes—Zaphrire, Tihare, Telane, and Lilin—The demons execute the will of the Creator—The origin of demons—Souls without bodies—The demons inhabit the earth—The struggle of the angels with the demons—Demonology in the Ethiopic *Book of Enoch*—The demons proceed from the giants—Sammael, chief ruler of the demons—The angel Fanuel and the Satans—Lilith, Queen of Night—The long-haired and winged enchantress—She is the first wife of Adam—Her quarrel with Adam—Lilith and the angels Senoi, Sansenoi, and Sammangelof—Her promise to spare the infants—Amulets to ward off Lilith—Makhlath and Agrath—The story of Ashmedai—Ashmedai and King Solomon—The building of the Temple—The Shamir—The defeat and capture of Ashmedai—His strange behaviour—The moor-cock—The King and the demon—Ashmedai takes his revenge—The return of the King and the flight of Ashmedai.

WE have seen that the angels are divided into two groups, angels of good and angels of evil, that is angels of light and angels of darkness, or fallen angels.

Real Judaism does not admit the existence of a principle of evil, *per se*; such a principle has no place in the absolute, and consequently this dualism of powers is practically opposed to Judaism.

The popular imagination, however, eagerly took hold of the idea that evil is independent of human action, and that there exist beings who are not only the incarnation of evil but also at war with the Creator himself. This is a concession made by Judaism to foreign ideas and influences.

Besides the fallen angels, Jewish myth also knows of demons, or evil spirits.

The demonology of the Talmud and of Rabbinic folklore has been influenced not by the Babylonian cult of Marduk-Bel, but by that of Ormuzd and Ahriman. The Persian devas, the devas of Ahriman, have invaded Jewish folklore and acquired citizen right in Jewish myth and legend.

The demons of the Jews, like the devas of Ahriman, male and female, fill the world, and in hosts of tens of thousands surround man in all shapes and forms, spreading disease and suffering among mortals. From birth to death these devas, demons who multiply continually, lay siege to men and give them no respite.

Persian influence is thus noticeable in the Jewish legends about evil spirits. Cunning and malicious, they are dangerous to man, but they are not always absolutely evil. Sometimes they are, like the sprites of fairy tales, like the elves, hobgoblins and gnomes, even serviceable and kind, and may be made not only innocuous but obedient to man.

They are divided into *Shedim*, *Roukhin*, *Mazikin*, and *Lilin*. They propagate themselves, and their number is unlimited. In three things they resemble man, whilst in three they are like angels. Like man they take nourishment, propagate themselves, and die. But like angels they have wings, pass through space unhindered, and know the future.

" For six things have been said about demons: they are like angels in three particulars, but resemble men in three others. Like angels they have wings, are able to fly from one end of the world to the other, and know the future. Whilst, however, the angels have the future revealed to them, they learn it by listening behind the veil. Like men, however, the demons eat and drink, marry and beget children and increase and ultimately die." [1]

They assume either the form of human beings or any

---

[1] *Hagigah*, 16a; see S. Louis, in *Proceedings of the Society of Biblical Archæology*, Vol. IX (June, 1881), pp. 217–228.

other form. They lodge in trees, caper bushes, in gardens, vineyards, in ruined and desolate houses, and dirty places.

To go alone into such places is dangerous, and the eves of Wednesday and Saturday were considered dangerous times.[1] The evil spirits and demons, the Shedim, Roukhin, Mazikin, and Lilin, can be mischievous, but they can never create anything themselves.

The demons have no power over anything that is sealed, counted, measured or tied up.[2] The pronouncing of the " Ineffable Name " (the *Shem hameforash*) has a paramount influence over them, and by it they can always be conquered.

Thus King Solomon conquered Ashmedai by the power and the virtue of the Ineffable Name.

These evil spirits are supposed to lurk everywhere around man. They crowd the academies and are to be found by the side of the bride. They are said to be found in the crumbs we throw on the floor, *in the water we drink, in the diseases which attack us*, in the oil, in the vessels, in the air, in the room, at every moment of day and night. No mortal could survive it, if he saw their number, for they are like the earth that is thrown up around a bed that is sown.[3]

Here, it may be pointed out, *en passant*, we have some trace of the idea of microbes and of the first indications of microbiology of which modern science is so proud.

The Shedim, Roukhin, Mazikin, and Lilin, are both male and female spirits. The hurtful spirits are known as *Malakhe Khabalah*, or angels of destruction; they exercise their power either by day or by night and are divided into different classes. They are called: *Zaphrire*, morning spirits; *Tihare*, midday spirits; *Telane*, evening spirits; and *Lilin*, night spirits, according to the time during which they are active.

With regard to myths and legends about demons, genii,

---

[1] *Pesachim*, 112b. [2] *Hullin*, 105b. [3] *Berachoth*, 6a.

and evil spirits, pre-exilian Judaism knows but little about them. Judaism, as represented in the Old Testament, knows no evil principle. The spirit of darkness and wickedness which rebels against and opposes the omnipotent Creator according to the Scriptures is not the result of a necessary emanation, but is the voluntary act of an omnipotent Creator. The tempter, the principle of evil, is not a power equal to and waging war against the omnipotent Creator, but a created being and a rebel.[1]

Thoroughly monotheistic, pre-exilian Judaism could not tolerate any idea harbouring upon polytheism. Thus Satan, or Sammael, is, unlike in the dual religion of Persia, not an independent original power waging war against Divinity, but a created being, a personification of the principle of evil, created for the purpose of testing the moral strength of man.[2]

In consequence of Babylonian and Persian influences the old Oriental beliefs, against which monotheism had fought and still continues to do so, received a new impetus.

Angels and demons acquired citizen rights in Jewish folklore, in Jewish myths and legends. The Psalmists and prophets who shared the exile may have protested against the invasion of foreign elements, and repeatedly declared themselves against any dual principles. But popular imagination and folklore seized upon the elements which were to some extent related to the old Oriental beliefs lingering among the people, and interwove them into Jewish myths and legends with a strongly monotheistic background.

And just as the angels in Jewish myth and legend are not independent beings but executors of the will of the One God, His messengers and ministering spirits, so also are their opposites. The spirits and demons, the inhabitants of the realm of darkness and destruction, of negation, of morally-evil, the

---

[1] *Targum, Ps.* 121, 6; *Targum Pseudo-Jonathan, Deuteron.,* 32, 24; *Targum Canticles,* 4, 6. [2] E. Bischoff, *Elemente der Kabbalah,* p. 224.

devils and demons, are the servants of the One God, doing His bidding. Unlike the devas of Persia, whence the Jewish demonology has been derived (although sufficient elements existed in Judaism to develop it independently) who are to some extent independent beings and opponents of Ormuzd, so the Shedim are servants of the Creator, submissive and obedient subjects.

And as the Shedim in Jewish myth are not opponents of the will of the Creator, and not in constant fight with the inhabitants of the realms of light, like the Persian devas, they are not so badly treated as are the Persian devas.

In Jewish myth and legend the Shedim, too, serve to glorify the One Creator and to testify to His omnipotence.[1]

Various theories are expounded in Jewish literature with regard to the origin of demons and evil spirits. According to some mythographers, the demons are the living souls which the Lord of the Universe created in addition to the beasts of the earth, the cattle and creeping things. Every day He created several things: Heaven, earth, and light on the first day; the firmaments, hell, and the ministering angels on the second; trees, herbs, and rivers on the third; sun, moon, and stars on the fourth day; the fishes, Leviathan, and the birds on the fifth day. But on the sixth day He had to produce twice as many creatures, doing the work also of the seventh day, which is the Sabbath and a day of rest. On the sixth day He created Adam and Eve and many creatures. He also produced many other souls for new creatures, but was interrupted by the arrival of the Sabbath and these creatures remained unfinished and incomplete.

These beings are the demons and spirits. The Lord had created their souls, but their bodies were not completed on account of the Sabbath on which the Lord of the Universe rested, and so they remained souls without bodies.[2]

---

[1] *Talmud Jerushalmi, Berachoth; Yalkut, Leviticus,* § 665. [2] *Genesis Rabba,* 7.

In other sources, however, we read that the demons were created long before man came into existence. They were the inhabitants of the earth and its masters. Dry land and sea were alike full of demons who lived happily for æons in peace and tranquillity, for the whole planet was their domain. They were obedient and did the bidding of the Lord. But a day came when wickedness and evil deeds increased among the demons, and they ignored the commandments of the Creator, and earth was full of their iniquity, and it cried to the Lord. And the Creator decided to put an end to the reign of the demons. He sent down a host of angels who waged a terrible war against the wicked and evil-doing demons and drove them from the face of the earth. Many of these demons the angels took captive, and among the latter was also Sammael, the chief leader, the curse and enemy of man. He was a youth in those days and knew not to distinguish between good and evil.

But he learned the way of the angels who spread over the planet and peopled it, and he acquired much wisdom and in time became the chief and leader of the angels. But the reign of the angels also came to an end, for in His great wisdom the Creator decided to send man and the sons of man to inhabit and people the earth. But the angels who were then the masters and rulers of the earth refused to leave it, for they were very happy there. And thus they spoke: " O Lord of the Universe! Thou dost intend to place upon earth man, as lord of creation, who will one day commit wicked deeds, do much evil and shed innocent blood. He will take our place and follow in the ways of the demons and the children of Satan. We are praising Thy holy name every day, and are proclaiming Thy glory in the upper and netherworlds." But the Creator carried out His purpose, and created man.[1]

---

[1] Kalonymos ben Kalonymos, *Iggeret baale Hayyim* (on the animals); see Julius Landsberger, *Abhandlung über die Thiere*, 1882.

According to the Ethiopic *Book of Enoch* the demons proceeded from the giants, the offspring of the fallen angels who lusted after the daughters of men. They now accomplish man's moral ruin, and their power will last until the day of final judgment.

There is not one Satan in the *Book of Enoch*, but many Satans, and Jequn was the first to lead astray all the children of the angels, bring them down to the earth and lead them astray through the daughters of men.

Fanuel, one of the four angels of the Presence, prevents the Satans from appearing before the Lord of Spirits to accuse man. They are all members of a kingdom of evil, in opposition to God, of a realm of darkness which is ruled under the name of Satan. This kingdom of evil existed already before the angels fell by corrupting themselves with the daughters of man.

On the great day of judgment the four angels Michael, Gabriel, Rufael, and Fanuel will take hold of these Satans, and cast them into a burning furnace, so that the Lord of Spirits may take vengeance on them for their unrighteousness in becoming subjects to Satan and leading astray those who dwell on the earth.[1]

The Satans thus have a right of access to Heaven, where they appear before the Throne of Glory to accuse men.

They are at once tempters, accusers, and punishers or executioners. The view of the *Book of Enoch* to a certain extent coincides with the views expressed in the Talmud and in the Midrashim.[2] Satan or Sammael, who was jealous of Adam and of Eve and caused the serpent to seduce the woman, coalesce into one personality. The supreme ruler of the evil spirits and demons, as of all the fallen angels, is thus Sammael, although there are other princes and kings of demons.

---

[1] R. H. Charles, *The Book of Enoch*, 54, 6.
[2] See Whitehouse, article *Satan* in Hastings' *Dictionary of the Bible*, Vol. IV, p. 409.

Legions innumerable of Shedim and Roukhin, of demons and spirits, obey their commands. For the spirits of evil who surround man are legion. They are hostile both to his body and to his soul, and constantly seek to do him harm. From the very birth of man, they lurk in the shadow, watching for an opportunity to undo him. These demons are even responsible for the terrible phantoms which appear to man and the evil thoughts which crowd his brain. They are everywhere, and no man could bear the sight of all the demons who surround him. They are everywhere on land and in the water, and every drop of water we drink contains numerous evil spirits.

They are very powerful, for they are more numerous than mankind. At every moment a war is being constantly waged between the demons and the angels, who are appointed to protect man against the evil influence of the demons.

THE STORY OF LILITH

Queen of the demons is Lilith, long-haired and winged.[1] She is supposed to have been the first wife of Adam. She had been one of the wives of Sammael, but of a wild, heroic and passionate nature she left her spouse and joined Adam. From their union issued the demons or Shedim, who rove about in the world as wicked spirits, persecute and plague men, and bring upon them illness, disease, and other sufferings.

Lilith, like Adam, had been created from the dust (Adamah) of the earth. But as soon as she had joined Adam they began to quarrel, each refusing to be subservient and submissive to the other. " I am your lord and master," spoke Adam, " and it is your duty to obey me." But Lilith replied: " We are both equal, for we are both issued from dust (Adamah), and I will not be submissive to you." And thus they quarrelled and none would give in. And when Lilith saw this she spoke

---

[1] *Niddah,* 16b; *Erubin,* 100b

the Ineffable Name of the Creator and soared up into the air. Thereupon Adam stood in prayer before the Creator and thus he spake: " O Lord of the Universe, the woman Thou hast given me has fled from me."

And the Holy One, blessed be His name, sent at once three angels whose names were Senoi, Sansenoi, and Sammangelof, to fetch and bring Lilith back to Adam. He ordered them to tell her to return, and if she refused to obey then a hundred of her offspring would die daily. The three aforementioned angels followed Lilith, and they found her in the midst of the sea, on the mighty waves (which were once to drown the Egyptians).

They communicated to her the command of the Eternal, but she refused to return. And the angels spake to this rebel, this she-demon: " We will drown thee in the sea." But she made answer: " Know ye not that I have been created for the purpose of weakening and punishing little children, infants and babes. I have power over them from the day they are born until they are eight days old if they are boys, and until the twentieth day if they are girls." And when the three angels heard her speech they wished to drown her by force, but she begged them to let her live, and they gave in. She swore to them in the name of the living God that whenever she came and saw the names or images or faces of these three angels, Senoi, Sansenoi, and Sammangelof, upon an amulet or cameo in the room where there was an infant, she would not touch it. But because she did not return to Adam, every day a hundred of her own children or spirits and demons die.

The legend of Lilith and the message of the three angels is found in several sources of Rabbinical lore in some of which it is quoted from the *Alphabetum Siracidis*.[1]

---

[1] *Alphabetum Siracidis (Sepher Ben Sira)*, edit. Steinschneider, 1858. See on Lilith. Gaster, in *Monatsschrift für Gesch. u. Wissenschaft d. Judent.*, Vol. XXIX (1880), pp. 553–555,

The book known as the *Sefer Rasiel* describes the formula to be written upon amulets or cameos and to be placed in the rooms where there are new-born babes. It refers to Lilith as the *first Eve*, and conjures her in the name of the three angels and the angel of the sea to whom she had sworn not to harm the babes in whose rooms she found written on paper the names of the three angels.[1]

Lilith is thus a female night demon, and is also known under the name of *Meyalleleth*, or the howling one.

The she-demon *Makhlath* (the dancer) and her daughter *Agrath*[2] are two female demons who live in strife with Lilith. Lilith is accompanied by four hundred and eighty hosts of evil spirits and destroying angels, and she is constantly howling. Makhlath is accompanied by four hundred and seventy-eight hosts of evil spirits. She and her daughter Agrath, from the Zend word *Agra* = beating, are in constant enmity with Lilith.

Constant war is waged between them, and they meet on the day of atonement. Whilst they are thus engaged in quarrel and strife, the prayers of Israel ascend to Heaven, whilst the accusers are absent, being otherwise engaged.[3]

Agrath commands hosts of evil spirits and demons, and rides in a big chariot. Her power is paramount on Wednesdays and Saturdays, for on these days Agrath, the daughter of Makhlath, roves about in the air accompanied by eighteen myriads of evil spirits.[4]

THE STORY OF ASHMEDAI

King of the demons is Ashmedai or Asmodaeus. The name of Ashmedai is never mentioned in the Talmud of Jerusalem nor in the older Palestinian sources.

He is very cunning and malignant. Of immense strength

---

[1] Elia Levita, *Tishbi*, s.v. Lilith.   [3] *Pesachim*, 112b; *Numbers Rabba*, 12.
[2] *Yalkut Chadash*, s.v. *Keshaphim*, No. 56.   [4] *Pesachim*, 112b.

and very powerful, he is intent upon doing harm to man. And yet he is frequently ready to perform deeds of kindness. Ashmedai fore-knows the future, and by the use of the Ineffable Name he can be made serviceable unto man and compelled to do what is bidden by those who pronounce the Ineffable Name. Thus, by the power and in virtue of his signet ring on which was engraven the Ineffable Name, King Solomon gained power over Ashmedai and made him do his bidding. The legend of King Solomon and Ashmedai runs as follows:

King Solomon, the son of David, was about to build the Temple of the Lord. " And the house, when it was in building, was built of stone made ready before it was brought thither." [1]

Now before the operation was begun King Solomon consulted with the Rabbis and asked them: " How shall I accomplish this without using tools of iron?" as no iron was to be used in the construction of the Temple. And the Rabbis remembered that an insect existed since the creation of the world which possessed the power of cutting stones, for even the hardest substance could not resist the power of this insect. The Rabbis therefore replied to the King: " There is an insect called *Shamir* with which Moses once cut the precious stones of the *Ephod*." [2] Hearing these words the King asked: " And where may this Shamir be found?" To which the Rabbis made answer as follows: " Conjure up a male and a female demon and coerce them; perchance they know where the Shamir is now to be found and they will reveal the secret unto thee." And the King did as they had counselled him. He conjured up into his presence a male and a female demon, and when they refused to reveal unto him the whereabouts of the Shamir he gave orders to torture them.

But all this was in vain, for the male and the female demon both declared that not knowing the whereabouts of the Shamir

[1] *I Kings*, 6, 7.   [2] *Leviticus*, 8, 7.

they could not reveal the secret to King Solomon. " But perhaps," they continued, " Ashmedai, the king of the demons, knows the hiding-place and will reveal the secret to the King."

The King thereupon urged them to tell him where Ashmedai might be found. And the male and female demon answered as follows: " Ashmedai's residence is on a high mountain, where he has dug a deep pit which serves him as a cistern. This he has filled with water. Every morning before ascending to Heaven, to study in the school of wisdom there and to listen to the decrees of the Upper Assembly, he covers his cistern over with a stone and seals it with his own seal. Every day when he returns from his celestial visit, he carefully examines the seal, and on finding that it has not been broken, he drinks, quenches his thirst and finally covers it again with the stone, seals the stone with his own seal and takes his departure." Thus spoke the male and female demon, and King Solomon decided to test the truth of their assertions.

He thereupon sent his trusty servant Benaiah, the son of Jehoiada, and enjoined him to capture Ashmedai, the king of the demons. Benaiah armed himself with a magic chain and a ring upon which the Ineffable Name was engraved, and went out to execute the command of King Solomon. He also provided himself with skins of wine and a fleece of wool.

When he arrived at the mountain where Ashmedai had his abode, Benaiah at once cunningly set to work. He first dug a pit below that of Ashmedai, and into it he drained off the water from the pit of the demon, and plugged the hole with the fleece he had brought. He then dug another pit higher up, and in it he made a channel through which he filled the emptied pit of Ashmedai with the wine from the skins he had brought. He thereupon levelled the ground so as not to arouse the suspicion of the demon king, and withdrew to a tree nearby, where he waited for the return of Ashmedai, and for an opportunity to seize him.

And when he had waited a little while, he heard a noise in the air as of the beating of gigantic wings. Benaiah soon perceived Ashmedai, who was descending from Heaven whither he had gone to study in the school of wisdom and to listen to the decrees of the Upper Assembly. The demon king examined his seal, and seeing that it had not been tampered with, raised the stone. But lo! to his surprise he found the cistern filled with wine. Now Ashmedai, like all other demons, hates wine, and usually abstains from drinking it. He was therefore unwilling to drink from the cistern, muttering to himself that " wine is a mocker; strong drink is raging, and whosoever is deceived thereby is not wise ". At last, however, being thirsty, the demon king could not resist the temptation to drink and proceeded to quench his thirst. When he had drunk his fill, Ashmedai, demon king though he was, became intoxicated and lay down to sleep. Thereupon Benaiah quickly came forth from his hiding-place and stealthily approached the sleeping demon. He took up the magic chain he had brought with him and upon which was engraved the Ineffable Name of God, and fastened it round the neck of the sleeping demon. At last Ashmedai awoke from his sleep. He was mightily wroth and roared like a lion in his fury, when he saw himself bound and fettered.

He seized the chain to break it, but Benaiah called out to him and warned him: " The name of the Lord is upon thee." Ashmedai, cowed and conquered, desisted. And thus Benaiah, the trusty servant of King Solomon, secured the king of the demons, and made him prisoner. He thereupon proceeded on his return journey, leading the demon king with him. As they travelled along they passed a palm tree and Ashmedai rubbed himself against it, but by so doing uprooted the tree and threw it down. Walking a little farther they drew near to the hut of a poor widow; she came out and implored the demon not to rub himself against her hut as he might uproot

it. Ashmedai complied with the request of the poor woman,
and as he was bending back rather quickly, he broke a bone
in his body, whereupon he said: " This is that which is written:
' And a gentle answer breaketh the bone '." Proceeding
farther on their way they saw a blind man straying out of his
way, whereupon the demon king hailed him and directed
him aright. When a little farther he descried a drunken man
who was in a similar difficulty, he again showed him the road.
A wedding party then passed along, rejoicing and making
merry, but at the sight of the merry-makers Ashmedai wept.
And when a little farther on he heard a man ordering at a
shoemaker's a pair of shoes that would last him seven years,
he burst out into a peal of uncontrollable laughter. He shrieked
and jeered and muttered words of scorn when he saw a magician
at his tricks. Benaiah wondered greatly and asked the demon
king to explain unto him the reason of his strange and almost
incomprehensible conduct. " Why didst thou so promptly
help the blind man, guiding him and putting him aright when
he strayed?" asked Benaiah. And Ashmedai made answer:
" Because I heard it proclaimed in Heaven that this blind
man was perfectly righteous and would inherit the world to
come, and that whosoever rendered him a service would also
earn a claim to a place in the world of the future." " And
why," queried Benaiah, " didst thou put right the man who,
overcome with drink, was wandering out of his way?" " Because," replied Ashmedai, " I have heard it proclaimed in
Heaven that this man was wholly and entirely bad and wicked,
and so I rendered him a good service so that he might not lose
all, but, at least, receive some good in the world that now
is."

" And why," continued Benaiah to question his prisoner,
" why didst thou weep when thou didst see the rejoicing
wedding party pass?" " The bridegroom of that wedding
party," replied Ashmedai, " is destined to die within thirty

days, and his newly wedded wife will soon be a widow and
will needs wait thirteen years for her husband's brother who
is now only an infant.[1]" " And why didst thou laugh when
thou didst hear the man ordering a pair of shoes that should
last him seven years?" again queried Benaiah. " Because,"
Ashmedai replied, " the man was not sure of even living
seven days." " And why thy jeers and scorn when thou sawest
the magician at his works?" " Because," was the answer of
the demon king, " at that very moment the magician was
sitting upon a vast treasure hidden in the soil underneath
him, and yet he knew it not, although he pretended that he
could foretell the future and unravel mysteries."

And when the demon king was brought into the royal
city, he was kept three days before being led into the presence
of the King of Israel. " Why am I not being led into the
presence of the King?" he queried. And the answer was that
the King had drunk too much wine and could not receive
him, as the wine had overpowered him. Thereupon Ashmedai
took up a brick and placed it upon the top of another brick.
When this action of the demon was in due course communicated
to the King of Israel, the latter said: " By this action Ashmedai
meant: if the wine has overpowered him, go and make him
drunk again."

On the following day the demon king once more asked:
" And why am I not being led to-day into the presence of
the King?" And the answer was that the King had eaten
too much and was resting. Thereupon the demon went and
removed the brick he had placed on the top of the other.
And when in due course this action of the demon was again
reported to the King, he replied: " By this action Ashmedai
meant: if he has eaten too much let him keep diet, be stinted
in his food for a day."

At last, on the third day, the demon king was introduced

---

[1] *Deuteron.* 25, 5–10.

to the King of Israel. Ashmedai then measured off four cubits upon the floor with a stick, and thus he spoke to King Solomon: " When thou diest, thou wilt rest in thy grave and possess in this world not more than four cubits of earth. But now, although thou hast conquered the world, thou art not yet content and must needs overcome me, too, and make me prisoner." To which the King of Israel made reply: " I have made thee prisoner because I wish to build the Temple, and, as I am not allowed to use iron tools, I must have the Shamir by virtue of which I can have the stones split. I have made thee prisoner so that thou mayest reveal to me the place where the Shamir is to be found." Thus spake the King.

But Ashmedai answered: " I do not have the Shamir in my possession, for it has not been committed to my charge. Know then, O King, that the Shamir was committed to the charge of the Prince of the Sea who entrusted it to the moor-cock; and the moor-cock has promised upon oath that he would return it again to the Prince of the Sea." Thus spoke Ashmedai, and the King of Israel, marvelling greatly, asked: " And what does the moor-cock do with the Shamir?" " The moor-cock," replied the demon, " carries the Shamir to some bleak rocky mountain which he cleaves asunder by means of the Shamir, to which, as thou well knowest, no substance however hard can resist. And into the cleft thus formed the moor-cock carries verdant grass, herbs, and seeds of various plants and trees. Thus when the valley is clothed with grass and green it becomes a place fit for habitation."

Thereupon King Solomon sent out his servants to search for the nest of the moor-cock. At last Benaiah found the nest, and saw that it contained a young brood. Covering the nest with a glass globe, he awaited the return of the moor-cock.

When the bird came and saw its young but was unable to get at them, the nest being impenetrably covered with the glass globe, he went and fetched the Shamir so as to apply it to the glass and break it. At the very moment when the moor-cock was about to apply the Shamir to the glass in order to cut it, Benaiah gave a shout, and the moor-cock was so frightened that in his agitation he dropped the Shamir.

Snatching it up Benaiah went off with it. The moor-cock, however, finding that he was now unable to keep his oath, according to which he was bound to return the Shamir to the Prince of the Sea, went and strangled himself.

And now Ashmedai remained in the power of Solomon, who detained him until the building of the Temple was completed. Once, however, Ashmedai got the better of Solomon.

One day, when Ashmedai was alone in the presence of the King, the latter said: " Thou seest now that the demons are but little superior to men, and have no power over them, for I have conquered thee and made thee prisoner." To this Ashmedai replied: " If thou wilt take this chain from my neck and give me for a while thy signet ring I will show thee my superiority." Foolishly, Solomon decided to put Ashmedai to the test, took off the chain from his neck and handed him the signet ring; but no sooner had he done this when he had cause to regret his rash action.

Snatching him up, Ashmedai swallowed the King, then he stretched out his wings, so that one touched Heaven and the other the earth, and vomited out the King of Israel in a distant land, four hundred miles away. Ashmedai then gave himself out as King Solomon and took his place, whilst the King himself was far away in a strange country and obliged to beg his bread from door to door. Thus Solomon wandered for many years until he came back to Jerusalem. He went to the house of the Sanhedrin and said: " I, the preacher, was King over Israel in Jerusalem," but the members of the Sanhedrin thought that he was mad, and would not believe him.

When, however, he came every day repeating the same thing, they began to reason and to ask themselves what he really meant by his words. They accordingly sent for Benaiah, King Solomon's trusted servant, and asked him: " Does the King ask thee now into his presence?" to which Benaiah replied that he had not been asked into the King's presence for some time. The members of the Sanhedrin thereupon made inquiries whether he who, according to the stranger, had taken the King's place, ever visited the royal harem. And when the ladies of the harem replied that he did visit the harem, the members of the Sanhedrin sent instructions that they should watch his feet, and see whether his feet were like those of a cock.

But the answer came back that the King visited his harem in stockinged feet and wearing slippers. Thereupon the Rabbis felt sure that the stranger had spoken the truth and that Ashmedai had taken the place of Solomon, the son of David, King of Israel. They escorted the King to the palace, and here restored unto him the chain and the ring on both of which the name of God was engraven. Then Solomon straightaway advanced into the presence-chamber, where Ashmedai, arrayed in Solomon's royal garments, was sitting on the throne. No sooner did he see Solomon enter than he took fright, and uttering a terrible shriek he raised his wings and flew away into space.[1]

[1] *Gittin*, 68b; Jellinek, *Beth-Hamidrash*, Vol. II, pp. 86–87; see also *Sotah*, 48b.

CHAPTER VIII

The Spirits of the Air

The demon Ornias and the foreman's little boy—The archangel Michael and the signet ring—The capture of Ornias—He is condemned to hew stones for the Temple—The angel Uriel and the big whales—Beelzeboul, prince of the demons—The female demons—The she-demon Onoskelis—The arrogant reply of Asmodeus—The liver and gall of the fish *Glanos*—Asmodeus is condemned to prepare the clay for the Temple—The son of Beelzeboul who is dwelling in the Red Sea—Beelzeboul is condemned to saw Theban marbles—The cloud of dust—The spirit of ashes—The seven female spirits—The headless demon who is wholly voice—The big hound Rabdos—He leads the King's servant to a mine of green beryl—The headless demon is condemned to cast a light on the artisans at work—The roaring lion.

NOT only Ashmedai, however, but all the spirits of the air, on the earth, and under the earth, and all the demons were controlled by King Solomon, and it was with their help that he was able to build the Temple.[1] It happened, when King Solomon was building the Temple, that the demon named Ornias came every day at sunset among the artificers. He took away half of the pay of the foreman's (*proto maistros*) little son and also half of his food. He then sucked away the life blood of the boy by sucking the thumb of his right hand, so that the child grew thinner every day and began to pine away. And when King Solomon, who loved the boy, inquired after the reason of his thinness and his ailment, the boy thus spake: "O mighty King! an evil demon named Ornias takes

---

[1] The following legends are related in the *Testament of Solomon*. See F. F. Fleck, *Wissenschaftliche Reise*, II, 3; Bornemann in *Zeitschrift für historische Theologie*, 1844 (Germ. transl.); and Conybeare in *Jewish Quarterly Review*, Vol. XI, pp. 1–45; see also Fabricius, *loc. cit.*, I, p. 1047; Migne, *Patrologia Graeco-Latina*, Vol. CXX, col. 1315–1362.

away every day at sunset half of my food and he also sucks the thumb of my right hand."

When King Solomon heard these words he was very grieved, and prayed to the Lord of Hosts that he might deliver into his hands and give him authority over the evil demon Ornias. The prayer of the King was heard, for soon the angel Michael appeared to him and brought him a signet ring with a seal upon which the Ineffable Name was engraved.

And the archangel Michael thus addressed King Solomon: " Take this ring, O King, which is a gift sent to thee by the Lord of Hosts. The engraving of the seal consists of five *A's* interlaced; and as long as thou wilt wear this ring thou wilt have great power over all the demons in the air, upon the earth, and under the earth, be they male or female." When the King heard these words spoken by the archangel Michael, and saw the ring sent to him as a gift by the Lord of Hosts, he rejoiced in his heart and gave thanks to the Creator, glorifying His name. Thereupon King Solomon called the boy who was the son of the foreman of the artificers, and thus he spake unto him: " Take this ring, my child, and when at sunset the fierce demon comes to visit thee, *throw* the ring at his chest and command him to appear in my presence. And thus thou shalt speak unto him: ' In the name of God, the Lord of the Universe, King Solomon calls thee hither.' When thou wilt have spoken these words thou wilt at once run and come to me and not be afraid of the demon whatever he may say." Thus spake King Solomon. And the boy took the ring and did as the King had commanded him. When at sunset Ornias descended upon him and prepared to take away his pay and his food, he threw the ring at the demon's chest, and commanded him in the name of God to appear before King Solomon. Thereupon he went off and ran to the King. When the demon heard the words of the boy and the command of the King, he was greatly perturbed and begged the child to take off the ring, and not to lead him before the King, promising him as a reward all the gold of the earth. But the boy, remembering the instructions he had received, would not listen to Ornias. And thus, greatly rejoicing, he brought the demon before the gates of the royal palace. When the King heard what had happened he was greatly rejoiced. He rose up from his throne and went out into the court of his palace where he beheld the demon Ornias greatly troubled and trembling. And the King thus spake unto Ornias: "Tell me, O demon, who art thou, what is thy name and to what sign of the Zodiac dost thou belong and art subject?" To this the demon made answer: "My name is Ornias, and I am subject to the Zodiacal sign of the waterpourer." He further informed the King of Israel that he often took the shape of a comely female leading man into temptation, and that he also metamorphosed himself into a lion, when he served and helped other demons to carry out their designs. "And whose offspring art thou?" queried the King. To which Ornias replied: "I am the offspring of the archangel Uriel." When Solomon heard these words from the mouth of the demon named Ornias, he glorified the Lord of Hosts, the God of Heaven and of earth, and greatly rejoiced in his heart.

He thereupon sealed the demon and set him down to hew stones for the Temple, all the stones which had been brought to Jerusalem by the sea of Arabia, and were lying along the shore. But Ornias was loth to be subject to King Solomon, and being fearful of iron, as all demons are, implored the King of Israel to let him go free, which request, however, King Solomon would not grant. Thereupon the King prayed unto the archangel Uriel to come down and help him subdue the rebellious demon. And the archangel Uriel descended from the heavens and appeared before King Solomon. He informed the latter that all the angels and demons had their destinies, for from all eternity it is written down and destined what powers they may exercise and what acts they are to perform and to whom they are to be subject. He (the archangel Uriel) thereupon commanded all the big whales of the sea to come out of the deep, and having cast the destiny of Ornias upon the ground, he announced that it had been destined from all eternity that the demon Ornias should be subject to King Solomon and do his bidding. Thereupon the angel Uriel commanded the demon Ornias to obey the commands of the King of Israel and to hew the stones for the Temple, the huge stones which had been brought from Arabia by sea, and were lying along the shore.

And the King of Israel, to whom Ornias was subject, even according to his destiny, thus spake unto the demon: " I command thee to take this ring and to hie thee to the prince of all the demons and to bring him hither." Whereupon Ornias took the signet ring of the King, and taking to his wings sped away to the prince of the demons whose name is Beelzeboul. To him he spoke: " Hie thee to King Solomon for he bids thee appear in his presence." And when the prince of demons refused to obey the summons, Ornias, as he had been instructed, threw the signet ring at his chest and repeated: " In the name of God, King Solomon commands thee to appear before him." Beelzeboul uttered a cry of rage, and from his mouth issued a burning flame and a veritable river of fire; but he was bound to obey the command, and he followed Ornias before King Solomon. When this mighty prince of demons appeared before the King of Israel, the latter praised the Lord and glorified Him, giving thanks to the Creator who had subjected unto His servant all the spirits of the air and all the demons upon earth and under the earth.

Then King Solomon addressed the prince of the demons, and thus he spake unto him: " O mighty demon, tell me, who am King of Israel, who art thou and what is thy name?"

To this the prince of the demons made answer: " I am Beelzeboul, and *exarch* of the demons. It is I who have the power to make appear before thee all my subject spirits." He then promised to the King to make manifest the apparition of all the demons of the air and upon earth, and to make them subject to the King.

Thereupon the King inquired of Beelzeboul whether there were many female demons, to which Beelzeboul made answer that there were many more females among the demons than males. The King, therefore, expressed the wish to behold one of these female demons. Beelzeboul at once took to his wings and hied himself to distant regions, but soon he returned bringing with him a fair and comely she-demon, fair of skin and lovely of countenance. And when King Solomon beheld this female demon he asked her: " Who art thou?" to which she replied that her name was Onoskelis, and that in the shape of a beautiful woman she worked mischief among men, leading them into temptation. She was born of an echo in a wood, and her dwelling-places were ravines, caves, and precipices.

And when King Solomon asked her to name the angel who usually frustrated her evil designs, she replied: " The angel who frustrates my designs is dwelling in thee, O King."

When the King heard these words he thought that Onoskelis was mocking him and he waxed angry, and ordered one of his soldiers to strike her. But Onoskelis assured the King that it was even so. " Be assured," she cried, " that by the wisdom of God given unto thee, I am subject to thy will, O Solomon, son of David." Thereupon King Solomon sealed and bound the female demon named Onoskelis, and commanded her to spin the hemp for the ropes to be used in the Temple.

And night and day she stood there and did the bidding of the King, spinning the hemp. Thereupon King Solomon commanded that another demon be brought to him. And immediately the demon named Asmodeus was brought before him. Asmodeus was bound and looked furious and enraged. " Who art thou?" queried the King of Israel. " And who art thou?" asked Asmodeus by way of a reply. " This is an arrogant reply," said the King. But Asmodeus said: " How shall I answer thee? Art thou not a son of man? I, Asmodeus, am the offspring of an angel out of his marriage with a daughter of man. Any answer which I, Asmodeus, who am of celestial origin, may choose to make to one earthborn can never be called arrogant. Is not my star bright in heaven, the star which some men call the dragon's child? Do not, therefore, O Solomon, son of David, ask me too many questions, for thy glory is only of short duration. After a little time thy kingdom will be destroyed and thy tyranny over us demons will be short. And then we shall once more have a free field among men, who will revere us as if we were gods, ignorant as they are of the names of the angels who command us and frustrate our designs." Thus spake Asmodeus, and his glance was full of anger.

And when King Solomon heard this speech he bade his soldiers to bind the demon even more carefully, and to flog him with thongs of leather (ox-hide). He then commanded the demon to be more humble in his speech and to tell him now what was his name and what his business. To which the demon made answer: " Among mortals I am called Asmodeus, and it is my business to estrange the hearts of newly-wedded couples and to alienate their affections. I waste away the beauty of young women and estrange the hearts of men." " And is this thy only business?" queried the King. " No," replied the demon. " My business is also to lead men who are wedded into temptation, to make them abandon their lawful wives and seek out the wives of other men, to commit grievous sins and even murderous deeds."

And when King Solomon heard these words, he said unto Asmodeus: " I command thee, Asmodeus, to tell me the name of the angel who has the power to subdue thee and to bring to nought thy designs." Whereupon Asmodeus replied: " The name of the archangel who has the power to frustrate my designs is Raphael, he who stands before the Throne of Glory." He then told the King that the liver and gall of a fish called the *Glanos*, when smoked over the coals of a tamarisk, would put him to flight. But the King queried still further: " Art thou sure, Asmodeus, that thou hast spoken the whole truth and that thou didst hide nothing from me?" Whereupon the demon cried out and said: " Whatever I have told thee, O King of Israel, is true, and the power of God, which hath bound me with indissoluble bonds, knoweth this full well. And now, O King, I pray thee not to condemn me to work in or upon water." But the King only smiled and said: " Thou shalt carry the iron, but also prepare the clay for the construction of the Temple, tread it with thy feet and carry the water for it." And he ordered his servants to give to Asmodeus ten water jars wherein to fetch and carry the water for the clay. And he also burned over Asmodeus the liver and the gall of the fish *Glanos*, and thus the malice and unbearable rage of the demon were frustrated. And groaning loudly the demon carried out the commands of the King.

Thereupon King Solomon once more summoned before him Beelzeboul, the prince of the demons, and seating himself upon a magnificent throne, he thus addressed the chief of the demons: " Tell me, O Beelzeboul, why art thou alone prince of demons?" To this Beelzeboul made answer: " Because I alone am left of all the angels of Heaven who came down upon earth. I was the first angel in the first heaven, my name being Beelzeboul; and now I am the prince and ruler of all those who are bound in Tartarus. I also have a child whose abode is the Red Sea. He is subject unto me, and at certain times he comes up, revealing unto me all he has done, and I give him new courage." "And what is thy business?" queried the King. "I," replied Beelzeboul, "am the ally of foreign tyrants; and furthermore, I excite evil desires and wicked inclinations in the hearts of the chosen servants of God. They commit grievous sins, and I thus lead them to destruction. It is I, too, who place envy and wicked thoughts in the hearts of men, and am the cause of envy, murderous deeds, and wars. Thus, I destroy the world, and all those who contribute to the destruction of this world are my servants and act thus because I have inspired them."

Thereupon the King said unto Beelzeboul: "Bring before me thy son who dwelleth in the Red Sea." The prince of the demons then replied: "I will not bring my son before thee, but another demon shall come to me, a demon whose name is Ephippas. Him thou mayest bind and he may bring up my son from the depth of the sea." "And how comes it," queried the King, "that thy son can live in the depth of the sea, and what is his name?" The prince of demons replied: "Ask me not, O King, for thou wilt not learn it from me, but by my command my son will come to thee and he will tell thee."

Thereupon the King set Beelzeboul to saw Theban marbles, and when the other demons beheld their chief sawing Theban marbles they howled aloud in their joy.

The King then commanded another demon to present himself before him. And lo! there appeared one who carried his head high up, whilst the remaining part of that spirit was curled up like a snake. Breaking through the few soldiers, this demon raised up a fearful cloud of dust which he hurled upwards and downwards so as to frighten the King.

But Solomon stood up and spat on the ground right in that spot where the cloud of dust was raised, and sealed the spot with the ring he had received from the archangel.

Thereupon the dust wind at once ceased. The King then asked the spirit: "Who art thou and what is thy name?" The demon once more raised a dust, and answered: "What is thy desire, O King?" "Tell me thy name, so that I may ask thee a question," replied the King. "Tell me also thy employment and pursuit." And the demon replied: "I am the spirit of ashes: I set fire to fields and destroy houses; and my principal occupation is during the summer, when I am particularly busy." "And under whose authority," asked the King, "dost thou do harm?" "Under the authority of the archangel Azael," replied the demon; whereupon the King summoned Azael and set a seal upon the demon. He then commanded the demon to seize huge stones and throw them up to the work people on the top of the structure. And the demon was compelled to do the King's bidding.

Thereupon King Solomon ordered another demon to come before him. And lo! there appeared seven female spirits, fair and comely to behold and beautiful in appearance. And the King questioned them as to their names and their employment. "We are of the thirty three elements of the ruler of darkness," they answered all at once. But the King questioned them one by one, beginning with the first and ending with the seventh.

And the first of these seven female spirits said: "I am Deception. I deceive and excite evil inclinations, but my designs are frustrated by the angel Lamechalal." And the second female spirit said: "I am Strife, the strife of strifes; but the angel who frustrates me is called Barnchiachel." And the third spirit said: "I am called Klathon, that is battle, and my business consists in causing honourable and decent people to quarrel and to attack one another; and Marmarath is the name of the angel who frustrates all my designs." The fourth spirit then said: "I am Jealousy; I cause men to lose their reason, I divide them and make them hostile to one another, and whenever Strife follows me I even alienate husband and wife, estrange parents and children, and tear brothers from sisters. Alas, however, I have an angel who frustrates my designs and his name is Balthial." And the fifth female spirit said: " I am Power; I raise up tyrants, I sweep kings out of the way by power. I also lend power to rebels, but the angel who is opposed to me is Asteraoth." And the sixth spirit said: " I am Error (Seduction). I induce men into error, and I will induce thee, too, into error, O King Solomon, as I have already done once when at my inspiration thou didst slay thine own brother. I also lead men into error, so that they pry into graves. I also instruct the thieves, and I lead men away from piety, and I do many other evil things, but I have an angel who frustrates me and his name is Uriel."

" I am the worst of all," said the seventh female spirit. " I can make even thee worse than thou art. Our stars are in heaven and we live together and we change our places together. We live together, sometimes in Lydia, sometimes in Olympus, and sometimes in a high mountain." The King heard these words of the female spirits and wondered greatly. Thereupon he sealed them with his ring, and because they were many he set them to dig the foundations of the Temple, which was two hundred and fifty cubits in length. He ordered them to be very industrious, and although they grumbled and protested they immediately started to perform the task set to them.

The King then bade another demon come to him.

And lo! there was brought before him a demon who had the limbs of a man but no head. And when the King beheld him he said to him: " Who art thou?" " I am a demon," replied the headless spirit. " I am called Envy, and it is my delight to swallow heads so that I may secure one for myself. But I am anxious to have such an head as thou hast, King Solomon." And when the King heard these words he swiftly stretched out his hand against the demon's chest and sealed

him. Whereupon the headless spirit threw himself upon the
ground and exclaimed: " Woe unto me, whither have I come
through the traitor Ornias?" The King then asked him: " How
dost thou manage to see, and how dost thou manage to speak,
having no head, no eyes, and no tongue?" But the spirit,
whose voice nevertheless came up to the King, made answer:
" I am able to see by means of my feelings, and manage to
speak because I am wholly voice, having inherited the voices
of many men. I smash the heads of many, and when I encounter some at the crossways I seize their heads, cutting
them off with my hands as if with a sword. Then I put these
heads upon myself, but the fire that is in me comes up through
my neck and devours them." " Tell me now," queried the
King, " the name of the angel by whom thou art frustrated?"
To which the headless demon replied: " He is the fiery flash
of lightning."

Thereupon the King bade another demon to appear in
his presence. And lo! there came a big hound and spoke
with a loud and powerful voice: " Hail thee, O King Solomon,
son of David!" The King was greatly astounded and even
frightened, and he asked the hound: " Who art thou, O hound?"
To which the demon, in the shape of a hound, made answer:
" Alas, I do appear to thee to be a hound, but even before
thou wast, O King Solomon, I was a man, committing many
evil deeds in the world. I was greatly learned in letters and
even dared to hold back the stars of heaven, and to accomplish
other divine works." " And what is thy name," queried the
King, " and thy pursuit?" " My name," replied the demon,
" is *Rabdos* (staff)." And he proceeded: " If thou, O King,
wilt send thy servant with me I will lead him to a spot in the
mountains and there he will find a mine of green beryl, which
thou canst take away, so that thou mayest adorn the Temple
with it." When the King heard these words, he bade his servant
to accompany the hound to the spot in the mountains. " Take

this signet ring," he added, " and whoever will show thee
the green stone, him shalt thou at once seal with this signet
ring. Mark with great care the spot and bring the demon
back with thee." And the servant set off, accompanied by
the hound, who showed him the spot where there was a mine
of green stones. When the servant returned with the huge
hound, the King bound both the headless demon and the
hound, and set the latter to keep guard over the headless
fiery spirit, so that the light emitted by him through his maw
by day and night be cast on the artisans at work in the Temple
of God. Thereupon the King took two hundred shekels
from the treasure of the mine for the supports of the altar,
and then closed the treasure of the mine. He then commanded
the demons to cut marble for the Temple.

King Solomon thereupon bade another demon to appear
before him, and there came one in the shape of a roaring
lion. And the spirit thus addressed the King: " I am a spirit,
O King, incapable of being perceived, although it is my business to enfeeble men who are lying sick. I am, however, also
able to cast out demons, legions of them being under my
control." " What is thy name," asked the King, " and what
is the name of the angel by whom thou art frustrated?" " My
name," replied the spirit in the form of a roaring lion, " is
Lion-bearer, but I cannot tell thee the name of the angel
who frustrates me, for in so doing I would bind not only myself but also the legions of demons who are under my control."
But the King adjured him in the name of God to tell him the
name of the angel by whom he was frustrated, and the spirit
answered: " I am bound by him who is the greatest among
men and whose name is the figure 644." The King thereupon set all the legions under his control to carry wood from
the forest, but the roaring lion himself he bade saw the wood
into small pieces with his teeth, for burning it in the furnace
for the construction of the Temple.

CHAPTER IX

King Solomon and the Serving Demons

The three-headed dragon—The treasure at the entrance of the Temple —Obizuth, the she-demon with invisible limbs—The winged dragon with the face of a man—Enepsigos, the she-demon with three heads—The demon who is half horse and half fish—The thirty-six spirits—The old workman and his son—The prediction of Ornias—The demons are able to foretell the future—The weakness and fall of demons—Adares, King of Arabia—His message to the King of Israel—The demon in the shape of a fierce wind—The capture of the demon by means of the signet ring and a leather flask—The demon Ephippas lifts the huge stone—Abezithibod, the demon dwelling in the Red Sea.

AND it came to pass that King Solomon bade another demon appear before him, and one day there came forward a terrible three-headed dragon. " I am a most terrible spirit," he said, " for I blind children in their mother's womb and make them deaf and mute. I also cause men to fall down and to grind their teeth and to foam." And he further said: " At the entrance of the Temple which thou hast begun to build, O King, there lieth hidden a treasure of gold; dig it up, O Solomon, son of David, and carry it off." Thus spake the three-headed dragon, and the King ordered his servants to dig up the treasure at the entrance of the Temple, and they found much gold, even as the demon had said. The King then sealed him with his signet ring, and bade him make bricks for the construction of the Temple.

Thereupon there came before the King another demon

who had the form of a woman. She had a head, and her hair was dishevelled, but her limbs were invisible.

And the King said unto this spirit: " Who art thou, and what is thy name?" To this the she-demon replied: " And who art thou and why art thou anxious to know all concerning me? As I am here, bound before thee, I will, however, tell thee, O King, and thou shalt learn who I am. I am called Obizuth, and I never sleep, for I roam about in the world, visiting women in childbirth. Not a single night am I idle, for if I am not successful in one place I visit another and strangle the newly-born babes. I roam about everywhere, east and west, and I have many names and many shapes and forms. Although I am standing before thee thou canst not command me, for my sole employment is the destruction of new-born babes."

And the King marvelled greatly at the appearance of this female demon, for, although the head of the spirit was that of a woman, the countenance bright and greeny, and the hair dishevelled like that of a dragon, the limbs and the body remained invisible. " Tell me," queried the King, " what is the name of the angel by whom thou art frustrated?" To which the female demon replied: " The name of the angel by whom I am frustrated is Apharoph, which is Raphael. And if any man knoweth his name and doth write it over a woman in childbirth, then I am not able to approach or harm her." The King then commanded that the hair of the female demon be bound, and that she be hung up in front of the Temple of God, so that everybody might see and praise the Lord, who had vouchsafed wisdom and power to the King of Israel through the signet ring.

And there appeared again before King Solomon a spirit which had the appearance of a dragon, but his face and feet were those of a man; and he also had wings on his back. " I am the winged dragon," said the spirit, " and alas, I have been subdued by thy ring and the wisdom which has been vouchsafed unto thee, O King." And when the demon said this the breath issuing from his mouth set fire to the wood of the frankincense tree, and burned and consumed all the wood collected, and placed in the Temple. And the King, seeing what this demon had done, marvelled greatly, and asked him to tell him the name of the angel by whom he was frustrated. The winged dragon made answer: " I am frustrated by the great angel who dwelleth in the second heaven called Bazazath." Thereupon the King invoked this angel, and by means of his signet ring he bound the winged dragon and condemned him to saw up blocks of marble for the construction of the Temple. He then bade another demon to appear before him. And lo! there appeared one that had the shape of a woman, but on her shoulders she carried two other heads with hands. " Who art thou?" queried King Solomon. " I am Enepsigos, but I have numerous other names." " And what is the name of the angel who subdues thee?" asked the King. " Why dost thou ask, what seekest thou?" said the spirit, by way of reply, " my shapes are numerous; like the goddess that I am called, I undergo changes and assume different shapes. Seek not, therefore, to know all about me. But this much thou mayest know, so hearken unto my words: I dwell in the moon and therefore possess three forms. I am sometimes invoked by the wise as *Kronos*, but at other times I come down and appear in another shape, whilst at others I appear in the form as thou seest me now. The angel to whom I am subjected sits in the third heaven and his name is Rathanael." The King at once invoked the angel Rathanael and bound the spirit with a triple chain.

Thereupon there came before the King another spirit who had in front the shape and form of a horse but behind that of a fish. " I am a mighty and fierce demon of the sea," he called in a loud and terrible voice, " and I seek to seize gold and

silver. Changing myself into waves I am busy over the wide
expanses of the sea and of the waters, where I whirl ships
round and round, destroying them and throwing men into the
sea. I get hold of men and money. The money I take to the
bottom of the sea, but the bodies of the men I cast out upon
the shore. And I came up from the depth of the sea to take
counsel with Beelzeboul who is the ruler of the spirits in the
air, upon the earth, and under the earth, but he bound me and
delivered me into thy hands, O King. But in two or three
days I shall no longer be able to converse with thee, because
I shall have no water which is my element. Jameth is the angel
who frustrates my designs." Thus spake the spirit of the
sea. Thereupon King Solomon commanded that the demon
of the sea be thrown into a phial containing sea-water, to
seal this phial with marbles and asphalt and pitch, and to
deposit it in the Temple.

And there appeared again another demon in the shape of
a man with bright, gleaming eyes, carrying a blade in his hand.
" I am the descendant of a giant who was killed during the
massacre of the giants," said he, " I often dwell among the
tombs and assume the form of the dead, destroying with my
sword all those whom I manage to catch." And when the
King had shut up this demon there appeared before him
thirty-six spirits with ugly, shapeless heads, but human in
form. There were some who had the faces of oxen, some
those of asses, and others the faces of birds. Marvelling greatly,
the King asked them who they were. To this they made
answer: " We are the thirty-six elements, the rulers of darkness,
and we have come before thee, O King, because the Lord
of the Universe has given thee authority over all the spirits
in the air, on the earth, and likewise under the earth." And
the first of them said: " I am the first leader of the Zodiacal
sign and am called the *ram*." And all these thirty-six spirits
King Solomon caused to be bound, setting them to fetch

water for the Temple. Some of the demons he condemned to drudgery and heavy work in the Temple, whilst others were shut up in prisons, so that they were made harmless.

And it came to pass that one day an old workman appeared before the King and complained against his only son who did insult and ill-treat him. He beseeched the King to avenge him and to condemn the son to die, as was the law.[1] And just as the King was about to pronounce sentence in this matter, the demon Ornias laughed aloud. The King thereupon commanded the demon to be brought before him, and he thus addressed him: " Accursed demon, how didst thou dare to laugh at me and in my royal presence?"

To this the demon Ornias made answer: " Be not angry, O mighty King. I did not laugh at thee or because of thee, but because of the old man and his wretched son. The old man is anxious to have his son condemned to death, but in three days the boy will anyhow die an untimely death." And the King marvelled greatly at the words of the demon, and asked: " Is this so? dost thou speak the truth?" " It is true, O King," replied the demon Ornias. " And how dost thou know this?" queried the King. " We demons," replied Ornias, " often ascend into the firmaments; there we fly about among the angels and the stars, and we hear the sentences which are proclaimed, and which go forth upon the souls of men." " And how can you demons ascend to Heaven and intermingle with the holy angels and the stars?" further queried the King. To this the demon replied: " Whatever happens in Heaven also occurs upon earth. We demons fly about in the air beneath the lower firmament, where we contemplate all the heavenly powers and hear their voices and the voices of all the heavenly beings. But we have nowhere to alight and rest, and thus we lose our strength and grow tired, and on account of our weakness, finding nowhere anything to lay hold of, we fall down

[1] *Deuteron.*, 21, 18-21.

like lightning in the depth of night, or like leaves from the trees. People seeing us fall down imagine that stars are falling, but it is not so, O great King. The stars having firm foundations in the firmaments do not fall, but it is only one of us demons falling from on high. We fall and set on fire cities and fields." Thus spake the demon, and the King marvelled greatly. The King, therefore, sent the old man home, commanding him to appear once more in his presence in five days. And when five days had passed, the King sent again for the old man. The latter appeared with sad face and in a great grief. "Alas, great King," wailed the old man, "I am childless and sit in despair by the grave of my boy who died two days ago." The King on hearing these words, knew that Ornias had spoken the truth and that demons are in reality able to foretell the future.

The power of Solomon over the demons became so great that he could subdue even the fiercest among them. Thus one day, Adares, the King of the Arabians, sent a message to King Solomon, of whose wisdom and power over all the spirits of the air he had heard, begging him to deliver Arabia from a terrible demon, who, in the shape of a fierce wind, blew over the country from early dawn until the third hour. "Its blast," wrote the King of Arabia, "is so terrible and so harsh that neither man nor beast can withstand it but are slain." The King of Arabia, therefore, begged the King of Israel to send a man and capture this terrible demon, promising in return for this act of righteousness, that he and his people and all his land would serve King Solomon, and that Arabia would live in peace with him.

Thereupon King Solomon called one of his trusted servants, and ordered him to take a camel and also a leather flask, and to betake himself to Arabia where the evil spirit, fierce and terrible, was blowing. Solomon also gave his trusted servant his signet ring and thus he spoke: " When thou wilt reach Arabia and the place where the evil spirit bloweth so fiercely, place the signet ring in front of the mouth of the leather flask, and hold both of them towards the great and terrible blast of the spirit. When thou wilt see that the flask is blown out then hastily tie up its mouth, for the demon will be in it. Then thou wilt seal the flask with the seal-ring very securely, and placing it upon thy camel bring it hither. On the way, no doubt, the demon will offer thee gold and silver and much treasure to let him go free. Take heed not to be persuaded, but try to find out from the demon and make him point out the places where there are treasures and gold and silver. Now, fare thee well, and bring the demon from Arabia hither without fail." Thus spake King Solomon, and his trusted servant did as he had been bidden, and set off into Arabia to the place where, fierce and terrible, the demon was blowing and blasting.

And when he arrived into this region of Arabia he waited till dawn, when the fierce and evil spirit began his daily blast. Facing the demon's blast, the messenger from King Solomon placed the leather flask upon the ground and held the ring on the mouth of the flask, so that the demon blew through the finger ring into the flask and blew it out. And when the servant of King Solomon saw that the flask was blown out, he knew that the demon was in it, and he promptly drew tight the opening of the flask in the name of the Lord God. He then sealed the flask securely with the seal ring, even as his master had bidden him do, but he tarried three days in the country to make trial. And lo! the fierce and terrible wind had ceased, for the demon now shut up in the leather flask no longer did blow against the city. And the Arabs marvelled greatly and praised the Lord God who had given such wisdom and power to King Solomon.

They then heaped gifts upon the servant of King Solomon, and sent him away with much honour. And when the messenger returned to Jerusalem he placed the leather flask containing the demon of Arabia in the Temple.

Now it came to pass that just at this moment King Solomon was in great distress. The Temple was being completed, but there was an immense corner stone which had still to be placed on the pinnacle of the Temple, and this work neither workmen nor demons had as yet been able to accomplish. Work as they might, they were not strong enough to stir it and lift it up to put it in its allotted place. Now on the next morning, after the return of his messenger from Arabia, the King went into the Temple and sat in deep distress, thinking about the heavy stone which neither workmen nor demons had been able to stir from its place. And lo! the flask containing the fierce demon from Arabia stood up, walked around seven steps, then fell down and did homage to King Solomon. The latter commanded the demon in the flask to stand up and tell him his name and employment. King Solomon then said to the demon: " Who art thou and by what angel art thou frustrated?" And the demon replied: " I am the demon called Ephippas and I am able to remove mountains and to overthrow them." " Canst thou raise this stone," asked King Solomon, " and lay it in its place?" " Verily," said the demon, " I can do this, and with the help of the demon who presides over the Red Sea, I can bring up a pillar of air and support the gigantic stone." Thereupon King Solomon commanded Ephippas to become flat, and the flask to appear as if depleted of air. He then placed it under the stone, and behold, the demon lifted up the stone on the top of the flask, and put it in its appointed place. And then the demon who presides over the Red Sea appeared and raised a column of air and the pillar remained in mid-air supporting the stone. King Solomon asked the spirit who had come up from the depth of the Red Sea to tell him who he was and what was his business. And the spirit replied: " I, O King Solomon, am called Abezithibod, and I once sat in the first heaven, being the descendant of an archangel. Fierce and winged I was, but I plotted against every spirit in Heaven. It was I who hardened the heart of Pharaoh, when Moses appeared before him; and also in the time of the exodus of the Children of Israel, it was I who excited the heart of Pharaoh and caused him and all the Egyptians to pursue the Children of Israel through the waves of the Red Sea. And it came to pass that when the Children of Israel had passed through the waves of the Red Sea, the waters came over the hosts of the Egyptians and hid them, and I, too, remained in the Sea." Thus spake the demon Abezithibod; and King Solomon wondered greatly, and praised the Lord.

CHAPTER X

Paradise, or the Abode of the Just

The two parks—Paradise in Heaven, and Paradise upon earth—Persian influence — Zoroastrian dualism — Egyptian and Greek doctrines — The realm of the dead, and the dog Anubis—Favourite persons visit Paradise and Hell during their lives upon earth—Orpheus and Ulysses—Enoch and the prophet Elijah—The three walls of Paradise—The just and pious men of the Gentiles—The sinners who repented—The seven compartments of Paradise—The tree of life—The river Jubal—Enoch-Metatron wanders through the city of the just—The Seat of Judgment—Description of Paradise in *Yalkut Rubeni*—The ten compartments—Rabbi Joshua ben Levi, the hero of a Jewish *Divina Commedia*—The angel of death leads Rabbi Joshua ben Levi to the gates of Paradise—The Rabbi enters Paradise alive —The complaint of the angel of death—Rabbi Joshua's description of Paradise—The reception of the just—The rivers of oil, balsam, wine and honey—The transformation of the Just—Childhood, adolescence, and old age—The thrones of gold and pearls—The purple covers woven by Eve— The compartment of the Messiah—Elijah comforts the Messiah—Rabbi Chanina and the angel of death—Moses visits Paradise and Hell—The thrones of the Patriarchs—The thrones of copper for the wicked whose sons are just and pious.

IN Rabbinic, Talmudic, and Midrashic literature, as well as in the apocryphal and pseudoepigraphic writings, the ideas with regard to Paradise and Hell, Garden of Eden, and Gehinnom, are numerous and varied. Some regarded Paradise as being on the earth itself, whilst for others it was in Heaven. Others again assumed two Paradises, one in Heaven for those who are perfect in holiness, and one on earth for those who are not quite perfect, or at least come short of perfection. There is no mention whatever of the myths of Paradise and Hell in the Holy Writ, in the Books of Moses or in the Prophets. The legislator promised his nation reward and punishment in this world, and even the Prophets speak only of a life here below. The author of *Ecclesiastes* recognizes the immortality of the soul,[1] but there is no question of Heaven, Paradise, or Hell.

The majority of the Rabbis of the Talmud speak of the immortality of the soul, but rarely indulge in descriptions of Paradise or Hell. The myths and legends about Paradise and Hell all took their origin upon Persian soil. Influenced by Zoroastrian dualism, the Babylonian exiles applied it in a truly Jewish spirit, that is in an ethical manner, not only to the doctrines of angels and demons, but also to reward and punishment after death. Foreign influence became even more pronounced under the rule of the Seleucidæ and the Ptolemies, when the Jews of Egypt came into close contact with the ideas of Greece and Egypt. From the Egyptians, they learned the doctrine of the realm of the dead whither the souls of the departed are led by the dog Anubis. From the Greeks they learned the existence of two realms, Elyseum, where the pious and just dwell, and Tartarus where the shadows of the wicked roam about. The Jewish mythmakers of the Persian and Hellenistic periods also created two cities, one the abode of the just and the other the dwelling of the wicked, whither the souls of the departed are taken by the angel Dumah.[2]

And just as in Greek myth many favoured persons were supposed to have visited Paradise and Hell during their lives and to have become the heroes of a *Divina Commedia*, so in Jewish myth, too, we meet with favoured personalities who were translated to Paradise before they had " shuffled off this mortal coil ". Some of them, as we shall see later, recorded their visions and gave a minute description of Heaven and Paradise. Rabbi Joshua ben Levi visited the lower Paradise, that is Paradise upon earth. Alexander the

---

[1] *Ecclesiastes*, 12, 7.   [2] Silence; see on *Dumah, Berachoth*, 18b; *Sanhedrin*, 94a.

Great knocked at its gates, but was not admitted. The Prophet
Elijah and Enoch are supposed to have been translated into
the lower Paradise, although in various places of the *Book of
Enoch* the latter is described as having been carried to the
upper Paradise, where also the Prophet Elijah dwells. But
whilst in Greek myth living personalities are allowed to visit
Hades and to return to the upper world, few, if any, persons
in Jewish myth are supposed to have had a peep into Hell.
Thus Orpheus goes down to Hades to fetch his wife Eurydice,
and Ulysses undertakes the journey to consult the seer
Tyresius. Moses was allowed to visit Hell; but it is only with
difficulty that Rabbi Joshua, the son of Levi, obtained the
permission to cast a glance upon the doings in Hell.

It is especially in Jewish mysticism, which is a more modern
development of ancient mythology, that the descriptions of
Paradise and Hell abound. Jewish mysticism teaches that
there are two Paradises, one in Heaven and one upon earth.
In the *Book of Enoch* and in the *Fourth Esra* both a lower
Paradise and an upper Paradise are mentioned.[1] It is the
garden of justice, or the city of the just, where the just and
pious dwell. Various descriptions of both the upper and the
lower Paradise are to be found in Midrashic lore. In one
Midrash it is described as follows: The Garden of Eden
has three walls all made of fire. The outer wall, of black
fire, is visible and invisible, and a flaming sword is constantly turning round this wall. There are four gates in this
wall at a distance of 120 yards one from the other. And
the flaming sword, turning round and round night and day,
never rests and devours all grass and everything that approaches
the outer wall within one mile. And at a distance of 600 yards
is the second wall. And there dwell the just and pious of the
Gentiles and heathens, all the proselytes who were not suffi-
ciently firm in their fear of the Lord. And every day at the

---

[1] R. H. Charles. *The Book of Enoch.* 65, 2; 106, 8; 77, 3; 60, 8; 87, 34; 89, 22.

time of the afternoon prayer the evil spirits and malignant angels assemble and endeavour to expel them and lead them straight into Hell. But they raise a loud cry, and the angel Azriel arrives and saves them from the clutches of the malignant spirits. Near that second outer wall dwell also all those who had given alms and done good deeds in the world publicly so as to gain fame, but not out of goodness of heart and for the sake of the Lord. Three times a day the malignant spirits and demons come to torture them, but the protecting angels save them from their hands. And all the sinners who had thought of repentance before leaving the earth are brought into the space between the two walls, and the angel, whose name is Mahariel, shows them from afar the abode of the just and of the blessed. The second wall is of green and red fire, and within that wall dwell all those who had striven to make their children study the law, although they did not succeed in their endeavour. Here also dwell those who, under the impulse of the moment, had performed a good deed. The light from the grace of the just shines upon them, but only for one moment when it is hidden again. The third wall consists of light mixed with darkness, and it is within the Garden of Eden, and within this wall is the abode of the just and of the blessed. And as soon as they enter this abode they become as light as air and part of it, and are robed in air as in a pure and holy garment. This garment resembles in shape and form the garments they had worn in the netherworld, so that they can recognize one another by it.[1] Another description runs as follows: The Garden of Eden forms the east of the world, and it measures æons, and therein dwell seven different kinds of the just and pious, and it contains houses built as dwellings for the just. The first house is the one wherein the prophets of justice have their abode. This house is built of the wood of cedars. In the second house the rafters are of cedar

---

[1] Jellinek, *Beth-Hamidrash*, Vol. III, pp. 131–132.

and the walls of silver, and therein dwell the sinners who repent and who are purified of sin, even as silver is free from all spots. And the third house is built of silver and fine gold, and ornamented with pearls and precious stones, and it is very vast, and all that is good upon earth or in heaven is to be found in this house, for all the delights and perfumes are planted therein, and in its midst stands the tree of life. From the tree issues the river Jubal dividing itself into four parts, Gihon, Hiddekel, Pishon, and Phrat. And the fourth house is built of olive wood, and therein dwell all those who had suffered upon earth, but had not rebelled or grumbled against Providence and the Creator, remaining humble, meek, merciful, and just.[1]

Before being crowned by the Lord of the Universe, Enoch, who afterwards became Metatron, wandered through the celestial regions led by Michael. He made a circuit of the heavens, wandering west and east, and saw the wonders of Heaven, its secrets and delights. On the west he saw a great and lofty mountain, a strong rock and four delightful places. It was both deep and dark to behold, but internally it was capacious and very smooth as if it had been rolled over. One of the holy angels who was with him informed Enoch that these were the places of delight where the spirits and souls of the dead would be collected. All the souls of the sons of men who were righteous would be collected in these delightful places formed for them. They would occupy these places until the day of judgment, which will be long. But the spirits of the dead are separated one from another. Three separations have been made between them, and they are separated by a chasm, by water, and by light above it. And the sinners, too, are separated one from another when they die and judgment has not overtaken them in their lifetime. Their souls are separated in Heaven. Enoch-Metatron then went from

---

[1] *Midrash Konen*, Jellinek, *Beth-Hamidrash*, Vol. II, pp. 28-29.

thence to another place at the extremities of the earth towards
the west. Here he saw a fire blazing and running without
ceasing, continuing by day and night, never intermitting its
course. It was the fire of all the luminaries of Heaven. He
then proceeded to another place, there he saw a mountain
of fire flashing unceasingly by day and night. Approaching
a little nearer he saw seven splendid mountains all different
from each other. The stones of all the mountains were splendid
and brilliant to behold, and their surface was very beautiful.
Three of these mountains placed one upon another were
towards the east, whilst three others, equally placed one upon
another, were towards the south. The seventh mountain was
in the midst of them. Surrounded by delightfully smelling
trees, the mountains resembled the seat of a throne. And
among the delightfully smelling trees surrounding the mountains there was one tree of an unceasing smell, not even
among the trees which were in Eden was there a tree which
was so fragrant. Its fruit was beautiful to behold, and neither
bark, nor flower and leaf ever withered. Its fruit resembled
the cluster of a palm, it was pleasing to behold and a delight
to the eye. It was the mountain which will be the seat on
which shall sit the great and holy Lord of Glory, the Everlasting King, on the day when He shall come and descend to
visit the earth with goodness. And Enoch was informed by
the angels in whose company he was that on the day of judgment, when all shall be punished and consumed, the fruit of
this tree of an agreeable smell shall be bestowed on the elect,
the righteous and humble. Enoch then proceeded to the
middle of the earth, and here he beheld a happy and fertile
spot, containing branches continually sprouting from the
trees which were planted in it. There were two holy mountains and underneath them water flowed, and between them
there was a deep valley. It was the place where, on the day
of judgment, all who utter with their mouths unbecoming

language against God and speak harsh things of His glory will be collected.[1]

The *Yalkut Rubeni* gives the following description of the upper Paradise. Paradise consists of ten compartments, and they are inhabited by the souls of the departed pious and just, according to the degree of their respective piety. Here they dwell without being swayed by any of the passions which cause so much trouble to mortal man. Without food or drink, care-free they live happily, enjoying the Divine radiance, wisdom, and benevolence, having free access to the treasures of knowledge, and learning the secrets of nature. The first compartment is the seat of the simply pious souls, of those who upon earth kept the covenant, fought valiantly against every evil inclination, and scrupulously observed the law. This compartment is presided over by Joseph, the viceroy of Egypt, who is assisted by the angel-group known as *Erelim*. The second compartment is inhabited by the souls of the departed who, upon earth, have done more than strictly adhere to the law. The inmates of this compartment are presided over by Phinehas, the son of Eleazar, who is assisted by the angel-group known as *Hashmalim*. In the third compartment dwell pious men, a shade more perfect. They are presided over by the High-priest Eleazar, who is assisted by the angel-group known as *Tarshishim*. The fourth compartment is the abode of the really holy souls. Here celestial music is constantly heard, and the Divine radiance is often visible. The compartment is presided over by the High-priest Aaron, who is assisted by an angel-group known as *Seraphim*. The fifth compartment is the abode of the sinners who have repented. They enjoy special favours, and are esteemed even higher than the inmates of the fourth compartment, enjoying even more frequently the manifestation of Divine radiance. The president of this compartment is the King Manasseh, who

[1] R. H. Charles, *The Book of Enoch*.

has at his disposal an angel-group known as the *Ophanim*. In the sixth compartment dwell the souls of the innocent, early deceased children. Their president, guardian, and teacher, is the great angel-prince Metatron himself. Daily he visits these innocent souls, teaching and instructing them. The ministering angels of the children are the *Cherubim*.[1]

The hero of a Jewish *Divina Commedia*, and who frequently describes the life in Paradise and Inferno, was the famous Rabbi Joshua ben Levi, although he was not the only one who was allowed to have a peep into Paradise and Hell. He lived in the third century of our era, and has left a description of Paradise and Hell which occupies a prominent place in Jewish apocalyptic literature. He became the recorder, long before Dante started to write his *Divina Commedia*, of myths on Paradise and Hell.

The Story of the Angel of Death and Rabbi Joshua ben Levi

The legend of this Rabbi—who in his lifetime visited Hell and explored and entered Paradise where he remained alive, thus never tasting death and the power of the angel of death—runs as follows: He entered Paradise not by the door, but by leaping over the wall. When his earthly life was drawing to a close, the angel of death was instructed to visit the Rabbi, but to show deference to him and to respect all his wishes. And when Rabbi Joshua, the son of Levi, noticed how courteous and humble the angel of death showed himself, he asked the latter whether he would consent to do him a favour. " If it is in my power," replied the angel, " I will gladly grant thy petition." " Let me, before thou takest my life, contemplate from afar my place in Paradise." The request was granted by the angel of death, and he promised to let Rabbi Joshua

[1] Cf. Jellinek, *loc. cit.*, Vol. II, pp. 28–29; Vol. III, pp. 52–53.

have a glimpse of Paradise and point out to him the seat he
was going to occupy there. As a proof of his good faith, he
handed over to Rabbi Joshua his sword, which the Rabbi was
allowed to keep during their journey and until they reached
the gates of Paradise. Thus the two set out on the journey,
and having travelled a long way finally halted before the gates
of Paradise, outside that celestial city of the just, where the
pious, after having shuffled off mortal coil, enjoy heavenly
bliss. With the assistance of the angel of death Rabbi Joshua
climbed up the wall of the celestial city, and peeped down
into the abode of the blessed. The angel of death pointed
out to him the place he was destined to occupy after death.
Suddenly Rabbi Joshua ben Levi threw himself over the wall
and was inside Paradise to the surprise and amazement of
his companion, the angel of death. Seizing the Rabbi Joshua
ben Levi by the skirt of his garment the angel of death urged
him to return. But the Rabbi swore an oath that he would
not return. Thereupon the angel of death ascended to Heaven
where he complained before the tribunal of justice. And the
heavenly decree was issued that as the Rabbi had never during
his earthly career broken his word and much less his oath,
and had never even sought to be relieved of the obligation
of a promise or of an oath, he had deserved not to be compelled to commit perjury within the precincts of the city
of the just. The angel of death had, therefore, to be content when the Rabbi returned unto him his sword, which
he at first had declined to give up. He yielded only when
a voice from Heaven ordered him immediately to restore the
sword.[1]

The angel of death, greatly vexed, went to Rabbi Gamaliel
and complained against Rabbi Joshua, the son of Levi, who
had deceived him and taken his place in Paradise whilst alive.

[1] *Ketubot*, 77*b*; see Jellinek, *loc. cit.*, Vol. II, pp 48–51; Bacher, *loc. cit.*, I, 192–194;
see also *Kol Bo*, fol., 136*d*–137*a*.

But Rabbi Gamaliel made answer: "Rabbi Joshua served thee quite right." Thereupon he asked the angel of death to go and request the Rabbi in his name to make a diligent search through Paradise and Hell, learn all its mysteries and send him a description. And the angel of death complied with the request of Rabbi Gamaliel and took his message to Rabbi Joshua who was now dwelling in Paradise. And Rabbi Joshua ben Levi gave the following description: Paradise has two gates of carbuncle, and sixty myriads of ministering angels are set to keep watch over them. And the lustre of the countenance of each angel is like the lustre of the firmament. And these angels are standing and waiting with crowns of gold and precious stones, and with myrtle wreaths in their hands, ready to welcome the righteous. And when a just man approaches the gates of Paradise, the ministering angels immediately divest him of the clothes in which he had been buried, and they array him with eight garments woven out of clouds of glory, and upon his head they place two crowns, one of precious stones and pearls, and the other of pure gold. Into his hands they place eight branches of myrtle, and they make him enter into the abode of the just, where eight rivers of water flow among eight hundred essences of rose and myrtle. And everyone of the just who enters the abode of the just has a canopy whence issue four rivers of oil, balsam, wine, and honey, and every canopy is overgrown by a vine of gold, thirty pearls hanging down from it. In every canopy there is a table of precious stones and pearls, and sixty angels minister to everyone of the just in the city of the just. And there is neither night nor day in the city of the just. The just also undergo three transformations, passing through the stages of childhood, adolescence, and old age. The just man is at first a child and enters the compartment of the children where he tastes the joys of childhood. He is thereupon changed into a youth, and the delights and pleasures of youth are his lot,

which he is allowed to enjoy. He is then changed into an old
man, and entering the compartment of aged people he is
allowed to enjoy all the pleasures of mature age. And there
are eighty myriads of trees in every corner of Paradise,
and the smallest of these trees is more magnificent than a
whole garden of spices. There are also sixty myriads of ministering angels in every corner of the Garden of Eden, who are
singing with sweet and lovely voices. And in the middle of
the Garden of Eden stands the tree of life, overshadowing the
whole of the Paradise. The fruit of this tree has 500 thousand
tastes, one taste being different from the other, and the perfumes thereof vary likewise. Seven clouds of glory hang over
the tree of life, and its odours are wafted from one end of the
world to the other. Underneath the tree sit the just and the
scholars and explain the law.

And Rabbi Joshua went and searched through Paradise,
and found therein seven compartments, each measuring both
in width and length twelve myriads of miles. The first compartment is just opposite the first door of Paradise, and here
dwell all the proselytes who have embraced Judaism not from
compulsion but of their own free will. The walls of this compartment are of glass, and the wainscoting is of cedarwood.
And when the Rabbi tried to measure it, the proselytes inhabit-
ing this compartment arose and wanted to prevent him from
doing so. But the prophet Obadjah, who presides over them,
rebuked them, and they ultimately allowed the Rabbi to
measure the compartment.

The second compartment facing the second door of Paradise is built of silver, and its wainscoting is of cedar, and here
dwell all the sinners who repent, and Manasseh, the son of
Ezekiah, presides over them.

The third compartment is facing the third door of Paradise,
and is built of silver and gold; and here dwell Abraham,
Isaac, and Jacob, and all the Israelites who came out of Egypt,

and the generation that had lived in the desert. Here are also all the royal princes, with the exception of Absalom, and David and Solomon, and all the kings of Judah. And Moses and Aaron preside over the inmates of this compartment. And in this compartment Rabbi Joshua also saw precious vessels of silver and gold, and jewels and precious stones and pearls, and lamps of pure gold. And there were thrones, and canopies, and beds, all prepared for those who still dwell in the world of mortals, but who, after death, would obtain the merit of their good deeds.

And the fourth compartment, facing the fourth door of Paradise, is built beautifully, its walls being of glass and its wainscoting of olive wood. And here dwell all the just and perfect to whom life upon earth has been bitter even as olives.

And the fifth compartment of Paradise is of silver and re-fined gold, of crystal, and bdellium, and the river Gihon flows through its midst. The walls of this compartment are of silver and gold, and it is pervaded by delicious perfumes which are more exquisite and delightful than all the perfumes of Lebanon. There are beds of gold and silver with covers of purple and violet woven once by Eve, and they are mixed with scarlet made of hair of goats and woven by angels. In this compart-ment there dwell the Messiah and the prophet Elijah, seated under a canopy made of the wood of Lebanon. The pillars of this palanquin are of silver, the bottom of gold, and the seat is purple. And the prophet Elijah comforts the Messiah and assures him that the end draweth near. And the Patriarchs, too, and the fathers of the tribes, and Moses, and Aaron, and David, and Solomon all come to visit the Messiah and weep with him and comfort him, saying: " Rely upon the Creator, for the end draweth near."

And in the sixth compartment there dwell those who died because they performed a pious deed.

In the seventh compartment dwell those who died on account of the sins of Israel.[1]

But Rabbi Joshua was not the only one who was allowed to converse with the angel of death and to be shown his place in Paradise. Another Rabbi also enjoyed this privilege according to legend. His name was Rabbi Chanina, the son of Paffa, and he lived in the third century. When he was about to die, the angel of death was instructed in celestial regions to go and visit the pious Rabbi, and if necessary to render him a kindly service. The angel of death accordingly descended upon earth and made himself known unto Rabbi Chanina, the son of Paffa. " Leave me for thirty days," spoke the Rabbi to the angel, " until I have repeated all that I have studied here, for I am anxious to appear in the world above with all my studies of the Sacred Law in my hands, as it is said: ' Blessed is he who comes here with his studies in his hand '." And the angel of death, faithful to instructions received, granted the service which the Rabbi required of him. After thirty days he returned again, and the Rabbi now asked to be shown his place in Paradise while he was still alive. This, too, the angel of death consented to do. They accordingly set out on their journey. " Lend me thy sword," said Rabbi Chanina unto the angel of death, " that I may keep it until we reach Paradise, lest thou cheatest me on the road and dost deprive me of my expectation." But this the angel of death, remembering his experience with Rabbi Joshua ben Levi, refused to grant. " Dost thou mean to imitate the example of thy friend," he queried, and he did not entrust the sword to Rabbi Chanina, but he showed him his place in Paradise.[2]

But already before Rabbi Joshua ben Levi, Moses is supposed to have seen the two parks, Paradise and Hell, the city of the just, and the abode of the sinners. And Moses, modest

---

[1] Jellinek, *Beth-Hamidrash*, Vol. II, pp. 49–53; see also Gaster, *Journal of Royal Asiatic Society*, 1893, pp. 596–598.   [2] *Ketubot*, 77b.

as he was, exclaimed: " O Lord of the Universe, I am only flesh and blood, and am afraid to enter the blazing fire of Hell." But the Almighty God assured the son of Amram that he could tread the blazing fire of Hell and yet his feet would not be burned. When Moses entered the place of Hell, the fire drew back, and the master of Hell exclaimed: " Son of Amram, thy place is not here." But a voice from the Throne of Glory called out and commanded the master of Hell to show the son of Amram the horrors of Hell and the punishment of the sinners. And Moses heard Hell crying with a loud voice and clamouring for the sinners that it might destroy them. Moses then witnessed the punishment of the sinners who had committed murder, theft, and adultery; who were guilty of pride and slander; who had oppressed the poor and per-secuted the orphan. And he saw how the wicked were punished by fire and snow and how they had no rest except on the Sabbath and festival days. And Moses prayed unto the Lord to save the sinners and forgive them.

And Moses again lifted up his eyes and beheld the angel Gabriel standing near him, who thus spoke unto him: " Come, O Son of Amram, and I will show thee Paradise." The angels watching at the gates of Paradise would not allow the son of Amram to enter the park created for the righteous. But a voice from the Throne of Glory commanded the minis-tering angels to open the gates of Paradise for the son of Amram who had come to witness the reward of the pious and the just. And when he entered Paradise Moses saw an angel sitting under the tree of life. He was the guardian of Para-dise, and he thus addressed the son of Amram: " Why didst thou come hither?" " I have come," replied Moses, " to witness the reward of the pious in Paradise." Thereupon the guardian of Paradise, who was sitting under the tree of life, took Moses by the hand and led him through Paradise. He showed him the thrones of precious stones, of sapphires and emeralds, of diamonds and pearls, all surrounded by ministering angels who were guarding the thrones. They were the thrones of Abraham and of Isaac, and of other pious men. Thereupon Moses asked his guide to tell him for whom the thrones of pearls were prepared; and the guardian angel answered: " These thrones are for the scholars who study the law; the thrones of rubies are for the just; the thrones of precious stones are for the pious; and the thrones of gold are for the sinners who repent." He also beheld thrones of copper and asked the angel who accompanied him: " For whom are these thrones of copper?" And the angel replied: " These thrones of copper are for the wicked men whose sons are just and pious. Although they were wicked themselves and sinned, they obtain a portion of heavenly bliss through the merit of their sons who are just and pious, and God, in His mercy, grants them a modest place in Paradise." Moses thereupon beheld a spring of living water flowing from underneath the tree of life and dividing itself into four streams. And Moses felt great joy when he beheld all the pleasant things prepared for the pious in the city of the just.[1]

THE LEGEND OF RABBI BEN LEVI

Rabbi ben Levi, on the Sabbath, read
A volume of the Law, in which it said,
" No man shall look upon my face and live ".
And as he read, he prayed that God would give
His faithful servant grace with mortal eye
To look upon his face and yet not die.

Then fell a sudden shadow on the page,
And, lifting up his eyes, grown dim with age,
He saw the angel of death before him stand,
Holding a naked sword in his right hand.
Rabbi ben Levi was a righteous man,
Yet through his veins a chill of horror ran.

[1] *Journal of Royal Asiatic Society*, 1893.

With trembling voice he said: " What wilt thou here?"
The angel answered: " Lo! the time draws near
When thou must die; yet first, by God's decree,
Whate'er thou askest shall be granted thee."
Replied the Rabbi: " Let these living eyes
First look upon my place in Paradise."

Then said the Angel: " Come with me and look."
Rabbi ben Levi closed the sacred book,
And rising, and uplifting his grey head,
" Give me thy sword," he to the angel said,
" Lest thou shouldst fall upon me by the way."
The angel smiled and hastened to obey,
Then led him forth to the celestial town,
And set him on the wall, whence, gazing down,
Rabbi ben Levi, with his living eyes,
Might look upon his place in Paradise.

Then straight into the city of the Lord
The Rabbi leaped with the death-angel's sword,
And through the streets there swept a sudden breath
Of something there unknown, which men call death.
Meanwhile the angel stayed without and cried:
" Come back!" To which the Rabbi's voice replied:
" No! in the name of God, whom I adore,
I swear that hence I will depart no more!"

Then all the angels cried: " O Holy One,
See what the son of Levi here has done!
The kingdom of Heaven he takes by violence,
And in Thy name refuses to go hence!"
The Lord replied: " My angels, be not wroth;
Did e'er the son of Levi break his oath?
Let him remain: for he with mortal eye
Shall look upon my face and yet not die."

Beyond the outer wall the angel of death
Heard the great voice, and said, with panting breath:
" Give back the sword, and let me go my way."
Whereat the Rabbi paused and answered: " Nay!

THE RABBI WITH THE DEATH ANGEL'S SWORD

Facing page 124, Vol. I

Anguish enough already has it caused
Among the sons of men."   And, while he paused,
He heard the awful mandate of the Lord
Resounding through the air: " Give back the sword!"

The Rabbi bowed his head in silent prayer;
Then said he to the dreadful angel: " Swear,
No human eye shall look on it again;
But when thou takest away the souls of men,
Thyself unseen, and with an unseen sword,
Thou wilt perform the bidding of the Lord."

The angel took the sword again, and swore,
And walks on earth unseen for evermore.

H. W. Longfellow.

CHAPTER XI

Alexander the Great at the Gates of Paradise

Alexander the Great reaches the silent river—The agreeable taste of the salt fish—The entrance to the city of the blessed—The voice of the guardian of Paradise—The king is refused admittance—He asks for a gift—The fragment of a human skull—The king's disappointment—The advice of the learned man—The skull is weighed against gold and silver—It overbalances the gold—The socket of a human eye—It is covered with earth, and the scales containing the gold go down.

ALEXANDER THE GREAT is also supposed to have reached the gates of Paradise on earth. Alexander the Great was pursuing his journey through dreary deserts and uncultivated lands, when at last he came to a small rivulet, gliding peacefully between shelving banks. The smooth undisturbed surface of the waters was the image of peace and contentment. In their silence the waters seemed to say: "This is the city of peace, the abode of tranquillity." Nature was hushed, all was still and not a sound was heard. The waters seemed to murmur into the ear of the traveller: "Come and dwell here in this abode of peace and happiness and tranquillity, of forgetfulness and bliss, far from the turmoil of the world. Leave the valley of misery, the world where sin and crime are practised, where bloodshed and massacres, slaughter, and rapine reign supreme, and where men are inspired only by greed, ambition, and envy." Alexander, however, remained untouched by the beauty of the spot, by the peace and tranquillity which reigned in this abode of happiness. He marched on. Soon, however, overcome by fatigue and hunger, he stopped and seated himself on one of the banks of the river flowing through this veritable abode of the blessed. Provided with salt fish he ordered some of it to be dipped in the waters of the peaceful river so as to take off the briny taste. And when the Macedonian conqueror tasted the fish, he was surprised to find that it had a finer and much more agreeable taste than on other occasions. He marvelled greatly and concluded that the river must flow from some very rich and luxuriant country. Thereupon he decided to explore and march to the place where the river took its origin. Onward he marched, following the course of the river. At last he arrived before the gates of Paradise. The gates being locked, the Macedonian conqueror knocked impetuously, demanding immediate admittance. At length a voice was heard from within the garden, asking: " Who is there?" " It is I, Alexander of Macedon, the great conqueror, the Lord of the Earth, the mighty ruler. Open the gates." But the voice replied: " This is the abode of the just, the city of peace; none but the just, those who have conquered their passions, may enter the abode of the blessed. We make no exceptions here for the conquerors of the earth, for the rulers of men, for the men who have been swayed by the will to power. Nations may have paid homage to thee, but thy soul is not worthy to be admitted within the gates of the abode of the just. Go thy ways, endeavour to cure thy soul, and learn more wisdom than thou hast done hitherto." Thus spake the voice from within the city of the just, the abode of the blessed, and all the great conqueror's pleading and insistence were of no avail. At last he asked the guardian of the city of the blessed to give him some gift, so that he might show it to the world, and prove that he, the great conqueror, had ventured as far as the abode of the blessed and been there where no mortal had ever been before. The guardian smiled and handed him something with the words: " Take this, may it prove useful

unto thee, and teach thee wisdom, more wisdom than thou
hast acquired during thy ambitious expeditions and pursuits."
Alexander took the gift and returned to his tent. On examining
the gift he found, however, that the guardian of the gates of
Paradise had given him nothing but the fragment of a human
skull. He was greatly disappointed and in a fit of rage threw
it to the ground.

"This," he exclaimed, "this fragment of a human skull is
all that they found worthy to offer to a mighty king like me,
to the renowned conqueror, the Lord of the Earth!"

A learned man, however, who was present, thus addressed
the king: "Mighty ruler! thou mayest be wrong to despise
this gift, for, however despicable it may appear in thine eyes,
it possesses nevertheless great qualities; order, please, that this
fragment of human skull be weighed on the scales against gold
and silver."

The king followed the advice of the learned man, and
a pair of scales were brought before him. Thereupon the
fragment of the human skull was placed in one, and a quantity
of gold in the other. But lo! to the king's great astonishment
and to the astonishment of all present, the fragment of the
human skull overbalanced the gold. More gold was added
and again more gold, but the more gold was put in the one
scale, the lower sunk the other scale which contained the
fragment of the human skull.

"This is truly strange," exclaimed the king, marvelling
greatly. "It is strange indeed that so small an object should
outweigh so much gold. Is there anything that would outweigh
this small portion of matter handed to me by the guardian of
the city of the just?"

"Yes, there is," said the learned man. "This fragment,
great king, is the socket of a human eye which, though
small in compass, is unbounded in desire. The more gold it
has, the more it craves for and is never satisfied. But once

it is laid in the grave, there is an end to its lust and ambition. If thou wilt order that a little earth be brought and the fragment of the skull, the socket of the human eye, be covered with it, then thou wilt see that the scale containing it will ascend." The king acted upon the advice of the learned man, and the socket of the human eye was covered with earth. And lo! the gold went down immediately and the scale containing the fragment of the skull ascended.[1]

[1] *Tamid,* 32b; see also Israel Levi, *La légende d'Alexandre dans le Talmud et le Midrash,* Paris, 1883.

CHAPTER XII

Hell, or the City of the Shadows

Jewish legends about Hell—Greek influence—The seven degrees of torment—Rabbi Joshua ben Levi describes the torments in Hell—The angels Komam and Kinor—The seven torments in Mohammedan tradition—Gehennom, Ladha, Hothama, Saïr, Sacar, Gehin, and Haoviath—The story of Enoch (Edris) in Mohammedan legend—Edris and Azrael, the angel of death—Edris visits Paradise—Ridhwan, the gatekeeper of Paradise—Persian and Indian influence—The description of Paradise in the *Mahabharata*—The description in the *Ardai-Viraf*—Paradise in Teutonic legend—The city of Asgard—Valhalla—The three fairies: Urda, Verandi, and Skulda.

WHILST the Holy Scripture, i.e. the Old Testament, only speaks of temporal reward and punishment for virtue and vice, of untimely and ignominious death, of cutting off, excommunication, of barrenness of land, captivity and slavery, the Talmud and later Rabbinic literature show clearly the belief in Hell obtained among them to a great extent. There is but little doubt that the Jews received these opinions round which so many myths and legends have gathered from the Greeks, when they became conversant with the latter. There are supposed to be seven degrees in Hell, for it is called by seven different names, and when the wicked are sent to this place of torment, they pass through a great diversity of suffering. No one is to remain for ever in this place of torment, for after one year in purgatory he is taken out and brought to the gates of the Garden of Eden. But three sorts of persons are condemned to eternal suffering in Tofet, or Hell. They who deny the existence of God, who deny the Divine authority of the Law, and who reject the resurrection of the dead. After a certain time, however, some souls of the wicked are annihilated altogether. Different torments are the lot of the wicked who are sent to Hell. Cold, heat, and despair are their lot. Hell is traversed by rivers of fire and of ice, and it is from the fire of Hell that the Creator took afterwards the fire which burnt down Sodom and the water with which the earth was overflowed at the deluge.

Rabbi Joshua, the son of Levi, is again the principal recorder of Hell. After visiting Paradise, he asked permission to look into Hell, but this permission was denied unto him, because the righteous are not allowed to behold Hell. He thereupon sent to the angel who is named Komam so that he might describe Hell unto him. But, as this angel could not go with him, he went afterwards with the angel named Kinor or Kipod who accompanied him to the gates of Hell which were open. He saw compartments ten miles in length and five in width, and they were full of mountains of fire and consuming the sinners. And in one compartment he saw ten nations from the heathens, and Absalom, the son of David, presides over them, and they say unto Absalom: " Our sin is because we have not accepted the Law, but what is thy sin and why art thou punished, seeing that thou and thy parents accepted the Law." And Absalom replied: " I am punished because I did not hearken to the commandments of my father." And after seeing this, the Rabbi returned to Paradise where he wrote a description of both Paradise and Hell and sent it to Rabbi Gamaliel, telling him what he had seen in Paradise and in Hell, and this is what he wrote about Hell: " I saw at the gates of Gehennom persons hung up by their noses, others by their hands. Some there were who were hung up by their tongues, whilst others were hung up by their eyelids or feet. I saw men devoured by worms but never dying, whilst at other places I saw some whose inner parts were burnt up by coals of fire. There were some whose food was dust which broke their teeth (because upon earth they had lived on stolen goods); whilst others there were who were cast from fire into ice and from ice into fire. And I saw angels appointed to chastise each sin, and the three deadly sins are: adultery, insulting a fellowman in public, and abusing the name of God. And the faces of the inhabitants of Hell are black. But in the midst of their sufferings, some of the Jewish sinners declared that God, the Lord of the Universe, was a just God, and they were forgiven and rescued after twelve months." [1]

Long before Dante visited the Inferno, the topic occupied the mind of mythographers. The descriptions in Jewish myths have their analogies in the traditions of other nations.

Just as Jewish myths and legends acknowledge seven degrees of torments in Hell (and seven houses), so the Moslems, too, speak of seven gates. These are: *Gehennom*, the first degree of torment for Moslems; *Ladha*, for Christians; *Hothama*, for Jews; *Saïr*, for Sabians; *Sacar*, for Magians, or Guebres; *Gehin*, for idolaters and pagans; *Haoviath*, the seventh and deepest part of the abyss, is reserved for hypocrites, who, disguising their religion, conceal one in their hearts different from the one they confess.

As for Paradise, a parallel to the story of Rabbi Joshua ben Levi is also found in Mohammedan legend. There it is told about Enoch who dwells in Paradise, whither he came during his lifetime. He, too, in company of the angel of death visited Paradise and Hell, and witnessed the bliss of the righteous and the torments of the wicked. He is called Edris by the Arabs, and is said to have been born in Hindostan, and to have lived in Yemen, where he was an accomplished tailor, author, and prophet. He knew how to sew, but also wrote many books and prophesied in the name of Allah.

---

[1] Jellinek, *Beth-Hamidrash*, Vol. II, pp. 50–51; Vol. V, pp. 43–45; Gaster, *Journal of Royal Asiatic Society*, 1893, pp. 572–620; *Jewish Quarterly Review*, VII, 596.

Men, in the days of Enoch-Edris, worshipped fire and many idols, and God sent Enoch to turn them from their wicked ways, and to induce them to abandon the worship of idols, but they would not listen unto him. There were indeed very few men in the days of Noah who worshipped the true and living God. Jared, the father of Enoch, had already fought the prince of evil, that is Iblis, captured him and led him about in chains. Now Enoch, seeing that men would not listen to him, began by first instructing them in various crafts and handiworks. He taught them the arts of tailoring and shoemaking; he showed them how to cut skins, sew them together and make garments and shoes, and men, being grateful to Enoch for this blessing and for the knowledge he had given them, were ready to listen to his books and to his words of wisdom. He thereupon read to them the books of Adam and his own books, and endeavoured to make them abandon idolatry and bring them back to the worship of the true and living, the only God. And when Enoch had passed many years in prayer, the angel of death appeared unto him, and thus he spake: " I am the angel of death and would fain be thy friend, Enoch, son of Jared. Thou mayest make a request unto me which I will for a certainty grant at once." " Take then my soul," said Enoch. " Thy time," replied the angel, " hath not yet come and I cannot take thy soul. It is not for this purpose that I have come to visit thee." " Take it away, then," said Enoch, " for a little while and restore it to me." " I cannot do this either," said Azrael, the angel of death, " without the consent of Allah." He thereupon presented Enoch's request to Allah, and having obtained the latter's permission took away for a short time the soul of Enoch which the Eternal at once restored to him. From that time the angel of death, having become a friend of Enoch, often came to visit him. One day, Enoch said again to the angel of death: " I have another request to make to thee." " If I can grant

it," said Azrael, "I am quite ready to do it." "I would visit
Hell," said Enoch, "for the sensations of death I already
know, having undergone it once, as thou dost well remember."
"I cannot grant thy request," replied the angel of death,
"without the special permission of the Eternal." But Allah
having granted the request of Enoch, the latter was borne
upon the wings of Azrael, who showed him Hell and its seven
stages. Enoch saw the torments inflicted upon sinners, and
was greatly impressed. After a while, he again requested
Azrael to show him Paradise. Once more Azrael had to obtain
the permission of Allah before granting Enoch's request.
The Almighty having replied that it should be even as his
faithful servant Enoch had desired, Azrael bore his friend
to the gates of Paradise. Here, however, Ridhwan, the gatekeeper refused to grant them admittance. "No man," said
he, "can enter Paradise, without having tasted death. Thou
canst therefore not enter Paradise as yet, Enoch, son of Jared."
Thus spake Ridhwan, the gatekeeper of Paradise. But Enoch
replied: "I have already tasted death, O Ridhwan; my soul
had left my body, but God hath resuscitated me." Ridhwan,
however, was obstinate, and refused to do what Enoch asked
him, without a higher authority. An order, thereupon, arrived
from Allah, bidding the gatekeeper to admit Enoch into Paradise. "Go in," said Ridhwan, "cast a glance upon Paradise,
but hurry back, for thou mayest not dwell there before the
Resurrection." Enoch promised to do so. He entered Paradise, viewed it, and speedily came out again. At the moment
of passing the threshold he said to Ridhwan: "I have left something in there, O Ridhwan, allow me to turn back and fetch it."

Ridhwan, however, refused to grant this request of Enoch,
and as the latter insisted, they began to quarrel. Enoch pretended that he was a prophet, and that Allah had promised
him Paradise. He had already tasted death and seen Hell,
and now that the gates of Paradise had been open to him

and that he had entered the place, he refused to leave it. The dispute between Enoch and Ridhwan was long, and was only put an end to by Allah who ordered the gatekeeper to reopen the gate of Paradise and readmit Enoch who still dwells there.[1]

The descriptions of Paradise and Hell in Jewish myth, which in a later age becomes mysticism, are also due to Persian and Indian influences. In the *Mahabharata* we find the following description of the heavens of Indra, Yama, and Varuna. These heavens recall the " Islands of the Blest " of Greece and the Celtic otherworld, where eternal summer reigns. They are also reminiscent of the Teutonic Valhalla.[2]

Narada spoke. " The celestial assembly-room of Shakra is full of lustre. It is full one hundred and fifty *yojanas* in length, and an hundred *yojanas* in breadth, and five *yojanas* in height. Dispelling weakness of age, grief, fatigue, and fear; auspicious and bestowing good fortune, furnished with rooms and seats, and adorned with celestial trees, it is delightful in the extreme. On an excellent seat there sitteth the lord of celestials, with his wife Shachi and with beauty and affluence embodied. Assuming a form incapable of description for its vagueness, with a crown on his head and bright bracelets on the upper arms, attired in robes of pure white, and decked in floral wreaths of many hues, here he sitteth with beauty, fame, and glory by his side. He is waited upon by the marutas, each leading the life of a householder in the bosom of his family. And the celestial Rishis, and the marutas of brilliant complexion and adorned in golden garlands, all wait upon the illustrious chief of the immortals, and the celestial Rishis also, all of pure souls, with sins completely washed off, and resplendent as the fire, and possessed of energy, and without sorrow of any kind, and freed from the fever of anxiety, also wait upon and worship Indra."

---

[1] *Tabari, loc. cit.*, I, Ch. 35.   [2] See Mackenzie, *Indian Myth and Legend*, p. 59.

The heaven of Yama is described as follows: Narada spoke: " The assembly-house of Yama is bright as burnished gold, and covers an area of much more than an hundred *yojanas*. Possessed of the splendour of the sun it yieldeth everything that one may desire. Neither very cool nor very hot, it delighteth the heart. There is neither grief nor weakness of age, neither hunger nor thirst. Every object of desire, celestial or human, is to be found in that mansion. And all kinds of enjoyable articles, as also of sweet, juicy, agreeable and delicious edibles are there in profusion, and are licked, sucked, and drunk. Of the most delicious fragrance are the floral wreaths in that mansion, and the trees that stand around it yield fruits that are desired of them. And there are both cold and hot waters and these are sweet and agreeable. And royal sages of great sanctity and Brahmana sages of great purity are in this mansion where they cheerfully wait upon and worship Yama, the son of Vivaswat.

The celestial Sabha of Varuna is also described by Narada who was capable of going into every world at will and at home in the celestial regions.

Said Narada: " The wells and arches of the celestial Sabha of Varuna are all of pure white. It is surrounded on all sides by many celestial trees made of gems and jewels, and yielding excellent fruit and flowers. And many plants with their weight and blossoms, blue and yellow and black and darkish, and white and red that stand there, form excellent bowers around. And within these bowers hundreds of thousands of birds of divers species, beautiful and variegated, always pour forth their melodies. And there are many rooms in the assembly-house of Varuna and many seats. Varuna, decked with jewels and golden ornaments and flowers, is throned there with his queen. The Nagas, or hooded snakes with human heads and arms, and the Daityas and Ianavas (the giants and demons) who have been rewarded with immortality, are there.

And so are the holy spirits of rivers and oceans, of lakes and springs, and the personified forms of the points of the heavens." [1]

And in the Persian book, entitled *Ardai-Viraf* (translated by Haugh and West), we read of the righteous man being allowed to glance at Heaven and Hell.

Heaven and Hell have three compartments, according to the three grades of good or bad thoughts, words, and actions. The uppermost heaven is full of light for the good God Ahuramazda; whilst there is also a nethermost and darkest hell for the bad spirit Ahriman and all his associate spirits. The three divisions of heaven are called the Sun, the Moon, and the Stars, and the dwelling place of Ahuramazda is above that of the Sun. We read also of the rivers of oil and wine which flow for the righteous, and of the terrible punishments meted out to the wicked. The lake of Tears is found in the Persian Inferno, and the lake Acheron, that great river of Hades which we meet in Greek mythology, is to be met with in the Sibyllines. [2] Another analogy to the Jewish myths about Paradise and Hell may also be found in Teutonic myth.

There exists in Heaven, near the city of Asgard, a vast room, called the Valhalla, where the courageous are received after their death. This room has 504 gates (or doors) through each of which eight dead warriors leave to engage in combat. These valiant dead shadows fight and then return to partake of a meal together. They drink of the milk of the goat Heidruma, which devours the leaves of the tree Loerada. This milk is in reality hydromel, and a jug is filled every day which the dead heroes drink and get drunk. They eat of the flesh of a marvellous boar which is cooked and eaten every morning, but is whole again in the evening to serve for the repast of the next day. There is also in Heaven the tree of Igdrasil, which

---

[1] *Mahabharata*, Sabha-Parva, Sections VII–X (Roy's Translation). See also D. A. Mackenzie, *Indian Myth and Legend*, pp. 57–59.

[2] Book I, 302; II, 341. See also *Jewish Quarterly Review*, Vol. VII, p. 605.

spreads over the whole world and has three roots; one in Heaven, one on earth, and one in Hell where it is gnawed by the infernal serpent. The tree is watered by three fairies: Urda, Verandi, and Skulda (past, present, and future). A beautiful squirrel constantly ascends and descends the tree to see what the serpent in Hell is doing, and then he tells it to the eagle of Heaven. Two black ravens daily report unto Odin all that they have seen in the world. After the death of Ymer the gods built Midgard, where later on they wish to erect a citadel against the giants.[1]

[1] Collin de Plancy, *Légendes de l'Ancien Testament*, 1861.

CHAPTER XIII

The Creation of our First Parents

The creation of man—The protest of the angels—Adam gives names to all the beasts—The dust from which Adam was created—Red, black, white, and yellow clay—The creation of man in Moslem legend—The protest of the earth—The angel Azrael brings seven handfuls of dust—The creation of man takes place slowly—Adam's stature—His head reaches the sky—God reduces him by a thousand cubits—The angels are ready to worship Adam—The impression produced upon the beasts of the earth—They come to worship Adam—Adam praises his Maker—He composes *Ps.* 104—The stature of Adam in Moslem legend—The angels, except Iblis, all admire the lifeless body of Adam—The breath of life enters the body of first man—The soul refuses to enter the body of Adam—It is enticed by the music of Gabriel—The angels do homage to Adam—Iblis alone refuses—The story of Adam in Christian works — *The Cave of Treasures* — The arrogance of the chief of the lower order of celestials—Satana, Sheda, and Daiwa—The angel Rasiel gives a book to Adam—The wisdom contained in the book—Adam knows all handicrafts—He makes a present of seventy years to David—The creation of Eve—Earth's protest—Why Eve was created from Adam's rib—The wedding of Adam and Eve—The banquet in Eden—Man created double, male and female—The story met with in the *Bundehesh*—Mashya and Mashyana—The story of primordial androgyns in the *Banquet* of Plato—The creation of Eve in Moslem legend—Adam's dream—He asks permission to take Hava as his wife.

WHEN the Creator wished to make man he consulted with the angels beforehand, and said unto them: " We will make a man in our image." The angels asked: " What is man that thou shouldst remember him, and what is his purpose?" " He will do justice," said the Lord. And the ministering angels were divided into groups. Some said: " Let man not be created." But others said: " Let him be created." Forgiveness said: " Let him be created, for he will be generous and benevolent." Truth said: " Let him not be created, for he will be a liar." Justice said: " Let him be created, for he will

bring justice into the world," whilst Peace objected and said:
" Let him not be created, for he will constantly wage wars."
The Creator hurled Truth from Heaven to earth, and in spite
of the protests of the ministering angels man was created.[1]
" His knowledge," said the Creator, " will excel yours, and
to-morrow you will see his wisdom." The Creator then gathered
all kinds of beasts before the ministering angels, the wild and
the tame beasts, as well as the birds, and the fowls of the
air, and asked the ministering angels to name them, but they
could not. " Now you will see the wisdom of man," spake
the Creator. " I will ask him and he will tell their names."
All the beasts and fowls of the air were then led before man,
and when asked he at once replied: " This is an ox, the other
an ass, yonder a horse or a camel." " And what is your own
name?" " I," replied man, " should be called Adam because
I have been created from *adamah*, or earth." [2]

The dust from which man was made was gathered from
various parts, for the whole earth is man's home, and earth
is the mother of man. The dust of Babylon, the earth of the
country of Israel, and the clay of other countries were all
employed to fashion the head, body, and limbs of man.[3] The
Creator, we read in the *Pirke de Rabbi Eliezer*,[4] commanded
His ministering angels to bring Him dust from all corners
of the earth, red, black, white, and yellow, out of which He
intended to fashion man, for the whole earth and all that
moves and lives upon it and its entrails will be subject to
man. The angel whose mission it was to bring the dust for
the creation of man took a handful from the place where the
Temple was once to stand, and some from other parts of the
world, and this dust the Creator mixed with drops from all
the waters of the world and fashioned man.[5]

[1] *Genesis Rabba*, 8.
[2] *Genesis Rabba*, 17; *Midrash Tehillim*, Ps. 8; see Geiger, *Was hat Mohammed aus dem Judentum genommen*, p. 99-100.   [3] *Sanhedrin*, 38b.
[4] *Pirke de Rabbi Eliezer*, Ch. 11 and 20.
[5] Gaster, *The Chronicles of Jerahmeel*, 6, 7; see also *Targum Jerushalmi*, Genesis, 2, 7.

First man was thus created from red, black, white, and yellow, or green clay. God fashioned the blood from the red dust, the entrails from the black, the bones from the white, and the body from the yellow dust. And the Creator thought: " A man might come from the east to the west, or from the west to the east, and his destiny would be to depart from the world. But the earth in that place shall not say: ' Return to the place whence thou wast created, I refuse to receive thee, for the dust of thy body was never taken from me.' But now, wherever man will go, to any place upon earth, and his hour will come to depart from the world, he will find the dust whence he was created and to which he will return.[1]

According to Moslem legend, God prepared, by rains of long continuance, the slime out of which He intended to fashion Adam. He then sent the angel Gabriel and commanded him to take a handful of earth from each of its seven layers. Gabriel obeyed and declared to the earth that he had received from the Creator the order to extract out of her entrails the substance out of which man was to be formed, man who would be monarch and ruler over her.[2] Amazed at such a proposition, the earth desired Gabriel to represent to All-Father her fears. One day, she maintained, the creature which was to be formed out of her bosom would disobey the commands of God, rebel against Him, and draw down upon herself the curse of the Creator. The angel Gabriel withdrew and reported to God earth's fears and remonstrances. God, having nevertheless resolved to execute His design, dispatched the angel Michael with the same commission, but Michael, too, was moved by earth's remonstrances, and returned empty-handed, reporting earth's excuses and her absolute refusal to contribute to the formation of man.

The Creator of the Universe then sent the angel Azrael

---

[1] *Pirke de Rabbi Eliezer*, Ch. 11.

[2] Abulfeda, *Historia Ante-Islamica*, p. 13; Weil, *Biblische Legenden der Muselmänner*, 1845, pp. 12–16.

to fetch a little mud. Once more the earth swore an oath that neither clay nor dust nor stone shall he take from her. But Azrael did not respect her oath and did not retire: " I must obey the command of God," said he, and violently tore out seven handfuls of dust out of seven different beds of earth. He carried off by force out of the mass belonging to earth the matter required for the formation of man. These seven handfuls, the angel Azrael carried away to a place in Arabia which is situated between Mecca and Taief. As a reward for his action, Azrael received the commission to separate the souls of men from their bodies, for which reason he is now called the angel of death.[1]

The creation of man took place slowly and by degrees.[2] At the first hour of the day the Creator collected the dust out of which he designed to compose the body of first man, and He so disposed it as to receive the form which he intended to give it. At the second hour Adam, or first man, stood upon his feet, at the third hour he gave names to the animals, the seventh hour was employed in the marriage of Adam and Eve, and at the tenth hour Adam sinned.[3] The form and stature of man were immense. He was so tall that his head reached to the sky. And when the ministering angels saw man and how tall he was they trembled and fled before him. " Lord of the world," they cried, " there seem to be two sovereigns, one in Heaven and one upon earth." [4] Then the Creator placed His hand upon the head of Adam and reduced him by a thousand cubits.[5]

Adam's body was beautiful and resplendent, and his spirit was unlike the spirit of all men who came after him. For all the souls and spirits and intelligences created before Adam and dwelling in Heaven, 600,000 in number, were

---

[1] Herbelot, *Bibl. Orientale, s.v. Adam.*
[2] *Pirke de Rabbi Eliezer*, Ch. 11. See also L. Ginzberg, *Die Haggada bei den Kirchenvätern*, p. 50; Kohut, *Z.D.M.G.*, XXV, pp. 59–94.
[3] *Midrash Tehillim, Ps.* 92; *Sanhedrin*, p. 38; *Abot de Rabbi Nathan*, Ch. 1.
[4] *Yalkut Shimeoni*, I, § 120.   [5] *Hagigah*, 12a; *Sanhedrin*, 38b.

THE CREATOR PLACES HIS HAND UPON THE HEAD OF ADAM

Facing page 142, Vol. I

all connected with the soul of Adam.[1] The aspect of man
and his splendour brought awe and wonder into the hearts
of all beings, celestial and terrestrial. When the ministering
angels saw the splendour of man, made in the image of the
All-Father, they quaked and were amazed. The sun, seeing
the size and splendour of Adam, was filled with dismay; and
the angels were frightened and prayed to God to remove the
mighty being He had made. Some of the angels, however,
were ready to worship Adam, and some even bowed before
him whose face was brighter than the brightness of the sun,
and said three times: " Holy." Thereupon God cast a deep
sleep on man, and the ministering angels knew that he was
only mortal and helpless, and they no longer feared him.[2]

In other sources we read that the angels, seeing Adam
so mighty and great, and shining brighter than the sun, were
all ready to worship him. Whereupon the Creator, in order
to prove to them the weakness and helplessness of man, cast
a deep sleep upon Adam, and during his sleep reduced him
to smaller proportions. Great pieces of his flesh were cut
off, and when Adam awoke and saw these pieces of flesh
scattered round him, like the shavings in a carpenter's shop,
he wailed and exclaimed: " O Lord of the Universe, how
hast Thou robbed me." But God answered: " Take these
pieces of thy flesh and carry them into all lands, and where
ever thou wilt drop them and lay them in the earth, that land
will I give to thy posterity." [3]

Profound was the impression produced by the aspect
of Adam upon the beasts of the earth and the fowls of the
air. They all came and fell down before him and desired
to worship him. But Adam said to the beasts of the earth
and to the fowls of the air: " Why have ye come to worship
me who am only a creature of clay, fashioned by the Creator

[1] Isaac Luria, *Sepher Hagilgulim*, fol.1c; *Emek hamelekh*, fol. 171c.
[2] *Genesis Rabba*, 8; see *Midrash Tanchuma*, section *Pekkude*.
[3] *Sepher Chassidim*. See Eisenmenger, *Entdecktes Judentum*, Vol. I, p. 369.

of the Universe? Come ye and let us all clothe ourselves with power and glory, and let us praise the Lord and let us acknowledge Him as King over us, for He has created us. A people chooses a king, but a king does not appoint himself arbitrarily as monarch." Thus spoke Adam, and he chose God as King of all the world and as Ruler of the Universe. And all the beasts, fowls, and fishes listened to his word and did likewise.[1]

Thus the first act of Adam was to praise his Master and to acknowledge his Maker as King of the world. And when he witnessed the splendour of the world and all the creatures called into existence before him, he praised the Lord and said: " How wonderful are Thy works, O God."

The *Pirke de Rabbi Eliezer* [2] relates this incident as follows: Adam stood and gazed upwards to Heaven and downwards upon earth, and he beheld all the creatures which God had created. Wondering in his heart, he at once began to praise the Lord, to sing a hymn and to glorify the name of the Creator. He is said to have composed *Psalm* 104, which is a Psalm of creation. Thereupon all the creatures, seeing him adorned with the Divine image, came to prostrate themselves before him. But Adam said unto them: " Do not prostrate your-selves before me, but let us rather acclaim Him as our King." Thereupon he opened his mouth and acclaimed the Creator, and all the creatures answered after him and said: " The Lord reigneth and is apparelled in Majesty." [3]

Moslem tradition also knows of these legends relating to the creation of Adam. Adam's body, still lifeless, was stretched out and no one knew what he was. He was the object of the amazement and admiration of the ministering angels who passed the gates of Paradise where the lifeless body of man had been placed by the Creator, and where it remained for forty years.

---

[1] Eisenmenger, *loc. cit.*, Vol. I, p. 368.   [2] *Pirke de Rabbi Eliezer*, Ch. 11.
[3] *Ps.* 93, 1. Cf. *Rosh-ha-Shanah*, 31a.

But Iblis, who was jealous of man's beautiful face and figure and his intelligent and lovely countenance, said unto the angels: " How can you admire such a creature made of clay? Only weakness and frailty are the lot of such a creature." All the celestial inmates, however, with the exception of Iblis, admired in solemn silence the lifeless body of first man and praised the Creator. For man was so big that when he stood up his head reached to the first of the seven heavens.[1] Adam remained stretched out for another 120 years, when Allah gave him a soul and the breath of life. Before the breath of life had completely entered Adam's body, he tried to rise, but fell down, and when it entered his head he began to sneeze, and said: " Praise be unto Allah, the Lord of the worlds." [2]

Adam's soul had been created one thousand years before Adam, and it persistently refused to leave the heavenly regions and enter the body of man. Only through the music played by the angel Gabriel the soul, which had descended to listen, was enticed in a moment of ecstasy to enter the body of man. And because her union with the body of man was an involuntary one, it was decreed that she should leave it only reluctantly.[3] When Adam had received the breath of life blown into his nostrils by the Creator, God called all the creatures and living things, and taught him the names of all the beasts and fowls and insects and even the names of the fishes in the sea, and told him their natures and the purpose of their existence. Then the Father of All called the ministering angels and commanded them to bow before man, whom He had created in His image, for man was the most perfect of created beings. Israfil, one of the ministering angels, was the first to obey and to do the bidding of the Creator, and therefore he received as a reward the custody of the Book of Fate. All the other ministering angels followed the example of Israfil and bowed before man.

---

[1] Weil, *Biblische Legenden der Muselmänner*, p. 13.   [2] *Chronique de Tabari*, I, Ch. 22.
[3] See Collin de Plancy, *Légendes de l'Ancien Testament*, Paris, 1861, p. 55.

Iblis alone refused to do the bidding of his Maker. Arrogantly he spoke: " How can I, an angel made of fire, bow before a man, a creature fashioned of clay?" He was cast out from among the angels, and the gates of Paradise were forbidden unto him.[1]

When Iblis had been expelled, the angels stood before man in ten thousand ranks, and man spoke unto them and praised the omnipotence of the Creator and the wonders of His creation. And the angels were greatly amazed and saw that his knowledge by far excelled theirs, for he could name the beasts in seventy languages and knew all their names.[2]

The Syriac authors, too, know of these legends and refer to them. Thus in the work entitled *The Cave of Treasures*, the author of which belonged to the school of St. Ephrem, in the sixth century A.D., the creation of first man is related as follows: The ministering angels witnessed and saw how the Creator of All took a grain of dust from the entire earth, and a drop of water from the immensity of waters, and particles from the elements of air and fire, and fashioned man. And all the ministering angels saw how these four elements were combined and how out of them man was made. The Creator then took these four elements, so that all that is in the world should be subject to man; all the beings and natures that are in earth, water, air, and fire. When the ministering angels saw the glory of first man, and the beauty of his countenance and the brightness of his eyes, which was like the brightness of the sun, and the splendour of his body, which was like crystal, they were amazed and greatly moved. And all the wild and tame beasts, and the fowls of the air gathered before man and he gave them their names; they bowed their heads, worshipped man and served him. The ministering angels, too, bent their knees and worshipped man. And when the chief of the lower order of celestial beings saw what greatness

---

[1] Koran, *Sura*, 33, 70–85.   [2] Koran, *Sura*, 2, 29–36. See also Weil, *loc. cit.*, pp. 15–16.

had been given unto man, he was very jealous of him and refused to bend his knee and to worship man. Turning to his hosts he thus spake: " Do not worship man, and praise him not as the other angels do. It is for him to worship me who am fire and spirit, and not for me to bow before a creature of dust." Disobedient and refusing to listen to the command of the All-Father, the rebel was cast out of Heaven, he and his hosts, in the second hour of the sixth day. He was divested of his garments of glory and was named *Satana*, because he had turned from God, and *Sheda*, because he had been thrown down, and *Daiwa*, because he had lost his angelic garment of glory. Then man was raised and brought into Paradise in a fiery chariot, and angels sang before him, and Seraphs sanctified him, and Cherubim blessed him.[1]

By means of the light created on the first day, man could see from one end of the world to the other. But this light, which in later days was only vouchsafed to the just and the righteous, was hidden from the sinful.[2]

This Jewish legend finds a parallel in Moslem myths and legends. As soon as the spirit which the Creator blew into Adam reached his eyes, he opened them, and when it reached his ears, he heard the celestial music and the song of the angels. When at last the spirit of life reached the feet of man, he stood up, but the light from the throne of the Creator, shining directly upon man, blinded him and compelled him to shut his eyes, for they could not bear the great light. Covering his eyes with one hand and pointing to the throne with the other, Adam asked: " What light is this?" And the Creator made reply: " This is the light of a prophet who will spring from thee and come into the world in later ages. I swear by My splendour that the world has been created for him alone, Ahmed, the much praised, is his name in Heaven, and by

---

[1] *The Cave of Treasures*, Ed. C. Bezold, 1888, pp. 3–4. See also M. Grünbaum, *Neue Beiträge zur semitischen Sagenkunde*, 1893, pp. 57–58.
[2] *Hagigah*, 12a; *Yalkut Rubeni*, section *Ki-Tissa*.

the name of Mohammed he will once be known upon earth." [1]

Jewish legend further relates that, as soon as first man was created, the angel Rasiel handed him, at the command of the Creator, a book containing all divine and human wisdom. From this book Adam gathered knowledge; he learned the order of the world and of the planets, and the cause of their motion. This book contained 72 kinds of wisdom in 670 writings, and first man was thus enabled to receive 1500 keys to all the mysterious knowledge which was not given to all the inhabitants of Heaven. When the angels and spirits saw that first man was in possession of the keys to knowledge, which the Father of All had handed to him, they all gathered round, eager to listen and to be instructed. But Hadarniel, one of the ministering angels, came and warned first man. And thus he spake: " O man, the splendour of the Lord was hidden; it was not given to the ministering angels to know the mysteries but only to thee." Adam then took the book of wisdom and kept it hidden. He studied it daily and learned all the mysteries which the ministering angels were ignorant of. But when the day came on which he sinned, the book flew from him, and he wept bitterly. Raphael, however, brought the book back to Adam, and he studied it daily. On his death he left it to his son Seth. It was then handed from generation to generation, until it came into the hands of Enoch. [2] Adam also knew all handicrafts and had much knowledge. [3] He saw all his generations that would spring from him, and the history of man until the end of days. [4] He saw the generations of Israel and their rulers and preachers and kings. When David came before him, he saw that he was dead. Adam then asked: " O Lord! who is this man who has no life in him?" And the Master of the world replied:

[1] Weil, loc. cit., p. 14.
[2] See Sepher Rasiel, Zohar Genesis. See also Jellinek. Beth-Hamidrash, Vol. III, pp. 155-160.   [3] Genesis Rabba, 24.
[4] Sanhedrin, 38b; Abodah Zarah, 5a; Abot de Rabbi Nathan, Ch. 31; Exodus Rabba, 40; Midrash Tehillim, Ps. 139.

" This is King David." When Adam saw that David was so created, he made him a present of seventy years to be taken off from his own life.[1]

Adam thereupon drew up a legal document of transfer, and sealed it with his own seal, and God and the angel Metatron signed the deed likewise. And thus Adam lived 930 years instead of one thousand.[2]

This legend is one of those taken over by Mohammed from Jewish lore. We are told by Tabari and Ibn el-Atir that God showed unto Adam all generations. He acquainted him with the names and fate of all his posterity. And when Adam learned that only thirty years had been allotted to David, he said: " How many years are allotted to me?" " One thousand," said God. " Then I make a present to David of seventy years," said Adam. A formal document of resignation was drawn up on parchment, and was signed by Adam and countersigned by Michael and Gabriel as witnesses.[3]

THE CREATION OF EVE

Now Adam walked about in the Garden of Eden at his leisure and like one of the ministering angels. But the Maker of the Universe said unto Himself: " It is not good for man to be alone. For he is alone in his world, just as I am alone in my world. And just as I have no companion, Adam has no companion, and the creatures, seeing that he does not propagate, will say to-morrow: ' Adam is surely our Creator, for there is no propagation in his life.' I will, therefore, make a helpmate for Adam." [4] But when the earth heard this decision of the Lord of the Universe, the earth quaked and shook and trembled, and thus it cried before the Creator: " Lord of the Universe! Sovereign of all the worlds! How

---

[1] *Book of Jubilees*, 4, 30; *Yalkut*, § 41; see also Friedlaender's edition of *Pirke de Rabbi Eliezer*, p. 128, Note 11.
[2] See Hugo Winckler, *Ex Oriente Lux*, p. 183 (15); Bin Gorion, *Die Sagen der Juden*, Vol. I, p. 253. [3] Weil, *loc. cit.*, pp. 29-38.
[4] *Pirke de Rabbi Eliezer*, Ch. 12; Gaster, *The Chronicles of Jerahmeel*, VI, 13-15.

shall I be able to provide for the whole of humanity and feed all the multitudes that will issue from Adam? I have no power to feed all the multitudes!" Thus complained the earth. But the Lord of the Universe silenced the earth and replied:

"I and thou will feed together the multitudes that will issue from Adam and his wife." And God made a covenant with the earth, according to which the Creator of the Universe assists earth and waters it so that it yields fruit and thus provides food for all the creatures during the day. God also created the sleep of life, so that when man lies down and sleeps, he is strengthened, sustained, healed, and refreshed.[1]

Thereupon God created a helpmate for Adam. But He had pity upon man and, in order that he should not feel any pain, He caused a deep sleep to fall upon Adam, and during that deep slumber He took the thirteenth rib of man and flesh from his heart, fashioned woman and placed her before him.[2] Eve, however, was not created merely for the purpose of continuing the human species, for she enjoys a higher moral dignity. He, therefore, who remains single is without happiness, joy or blessing, peace and life. He is not called a man, and is like unto one who had committed murder.[3]

And when Adam awoke and saw Eve before him, his wonder and delight knew no bounds. He approached her and kissed her, and thus he spoke: "Blessed art thou before the Eternal. It is right and proper that thou shouldst be called Ishah (woman) for thou hast been taken from man (Ish)."

Jewish legend further relates that Eve was not created from the head of Adam, lest she should be vain; nor from his eyes, lest she should be wanton; nor from his mouth, lest she should be given to gossiping; nor from his ears, lest she should be an eavesdropper; nor from his hands, lest she

---

[1] *Pirke de Rabbi Eliezer*, Ch. 12; Gaster, *The Chronicles of Jerahmeel*, VI, 13–15.
[2] *Pirke de Rabbi Eliezer*, Ch. 12; *Targum Jerushalmi*, *Genesis*, 2, 21. See also *Lekach Tob*, *Genesis*, 2, 21.   [3] *Jebamoth*, 63*b*; *Genesis Rabba*, 17.

should be meddlesome; nor from his feet, lest she should
be a gadabout; nor from his heart, lest she should be jealous.
She was drawn from man's rib, which is a hidden part, so
that she might be modest and retiring. And yet, notwithstanding all the precautions taken by the Creator, woman
has all the faults God wished to guard her against.[1]

Thereupon the Lord made ten wedding canopies for
Adam in the Garden of Eden, all of which were out of gold,
and pearls and precious stones. This was done in order to
bestow special honour upon our first parents. And angels
came into the Garden and played heavenly music. Then the
Holy One said unto His hosts and ministering angels: " Come
let us descend and do honour and render a loving service to
the first man, who hath been created in My image, and to
his helpmate, for it is only through loving kindness and the
service of loving kindness that the world will exist. It is love
and not burnt offerings that I will require of man." [2] And
the ministering angels descended into the Garden of Eden,
and walked before the bridal pair, the first man and his wife,
and guarded the wedding canopies, and the Holy One, blessed
be His name, blessed Adam and his helpmate.[3]

The Cabbalists give in glowing terms an imaginative
description of the marriage ceremony of Adam and Eve, and
of the banquet in Eden. Accompanied by myriads of ministering angels, who sang and played, Eve was brought to Adam.
The entire host of Heaven descended into the Garden of Eden.
Some of the ministering angels played upon harps, cymbals
and cithers, whilst the sun and the moon danced in honour
of Adam and Eve.[4] Here, we evidently see Babylonian astral
influences which the imagination of the Jews has made use
of in its own way.

[1] *Genesis Rabba*, 18.
[2] *Pirke de Rabbi Eliezer*, Ch. 12; Gaster, *The Chronicles of Jerahmeel*, XII. 1–2; *Menorath ha-Maor*, § 205.
[3] *Pirke de Rabbi Eliezer*, ibid.; *Midrash Tanchuma*, ed. Buber, I, 58b; cf. *Abot de Rabbi Nathan*, Ch. 1.   [4] *Othioth de Rabbi Akiba*, Venice, 1546, fol. 6.

In some Jewish legends it is maintained that first man was created double with a woman at his back, and that God cut them apart. Adam was thus originally a male on the right side and a female on the left, but subsequently the Creator removed one half of him to make Eve.[1] The complete man thus consists of both sexes.

The idea that the first human pair had originally formed a single androgynous being with two faces, separated later into two personalities by the Creator, is met with in the myths and legends of other nations. It is found among the Indians, among the Greeks, and the Persians. Thus in the *Bundehesh*, a book written in the Pehlevi tongue and containing the exposition of a complete cosmogony, we read the following account of the creation of Mashya and Mashyana, the first man and the first woman.

His first act of creation Ahuramazda completed by producing simultaneously Gayômaretan or Gayômard, the typical man and the typical bull, two creatures of perfect purity. They lived 3000 years upon earth in a state of happiness, fearing no evil. But the time came when Angrômainyus, the evil principle, made his power felt in the world. Having struck the typical bull dead, useful plants and domestic animals sprung from his body. Thirty years later Gayômaretan, too, perished, struck by Angrômainyus. But at the end of forty years the seed of Gayômaretan, the typical man, shed upon the ground at the time of his death, germinated and brought forth a plant. A plant of reivas came forth from the ground and grew up. And in the centre of this plant a stalk rose up which had the form of a man and of a woman joined together at the back. They were divided by Ahuramazda, who endowed them with motion and activity. He placed within them an intelligent soul and bade them observe the law and be humble of heart, pure in thought, pure in speech, and pure in action.

---

[1] *Berachoth*, 61a; *Erubin*, 18a; see also *Genesis Rabba*, 7.

They were called Mashya and Mashyana, the human pair from whom all human beings are descended.[1]

Brahma, we read in Indian myth, engaged in the production of beings, saw Kaya divide itself into two parts, each part being a different sex, from whom the whole human race sprang.[2]

In the *Banquet* of Plato, Aristophanes relates the history of the primordial androgyns, who were subsequently separated by the Gods into man and woman. " In the beginning there were three sexes among men, not only two which we still find at this time, male and female, but yet a third, partaking of the nature of each, which has disappeared, only leaving its name behind. Filled with pride, this race attempted to scale Heaven. The Gods then decided to reduce their might and punish their temerity, and they were hewn asunder, so that each half had only left two arms and a pair of legs, one head and a single sex. They were made into male and female who desire to come together, in order to return to their primitive unity." [3]

The myths and legends about Adam and Eve were taken over from Jewish sources by the Moslems, and are related in different versions by the Arab commentators, such as Tabari and Masudi.[4] Thus Tabari relates that Adam was roaming through Paradise and eating from the fruit of the trees, when suddenly he fell fast asleep. When he opened his eyes he saw Eve before him and wondered at her presence. " Who art thou?" he asked. " I am thy wife," replied the lady; " God has created me out of thee and for thee, so that my heart might find repose." Then the angels said to Adam: " What thing is this, and what is her name?" To which Adam replied: " This is Eve." [5]

---

[1] See *Bundehesh*, trans. by West, in Sacred Books of the East, Vol. V, Chapters 1, 4, 14, and 15.

[2] *Bhagavat*, 3, 12, 51; Mackenzie, *Indian Myth and Legend*; F. Lenormant, *Les Origines de l'Histoire*, Ch. 1.   [3] Plato's *Banquet*, Jowett's Transl.

[4] See Grünbaum, *Neue Beiträge zur semitischen Sagenkunde*, pp. 60–67: Weil, *Biblische Legenden der Muselmänner*; Geiger, *Was hat Mohammed aus dem Judentum genommen*, pp. 99–102.   [5] *Chronique de Tabari*, I, Ch. 26.

Another Moslem version of the creation of Eve runs as follows: As a reward for his having preached to the angels, Adam received a bunch of grapes. Having eaten of the grapes, he fell asleep, and whilst he slept God made Eve and placed her beside Adam.[1] She resembled him exactly, but she was more beautiful, her features were more delicate, her eyes softer, her form more slender, her voice sweeter, and her hair longer, being divided into seven hundred locks. Adam had in the meantime been dreaming that he had a wife and a helpmate, and great was his joy when, upon his waking, he found his dream a reality. Putting forth his hand, Adam tried to take hold of that of Hava, for that was the name God had given her. The woman, however, withdrew hers, and would not listen to Adam's words of love: " God is my master," she said, " and without His permission I cannot listen to thy words of love, nor give my hand to thee. Besides, it is not proper for a man to take a wife without first making her a wedding present." Thereupon Adam dispatched the angel Gabriel to go and ask for him God's permission to take Hava as his wife. Soon Gabriel returned and informed Adam that Hava had been created to be his wife and helpmate, but that he was to treat her with love and kindness. Thereupon Ridhwan, the gatekeeper of Paradise, brought to Adam the winged horse called Meimun, and a lightfooted she-camel to Eve. Helped by Gabriel, they mounted the animals and were led into Paradise where they were greeted by the angels and all the creatures with the words: " Hail, father and mother of Mohammed." Then Adam and Eve were placed upon a throne in a green silk tent supported on gold pillars. They were then bathed in one of the rivers of Paradise and brought into the presence of God, who bade them live happily in Paradise which He had prepared for them as their home.[2]

[1] Weil, *Biblische Legenden der Muselmänner*. pp. 17–18,   [2] Weil, *loc. cit.*

ADAM IN PARADISE

God Warns Adam

Tunc figura vocet Adam propius, et attentius ei dicat:
Escote, Adam, e entent ma raison;
Io t'ai formé, or te doerai itel don:
Tot tens poez vivre, si tu tiens mon sermon,
E serras sains, nen sentiras friczion;
Jà n'avras faim, por bosoing ne beveras,
Jà n'averas frait, jà chalt ne sentiras;
Tu iers en joie, jà ne te lasseras
E en deduit, jà dolor ne savras.
Toute ta vie demeneras en joie;
Tut jors serras, n'en estrat pas poie.
Jo l'di à toi, e voil que Eva l'oie;
Se n'el entent, donc s'afoloie.
De tote terre avez la seignorie,
D'oisels, des bestes e d'altre manantie.
A petit vus soit qui vus porte en vie,
Car tot li mond vus iert encline.
En vostre cors vus met e bien e mal:
Ki ad tel dun n'est pas liez à pal.
Tut en balance ore pendiez par egal
Creez conseil que soiet vers mei leal,
Laisse le mal, e si te pren al bien,
Tun seignor aime e ovec lui te tien,
Por nul conseil ne gerpisez le mien.
Si tu le fais, ne peccheras de rien.

Adam, Drame Anglo-Normand du XIIᵉ Siècle, publié par
Victor Luzarche (Tours, 1854), pp. 5–6.

CHAPTER XIV

The Plot of Sammael, or Paradise Lost

The plot of the angels—Sammael, the angel of light—His jealousy—
Sammael and the serpent—Sammael inspires the serpent—The sin of
Eve—The story of the bird Hol, or Milham (the Phœnix)—The story of the
fox and the weasel—Leviathan sends the large fishes to bring the fox—How
the fox cheated the fishes—The punishment of Adam and Eve—Sammael
is cursed—What Adam lost—He seeks shelter—The story of the Fall in the
Iggeret Baale Hayyim—Adam and the Sabbath—Paradise and the Peri.

WHEN the ministering angels saw the glory and power of
man, and how beloved he was by the Creator, they said unto
themselves, that they would never prevail against him, unless
they led him into temptation.[1] Foremost among the angels,
who were jealous of man and anxious to lead him into temptation, was Sammael, an angel of light, a Seraph with six wings.[2]
Sammael and the angels saw that man was powerful and
beloved by the Creator; they knew that only through a ruse
could they encompass his sin and bring about his perdition.
Then Sammael, accompanied by a host of rebels, descended
from his celestial abode and gathered all the living creatures.
None he found so wily as the serpent and so apt to do wicked
and evil deeds. Thereupon Sammael mounted the serpent
like a rider mounts a swift steed, inspired him with his spirit
and sent him to Eve, the first woman, and wife of Adam. "Man,"
said Sammael, "will not listen to thee, but woman will listen
unto thee, because she easily lends an ear to all creatures."[3]

[1] *Pirke de Rabbi Eliezer*, Ch. 13; Gaster, *The Chronicles of Jerahmeel*, 22, 1.
[2] *Hagigah*, 12b; *Yalkut, Genesis*, § 25.
[3] *Pirke de Rabbi Eliezer*, Ch. 13; *Midrash Haggadol* (ed. Schechter), col. 87; *Genesis Rabba*, 17.

The serpent walked on two feet and was as erect as a reed.[1]
It was superior to all other animals, and its physical strength
and wisdom and intelligence were great. Had the serpent
not been cursed, but retained its primeval shape and form
and its intellectual powers and its power of speech, it would
have rendered innumerable services to man. For like a camel
the serpent would have fetched and carried and brought
pearls and precious stones from the far East.[2]

And the serpent, too, was very jealous and envious of
Adam. It harboured the plan of killing Adam and of marrying
his widow and then of ruling over the world.[3] The serpent
then came and sat down by the side of Eve and began to converse and thus it spoke: " The Creator has eaten from this
tree (the tree of wisdom), and created the world, but He
commanded you not to eat from this tree, for fear that you, too,
might create new worlds. You should eat of the fruit of this
tree, before He destroys you and creates new worlds.[4] If,
as you tell me," the serpent continued, " the Creator has
commanded ye not to touch this tree, then behold, I touch
it, and yet I am alive, and you, too, will never die, if you
touch it." Thus spoke the serpent. But the serpent was only
a vessel, and it was Sammael who spoke through its mouth,
having mounted it like a rider mounts a horse.[5] When Sammael
mounted the serpent and rode upon it, the voice of justice
(the voice of the law) cried out aloud: " It is wicked, O
Sammael, now that the world has been created, to rebel against
the omnipotent Creator, for He is omnipotent and omni-
present, and in His loving-kindness has He created the world
and man to inhabit it." [6]

But Sammael inspired the serpent to go and argue with
Eve and to lead her into temptation. Thereupon the serpent,

---

[1] *Genesis Rabba*, 19.   [2] *Abot de Rabbi Nathan*, Ch. 1; *Sanhedrin*, 59b.
[3] *Abot de Rabbi Nathan*, Ch. 1.   [4] *Midrash Debarim Rabba*, 5.
[5] *Pirke de Rabbi Eliezer*, Ch. 13; see also *Abot de Rabbi Nathan*, Ch. 1.
[6] *Pirke de Rabbi Eliezer*, Ch. 13.

who was more subtle than all other beasts in the field, went
to Eve, for he said unto himself: " Man is not so easily persuaded or swayed as is woman. Man is evil and churlish in
his doings.[1] I will, therefore, approach woman who is by
nature more kind hearted and simpler than man." [2] Then
Sammael rose and touched the tree with both hands and
feet and shook it. And the tree cried aloud and exclaimed:
" Touch me not, thou accursed one." [3] When Sammael saw
that Eve still hesitated to touch the tree he took hold of her
and threw her against the tree and she touched it. Then he
spoke: " Thou seest, just as thou hast not died when thou
didst touch the tree, so thou wilt not die when thou wilt eat
of its fruit." [4] But when Eve was persuaded and touched the
tree, she suddenly perceived the angel of death.[5] She was
greatly troubled in her heart, and said unto herself: " Now
I shall of a certainty die, and the Creator will fashion another
woman and give her to Adam as wife. I will, therefore, per-
suade my husband to eat of the fruit with me. If we die, we
die together, and if we live we shall live together, and he will
not take another woman to wife." Eve, therefore, after having
eaten of the fruit, took thereof and gave it to Adam and they
both ate. Then their eyes were opened and they saw that
they were naked, and their teeth were set on edge.[6]

Eve was very subtle and had easily prevailed upon Adam
to partake of the fruit of the forbidden tree. " Do not think,"
she argued, " that if I die the Creator will fashion another
wife for thee. Neither shouldst thou imagine that thou wilt
be allowed to remain a widower and inhabit the earth in
solitude. For the earth has been created to be peopled. If
I die, the Creator will destroy thee and fashion another man." [7]

[1] *I Samuel*, 25, 3.　　[2] *Prov.* 9, 13.

[3] Menachem Recanati, *Commentary to the Pentateuch*, fol. 24b–25a; *Pirke de Rabbi Eliezer*,
Ch. 13; *Abot de Rabbi Nathan*, Ch. 1.

[4] *Genesis Rabba*, 19; *Midrash Haggadol, Genesis*, col. 88; *Pirke de Rabbi Eliezer*, Ch. 13.

[5] *Targum Jerushalmi, Genesis*, 3, 6; *Pirke de Rabbi Eliezer*, Ch. 13.

[6] Menachem Recanati, *loc. cit.*, fol. 24b–25a.　　[7] *Genesis Rabba*, 19–20.

Eve was also jealous of all the beasts who were in
Eden. Having partaken of the forbidden fruit, she gave it
unto all the animals, to the tame and wild beasts and to
the fowls of the air. All the beasts and fowls obeyed her,
with the exception of one bird who is called *Hol*.

THE STORY OF THE BIRD HOL, OR MILHAM (THE PHŒNIX)

All the animals and beasts in the field and fowls in the
air listened to the woman's voice, and ate of the fruit of knowledge, and were thus condemned to die. Eve then saw the
bird Hol, or Milham, and said unto it: " Eat thou, too, of
the fruit of which all the beasts in the field and the fowls of
the air have eaten." But the bird Milham said unto the woman:
" Is it not sufficient for you to have transgressed the command
of the Lord by eating of the fruit from the tree of knowledge
and to have caused all the animals and beasts in the field and
birds of the air to eat of it? Do you want to make me also
sin by transgressing the command of the Lord?" And the
bird Milham, who was very wise, did not listen to the voice
of the woman and alone of all the birds did not eat of the
fruit of the tree of knowledge.

Then a voice called from Heaven and resounded throughout creation and thus said unto Adam and Eve: " Ye received
My command not to partake of the fruit from the tree of
knowledge, but ye did not listen to My words and transgressed
My command and sinned. The bird Milham did not receive
My command, and yet it refused to listen to your voice and
it honoured My command. Henceforth of all living creatures
the bird Milham alone and its offspring in all eternity will
never die, but live for ever."

And the Creator, the Lord of the Universe, gave to the
angel of death power over all the living creatures. " All the
living creatures are in thy power," said the Lord, "but over
Milham alone thou shalt have no power, neither over it nor

over its offspring from now on unto all eternity." Then
the angel of death replied: " O! Lord of the Universe! Let
me separate this bird from all the living creatures, so that all
will know that Milham and its offspring are the just who will
never undergo the penalty of death or taste its bitterness."

The Lord of the Universe, the Creator and All - Father,
then commanded the angel of death to build a big town
and there to place the bird Milham and its offspring. And
the angel of death did as the Creator had commanded him.
He built a big town wherein he placed the bird Milham and
its offspring. He then sealed the gates of the big town and
said: " It is decreed from now unto all eternity that no
sword, neither mine nor that of any one else, shall have
power over the offspring of the bird Milham from now unto
all eternity. Never will the birds, the offspring of Milham,
taste the bitterness of death until the end of all generations."
And the bird Milham lives in the big town which the angel of
death had built at the command of the Lord of the Universe.
For one thousand years the bird Milham and its offspring
live, and they are fruitful and multiply like all other living
creatures. But every thousand years, when each bird grows
old, a fire is kindled in its nest and issues forth. It consumes
the bird and leaves only a part of it not bigger than an egg.
This egg then grows and changes into a new bird, and from
the ashes the bird rises rejuvenated and soars up like an eagle.
This is the bird Milham, or Hol, concerning which it has
been decreed by the Creator that it should never die.[1]

THE STORY OF THE FOX AND THE WEASEL

And it came to pass that when the angel of death had
closed and sealed the gates of the town he had built for the
bird Milham, the Lord of the Universe thus spake unto him:

[1] *Alphabetum Siracides* (ed.Steinschneider); see also Jellinek, *Beth-Hamidrash*, Vol. VI,
p. xii; *Monatsschrift*, 43, p. 219; *Genesis Rabba*, 19; *Midrash Samuel*, 12, 4; see also P. Cassel,
Der Phœnix und seine Aera.

"Throw into the sea a pair, male and female, from every species of the creatures I have created, and over all the others shalt thou have power." The angel of death obeyed and did as he had been commanded by the Lord of the Universe. He began to throw into the sea a pair from every species the Lord had created. When the fox—who was very wily—saw what was happening, he approached the angel of death and began to cry bitterly.

"Well, and why art thou crying so bitterly," asked the angel of death.

"I am weeping over my poor brother," replied the fox, "my brother whom thou hast just thrown into the sea."

"Where is thy brother?" inquired the angel of death.

The fox approached and came up to the water's edge, so that his image was reflected by the water, and pointing to his own image he said: "Here he is." When the angel of death saw the image of the fox in the water, he thought that he had already thrown one of the species into the sea. He therefore said: "As I have already thrown into the water one of thy species, thou canst go." And the fox ran away and was saved. On his way he met his friend the weasel, to whom he related what had happened and how he had cheated the angel of death and had escaped. The weasel greatly admired the cunning of the fox and did likewise. He, too, cheated the angel of death and was not thrown into the water.

Now it came to pass that after a time Leviathan, the king over all the creatures that live in the sea, gathered all his subjects round him, but he saw neither fox nor weasel among them. Greatly astonished, he asked the fishes why the fox and the weasel were absent and had not appeared in his presence. Then the fishes told Leviathan what had happened, how the fox and the weasel—who were both cunning and wily—had cheated the angel of death and been saved from the water. And Leviathan was very jealous of the fox and

envied him his cleverness and intelligence and cunning. He,
therefore, sent out the large fishes and commanded them to
go and fetch the fox and to use cunning so as to entice him
into the water and bring him before Leviathan. The large
fishes did the bidding of their King Leviathan, who is set
over all the fishes in the sea. They swam to the shore and
perceived the fox who was walking up and down along the
seashore. When the fox beheld the large fishes who had swum
up he wondered greatly.

" Who are you?" asked the fishes.

" I am the fox," he replied.

Then the fishes, who tried to be cunning, said: " Hail
King! Great honours await thee, for whose sake we have
come up to the surface of the waters and swum up to the
shore."

" How so," asked the fox. And the fishes replied:

" Our great King, Leviathan, who is the ruler of all the
creatures in the deep seas, is sick unto death. Feeling his end
near, he has decreed that none but thou shouldst succeed
him on his throne which will soon be vacant. He has
heard of thee and how clever and cunning thou art. And
he has dispatched us, the large fishes, to find and bring thee
before him that he might crown thee king and leave his
kingdom to thee for thou art cleverer than all the beasts of
the earth and all the fishes in the sea."

Thus spoke the fishes, and the fox was greatly flattered
and pleased to hear such tidings.

" But how can I go into the water," he said, " without
being drowned?"

" Do not trouble about this," said the large fishes. " We
will carry thee upon our backs, as befits a king. Right across
the waves and over the vast sea we will carry thee, until we
bring thee before our King Leviathan. And when thou wilt
have reached the abode of Leviathan thou wilt become king

over all of us, and thou wilt live happily for ever. For thy nourishment will be brought to thee daily, as it befits a king, and no longer wilt thou fear the wild beasts who are mightier and stronger than thyself."

And the fox listened to their voice and believed their words. He mounted upon the back of one of the large fishes who promised to carry him over the surface of the waters to the abode of Leviathan. But when the foam-crested waves began to beat mightily against him, the fox suddenly felt afraid; his heart fell and his ambition left him.

"Woe is unto me," he wailed. "What have I done? The fishes have deceived me and made a fool of me. I, who have deceived and misled other beasts, am now in their power, and who will save me?" And the fox thought deeply of means how to escape. Thereupon he addressed the fishes and said unto them:

"Tell me the truth, what is your purpose and what do you intend to do to me?" And the fishes said: "We will tell thee the real truth. Our King Leviathan, he who is the ruler over all the fishes in the deep seas, has heard of thee and how cunning thou art and he has said: 'I will cut open his body and swallow his heart, and be as wise and cunning as the fox.'"

Then the fox said unto the fishes: "Why did you not tell me the truth at once? I would then have taken my heart with me and offered it as a gift to the king. He would have honoured and loved me. But now evil will befall you, for your king will be angry, when he hears that you have brought me without my heart."

And the fishes marvelled greatly and said: "Is it really so that thy heart is not within thee and that thou hast come out leaving it behind?"

"Verily, it is so," replied the fox, "for such is the custom among us foxes. We leave our hearts behind us in a safe place, and we walk about without any heart. When once we need it, we go home and fetch it, but if we do not require it our hearts remain at home in a safe place." Thus spoke the fox. And when the fishes heard this, they were greatly troubled and perplexed, and did not know what to do. But the fox said unto them:

" My abode is on the shore of the sea, just where you met me. If you will take me back to the water's edge, I will run up and quickly fetch my heart where it is hidden. I will then return with you to King Leviathan and offer him my heart as a gift. He will be greatly pleased, and honour you and me. But if you refuse and bring me to him without my heart, he will be mightily angry with you and will swallow you up, for you have failed to carry out his commands. As for myself, I am not afraid, for I will tell him the truth. ' O Lord Leviathan!' I will say, ' these fishes thou didst send out did not tell me anything of thy desire. And when at last they did tell me the reason of their errand, I urged them to return and let me fetch my heart, but they refused, and so I cannot offer thee my heart which I would fain do.'"

When the fishes heard these cunning words of the fox, they said to one another: " Verily, he has spoken well." They returned to the seashore and brought the fox to the dry land. The fox immediately jumped upon the shore, threw himself upon the sand and began to dance for joy.

" Hurry up," urged the fishes, " and fetch thy heart where it is hidden, that we may return to King Leviathan."

But the fox laughed merrily and said: " Verily, you are fools. Do not you know that if my heart had not been with me I could not have gone with you upon the water and faced the foam-crested waves? Is there a creature upon earth that could walk about without a heart?"

And the fishes spoke: " Then thou hast deceived us." But the fox only laughed and said: " If I have been clever enough

SAMMAEL AND HIS BAND OF ANGELS HURLED FROM HEAVEN

to cheat the angel of death, how much easier was it for me to cheat you, stupid fishes." And so the fishes returned to King Leviathan empty-handed and were greatly ashamed. When Leviathan heard their story he said:

" Verily, the fox is very cunning, but you are very stupid and deserve punishment." He, therefore, ate them all. And ever since there are counterparts in the water of every species of beasts upon earth, even the counterparts of man and of woman, but there are none of either the fox or the weasel![1]

When Adam and Eve had eaten of the forbidden fruit, their eyes were opened, and they saw themselves naked.[2] Their glory then fled from them, for they lost their celestial garments and angelic endowments. Only sensible matters did they see and understand, but all divine and angelic wisdom was taken from them. Stripped of his garment which was a skin like finger nails, and a cloud of glory, man, after his sin, stood naked. Then the voice of the Creator resounded, calling upon Adam: " How art thou changed, O man!" And Adam said: " O Creator of the world, Lord of the Universe! I did not sin against Thee when I lived alone in Eden. The woman thou hast given me enticed me." But the woman replied that the serpent had beguiled her. And the voice of the Creator resounded once more through the whole world, and the mountains trembled and the earth quaked, and thus He spoke·

" All three of you shall be punished, for you have sinned and transgressed My commandment." And Sammael and his band of angels who followed him were hurled from Heaven. To the serpent the Creator spoke thus: " I made thee king over all the beasts in the field, and thou didst walk erect like a man. But now thou shalt drag thyself upon the ground with thy belly, and dust shall henceforth be thy food." And

---

[1] *Alphabetum Siracidis* (ed Steinschneider).
[2] *Pirke de Rabbi Eliezer*, Ch. 14; *Targum Jerushalmi, Genesis*, 3, 7.

the serpent was cursed above all the cattle and the living
beasts. It was ordained that its feet be cut off, and that it
should cast off its skin once in seven years and thereby suffer
great pain.[1] And the Creator further spoke: " Thou didst
harbour wicked thoughts in thy mind and evil in thy heart.
Thou didst say unto thyself: ' I will kill Adam and take
Eve to be my wife, and I shall be the Lord of creation and king
of the world.' But now I will put death and poison in thy
mouth, and a deadly venom, and will put hatred between thee
and the woman and her children. Instead of being king of
the world, walk erect and eat of all the agreeable and delightful food, thou shalt henceforth be cursed above all cattle,
creep on thy belly and eat dust." [2] The Creator thereupon
cursed Adam, and shortened his stature and took his glory
from him. Six things were taken from Adam as a punishment for his sin, and these things were: his splendour, his
stature, his life, the fruits of the trees, the fruits, and the
heavenly lights. And he was to sow wheat and reap thistles,
and earn his bread in anxiety, and his food by the sweat of his
brow.[3]

When Adam heard his sentence, that the earth should
produce thorns and thistles, his body trembled, tears welled
up in his eyes, and sweat poured down his countenance, and
thus he spoke before his Creator: " Lord of the Universe!
shall I and my ass eat alike from the same crib?" But the
Creator replied: " Since thou dost repent, and thy limbs did
tremble and thou didst weep and sweat poured down thy
countenance, thou wilt eat not grass, like the beasts in the
field, but bread." [4]

Furthermore, in consequence of the sin of our first parents,
the presence and splendour of the Creator (the Shekhina)

[1] *Targum Jerushalmi, Genesis,* 3, 14; *Yalkut Shimeoni,* § 27; *Pirke de Rabbi Eliezer,* Ch. 14;
Genesis Rabba, 20.
[2] *Abot de Rabbi Nathan,* Ch. 1. [3] Bin Gorion, *loc. cit.,* p. 111.
[4] *Pesachim,* 118a; *Genesis Rabba,* 24; *Abot de Rabbi Nathan,* Ch. 1.

which had manifested itself upon earth and dwelt in Eden, retired to the celestial regions. As the future generations and the descendants of Adam sinned once more, it retired farther and farther from the inhabitants of earth. Thus, after the fall of Adam, the Shekhina, or Divine presence, had retired to the first or lowest heavenly sphere. It ascended to the second after the crime of Cain, to the third in the time of Enosh, to the fourth in the time of the deluge, to the fifth when the tower of Babel was being constructed, to the sixth in the age of Sodom, and to the seventh, that is the highest heavenly sphere, when Abraham visited the land of Egypt. But when the just and pious men arose, the Shekhina once more descended gradually to dwell among men.[1]

After his fall Adam wandered about begging the trees to give him shelter, but they all refused. " Here is the thief," they said, " who has deceived his Maker." The fig tree alone offered him shelter, for it is of the fruit of the fig tree that he had eaten.[2]

All this had happened on the first day of his creation, and Adam had not yet witnessed the sunset, nor the approach of night and darkness. When he therefore suddenly noticed how the world was growing dark in the west, and the sun was disappearing upon the horizon, he was greatly perturbed and exclaimed: " Woe unto me! On account of my sin the Creator is sending darkness upon earth, and is throwing creation back into chaos." As yet, Adam was not aware that such was the course of the world, and he thought that it was death that was swiftly approaching. But when on the following morning the sun once more arose in all its radiance in the east, he was mightily glad, built altars and praised the Creator.[3]

---

[1] *Genesis Rabba*, 19; *Midrash Haggadol*, col. 90.
[2] *Genesis Rabba*, 15; *Midrash Haggadol*, col. 90.
[3] *Abodah Zarah*, 8a; *Abot de Rabbi Nathan*, Ch. 1.

SAMMAEL, THE ANGEL OF LIGHT

In the *Iggeret Baale Hayyim*,[1] the story of the Fall is related as follows: When the Lord of the Universe had created man, He commanded the angels to pay homage to him, and they all obeyed the command of their Master. But Sammael alone, who was arrogant and obstinate, refused to obey. He was greatly grieved and very wroth, when he heard that his rule on earth had come to an end, and his wrath knew no bounds. He was loath to leave his throne and to obey another ruler and lord, where he had hitherto ruled supreme; to submit to the will of another, where hitherto all had submitted to his will. And the Creator commanded the angels to place man in the Garden of Eden, in a lovely spot on the top of the mountains, where the air is delicious, and where winter and summer, and day and night are alike. There are lovely streams and flowers and trees, pleasant to the eye, in abundance. And high upon the mountains Adam and Eve wandered. They walked by the river banks, among flowers and trees, beautiful to behold. They lived without care or sorrow, for they neither toiled nor laboured, but ate of the fruit of delight and listened to the song of the lovely birds. When Sammael saw the happiness of man, his envy and wrath increased, and he sought to seduce man, lead him into temptation and thus deprive him of his happiness. He came to him with smooth speech and thus he spoke: " Well enough do I know that the Creator has placed thee above all creatures and lent thee much wisdom. But if thou wouldst follow my advice and partake of the tree of life, thou wouldst never die, but live for ever and ever in all eternity. And Adam listened to the voice of Sammael, the seducer, and was greatly tempted. He ate of the tree of life and tasted its fruit. Scarcely had he eaten of the tree of life, when his body became black and his

---

[1] Trans. by Julius Landsberger, 1882.

countenance was changed. His garment of light fell from him
and he was troubled by the heat of the sun. And all the animals,
when they saw how greatly Adam had changed, no longer
feared him.

And thus Adam and his helpmate did not remain long
in the Garden of Eden. According to Rabbinic legend,[1]
Adam entered Eden on Friday evening, and already at twilight
on the next day, he was driven forth, and went out. He would
have been sent out of Eden earlier, but he was saved by the
Sabbath day which arrived and became the advocate for our
first parent. The Sabbath day appeared before the Throne
of Glory and thus it spoke: " Lord of the Universe, Sovereign
of all the worlds, Thou hast blessed and sanctified the
Sabbath day more than all the days of the week. No one has
as yet been punished during the six days of creation, and shall
this happen on the Sabbath day? Where is then my sanctity
and where is Thy blessing?" And thus, by the merit of the
Sabbath, Adam was saved from judgment on the Sabbath
day.[2]

Thereupon Adam went forth outside the Garden of Eden,
and he dwelt upon the Mount Moriah, which is near to the
Garden of Eden.

PARADISE AND THE PERI

One morn a Peri at the gate
Of Eden stood disconsolate,
And as she listened to the springs
Of life within, like music flowing,
And caught the light upon her wings
Through the half-open portal glowing,
She wept to think her recreant race
Should e'er have lost that glorious place!

---

[1] *Pirke de Rabbi Eliezer*, Ch. 18; *Midrash Shokher Tob, Ps.* 92, 3; see, however, contra-
diction in *Pirke de Rabbi Eliezer*, Ch. 11.
[2] *Pirke de Rabbi Eliezer*, Ch. 19. See also *Midrash Shokher Tob, Ps.* 92, 3; cf. *Sabbath,*
118a.

" How happy," exclaimed this child of air,
" Are the Holy Spirits who wander there,
'Mid flowers that never shall fade or fall;
Though mine are the gardens of earth and sea
And the stars themselves have flowers for me,
One blossom of Heaven outblooms them all.

" Though sunny the lake of cool Cashmere
With its plane-tree isle reflected clear,
And sweetly the founts of that valley fall;
Though bright are the waters of Sing-su-Hay,
And the golden floods that thitherward stray,
Yet—Oh! 't is only the Blest can say
How the waters of Heaven outshine them all.

" Go, wing thy flight from star to star,
From world to luminous world, as far
As the universe spreads its flaming wall,
Take all the pleasure of all the spheres,
And multiply each through endless years,
One minute of Heaven is worth them all!"

The glorious angel, who was keeping
The Gates of Light, beheld her weeping;
And, as he nearer drew and listen'd
To her sad song, a tear-drop glistened
Within his eyelids, like the spray
From Eden's fountain, when it lies
On the blue flower, which—Brammissay—
Blooms nowhere but in Paradise.

" Nymph of a fair but erring line! "
Gently he said, " one hope is thine,
'T is written in the Book of Fate,
The Peri yet may be forgiven
Who brings to this Eternal Gate
The gift that is most dear to Heaven!
Go, seek it, and redeem thy sin—
'T is sweet to let the pardon'd in."

Thomas Moore (" Lalla Rookh ").

CHAPTER XV

In Exile

The prayer of Adam—The angel Rasiel brings the book back to Adam —Adam and Eve search after food—They decide to do penance—Eve goes to the Tigris and Adam to the Jordan—Eve is once more beguiled by Sammael—The story of Sammael's fall from Heaven—Eve gives birth to Cain— Her dream—Adam's sickness—His story of the Fall—Eve and Seth go to the Garden of Eden in search of the oil of life—Seth is bitten by the serpent —Eve's story of the Fall—The death of Adam—Angels come down to bury Adam—The death of Eve—The life of Adam in Moslem legend—The beasts show their pity—The locusts—Adam and Eve are forgiven—Iblis implores the grace of God—God makes a covenant with Adam.

ADAM AND EVE AFTER THE FALL

ADAM and Eve did not leave Paradise empty-handed. They carried with them various possessions, among these their garments, the rod which God had created on the eve of the Sabbath, and a book which the angel Rasiel gave them.[1]

When Adam was expelled from the Garden of Eden, he prayed unto the Creator and such was his prayer: " Eternal, Lord of the Universe! Thou didst create the whole world and all the creatures therein. Thy power is everlasting, and Thy glory goes from generation to generation. Nothing is hidden from Thee and nothing escapes Thine eye. Thou didst fashion me with Thine own hands and make me ruler over all Thy creatures. But the wily and cursed serpent seduced me and made me eat of the fruit from the tree of delight. And the wife of my bosom, she, too, seduced me. But Thou didst not inform me as to my fate and the fate of

---

[1] *Sepher Rasiel*, ed. Amsterdam, 1700.

my children after me, and as to what will happen to me and
to the generations who will come after me. I know that no
man is just before Thee, and who am I and what is my strength
that I should dare to resist Thee or rise up against Thee?
I dare not open my mouth to speak before Thee, or to raise
mine eyes, for I have sinned and transgressed Thy commandments and on account of my sin I am now driven forth and
expelled from Eden. And now I must plough and cultivate the
earth whence I have been taken. The inmates and inhabitants
of the earth no longer fear me nor do they tremble before me,
for since I have eaten of the fruit from the tree of knowledge
and transgressed Thy commandments my wisdom has been
taken from me, and I am a fool who knoweth not, and a stupid
who understandeth not what will happen and come to pass.
Now, merciful God, in Thy great mercy, turn to him who
is the chief and first of Thy creatures, to the spirit which
Thou didst breath into him and to the soul Thou didst give
him. Vouchsafe Thy mercy unto me, for Thou art gracious,
magnanimous, patient and rich in favour. May my prayer
ascend before the throne of Thy glory, and may my supplications reach the seat of Thy mercy, and mayest Thou be
merciful unto me. May the words of my mouth find favour
before Thee, and do not hide Thy countenance from me.
Thou who wast from the beginning and wilt be for ever,
Thou who didst reign and wilt continue to reign, have mercy
upon the work of Thine hands and let me understand and
know what will happen unto my offspring and to the generations
that will issue from me. Hide not from me the wisdom of
Thy help and the help of Thy ministering angels." [1]

Thus prayed Adam, and three days after he had thus
prayed, the angel Rasiel, who dwells near the river which
issues forth from the Garden of Eden, came to Adam and
manifested himself to him whilst the sun was hot. In his

---

[1] *Sepher Rasiel*, p. 3*a*; Jellinek, *Beth-Hamidrash*, Vol. III, p. 157.

hand the angel held a book and thus he spake unto Adam:
" Why art thou so troubled and why dost thou grieve?
Thy prayer and supplication have been heard, and I have
now come to teach thee the great wisdom through the words
of this holy book. Through it thou wilt know what will
befall thee until the day of thy death. And all thy offspring
and all those of thy children who will read and study this book
in humility of spirit and purity of flesh, and fulfil conscien-
tiously all that is written within its pages, will know for a
certainty what will happen unto them and befall them every
month and between day and night. Everything will be manifested unto them, and they will understand and know whether
misfortune or hunger, rain or drought, good or bad harvests
will come; whether sinners will rule in the world and whether
locusts will plague men; whether wars will be waged and
much blood be shed among men; and whether diseases will
break out and death mow down the children of man. And
now, Adam, approach and lend thine ear and I will teach
thee the secrets of the book and its holiness." Adam approached
and lent his ear, and the angel Rasiel, he who dwells by the
river that issues forth from the Garden of Eden, read unto
him the secrets of the book.[1]

And it so happened that when Adam heard the words
of the holy book as they issued from the mouth of the angel
Rasiel, he fell down upon his face greatly trembling. But
the angel of the Presence spake unto Adam and said: " Rise
up, Adam, and take heart, fear not, neither do thou tremble,
but take this book from my hands and guard it carefully, for
from this book thou wilt learn much knowledge and from
its source thou wilt draw intelligence and understanding that
thou mayest impart this knowledge to all those who will be
worthy of it." [2]

And it so happened that when Adam took the book from

---

[1] *Sepher Rasiel.*   [2] *Ibid.*

the hands of the angel Rasiel, a fire broke out on the bank of
the river, and in the flame the angel ascended to Heaven.
Then Adam understood and knew that he had been face to
face with an angel of the Presence, and that the book had been
sent to him by order and command of the holy King and
Ruler of the Universe. And he kept the book in sanctity and
purity.[1]

Thereupon Adam and Eve constructed a hut where they
passed seven days in sorrow and grief, in wailing and weeping.
When seven days had elapsed, they began to feel the pangs
of hunger, searched for food, but found none. Thereupon
Eve said to Adam : " My lord, I am hungry, go and find
some food for us that we may eat and live. And perhaps
God in His mercy will bring us back where we were before."
Then Adam went and searched for food seven days long, but
found none such as they had enjoyed in the Garden of Eden.
" My lord," said Eve, " if thou wouldst kill me, the Lord
will perhaps have mercy upon thee and take thee back to
Paradise, for it is solely on my account that He waxed wroth
with thee. Kill me, and then thou wilt return to Paradise."

Said Adam: " Eve, do not speak foolishly; how can I lift
my hand against my own flesh and blood. Let us rather wander
about in the land, perchance we may find food and not die." [2]
Thereupon they wandered about for nine days, but found
only food fit for animals and beasts of the earth. And Adam
said: " This is the food which the Lord has given to the beasts,
whilst we partook of the food of the angels when we dwelt
in Paradise.[3] Verily, the anger of God against us is great.
Let us, therefore, repent of our sin and do penance, perchance
He will have mercy upon us, forgive us and send us food that
we may live and not die. Thou, my dear Eve, canst not do
so much penance as I can, but do thou as much as thy health

---

[1] *Sepher Rasiel;* Jellinek, *Beth-Hamidrash,* Vol. III, p. 157.
[2] *Vita Adae et Evae,* ed. by W. Meyer in *Abhandlungen der bayrischen Akademie der
Wissenschaften, Phil.-philos. Classe,* XIV, 3, 1878, pp. 185 ff.   [3] *Ps.* 78, 25.

will permit thee. I will fast for forty days, but go thou to the river Tigris and remain in the water up to thy neck. Do not open thy mouth for speech, for we are unworthy to address the Lord and beg His pardon. Thus thou shalt remain for thirty-seven days and not quit the water. And I will go to the Jordan and there remain up to my neck in the water for forty days and do penance, perchance the Lord will forgive us our sin and have mercy upon us." Thus spake Adam.

And Eve went to the Tigris and entered the water, whilst Adam was doing penance in the Jordan. " Mourn with me, O waters of the Jordan," said Adam, " for I have sinned; gather round me all the living things that are in the Jordan and let them mourn with me and help me to do penance." Whilst Adam and Eve were thus doing penance, Sammael, who is Satan, grew angry and cast about how he might bring to naught their decision to undergo penance.

He decided to frustrate the intention of our first parents. On the eighteenth day he took upon him the form of an angel of light and flew over the Tigris where he perceived Eve crying. Pretending that he was moved by her distress, Sammael began to cry aloud. And thus he spoke: " Quit the water of the Tigris, Eve, and cry no longer. Why art thou and thy spouse Adam still sad and unhappy? The Lord has heard your joint prayers and has accepted your penance. We angels of light have all prayed the Lord to forgive you, and the Almighty has sent me to fetch you out of the water and to bring you the food which you enjoyed in Paradise. Quit now the water, and I will lead thee to a place where thou wilt find food in abundance." And Eve listened to the speech of Sammael who had taken the form of an angel of light, and scrambled out of the water. Her body was trembling from cold like a blade of grass. She fell upon the ground exhausted, but Sammael lifted her up and led her to Adam. When Adam saw Eve following Sammael, he was filled with dismay, beat his breast and wept aloud. "Eve, Eve," he cried, "what has become of thy penance? How couldst thou once more listen to the voice of our enemy and be beguiled by his deception?"

When Eve heard these words, she perceived that indeed it had been their enemy Sammael who had taken the form of an angel of light. She fell down upon the ground in great despair and cried bitterly: "Woe unto thee, O Satan," she exclaimed, "why art thou seeking to destroy us? What have we done unto thee that thou art our enemy? Why dost thou hate us? Have we taken from thee thy splendour and glory? Why dost thou hate us so fiercely?" Thus cried Eve.

And Sammael, sighing aloud, replied: "Adam! all my enmity, envy, and jealousy are directed against thee, because it is on thy account that I lost the glory which I enjoyed in Heaven among the angels of light. It is on thy account that I was expelled from Heaven and hurled down to earth!"

"How am I guilty of thy fall?" asked Adam.

"Because," replied Sammael, "when thou wast created and God had breathed the spirit of life in thee and thou wast made in the image of God, the angel Michael brought thee among the celestials and commanded them to pay homage to thee. 'Worship the image of God,' he said, 'and prostrate yourselves before him.' Michael himself worshipped thee, and all the other angels followed his example. He thereupon called me and said: 'Worship the image of God!' But I replied: 'I will not worship Adam, for he is younger than I am and inferior to me. It is for him to worship me, for was I not created long before him?'[1] And when the other angels heard my words they, too, refused to worship thee. Thereupon Michael said: 'If thou wilt not worship Adam, the anger of the Lord will fall upon thee.' But I was arrogant

[1] Raimund Martin, *Pugio Fidei*, ed. Lips., p. 536, quoted from *Midrash of Rabbi Moses ha-Darshan*. See, however, Ginzberg, *Die Haggada bei den Kirchenvätern und in der apokryphischen Literatur, Monatsschrift*, Vol. 43, p. 151-152.

and exclaimed: ' If He will grow angry with me, I will raise my seat above the stars of Heaven and be like the Creator Himself.' Thereupon God grew angry with me and with all the angels who followed me, and expelled us from Heaven, from among the angels of light. And thus it was that on thy account we lost our former splendour and glory, and were expelled from Heaven. When we saw thee so happy, living in Eden, our envy and fury grew even stronger, and we decided to deprive thee of thy joy and glory. I, therefore, approached thy wife and persuaded her to partake of the forbidden fruit, so that thou, too, wast deprived of thy glory, as I had been deprived of mine." Thus spoke Sammael, and Adam, on hearing his words, wept aloud. " Lord of the Universe!" he prayed, " save me from this arch-enemy who is trying to lead my soul into perdition." Sammael vanished, and Adam continued to do his penance, remaining in the water for forty days.[1]

Thereupon Eve said to her spouse: " My lord, thou shalt remain alive, because thou didst not commit either the first or the second transgression, but I am very guilty and ought to die." And Eve went out towards the west where she mourned and wept. But her time came near to give birth to a child, and her suffering and pains were great, and she travailed much. She prayed to the Lord to have mercy upon her, but her prayers were not heard. " Who will bring the tidings to my spouse," thought Eve, in her distress. And she thus addressed the heavenly lights: " When ye travel east, bring the news to my husband and inform him of my distress." Adam heard Eve's lament and came to see her. " Thy arrival, my lord," said Eve, " has gladdened my heart, and now pray to the Lord that He may assuage my suffering." Adam was sorry in his heart and suffered much for her sake, and when he saw the strait in which Eve was, he arose and

---

[1] See *Pirke de Rabbi Eliezer*, Ch. 20, where it is said: "He went into the waters of Gihon and fasted seven weeks of days until his body became like a sieve." See also Ginzberg, p. 218. A similar legend is related by Tabari and Ibn el-Atir. See Grünbaum, *loc. cit.*, p. 66.

prayed to the Lord, and lo, twelve angels appeared and one
of them, the angel Michael, touched Eve's face and said:
" Blessed be thou, Eve, the prayers of thy spouse have found
favour with the Most High and He has sent me to thee to
bring thee out of thy distress." Thereupon Eve gave birth
to a son whose countenance was radiant and shining. The
child at once rose up and brought a reed to his mother, and
they called his name Cain.[1] Adam then took his wife and
child and travelled east. Soon the angel Michael came and
brought different kinds of seeds to Adam, and taught him
how to till the ground and cultivate the earth so that it should
bear fruit. Then Eve bore another son whom they called
Habel.

Now one day, Eve awoke and told Adam the dream she
had, and said as follows: " My lord, I saw in a dream by
night, that the blood of our son Habel was poured into the
hand of our son Cain, which he drank and swallowed, and
therefore I was sad at heart." When Adam heard this he
said: " Woe unto us, I fear that Cain will slay Habel; let
us therefore make Cain a tiller of the soil and Habel a shepherd,
so that they may live apart." Thereupon Adam begat a
son whom he named Seth, and many other sons.

When Adam was nine hundred and thirty years old he
fell sick and he knew that his end was near. He called out
and said: " Let all my sons gather round me so that I may
behold them, speak to them and bless them before I die."
All the sons of Adam gathered round their father near the
place where they used to worship the Creator of the Universe.
And they asked him and said: " O our father, how is it with
thee and why dost thou lie upon thy bed?" Adam made
answer: " My sons, I am sick and suffer greatly." Then
Seth, his son, said unto him: " O my father, perhaps thou
cravest for the delightful fruit of Paradise which thou didst

[1] *Kanah* in Hebrew means reed. See *Genesis*, 4, 1.

eat, and because of that craving thou art so sorrowful and sick. If this be so, tell me, my sire, and I will go near the gates of Paradise. I will place dust upon my head, and loudly lament before the Garden of Eden and beseech the Lord. Perchance the Lord will hear the prayer of His servant, and send His angel to give me of the fruit after which thy heart desires." But Adam made answer: " I do not crave for the fruit of Paradise, but great pains and weakness beset me." " And what is pain, O my father?" asked Seth; " I do not know it, so tell us about it and do not hide it from us."

Then Adam said unto his sons: " Hear me, my sons. When God created me and your mother Eve, he placed us in Paradise, and He gave me the command to taste, eat, and enjoy all the fruits of the garden, but of the tree of knowledge between good and evil He commanded me not to taste. It so happened that God had given one part of the garden to me and the other to your mother; the fruits of the eastern and northern corners He gave to me, but the fruits of the southern and western corners He gave to you mother. Then God, the Creator, set two angels as our guardians, but an hour came when the angels left us to go and render homage before the Creator. Seeing that the angels had departed, the enemy, Satan, availed himself of this opportunity and came and conversed with your mother, seduced her and made her eat of the forbidden tree. When she had eaten of it, God was angry with me, and He spoke to me and said: ' Forasmuch as thou hast transgressed My command and not listened to My words, I will bring upon thy flesh many woes, seventy in number, pains of the head and afflictions of the eyes and ears, and such woes will befall all thy members down to the soles of thy feet.' "

When Adam had said all this to his sons he was seized with great pains, and he called aloud and said: " What shall I do, who am beset with such pains and woes?" And when

Eve saw her sire cry, she, too, wept bitterly, and said unto God: " O my God, give me all his woes and suffering, for it is I who transgressed." To Adam she said: " My sire, give me half of thy woes and suffering, for it is on my account that thou hast fallen into guilt." But Adam said unto Eve: " Do thou arise, my wife, and go with our son Seth near the garden and cast dust upon your heads and prostrate yourselves before the Lord and lament and beseech. Perchance He will have pity on me and send His angel to the tree of mercy from which proceedeth the oil of life, and give some of it to you that you may anoint my person therewith and that my pains may cease."

Seth and his mother at once arose and went near the garden. And when they were in the road, a beast suddenly appeared and beholding Seth it fell upon him and bit him. This beast was the serpent. Eve wept bitterly and said: " Woe to me, who am so unfortunate; I am cursed, for I have disobeyed the commands of the Lord and not kept the observance of His word." Looking at the serpent, she said: " Cursed beast, art thou not afraid to wage war against and throw thyself upon the image of God? Why did thy teeth bite him?" Then the serpent called out and replied in a human voice: " Eve, tell me why didst thou open thy mouth to eat of the fruit of the tree, of which God commanded you not to eat. Now thou canst not bear when I begin to accuse thee, but it is not from me that there was the beginning of evil." Thereupon Seth said to the beast: " Shut thy mouth and be silent, thou cursed enemy of truth, thou seducer; hold off from the image of God, until the day when the Lord will call thee to judgment." But the wild beast said unto Seth: " Behold, I stand aloof, as thou sayest, and hold off from the image of God." Then the beast let Seth go.

Thereupon Seth and his mother Eve went nigh to Paradise for the oil of pity wherewith to anoint Adam who was sick. When they reached the gates of Paradise they strewed dust upon their heads, prostrated themselves, and wept bitterly. They lamented and prayed to the Lord to have mercy upon Adam and to send His ministering angel who would give them oil from the tree of pity. Thus they remained for many hours, and lo, the angel Michael appeared and thus he spoke: " I have been sent by the Lord of the Universe, and I tell thee, Seth, to cease thy weeping and praying and not to worry concerning the oil from the tree of compassion wherewith to anoint thy father Adam. For I tell thee that in the present thou wilt not receive it. Go, therefore, Seth, to thy father, whose earthly life is now at an end. After six days his soul will leave his body; and when this will have happened thou shalt behold great wonders in Heaven and upon earth." When the angel of the Lord had said this, he left them and ascended to Heaven.

Then Eve and Seth returned to Adam who was lying sick. They told him of what had befallen them and how they had met the serpent who had bitten Seth. And Adam said to Eve: " What hast thou done unto me! Thou hast brought great suffering upon us and upon our whole race. Now when I am no more, tell our sons what thou hast done, for those who will come after us will curse us and say: ' Our first parents have brought all suffering upon us.' " When Eve heard this, she began to weep and lament bitterly.

EVE'S STORY OF THE FALL

Thereupon Eve said to her sons:

" Children, I will relate unto you how the enemy and adversary seduced us and robbed us of our bliss and delight and the Garden of Eden. When we dwelt in Paradise all the male animals were placed under you father's supervision in the north-eastern corner, whilst the female animals were under my supervision in the south-western corner. One day the adversary, who is Satan, came into the domain of your father where he found the serpent whom he approached, and thus he spoke: ' I hear that thou art wiser than all the other animals, and I will reveal unto thee what is in my mind. Thou art greater and wiser than all the other animals and yet thou dost worship one who is inferior to thee. Why dost thou feed upon grass, whilst Adam and Eve are partaking of heavenly food, and of the fruit of Paradise? Come, let us bring about that Adam be driven out of Paradise on account of his wife, even as we have been expelled from Heaven on his account.'

" Said the serpent to Satan: ' I fear to do this thing, for the Lord will be wroth with me.'

" ' Fear not,' said Satan, ' for thou wilt only be a vessel unto me,[1] and it is I who will deceive them by thy mouth through which I will speak and ensnare them.'

" Thereupon the serpent came and hung himself from the wall of the garden. When the angels, our guardians, went forth and ascended to Heaven to do homage to God, Satan at once took the form of an angel of light, and sang songs of praise. Looking up, I beheld him on the wall of the garden. He then said to me: ' Art thou Eve?' and I replied: ' Yes, I am.' ' And what mayest thou be doing in Paradise?' he asked. And I said to him: ' God placed us here to guard it and to eat of the fruit of its trees.' He then said to me: ' Ye do well, but ye do not eat of the trees which are in this garden.' ' It is not so,' I replied; ' for we eat of all the trees, except of a single tree which is in the middle of the garden, concerning which God commanded us not to eat of it, lest we die with death.' Thereupon the serpent said to me: ' Verily, my soul is full of sorrow because of thee, Eve, for thou and thy spouse are as ignorant as the cattle, and I will not leave thee in ignorance. Come and eat of the fruit of this tree and

[1] Cf. *Pirke de Rabbi Eliezer*, Ch. 13.

thou wilt forthwith know the power and worth of this tree.'
Thus spake the serpent, but I replied: 'I fear lest the Lord
be wroth with me, even as He commanded us.' But the serpent
replied: 'Fear not, Eve, for when thou shalt eat of the fruit
of this tree, thine eyes shall be opened, and ye, thy spouse
and thyself, shall become like Gods, knowing what is good
and evil. God knew that ye shall become like God, if ye eat
of the fruit of this tree, and out of jealousy He forbade ye to
eat thereof.'[1] And I lifted up mine eyes and saw the glory
of the tree. 'It is pleasant to behold,' said I, 'but I fear to
partake of its fruit.'

"'I will give it to thee,' replied the serpent. Thereupon
I opened the door of the garden of delight and the serpent
entered. He walked before me and I after him. After a little
while he turned to me and said: 'Swear unto me that when
thou hast eaten of the fruit of this tree, thou wilt also give to
thy husband to eat of the same.' 'I know not how to swear,'
I replied, 'but I will say whatsoever I know. On the Throne
of Glory, on the Cherubim, and on the tree of life, I swear to
thee that when I have eaten of the fruit of the tree, I will also
give to my husband to eat thereof.' And when the serpent
heard my oath he climbed up the tree and placed the poison
of his wickedness, that is desire, in the fruit.[2] He thereupon
bent the branches down to the earth, and I took of the fruit
and ate it. Mine eyes were at once opened, and I knew that
I was naked, divested of the righteousness with which I had
clad myself. Bitterly did I weep, saying unto the serpent:
'Why hast thou done this unto me, and thus deprived me of
my glory?' I also wept, because I remembered the oath I had
taken to give of the fruit to my husband. The serpent went
down from the tree and vanished, and I went about in the
garden to search for leaves wherewith to cover my shame.

[1] Cf. *Pirke de Rabbi Eliezer*, Ch. 13.
[2] See *Emek hamelekh*, fol. 23c—where it is said that on eating the fruit, Eve felt in herself
the poison of original sin, or *yezer hazā* (evil inclination).

There were none, for all the leaves upon the trees had disappeared, except those of the fig tree, and it was of the fruit of the fig tree that I had eaten.[1] I took the leaves and made a girdle to hide my nakedness. Thereupon I called your father and said : ' My lord, where art thou, come and I will show thee a wonderful thing and reveal unto thee a secret.' And I persuaded him to eat of the fruit of the tree, for Satan spoke out of my mouth. In the hour when your father had eaten the forbidden fruit, we heard the angel Michael sounding his trumpet and calling to all the angels: ' Come ye down, all angels, into the garden to hear the judgment by which the Lord will judge Adam.'

" Thereupon the Lord commanded His angels to drive us out of the garden. Your father then prayed to the Lord and said: ' O Lord of the Universe, remit unto me my transgressions and bestow on me of the fruit from the tree of life, that I may eat thereof before I go forth from the garden.' But the Lord replied: ' In the present thou shalt not receive of the fruit from the tree of life, for I have commanded the Cherubim with the flaming sword to guard the path and not allow thee to eat thereof and abide deathless for ever. But when, driven out of Paradise, thou wilt keep away from wickedness and be ready to die, when thy time comes, then, on the day of resurrection, I will raise thee up and give thee of the fruit from the tree of life and thou shalt abide deathless for ever.' We went forth from the garden and were placed on this earth."

Thus spoke Eve to her children, and wept bitterly, whilst Adam lay before them, afflicted in his sickness.

After six days, as the archangel Michael had foretold, Adam died. The sun and moon and stars lost their radiance and grew dark for seven days. Adam's soul was carried up in a fiery chariot, and angels went before the chariot. Then all

---

[1] Cf. *Genesis Rabba*, 15; *Midrash Haggadol, Genesis*, col. 90.

the angels prostrated themselves before the Throne of Glory, and beseeched the Lord to vouchsafe remission to Adam. " O Lord of the Universe," they prayed, " take pity on Adam who is Thine image and was fashioned by Thine own spotless hand."

And lo, the angel Michael appeared before the weeping Eve and the sorrowing Seth, and thus he spoke: " Arise now from the corpse of your father and husband, for God has taken pity on him who was fashioned in the image of the Lord." Thereupon one of the archangels blew his trumpet, and all the ministering angels called aloud: " Blessed is the glory of the Lord, for He has taken pity upon Adam." And Seth saw how God, having taken the soul of Adam, gave him into the hands of Michael saying: " Bear him unto the third heaven, and let him repose there until the great and terrible day, when I will change his suffering into joy."

Thereupon angels came down from Heaven and descended upon earth, and came to the spot where the body of Adam was lying. And the voice from the Throne of Glory called out: " O Adam, hadst thou not transgressed the commandment I gave unto thee, thine adversary, who has brought thee to such a state, would not rejoice now. But I say unto thee that I will turn the rejoicing of the enemy into sorrow, and thy sorrow into rejoicing." Then God commanded the angels Michael and Uriel to spread out fine linen cloths and enfold the body of Adam and to bury him, and the angels Michael and Uriel did as the Lord had commanded them. Thereupon they said unto Seth: " Thus shalt thou bury every man who shall die until the great day of the resurrection."

Six days after Adam's death, Eve, feeling that her end was near, gathered about her all her sons and daughters, and she prayed to the Lord not to separate her body from the body of Adam, her spouse, but to let her be near him, even as she had been together with him during their lives, and to let her be buried by the side of Adam from whose bones the Lord did fashion her.   Thereupon she enjoined her children to erect two slabs of clay and stone, and write on them the names and history of herself and of Adam. " For I have been informed by the angel Michael," she said, " that God has decided to bring upon the world a destructive fire and a flood. These slabs of clay and stone alone will escape destruction." Thus spoke Eve and passed away six days after the death of Adam. The angels buried her by the side of Adam, in the neighbour-hood of Paradise. Then the angel Michael appeared to Seth and said: " Do not mourn more than six days for thy dead, and rest and rejoice on the seventh, for on that day, which is the symbol of resurrection, God and His angels will receive the soul freed from all earthly matter." [1]

In Moslem legend the story of Adam's life after his fall and his expulsion from Eden runs as follows: After Adam had fallen he was excessively grieved and penitent, and his beard grew. He was greatly perturbed at this growth of hair upon his chin, and a voice from Heaven called out and said: " Be not grieved, O Adam, for the beard is man's ornament upon earth where it distinguishes him from the weak woman." And Adam's tears flowed abundantly, and not only did beasts and birds drink freely, but the tears that dropped from his eyes, of him who had partaken of the fruit of Paradise, flowed into the earth, producing gum-bearing trees and fragrant plants. And Eve, too, shed many tears in her great sorrow. Her tears, when falling into the sea, were transformed into costly pearls, and into fragrant and beautiful flowers when they sank into earth. Both Adam and Eve wept bitterly over the loss of the Garden of Eden, and they wailed so loud that their cries were borne from one to the other on the wings of

[1] See for the above: *Vita Adae et Evae*, edit. W. Meyer; C. Fuchs, *Das Leben Adams und Evas*, in Kautzsch, *Die Apokryphen*, Vol. II, pp. 506 ff. Tischendorf. *Apocalypses Apocryphae, Apocalypsis Moses*, 1866; Conybeare, *On the Apocalypse of Moses*, J.Q.R., Vol. VII, pp. 219 ff.

the east and west winds. And when they heard each other
weep, their sorrow increased.[1]

Eve clasped her hands above her head, whilst Adam put
his right hand under his beard. Then the tears poured
afresh out of the eyes of our first parent that they formed two
rivers, the tears out of the right eye the river Euphrates and
the tears out of the left the river Tigris. And all nature wept
with Adam, and the beasts and birds, who had hitherto shunned
him on account of his sin, were moved by his wailing and his
tears, and came to him to shôw him pity.

But the locusts were the first to arrive, because they had
been created from the handful of earth left over after Adam had
been created. The locusts, therefore, are privileged among
other animals. There are seven thousand kinds of them in
all colours and shapes, and they are ruled by a king whom
God commands and sends out whenever He wishes to punish
and destroy a sinful nation such as the Egyptians under Pharaoh.
The black characters on the locusts' wings signify in Hebrew:
God is one; He overcometh the mightiest; the locusts form
a portion of His hosts which He frequently sends out against
the wicked.

All nature was thus full of wailing and lamentation, for
all nature wailed and lamented with Adam, from the smallest,
almost invisible, insect to the angel who holds the earth in
one hand. Thereupon God sent his angel Gabriel unto Adam,
and he taught him how to cry and pray for forgiveness with
a penitent heart. (He was to say: 'There is no God but Thou;
forgive me for the sake of Mohammed, the great and last
prophet, whose name is engraved on Thy throne.') When
Adam had spoken these words with a penitent heart, the
gates of Heaven opened, and the angel Gabriel cried out:
" O Adam! God has accepted thy penitence; pray unto
Him alone and He will grant thy prayers and give thee all

[1] Weil, *Biblische Legenden der Muselmänner*, pp. 29-38.

that thou desirest, even thy return to Paradise, after a certain time." And Adam prayed unto God and said: " O Lord, protect me from further intrigues of mine enemy Iblis." And a voice from Heaven answered him: " Speak continually the words: ' There is no God but God;' these words will wound Iblis even like a poisoned arrow." And Adam asked: " Lord, will not the food and drink provided for me by this earth lead me into sin?" And the voice from Heaven again replied: " Drink water and eat only clean beasts, beasts which have been killed in the name of God, and build mosques for thy dwellings, and then Iblis will have no power over thee." But Adam still continued to query; " And if Iblis torments me at night with evil thoughts and dreams?" " Rise from thy couch," was the answer, " and pray." " O Lord," Adam continued, " how shall I ever be able to distinguish between good and evil?" And the Eternal replied unto him: " I will vouchsafe unto thee My guidance, and two angels shall always dwell in thy heart; they will warn thee against evil and encourage thee to do good." And Adam once more prayed: " O Lord! assure me also of Thy grace against future sin!" But the Eternal replied: " That thou canst only obtain by good works. But this I can promise thee, however, that evil shall be punished one fold, good shall be rewarded ten fold." [1]

In the meantime the angel Michael was sent to Eve to announce to her the mercy and grace of God. And Eve asked the angel: " With what weapons shall I, who am feeble and frail, lacking strength of heart and mind, fight against sin?" Spake the archangel Michael: " God has endowed thee with shamefacedness which will serve thee as weapon. And just as man is able to restrain his passions by virtue of his faith, so thou mayest conquer them by this shamefacedness." " And what," queried Eve, " will protect me against the strength of man who is stronger and more vigorous than I am, both

[1] Weil, *loc. cit.*

in body and in mind, and who will, moreover, be always privileged by the laws made by man?" " I have placed in the heart of man," answered Michael, " love and the feeling of compassion, and these will protect thee in future against man's brute force."

When Iblis saw the mercy vouchsafed to Adam and to Eve by the Almighty, his courage grew and he dared to implore the grace of God for himself, and to entreat the Almighty to ameliorate his lot. And the Creator decreed that Iblis should not be tormented in Hell until the day of resurrection, and that he should exercise unlimited power over all the sinners and the wicked who should reject the word of God.

" And where, O Lord," queried Iblis, " shall I dwell in the meantime?"

" Among ruins, in tombs, and in many other unclean places shunned by men!"

" And what will be my nourishment?" asked Iblis.

" All that is killed in the name of idols."

" And what will I drink when I am thirsty?"

" Wine and other intoxicating liquors."

" And in my hours of idleness what will be my occupation?"

" Music, dancing, and song."

" And what is my destiny?"

" The curse of God until the day of judgment."

" And how," asked Iblis, " am I to fight against man who will have received Thy revelation and to whom Thou hast given two angels for his protection?"

" Thy offspring," was the reply, " will be more numerous than the offspring of man, for to every man born in this world, seven evil spirits will come into the world." [1]

And the Creator then made a covenant with the progeny of Adam. He touched Adam's back, and from it crept

[1] Weil, *loc. cit.*

out all the generations which were to be born until the end of days. They were about the size of ants, and they came and ranged themselves on his right and on his left. And God said unto Adam: " All the disobedient of thy children, if they remain obstinate, will be condemned to Hell, but the believers shall enjoy eternal bliss in Paradise." " So be it," said Adam. And thus shall it be on the day of resurrection, when Adam will call every one by his name and pass sentence according to merit. And then God again touched Adam's neck and all his posterity returned into it again.[1]

ADAM AND EVE DO PENANCE

Þanne seyde Adam wiþ ruful ble:
Eue, let swiche wordis be,
   Þat god vs eft noȝt werye!
Eue, þow were mad of me,
Þerfore in no wyse how it be
   Þe wile y noȝt derye.

Bote rys, and go we eft wiþ mod
For to seken vs sum fod,
   Þat we ne deye for mys!
Þeȝ souȝten aboute wiþ sory mynde,
Bote swich myȝte þeȝ, nowher fynde
   As hy hadden in paradys.

Bote þer þeȝ founden such mete
As bestis and briddes ete.
   Adam tolde Eue his þoȝte:
Þis mete god ȝaf bestis to.
Go we sorwen and nomen also
   In his siȝt þat vs wroȝte.

And for oure trespas do penaunce,
Fourty dayes wiþouten distaunce,
   And praye god, kyng of riȝt,

[1] Weil, *loc. cit.*

Gif he vs wolde forȝeuen his mod,
And granten vs som lyues fod,
  Wherwiþ we lyuen myȝt.

Þus to Adam þo seide Eue:
Tel me, lord, at wordis breue,
  What is penaunce to say?
And how mowe we penaunce do?
Þat we namore byholen him to
  Þan we fulfelle may:

In aunter ȝif oure god dere
Wile noȝt heren oure preyere
  Bote turne his face fro vs,
For þat we oure penaunce breke.
Þan anon gan Adam speke
  And seide to Eue riȝt þus:

Fourty dayes þow myȝt do,
And y rede þow do so,
  For oure synnes sake,
And y fourty and seuene wile fulfelle,
Gif god wile of his guod wille
  On vs eny mercy take:

For on þe seuende day god made ende,
Of his work guod and hende
  He restyde him þat day.
Þerfore rys and tak a stone,
To Tygre flod gynne þow gon,
  And do as y þe say:

Vppon þat ston loke þat þow stonde,
Vp to þe nekke in þe stronde,
  Til fourty dayes don be,
Of þy mouth let no word reke—
We be noȝt worþy to god to speke:
  Oure lippes vnclene be,

For þeӡ byten þe appel aӡens his steuene,
And y shel fourty dayes and seuene
  Be in þe fflom Jordon,
Gif ӡit oure lord aboue þe sky
On vs wile haue eny mercy
  For oure mochel mon.

Canticum Creatione, MS. Trin. Coll., Oxford, 57, fol. 156
(written in 1375). See C. Horstmann, *Sammlung
altenglischer Legenden*, 1878, pp. 125–126.

CHAPTER XVI

The Quarrel of the Brothers

Cain and Abel—The jealousy of Cain—The twin sisters—The burial of Abel—The two ravens—The story of the fratricide in Christian and Mohammedan literature—Another version of the burial of Abel—The repentance of Cain—Cain is a son of Sammael—The death of Cain—His descendants—Cain was the first to build a city—Seth, into whom the soul of Abel passes—The Sethites and the Cainites—The sons of God and the daughters of man—The Nephilim, or the Fallen—The story of Seth in Christian and Mohammedan literature—Quotation from Suidas—Alexander the Great on the sepulchre of Cainan—God decides to destroy the world by water.

CAIN and Abel, the two sons of Adam and Eve, did not live in peace, but always quarrelled and never could agree, for whatever one brother had the other, too, wanted it at once. Abel, therefore, said unto his elder brother: " Let us divide our property, and thus we will live in peace, take thou the earth and all that is fixed, whilst I will take all the moveable property." But Cain was of a wicked disposition, and black envy and hatred always dwelt in his heart. He persistently persecuted his gentle brother and gave him no rest. " The earth is mine," he exclaimed one day, " and the plains are mine and I forbid thee to stand on my property." Greatly astonished at such a command from his brother, Abel meekly ran up the hills there to rest. But Cain called after him: " And the hills? Are not the hills mine too, for the whole earth belongs to me." [1] Thus the quarrel began.

One day the flock of Abel came to pasture near the ground

---

[1] See Bin Gorion, *loc. cit.* pp. 137 and 372; *Genesis Rabba*, 22.

which Cain was ploughing, and he bade his brother leave
the spot at once. " But thou, too," said Abel, " art using my
property. Hast thou not taken the skins of my sheep and
the wool of their fleeces and used them for thy clothing?
Have I ever grudged thee anything from my possessions?" But
Cain grew even more furious at the gentle words of Abel and
made up his mind to kill his brother.[1]

Cain, according to Rabbinic legend, was not the son of
Adam, but the child of Sammael, the beautiful, the resplendent
who had been hurled from Heaven into the region of darkness.
He had seduced Eve, and the son she bore, Cain, was not like
the earthly beings, but like unto the inmates of Heaven.[2]

Now Cain was jealous of his brother Abel, not only because
the latter's offering had been accepted and his own abhorred,
but because Abel's twin sister was the most beautiful of women,
and Cain desired her in his heart. He, therefore, conceived
the plan of slaying his brother Abel and of taking his twin
sister from him.[3]

When the deed had been accomplished, Adam and Eve
were sitting, mourning and weeping, in their great sadness
and grief of having lost Abel, their son. But they were yet
unaccustomed to burial, and did not know what to do with
the body. The dog which had guarded Abel's flock was still
guarding his master's dead body from all the beasts in the
field and all the fowls of the heavens. Now the Lord decided
to teach Adam what to do with the body. A raven had just fallen
dead by the side of Adam, and behold, another raven came,
took its fellow, dug it in the earth and buried it. And Adam
watched and wondered and said unto himself: " I will act
like this raven did act."[4] And he took the corpse of Abel,
dug a hole in the earth and buried it. The ravens who had

[1] Sepher Hajashar.
[2] Pirke de Rabbi Eliezer, Ch. 21, and Ch. 22. See also Targum Jerushalmi, Genesis 4, 1;
5, 3; Yalkut Shimeoni, Genesis, § 29 and § 35.   [3] Pirke de Rabbi Eliezer, Ch. 21.
[4] Pirke de Rabbi Eliezer, Ch. 21, Yalkut Shimeoni, Prov. § 963.

done the bidding of the Lord and taught man how to bury his dead received a good reward from the Maker of the Universe, for when his young ones cry the Almighty provideth their sustenance without lack.[1]

The legends relating to the quarrel between the two brothers are also found in Christian as well as in Mohammedan sources. Thus Eutychius, Patriarch of Alexandria, relates in his *Annales* the following story: After their sin and disobedience to the command of God, Adam and Eve were expelled from Paradise on Friday at the ninth hour. They were sent to a mountain in India and commanded to produce children and increase and multiply upon the earth. Thus it came to pass that Eve bore a boy named Cain and his twin sister named Azrun. Sometime afterwards Eve again gave birth to twins, a boy named Abel and a girl named Owain, or in Greek Laphura. Azrun, Cain's twin sister, was much prettier than Owain, Abel's twin sister. Now when the children had grown up, Adam said to Eve: " Cain shall marry Owain who was born with Abel, and Abel shall marry Azrun who is Cain's twin sister, for they should not marry their own twin sisters." Thus spoke Adam, but Cain grew angry when he heard these words of his father: " I will marry my own twin sister," he said to his mother, " and Abel will marry his."

Thereupon Adam said to his sons: " Take of the fruit of the earth and of the young of the sheep, and ascend ye the top of this holy mountain, there to offer the best and choicest to God." The two brothers did as their father bade them, and Abel indeed offered the best and fattest of his first born lambs. But when they were ascending the top of the mountain, Sammael, or Satan, came and whispered to Cain to kill his brother, so as to get rid of him and thus be free to marry his own twin sister Azrun. As his oblation had not been

---

[1] *Pirke de Rabbi Eliezer*, Ch. 21; *Midrash Haggadol*, col. 117; *Genesis Rabba*, 22, where another story is given of Abel being buried by Cain himself.

accepted by God, Cain grew even more enraged against his brother and made up his mind to kill him.

When they were descending the mountain, he rushed upon his brother and hurling a stone at his head killed him. For one hundred years Adam and Eve bewailed the death of their son Abel, whilst Cain had been cast out into the land of Nod. He carried off, however, his sister Azrun with him.[1]

The same legend is told in Moslem tradition. Thus we read in the *Chronicle of Tabari* that Adam and Eve had many children, and that every time that Eve bore she bare twins, one male and the other female. Kabil, or Cain, and his twin sister were born when Adam and Eve still dwelt in Paradise, whilst Habil, or Abel, and his twin sister were born after the expulsion of Adam and Eve from Paradise. Now it was the wish of Adam that each of the brothers, when he was old enough to marry, should take to wife the twin sister of his brother. But the twin sister of Cain was of surpassing beauty, and Cain was dissatisfied. Thereupon Adam said to his sons: " Go ye, my sons, and sacrifice to the Lord, and he whose sacrifice is accepted, shall marry the beautiful girl."

Abel, being a shepherd, took the fattest of the sheep, bore it to the place of sacrifice and offered it to God. Cain, however, who was a tiller of the soil, took only the poorest sheaf of corn he could find and placed it upon the altar. Thereupon a fire descended from Heaven and consumed the offering of Abel, whilst the sheaf of corn offered by Cain remained untouched. Adam then gave the maiden to Abel as wife, and Cain was greatly vexed. He made up his mind to kill his brother, and one day, when Abel was asleep on the summit of a mountain, he took a stone and crushed his brother's head. He threw the corpse upon his back and walked about with it, not knowing what to do with it. One day, however, he saw two crows fighting and one killing the other. Thereupon the

---

[1] Eutychius, *Annales*, I, 14.

crow that had killed its companion dug a hole in the earth
and buried the dead crow. When Cain saw this, he thought:
" I, too, will lay the corpse of my brother in the ground and
hide it." [1]

According to the *Pirke de Rabbi Eliezer*, it was Cain
himself who had buried his brother's corpse, so as to hide
what he had done from the eye of God, not knowing that
God can see everything. And when the Lord accused Cain
of the murder of his brother he exclaimed: " My iniquity
is too great to be atoned for, except by my brother rising
from the earth and slaying me, for my sin has no atonement." [2]
And this utterance was reckoned to him as repentance. The
Lord thereupon took one letter of the twenty-two letters of
the alphabet and put it upon Cain's arm, so that he should
not be killed. God had cursed Cain for his foul deed, but on
account of his repentance and his contrition, the symbol of
pardon was placed on his brow. Some say that it was a horn
which grew out of the midst of his forehead. And when Adam
met his son and seeing the token upon his brow, the symbol
of pardon, he wondered greatly and asked: " How hast thou
turned away the wrath of the Almighty?"

" By repentance and confession of my sin," replied Cain.

" Great is the virtue of repentance," cried Adam, " and I
knew it not. Had I known it, I might have altered my lot." [3]

And Cain wandered over the face of the earth, accompanied
by his wife, and at last settled in the land of Nod. But he did
not mend his ways, for the spirit of Sammael was in him.
He was not of Adam's seed, nor after his likeness, nor after
his image.[4] His soul was from Sammael, his body alone from
Eve. And all his children became demons of darkness, and
all his offspring rebels against their Maker. Cain himself
never changed his violent and passionate nature. He lived by

---

[1] *Chronique de Tabari*; Abulfeda, *Historia Ante-Islamica*, pp. 12–15. A similar story is told
by Masudi and Yakubi. See Grünbaum, *loc. cit.*, p. 69.
[2] *Pirke de Rabbi Eliezer*, Ch. 21.   [3] *Genesis Rabba*, 22.   [4] *Pirke de Rabbi Eliezer*, Ch. 22.

robbery and rapine and encouraged his children to lead a similar life. They corrupted the primitive simplicity of men by introducing weights and measures, by placing boundaries and walling cities.[1] Cain was at last killed by Lamech who once exclaimed to his two wives Adah and Zillah: " For I have slain a man to my wounding, and a young man to my hurt." [2] Lamech, who belonged to the seventh generation after Cain, had two wives, named Adah and Zillah. Zillah was barren till in her old age she bare Tubal-Cain and his sister Naamah. Now it came to pass that Lamech became blind in his old age and was led about by his boy Tubal-Cain. One day Tubal-Cain saw in the distance their great ancestor Cain. From the horn upon the latter's forehead, the boy supposed that it was a wild beast and he hastily exclaimed: " Father, span thy bow and shoot the wild beast." Blind Lamech quickly complied with the boy's request, discharged his arrow and killed his great-ancestor Cain. When at last he was informed by Tubal-Cain of their error and that he had in reality slain his ancestor Cain, Lamech smote his hands together in his despair, and in so doing accidentally struck his own son and killed him. And his wives were very wroth with him.[3]

In this song of Lamech, in which some authors saw a song of triumph, others see a song of menace, and others again an expression of remorse and penitence, the blind man thus indicating his deed by which he had killed both Cain and Tubal-Cain.

This legend of the deed of Lamech was known to St. Jerome, who relates that in his day there existed a tradition among the Jews, accepted, too, by certain of the Christians, to the effect that Lamech had killed Cain by accident.[4]

---

[1] Josephus, *Antiquities*, 1, 2.   [2] *Genesis*, 4, 24.
[3] *Tanchuma* to *Genesis*, 4, 14; *Rashi* to *Genesis*, 4, 23; *Yalkut, Genesis*, § 38; *Sepher Hajashar. Shalsheleth Hakkabbala.* See also Grünbaum, *Neue Beiträge zur semitischen Sagenkunde*, p. 70.
[4] St. Jerome, *Epist.* 26, *ad Damasum.* See also Lenormant, *Les Origines de l'Histoire,* 1, p. 188.

The offspring of Cain were very wicked indeed, for from him descended all the generations who sin against the Lord and rebel against the commands of the Creator. And the sons and daughters who descended from Cain defiled themselves with immorality, and their wickedness was great on the earth. The daughters of the generations of Cain were walking about like harlots, having neither modesty nor shame, and with painted eyes and naked flesh they led astray not only mortal men, but also the angels who had fallen from Heaven and walked amongst men. They saw the daughters of man of the generations of Cain, that they were fair, and they went astray after them.

It is also related that Cain knew his wife Qualmana and she bore him a son named Enoch. He thereupon built a city and called it Enoch after the name of his son. Cain was thus the first to build a city, to surround it with a wall and to dig trenches.[1] He was the first to build a city and to surround it with a wall, because he was afraid of his enemies. To this city Cain used to entice people and there rob and plunder them. It has rightly been pointed out by Lenormant,[2] that the idea which associated the formation of a city with a fratricide is one of the ideas common to most nations, and may be traced almost everywhere. It begins with Cain and ends with Romulus, who laid the foundations of Rome in the blood of his brother Remus. This city became very corrupt, and its inhabitants were very wicked, as were all the descendants of Cain.

THE SETHITES AND THE CAINITES

Now after the death of Abel Eve bore another son unto Adam, who was named Seth. Into the body of Seth passed the soul of the righteous Abel, and the same soul passed afterwards into Moses.[3] Seth, majestic in appearance and very

---

[1] Gaster, *The Chronicles of Jerahmeel*, p. 50, Ch. 24.   [2] *Loc. cit.* Ch. 4.
[3] *Shnee Loukhoth*, quoted by Eisenmenger, *Entdecktes Judentum*, Vol. I, p. 645.

handsome, was instructed by the angels who taught him much wisdom. He knew what would take place in the world, knew that men would be very wicked and their iniquity grow, so that they would, in the end, be destroyed by a flood.

It was revealed to him that the earth would be destroyed first by water then by fire. Thereupon Seth, lest those things revealed to him should perish from the memory of man, set up two pillars, one of brick and one of stone and wrote thereon all that he knew and all the science which he nad acquired.[1] Seth married his twin sister named Azura, or, according to others, Noba, or Noraea.[2] He became the father of all the generations of the righteous. But the generations descended from Cain were all wicked. Among them were Tubal-Cain and his sister Naamah. Naamah became afterwards one of the wives of Sammael, or, according to others, of Shomron, and bare unto him the demon Ashmedai.[3] Naamah invented all kinds of instruments for weaving silk, and was the first to play upon musical instruments in honour of the idols.[4]

Now, as long as Adam was still alive, the sons of Seth had never intermarried with the daughters of Cain. The former dwelt in the mountains not far from the Garden of Eden, whilst the latter lived in the fields of Damascus. But when Adam had died, the children of Seth, who were called the Sons of God, or the children of Elohim, grew wicked. They looked upon the daughters of man, or the seed of Cain, took wives from among them and begat the giants who peopled the earth in the days of Noah. It is thus from the descendants of Seth and the descendants of Cain that the giants came forth; wicked, corrupt, and haughty of spirit, they were swept away by the waters of the flood, and were also called the Nephilim, or the Fallen.[5] It has been pointed out that Seth is the

---

[1] Josephus, *Antiquities*, 1, 2.   [2] *Book of Jubilees*, 4, 11.
[3] See Hamburger, *Real-encyclopœdie für Bibel und Talmud*, Vol. II, *s.v. Ashmedai*.
[4] *Rashi* to *Genesis*, 4, 21; *Targum Jerushalmi* to *Genesis*, 4, 22.
[5] Gaster, *The Chronicles of Jerahmeel*, p. 52.

name of an Egyptian Sun deity, and subsequently identified
with Typhon. He was the chief god of the Hyksos or Shepherd
Kings.[1] Some of the legends contained in Talmudic and
Midrashic lore concerning Seth may be traced back to Egyptian
influence, who regarded Seth as the giver of light and civilization. Seth is also said to have dwelt in Heaven for forty
days and to have been instructed in the ethical law by the
angels. It was he who invented the art of writing, who gave
names to the five planets and divided time into months, weeks,
and years.[2]

The legends concerning Seth and the Sethians, and Cain
and the Cainites, play an important rôle not only among the
Jews, but also among Moslems, Samaritans, and Gnostic
Christians. Thus we read in Abulfaraj [3] that Seth discovered
letters and went to dwell upon Mount Hermon, where he
and his offspring served God and never associated with the
people of the land, abstaining to intermarry with them. It
is for this reason that the Sethites, or descendants of Seth,
were called the Sons of God.

This same idea, which, as has been pointed out, occurs
in the *Chronicles of Jerahmeel*,[4] is found in Suidas, under the
heading *Seth*, and in Christian pseudoepigraphic literature.
Thus Suidas writes: " The Sons of God went unto the
daughters of men, that is to say, the sons of Seth intermarried
with the daughters of Cain. Seth was called God in those
days, because he had discovered Hebrew letters, and also
the names of the stars. He was especially called so on account
of his great piety, so that he was the first to bear the name
of God." [5]

In other Christian sources it is related that the sons and
descendants of Seth lived upon the holy mountain, where
they led a life of piety and abstinence, pleasing to God. There

---

[1] J. Braun, *Naturgeschichte der Sage*, Vol. I, p. 264.
[2] See Fabricius, *Codex Pseudoepigraphicus, Vet. Test.*, Vol. I, pp. 141-147.
[3] *Historia Dynastiarum*, p. 5.   [4] Ch. 24.   [5] Suidas, *Lexicon, s.v. Seth*.

they heard the voices of the angels and their heavenly music, and joined in their praises of the Lord of the Universe. Later, however, in the days of Jared, the descendants of Seth began to lend an ear to the alluring songs of the seductive daughters of Cain who dwelt in the plain, at the foot of the mountain. Seduced by the alluring women, drawn by their song, many of the Sethites left the sacred mountain and descended into the plain. Here they saw women, attractive and shameless, their eyes painted like harlots, beautiful and walking about with naked flesh. Their passions were kindled, they desired them in sinful love and went astray with them.[1]

The mountain where dwelt the Sethites was called Hermon, because there they had made a covenant and sworn one to another to take wives from among the daughters of Cain.[2] Whilst, according to the *Pirke de Rabbi Eliezer*, and generally in Jewish tradition, the giants are considered to be the children of angels, who intermarried with the daughters of man, in the *Chronicles of Jerahmeel* they are the offspring from the sons of Seth and the daughters of Cain.[3] Gedalya Ibn Yachia, in his book *Shalsheleth Hakkabbala* (Chain of Tradition), explains, however, the Sons of God as the descendants of Seth. This opinion is also mentioned by Ibn Ezra and by Nachmanides in his Commentary.[4]

In the *Chronique de Tabari* we read that Seth was the greatest of the sons of Adam, that every day he made a pilgrimage to the Kaaba and ruled the world with equity. He and his followers waged a perpetual war against the giants, the sons of Kabil, or Cain. The Sethites dwelt upon a mountain, the Cainites in the plain. The former were allured by the songs sung to the playing of musical instruments invented by the Cainites. In spite of the injunction they had received

---

[1] Malan, *The Christian Book of Adam*, pp. 82-93; Eutychius, *Annales*, Vol. I, pp. 21-26; Bezold, *Die Schatzhöhle* (Cave of Treasures), p. 10.

[2] *Cedrenus*, ed. Bonn, 1, 19 (also in Migne, *Patrologia*, Vols. 121-122). See Grünbaum, *Neue Beiträge*, p. 73.

[3] *Pirke de Rabbi Eliezer*, Ch. 22; *Yalkut, Genesis*, § 44.   [4] Grünbaum, *loc. cit.*, p. 75.

from Adam to keep away from the daughters of Cain, who were very attractive, enhancing their beauty by various artificial devices, but very shameless and wicked, the Sethites at last came down from their mountain and fell.[1]

Yakubi also relates that in the days of Jared, the Sethites broke their oath, came down into the plain and sinned with the daughters of Cain.[2]

In one of his espistles, sent to his teacher Aristotle, Alexander the Great also wrote that in a province of India he had found men and women who lived on raw fish, and spoke a language very much like Greek. They informed him that in the islands there was the sepulchre of a most ancient king named Cainan, son of Enos, who knew that God would bring a flood in the days of Noah, wherefore he engraved all that was to take place on stone tables. Therein he had written that the ocean would overflow a third part of the world, an event which took place in the days of Enos, the son of Seth.[3]

And after the Sethites had intermarried with the Cainites, the earth was full of wickedness, and the Lord decided to destroy it by water.

THE PRAYER OF ABEL

Oh God!
Who made us, and Who breathed the breath of life
Within our nostrils, Who hath blessed us,
And spared, despite our father's sin, to make
His children all lost, as they might have been,
Had not Thy justice been so temper'd with
The mercy which is Thy delight, as to
Accord a pardon like a Paradise,
Compared with our great crimes: sole Lord of light!
Of good, and glory, and eternity;
Without Whom all were evil, and with Whom

---

[1] *Chronique de Tabari*, I, Ch. 34.   [2] Grünbaum, *loc. cit.*, p. 77.
[3] *Josippon* (Josephus Gorionides), ed. Amsterdam, 1771, Ch. 11, p. 33a; Fabricius, *Codex Pseudoepigraphicus, Vet. Test.*, Vol I, p. 157.

Nothing can err, except to some good end
Of Thine omnipotent benevolence—
Inscrutable, but still to be fulfill'd—
Accept from out Thy humble first of shepherd's
First of the first-born flocks—an offering,
In itself nothing—as what offering can be
Aught unto Thee?—but yet accept it for
The thanksgiving of him who spreads it in
The face of Thy high heaven, bowing his own
Even to the dust, of which he is, in honour
Of Thee, and of Thy name, for evermore!

Lord Byron—Cain a mystery, Act III, Scene 1.

THE REPENTANCE OF CAIN

My hand! 't is all red, and with—
What?
Where am I? alone! Where 's Abel? Where
Cain? Can it be that I am he? My brother,
Awake! Why liest thou so on the green earth?
'T is not the hour of slumber—why so pale?
What, hast thou!—thou wert full of life this morn!
Abel! I pray thee, mock me not! I smote
Too fiercely, but not fatally. Ah, why
Wouldst thou oppose me? This is mockery;
And only done to daunt me: 't was a blow—
And but a blow. Stir—stir—nay, only stir!
Why, so—that's well! thou breath'st! breathe upon me!
　　　　Oh, God! Oh, God!
The earth swims round me—What is this? 't is wet;
And yet there are no dews! 'T is blood—my blood—
My brother's and my own; and shed by me!
Then what have I further to do with life,
Since I have taken life from my own flesh?
But he cannot be dead!—Is silence death?
No, he will wake: then let me watch by him.
Life cannot be so slight, as to be quench'd
Thus quickly! he hath spoken to me since—

What shall I say to him? My brother!—No;
He will not answer to that name, for brethren
Smite not each other. Yet—yet—Speak to me;
Oh! for a word more of that gentle voice,
That I may bear to hear my own again.

Lord Byron—Cain, a mystery, Act III, Scene 1.

THE CURSE OF EVE

May all the curses
Of life be on him! and his agonies
Drive him forth over the wilderness, like us
From Eden, till his children do by him
As he did by his brother! May the swords
And wings of fiery cherubim pursue him
By day and night—snakes spring up in his path—
Earth's fruits be ashes in his mouth—the leaves
On which he lays his head to sleep be strew'd
With scorpions! May his dreams be of his victim!
His waking a continual dread of death!
May the clear rivers turn to blood as he
Stoops down to stain them with his raging lip!
May every element shun or change to him!
May he live in the pangs which others die with!
And death itself wax something worse than death
To him who first acquainted him with man!
Hence, fratricide, henceforth that word is *Cain*
Through all the coming myriads of mankind,
Who shall abhor thee, though thou wert their sire!
May the grass wither from thy feet! the woods
Deny thee shelter! earth a home! the dust
A grave! The sun his light! and Heaven her God!

Lord Byron—Cain, a mystery, Act III, Scene 1.

THE DEATH OF CAIN

LAMECH MISTOOK CAIN FOR A DEER

Lamech ledde long lif til ðan
ðat he wurð bisne, and haued a man
ðat ledde him ofte wudes ner,
To scheten after ðe wilde der;
Al-so he mistagte, also he schet,
And cain in ðe wude is let;
His knaþe wende it were a der.

An lamech droge is arwe ner,
And letet flegen of ðe streng,
Cain unwar(n)de it under-feng,
Grusnende, and strekende, and starf wið-ðan.
Lamech wið wreðe is knaþe nam,

Vn-bente is boge, and bet, and slog,
Til he fel dun on deders sevog.
Twin-wifing ant twin-manslagt,
Of his soule beð mikel hagt.

The Story of Genesis and Exodus (Early English Text Society),
Edited by Richard Morris, 1865, p. 14, l. 471–486.

THE DEATH OF ABEL

The seducer, with triumph in his look, remained near the dead. Elate with pride, he stretched his gigantic form to its full height, and his countenance was not less dreadful than the black pillars of smoke, arising from the half-consumed lumber of a lonely cottage, is to the inhabitants, who, returning from their peaceful labours, find all their conveniences, all their riches, the prey of the devouring flames. The seducer followed the criminal with his eyes, while a ruthless smile spoke his exultation. He then cast on the bleeding body a look of complacency. " Pleasing sight!" said he, " I see, for the first time, this earth wet with human blood. The flow of the sacred springs of Heaven, before the fatal hour when the Master of the Universe precipitated us from the seats of bliss, never gave me half this pleasure. Never did the harmonious harps of the archangels give me such delight, as the last sighs of a brother murdered by his brother. . . . His own brother has left him weltering in his blood. No! that honour is mine; I guided the arm of the fratricide. It is by action, such as Satan himself would boast, I shall rise above the populace of Hell. I hasten to the foot of the infernal throne. The vast concave of the fiery gulf will reverberate my praises."

The Death of Abel, by Solomon Gessner (Transl. by Mary Collyer, 1810, p. 125–126).

CHAPTER XVII

The Righteous Man in his Generation

The angels are jealous of Noah, called Menahem, or comforter—Noah preaches to the sinners—He builds an ark during fifty-two years—The giants and the ark—They mock and rail at Noah—The giants are alarmed—The wonders in Heaven—The angels gather all the animals and bring them to the ark—The rhinoceros—The tip of its nose is admitted in the ark—God closes and seals the gates of the ark—The giants try to stop the waters with their hands and the soles of their feet—The regret of the sinners—Noah's reply—The giant Og climbs up on the roof of the ark—The story of False-hood and Injustice who are admitted in the ark—The Patriarch and his sons are busy feeding the animals—The food of the grasshopper—The noise in the ark when the animals are fed—The bird Orsinia who is blessed with long life—The cat and the mouse—The story of Noah in Moslem legend—The oven of Noah's wife begins to boil—Canaan refuses to enter the ark—The story of Satan and the ass—Satan, or Iblis, catches hold of the tail of the ass—The pig and the cat—How they were created in the ark.

AND when the earth was filled with violence and wickedness, God resolved upon its destruction. Not only men, but also beasts were utterly wicked and demoralized.[1] Noah alone, who had found favour in the eyes of the Lord, he and his family, and one pair of all the beasts of the earth, were to be saved from the flood, whilst of every clean beast seven were to enter the ark.

Noah was the son of Lamech, born unto him by his wife Betenos, a daughter of Barakill. When Noah was born, his grandfather Methuselah said: "This son will comfort us for all our trouble and all our work."[2] By his grandfather the boy was called Noah, which signifies rest, because in his

---

[1] *Sanhedrin*, 108a.   [2] Charles, *The Book of Jubilees*, 4, 28.

days the land rested from the curse; but Lamech called his son Menahem, which means comforter.[1]

And the Lord said to Noah: " I have found thee alone a righteous man in this generation." But the angels were jealous of Noah and they asked the Lord of the Universe; " What is the virtue of Noah and what deed has he done that he has found favour in Thine eyes?" And the Creator replied: " When Enos, the son of Seth, was born, he was told to find sustenance for his old father, and he agreed to do so. But when he was told to feed also his grandfather Adam, he refused, saying: " I have enough to do to feed my father, and cannot trouble myself to find also sustenance for my grandfather." Cainan, too, and Mahalalel, Jared, Methuselah, and Lamech, none of them worked and fed anybody but their own fathers. When Noah came, he found sustenance for and worked and fed all his relatives."

Thus spoke the Lord, and when the angels heard this, they agreed that Noah was the most generous man of his generation. Thereupon the Lord said to Noah: " Go and speak unto all the men who have sinned and ask them to turn from their wicked ways and evil deeds and not to anger the Lord, lest He bring upon them the waters of the flood and destroy them all, and they perish from the face of the earth. If they repent and turn from their evil ways, I will refrain from bringing any punishment upon them."

Thus spoke the Lord to Noah. And Noah went and told Methuselah all that the Lord had spoken unto him. Thereupon these two righteous men, Noah and Methuselah, went out and preached to all the sinners, but none of them would repent. God then told Noah to build an ark, for in another hundred and twenty years a flood would come upon the earth. Noah did as the Lord bade him do, and he began to build the ark, making it during fifty-two years.[2] But the people

---

[1] *Sepher Hajashar.*   [2] *Pirke de Rabbi Eliezer*, Ch. 23.

and the giants mocked Noah and said: " If God brings from Heaven the waters of the flood upon us, behold we are of such high stature that the waters will not reach up to our necks, and if He bring the waters of the depth against us, behold, the soles of our feet can close up all the depths." Thereupon they put forth the soles of their feet, and closed up all the depths. But when the flood came, the waters of the deep were hot, burned their flesh and pealed off their skin.[1]

When the giants saw that Noah was proceeding with the building of the ark, they came again to watch and mock the old man. " Repent ye of your sins," said Noah, " for God is merciful and will listen to your prayers." But they only mocked him and replied: " We fear not thy God, for if He rains upon us fire, we will bathe our bodies in the blood of the Salamander, and fire will have no power over us." [2] Thus they spoke every day, and all mocked Noah and laughed at his ark.

Now Noah had worked for fifty-two years upon the ark, so as to give time to the wicked to repent of their ways, but they did not repent. In other sources it is said that Noah built the ark in 120 years.[3] When the days of the flood approached, the men of Noah's generation began to be alarmed, for they saw great wonders in Heaven and upon earth. The sun rose in the west and set in the east. Now it happened in those days that the virtuous Methuselah died, and all the beasts and fowls of the air came to accompany him to his last resting-place. Thereupon God said unto Noah: " Take to thee seven and seven of every clean beast, and of the beasts that are not clean two, the male and the female." [4] Then Noah said to the Lord: " Sovereign of all the worlds, I have never been a hunter in all my life, and I have not the strength

---

[1] *Pirke de Rabbi Eliezer*, Ch. 23.
[2] *Midrash Abkhir*, quoted in *Yalkut Shimeoni*, § 42; *Midrash Tanchuma*; *Pirke de Rabbi Eliezer*, Ch. 22; *Sanhedrin*, 108b; *Sepher Hajashar*.
[3] *Midrash Lekach Tob*, ed. Buber, p. 36.   [4] *Genesis*, 7, 2.

to collect all the animals into the ark." The angels, however, appointed over each kind, came down and gathered all the animals and with them all their food, so that the animals came of their own accord.[1]

Among the beasts which Noah brought to the ark was also the rhinoceros. When Noah saw this animal, who was only one day old, he understood that he could not lodge it in his ark. Being very large, forty-four and a half miles long, it would swamp the whole ark. He therefore made an aperture in the ark, took in the head of the rhinoceros, whilst the animal swam behind the vessel. Others say that even the head and the neck of the rhinoceros, which are three and a half miles long, could not be lodged in the ark. It was only the tip of the nose of the rhinoceros which Noah admitted into the ark. He also tied the horn of the animal to the side of the vessel lest the beast should slip off when the vessel lurched and thus perish.[2]

Now when seven days had elapsed after the death of Methuselah, and still the sinners continued in their evil and wicked ways, God sent a rain upon earth, saying: " If they repent, this rain will become a rain of blessing, but if they do not repent, it will turn into a flood and destroy them." The men, however, did not repent, and the flood at last burst out. Thunder and lightning came, and the earth trembled and was tossed about like a ship in mid-ocean; the arteries of the earth broke and spirted out water. Thereupon Noah and his family entered the ark, and the Holy One, blessed be His name, closed and sealed with His own hand the gates of the ark.[3] When the sinners saw that the flood was increasing, they at first tried to stop the waters with their hands and with the soles of their feet, and then they threw their children into the abyss to close up all the depths. Their efforts were all

---

[1] *Sanhedrin*, 108b; *Midrash Abkhir*, in *Yalkut*, § 42; *Genesis Rabba*, 32; *Pirke de Rabbi Eliezer*, Ch. 23. [2] *Zebachim*, 113b. [3] *Pirke de Rabbi Eliezer*, Ch. 23.

in vain, for stronger and stronger the flood came and covered the earth. The people thereupon gathered round the ark and tried to enter it, but a fire came down from Heaven and burned their feet, so that they drew back.[1] The sinners now implored Noah to take them in and give them shelter in his ark. "We repent of our sins," they cried, "only take us in that we may not die." But Noah only replied: "Now it is too late, for I had warned ye." The men thereupon tried to take the ark by force, but God sent wild beasts who fell upon them and drove them away from the ark.

Thus all living things were destroyed, except Noah and those who were with him in the ark.[2]

Among those who came to ask admittance to the ark was the giant Og. He climbed up on the roof of the ark, and refused to leave. Others say that he sat down on a piece of wood under the gutter of the ark, or on a rung of one of the ladders. He swore to Noah that if he allowed him to remain on the roof of the ark he and his posterity would always be the slaves of Noah and of his sons. The Patriarch allowed him to remain, and daily passed him his food through an aperture bored in the side of the ark.[3] Thereupon Falsehood, too, came to the ark and asked to be admitted, but Noah refused. "I admit the animals only in pairs," replied Noah; "go thou and find thee a mate and then thou, too, wilt be admitted." Falsehood, refused admittance, went away in wrath, and met Injustice.

"Why art thou so sad?" queried Injustice.

"Noah has refused to admit me in the ark," replied Falsehood, speaking the truth for once, "until I have found a companion. Now, if I have found favour in thine eyes, come and be my companion, and the pair of us will be admitted in the ark." Thus spoke Falsehood, but Injustice answered:

---

[1] *Berachoth*, 59; *Genesis Rabba*, 32.   [2] *Berachoth*, 59; *Sepher Hajashar*.
[3] *Pirke de Rabbi Eliezer*, Ch. 23.

FALSEHOOD AND INJUSTICE GAIN ADMITTANCE TO THE ARK

" And what will be my reward, if I agree to be thy companion? Thou knowest full well that never do I take companionship without prospect of gain."

" I will give thee all that I shall have earned through my lies," said Falsehood. Injustice agreed, and they both went to find Noah who had to admit the pair in his ark. Falsehood was very busy among the inmates of the ark and acquired much wealth by lying and cheating.

When the flood had ceased and all the beasts came out of the ark, Falsehood said to Injustice : " Where is all the plunder which I have acquired? I have done my work well, but I see no booty!"

" I have taken it," said Injustice. " Didst thou forget our agreement? Thou wast to spread the net and I to take the spoils." [1]

During the time of the flood the sun and moon had been locked up by the Lord, and did not shed their light upon the world. Noah, however, knew when it was day or night, because the pearls and precious stones which he had taken with him into the ark sparkled at night time, but lost their lustre during the day.[2] The Patriarch had to know when it was day and when night, on account of the animals. There were some animals who had to be fed during the day, whilst others, on the contrary, had their food only at night.[3]

During his sojourn in the ark Noah hardly ever slept, but was constantly busy feeding the animals. The Patriarch himself fed the beasts, Shem took care of the cattle, Ham of the birds, and Japheth of the insects, giving them their daily rations. God taught Noah not only what food he should give to each animal or bird, but at what hour to feed them and what quantity to offer. One day the Patriarch forgot to feed the lion, and the beast bit him in the leg, so that he became

---

[1] *Midrash Tehillim, Ps.* 7; see also *Monatsschrift*, Vol. 25, p. 449.
[2] *Pirke de Rabbi Eliezer*, Ch. 23. [3] *Genesis Rabba*, 34.

lame.[1] Noah knew nothing at first what food to offer to the
grasshopper. But one day, whilst cutting open a pomegranate,
a little worm fell to the ground, and the grasshopper swallowed
it. After that Noah soaked bran in water, and when the worms
began to grow therein he gave them to the grasshopper to eat.[2]

When Noah went round to feed the beasts and birds, the
noise that arose in the ark was tremendous. The inmates of
the ark roared and neighed, bleated, mewed, and chirped in
chorus, each calling for its daily ration. One day Noah noticed
the bird Orsinia lying still in a corner of the ark and not chirp-
ing like the other birds. The Patriarch wondered greatly and
asked: " Why art thou not asking for thy food?" But the
bird Orsinia replied: " I saw how busy and hard worked
thou art in feeding all the inmates of the ark, and I preferred
to suffer the pangs of hunger rather than increase thy work."
When Noah heard these words of the bird Orsinia, he said:
" Since thou didst have pity with me and didst wish to spare me
work, I will bless thee, and wish thee long life." And the Lord
heard the prayer of Noah and gave the bird Orsinia long life.[3]

It is also related that the cat and the mouse were at first
good friends and lived peacefully together in the ark, but
the mouse was jealous and said: " There is not sufficient
food for both of us." But the Lord said: " Thou wicked
beast, thou dost slander thy friend, because thou wouldst fain
eat the cat. Hast thou not learned a lesson from the case of
the sun and the moon? Both were equal in size, but the moon
having slandered the sun, I diminished her size. Thou, too,
didst slander thy friend, and wast eager to devour the cat,
therefore it is the cat that will devour thee." The mouse,
however, rushed and bit the cat, and the cat killed and ate
the mouse. And since that time, the mice tremble at the
approach of the cat which devours them.[4]

[1] *Genesis Rabba*, 30.　　[2] *Sanhedrin*, 108b.　　[3] *Ibid.*; see also *Yalkut Rubeni, Genesis*.
[4] *Alphabetum Siracidis*, ed. Steinschneider. Cf. Gaster, *Roumanian Bird Stories*.

In Moslem legend it is related that whilst Noah was building the ark, all the people came and mocked him. " Why art thou building this ark, thou stupid fool," they said. But Noah replied and said: " The day will come, ye sinners, when ye will regret your words, and it is I who will then rail at ye. Ye will then learn that God not only punishes the wicked in this world, but also in the next." [1]

Noah then built the ark according to the instructions given to him and with the assistance of the angels. He had planted a teak tree which grew to such a size in twenty years that he was able to build the whole ark out of it.[2] When the time of the flood arrived, the oven of Noah's wife began to boil, and water flowed out of it. Thereupon water flowed from all the arteries of the earth.[3] Noah thereupon embarked with his wife and his three sons, and their wives, the three daughters of Eliakim, the son of Methuselah, and he invited all those who dwelt on earth to embark with him in the name of the Lord. Noah then noticed that his grandson Canaan was not among those who had embarked and he called to him and said: " Come, embark, my child, do not remain with the sinners." But Canaan refused to come and replied: " I will ascend one of the mountains where I will be safe from the flood." " Thou canst never be saved except by the mercy of God," said Noah, but Canaan would not listen to him. A wave then came and submerged Canaan. Then all the animals that were to enter the ark were collected and wafted by the wind towards the vessel. Among those who came was also the ass. Satan, or Iblis, who wanted to enter the ark, caught hold of its tail just at the moment when the ass was about to enter the ark, so that it proceeded rather slowly. Noah, growing impatient, called out: " Come on, thou accursed one, come on quickly, even if Satan were with thee." Iblis at once entered the ark. When Noah beheld Satan, he exclaimed:

---

[1] The Koran, *Sura Hud.*   [2] *Chronique de Tabari.*   [3] Abulfeda, *loc. cit.*

" And what art thou doing here? By what right didst thou come?" " I came by thy own invitation," replied Iblis; " didst thou not say to the ass: ' Come on, even if Satan were with thee ' ?"

Two sorts of animals, however, left the ark without having entered it. They were the pig and the cat. God had created these animals in the ark for a special purpose. The vessel was becoming full of filth and human excrements, and the stench was such that it could no longer be endured. When the inmates of the ark complained to Noah, he passed his hand down the back of the elephant, and the pig issued forth and ate up all the filth that was in the ark. Thereupon the inhabitants of the ark once more came to Noah and complained against the rats who were busy in the ark and caused great annoyance. They ate up all the food, and plagued the travellers in many other ways. Noah thereupon passed his hand down the back of the lion. The king of beasts sneezed, and a cat leaped out of its nose. The cat at once ate all the rats, and the travellers had peace.[1]

AN ANGEL VISITS NOAH

It is an angel to thee sent,
Noah, to tell thee hard tiding:
For ever-ilk wight for-warks (him) wild,
And many [are] soiled in sin[n]is seir
And in felony fowly filed.
Therefore a ship thou dight to steer
With tree [and] timber, highly railed,
Of thirty cubits [hight], but feare.
Look that she draw, when she is drest,
And in her side thou shear a door
With fenesters full fifty fest,
And make chambers both less and more.

[1] Weil, *Biblische Legenden der Muselmänner.*

In earth [there] shall be such a flood,
That everylke life that is livand:
Beast and body with bone and blood,
They shall be stroied [in water and sand]
Al but thou, Noah, and thy brood,
[Thy wife] and their three wives in hand—
(For you are full righteous and good)
You shall be saved by sea and land.

Noah's Ark, or, The Shipwrights' Ancient Play or Dirge—
played at Newcastle-upon-Tyne. See The History of
Newcastle-upon-Tyne, by Henry Bourne.

NOE

(19)

Lord, at your byddinge I am bayne,
sith non other grace will gayne,
hit will I fulfill fayne,
for gratious I thee fynde.

A 100 wynters and 20
this shipp making taried haue I,
if through amendment any mercye
wolde fall vnto mankinde.

(20)

Haue done, you men and women all!
hye you lest this water fall,
that each beast were in his stall,
and into the ship broughte.

Of cleane beastes seaven shalbe,
of vncleane two, this God bade me;
this floode is nye, well may we see,
therfore tary you noughte.

The Chester Plays, The Deluge (p. 53), Early English Text
Society, Extra Series, LXII. Part I (1892).

CHAPTER XVIII

The Foolish Shepherd, and the Planting of the Vine

The mission of the raven—The protest of the bird—The dove and the olive leaf—The usefulness of the raven—Noah is anxious to be delivered from prison—His prayer—The desolation of the world—God rebukes the Patriarch—The foolish shepherd—The planting of the vine—The story of Satan who immolates a lamb, a lion, an ape, and a pig—The version of Ibn Yahya—The story of Satan and the vine in Moslem legend—The angel Raphael hands a book to Noah—Noah on the Mount Lubar—The suffering and complaint of Noah's children—The prayer of the Patriarch—The binding of the spirits—Mastema, the chief of the spirits, and his plea—Noah, the first physician—The angel Raphael teaches him the science of medicine—The secrets of the trees of healing—The knowledge of medicine spreads among the wise men of the east—The journey of Asklepinos and the forty learned men—They find the trees of healing and the tree of life—They are burned to ashes.

THE flood covered the whole earth, except the land of Israel which remained dry.[1] Now when Noah wished to know the state of the waters, he addressed himself to the raven and thus he spoke: " Go thou and see whether the flood hath ceased." But the raven replied: " The Lord hates me, for hath He not said that of my kind and of that of other unclean beasts thou shouldst only bring two into the ark? and thou, too, dost hate me, for thou seekest my destruction by sending me from among all other animals out of the ark. Now the prince of cold or of heat will meet me and kill me, and the world will have no raven for evermore." But Noah replied: " The world will well exist without thee, for thou art only an unclean beast." [2] Thereupon the raven went out, but finding

[1] *Zebachim*, 113a; *Pirke de Rabbi Eliezer*, Ch. 23.   [2] *Sanhedrin*, 108b.

the carcass of a man cast upon the top of a mountain it settled and remained to devour it, and it did not return to Noah with its message. Noah, therefore, sent forth the dove. She departed and without tarrying returned, for she had found no resting-place for her feet. But the second time the dove flew as far as the land of Israel where she came to the gates of Paradise. Here she saw the wonderful fruit and smelt the pleasant perfumes, but she had an olive leaf in her mouth when she returned. The dove wished to indicate that it is preferable to accept food that is bitter from the hand of God, rather than nourishment sweet as honey given by the hand of flesh and blood.[1]

In the meantime the raven returned to Noah, but the latter refused to admit it. But God said unto Noah: " Admit the raven once more into the ark, for in days to come the bird will be useful."

" When will this be?" asked Noah. " In another 1359 years," said the Lord, " when it will happen that a just man will stop the heavens from sending any rain upon earth. He will be in great straits, and I will send the ravens to feed him."

Noah had remained in the ark for twelve months, that is, a solar year, or one lunar year and eleven days, for the flood began on the 27th of Marcheshvan and ended on the 27th of this month a year later. During his life in the ark, he had worked assiduously, feeding all the animals, and very rarely slept. He naturally felt the strain and prayed to the Lord to release him: " Sovereign of all the worlds!" he prayed, " bring me forth from this prison, my soul being faint, because of the dread of the lions and the stench of the animals. All the righteous will crown Thee through me with a crown of sovereignty, because Thou wilt have brought me forth from this prison." [2]

But when Noah left the ark and saw how the world had

---

[1] *Pirke de Rabbi Eliezer*, Ch. 23; *Sanhedrin*, 108b; *Genesis Rabba*, 33; *Midrash Agadah*, ed. Buber, Vol. I, p. 19.   [2]*Pirke de Rabbi Eliezer*, Ch. 33.

been destroyed, he began to cry and said to the Lord: " Sovereign of the Universe! If it was because of the sinners that Thou hast destroyed the world, why didst Thou create them? Thou shouldst never have created the world, or not created man! And now where should I and my children go! The earth has been cursed, and its inhabitants have disappeared." But the Lord said unto Noah: " The inhabitants of the earth have been destroyed, but thou and thy children have been saved, and ye will increase and multiply." [1] Thereupon Noah rebuilt the altar which Adam had once built at the time when he had been cast forth from the Garden of Eden and had offered an offering upon it. Upon this altar Cain and Abel had also offered their offerings.[2]

Another version runs as follows: When Noah came out of the ark, and saw the destruction and the desolation of the world, he began to weep, and thus he said: " Sovereign of all the worlds! Merciful art Thou, but why hast Thou not pitied Thy children?" " Thou art a foolish shepherd," said the Lord. " Thou dost implore my clemency now, but when I told thee that I would bring a flood on the world thou didst say nothing. Thou didst know that thou wouldst be rescued in the ark, and didst care but little for the world. Hadst thou implored my clemency then, it would not have come to pass." And Noah's punishment was that he became lame and was abused by his son Ham.[3]

Then the Lord swore to Noah that thenceforth He would never bring the waters of the flood upon the earth.

Noah thereupon began to cultivate the earth and was the first who began to plant. It is related that he found a vine which had been cast forth out of the Garden of Eden. It had clusters of berries with it, and Noah, having eaten of them, desired the fruit in his heart. He thereupon planted a vine-

---

[1] *Yalkut Rubeni, Genesis.*
[2] *Targum Jerushalmi, Genesis,* 8, 20; *Genesis Rabba,* 34; *Pirke de Rabbi Eliezer,* Ch. 33.
[3] *Zohar Chadash;* see Bin Gorion, *loc. cit.,* p. 226.

yard, and on the selfsame day the fruit ripened, and Noah drank the wine.[1]

Another legend runs as follows: Noah was working very hard to break the hard clods, for the purpose of planting the grape. Suddenly Satan appeared before the Patriarch and said to him: " What art thou planting here?" " It is a vineyard I am planting," said Noah. " And what fruit will it bring forth?" " The grape," replied the Patriarch, " which gives joy to man and gladdens his heart." " Then let us work together," said Satan. Noah consented. Thereupon Satan brought a lamb, slaughtered it and poured its blood over the clods of earth. He then caught a lion, slaughtered it and again poured out the blood, drenching the soil with it. Noah looked and wondered. Satan thereupon caught an ape, slew it and poured the blood upon the clods of earth. At last he brought a pig, slaughtered it and fertilized the ground with its blood. And thereby Satan wished to indicate to Noah the following lesson: after tasting of the juice of the grape, drinking the first cup of wine, man becomes as mild and soft-spirited as a lamb; after the second cup, he becomes courageous as a lion, boasts of his power and of his might; after the third cup, he becomes intoxicated, dances, leaps, and gambols like an ape, making a fool of himself; but when he has drunk four or more cups of wine, he is like a pig, bestial, filthy and degraded—he is like a hog that wallows in mud.[2]

Ibn Yahya, in his *Shalsheleth Hakkabbalah*,[3] gives a different version of this legend. The Patriarch saw a goat eating sour grapes, and, becoming intoxicated, it began to gambol and frisk. He thereupon took the root of the vine branch, washed it with the blood of a sheep, a lion, an ape, and a hog, and planted it, so that it brought forth sweet fruit.

---

[1] *Pirke de Rabbi Eliezer*, Ch. 33.
[2] *Midrash Abkhir*, in *Yalkut Shimeoni*; *Midrash Agadah*, Vol. I, 22; *Genesis Rabba*, 36.— This story is also related in the *Gesta Romanorum*, Ch. 159, where, however, it is wrongly attributed to Josephus. [3] Ed. Amsterdam, 1697, p. 75a.

This legend is also found in Moslem tradition. Here we
are told that it was Ham who planted the vine, and that Satan
sprinkled the soil with the blood of a peacock, an ape, a lion,
and a swine. And thence it happens that the first glass of wine
makes a man to be like a peacock, red in colour and vivacious.
He is like an ape, leaping and dancing, when the wine has
risen to his head. When in an advanced stage of intoxication,
man becomes furious like a lion; whilst in a state of complete
drunkenness, he is like a swine, rolling in the gutter, soiling
his clothes, and wallowing in mud.[1]

Before Noah had entered the ark, the angel Raphael, the
holy prince, came to him and thus he spoke: " By the will
of the Lord of the Universe I have been sent to thee to heal
the earth and to proclaim the events which will happen, and
to tell thee what thou art to do so that thou mayest be saved."
And he handed unto Noah the holy book which had once been
in the possession of Adam, and taught him how to study it
and how to preserve and guard it in sanctity of spirit and in
purity of flesh. " Lo," said the angel of the Presence, " I give
to thee this book and from its holy pages thou wilt learn much
wisdom, also how to find the wood of gopher and to build an
ark, wherein to hide, thou and thy sons, and thy wife and the
wives of thy sons." And when Noah studied the holy book
and learned its secrets he gathered much knowledge. And
before he entered the ark which he had built, he hid the book.
When he had left the ark, Noah received another book on the
mountain of Lubar, in the mountains of Ararat. For in those
days the spirits of the bastards began to make an endeavour
to tempt and lead into sin the sons of Noah. They also sent
upon them all sorts of ills and diseases which bring suffering
and death unto man. And then the children of Noah and
his children's children came to the Patriarch and complained
of their ills and sufferings. Noah was sore at heart and very

[1] Collin de Plancy, *Légendes Bibliques*, p. 121.

grieved. He knew that it was on account of their sins that they had been visited by all kinds of ills and diseases. And Noah prayed before God, his Lord, and thus he spoke: " God of the spirits who are in all flesh, Thou who hast shown mercy unto me and saved me and my children from the waters of the deluge and didst not let us perish, as Thou didst cause to perish the children of evil and perdition, for great hath been Thy grace towards me, and great hath been Thy mercy to my soul. May Thy grace be lifted up over my children and the children of my children, and let not the evil and the malignant spirits rule over them and destroy them from the earth. Bless me and my children, so that we may grow, increase and multiply and fill the earth, and Thou dost know how Thy watchers who were the fathers of these spirits acted in my day; and I pray Thee to imprison the spirits which are living, and to hold them fast in a place of condemnation, so that they may not destroy the children of Thy servant. For verily, they are terrible and wicked and have been created to destroy. Thou alone knowest their strength, and let them not have power over the spirits of living men. Let them not have power over the just from now and for evermore." Thus did Noah pray, and the Lord of the Universe commanded His angels to bind the spirits. But Mastema, the chief of the spirits, came and thus he spoke: " O Lord of the Universe, Creator of the world, allow some of them to remain free before me, so that they may listen to my voice and do all that I may tell them. For if some of them are not left unto me how can I exercise the power and dominion of my will over the children of man? For verily, the wickedness of the sons of man is great." And then the Creator replied and decreed that a tenth part of the spirits remained before Mastema, but that nine parts descend into the place of condemnation.

And the Creator also commanded one of the angels of the Presence to teach Noah all the medicines, and he did the bidding of His Creator, the Lord of the Universe, and he taught Noah all the medicines of the diseases, and how he might heal them with the herbs of the earth. And the angels also did according to the words of the Lord, and bound all the malignant and wicked spirits and placed them in the place of condemnation, but one-tenth of them only they left upon earth where they might be subject unto Mastema who is called Satan.[1] The Creator of the Universe thereupon sent down the angel named Raphael who taught Noah all sorts of remedies, and how to prepare medicaments and physic from the trees of the earth and from the growth of the earth and roots. And he sent the princes of the spirits to teach unto Noah all the trees of healing and all the herbs and roots and seeds. And they taught him the secrets of all these trees and herbs and seeds, and the purpose for which they have been created and all their power to heal and give life. And Noah wrote all the words down into a book which he handed to Shem his eldest son.[2] It is from this book that the future sages studied medicine and the art of healing and wrote many books in various tongues. And thus the knowledge of medicine spread among the wise men of Hodus (India), of Greece, and Egypt. For the wise men of Hodus (India) travelled all over the world and studied the qualities of the healing trees and the balm trees, and the wise men of Aram discovered all kinds of herbs for healing purposes. The wise men of Greece began to heal men of various diseases; and the wise men of Egypt began to practise incantations, magic, and witchcraft by means of the images of the constellations and the stars. And they studied the books of the Chaldeans. And their wisdom was very vast, until one of the wise men of Greece, named Asklepinos (Asklepios) and forty learned men with him travelled far and wide, and went out to Hodus (India) and beyond it to the country which

[1] Book of Jubilees, Ch. 10; Kautzsch, Die Apokryphen, Vol. II, p. 58.
[2] Midrash Noah, Jellinek, Beth-Hamidrash, Vol. III, pp. 155-160.

lies east of Eden, there to find the trees of life, so that their glory and renown might increase and excel the glory and renown of the wise men of the land. And it so happened that when they arrived to the place east of Eden, they found the trees of healing and the wood of the tree of life. And they stretched out their hands to take it, but the flaming sword touched them, and they were all set aflame and were burned to ashes and none of them escaped. And thus the knowledge of physics and of medicine left the healers and physicians and rested for 630 years, until the days of another wise and learned man of Greece, whose name was Isppocrates (Hypocrates), and of other wise men, whose names were: Asaph, the Jew, and Dioscorides, and Galenos, the Kaphthorite, and many others who renewed the knowledge of medicine and the art of healing.[1]

DE INVENTIONE VINEARUM

Josephus in libro de causis rerum naturalium refert, quod Noe invenit vitam silvestrem, id est labruscam a labris terrae et viarum dictam. Que cum esset amara, tulit sanguinem quatuor animalium scilicet leonis, agni, porci et simee, quo terre mixto fecit fimum, quem ad radices labruscarum posuit. Sic ergo vinum lorum sanguine est dulceatum. Quo facto Noe postea de vino inebriabatur, et nudatus jacens a filio juniori derisus, qui omnibus filiis ejus congregatis dixit, se ideo sanguinem dictorum animalium posuisse hominibus pro doctrina.

Carissimi, per vinum multi facti sunt leones per iram, nec illo tempore habent discretionem, aliqui agni per verecundiam, aliqui sunt simee per curiositatem assumptam ineptamque leticiam; nam simea omnia coram se facta eciam facere proponit, sed destruit. Quam si capere nolueris, plumbeos calceos habeas, et dum te illos exuentem induentemque conspexerit et fortiter ligantem, similiter facit; que, cum currere temptat, torquetur gravedine et captitar; quod de multis hominibus est simile, qui dum singula temptant in ebrietatibus vix aliqua perficiunt, sed sicut simea destruunt et confundunt.

Gesta Romanorum, Ch. 159, p. 539. Edit. Oesterley, Berlin, 1872.

[1] *Midrash Noah*, Jellinek, *Beth-Hamidrash, ibidem.*

CHAPTER XIX

The Astrologers and the Boy in the Cave

The birth of Abraham—The banquet of Terah—The big star—The prediction of the astrologers—Nimrod sends for Terah—The boy in the cave—Nimrod reads the stars—The imprisonment of the pregnant women—The miracle in the case of Emtelai, the wife of Terah—The boy recognizes the existence of the Creator—The meeting of mother and son—The advice of Satan—Abraham is carried by the angel Gabriel to the gates of Babylon—The opinion of the magicians—Abraham warns Nimrod—The King sends away the boy unmolested.

It happened in the year 1948, after the creation of the world, in the month of Nissan. On a fine starlit night, several high dignitaries of the court of the great and famous King Nimrod, among whom were many magicians and astrologers, were returning home from a banquet offered to them by their friend Terah, one of the commanders of Nimrod's armies. He had invited his friends to rejoice with him on the occasion of the birth of his son Abraham, whom his wife Emtelai, a daughter of Carnebo, had borne unto him.[1]

Late at night, the guests were returning home when they were struck by an unusual phenomenon. Yonder in the east they perceived a great star swiftly moving along in the firmament. And lo! this big and unusually bright star suddenly swallowed up four other stars, one after the other. Greatly marvelled the courtiers, magicians and soothsayers of Nimrod, in distant Mesopotamia, at this phenomenon.[2]

[1] *Sepher Hajashar*; *Pirke de Rabbi Eliezer*, Ch. 26; *Baba Batra*, 91a.
[2] *Sepher Hajashar*. See also Josephus, *Antiquities*, II, 9, 2.

" Verily," they said, " this can be interpreted only in one way. One day the newly born son of Terah will be great and mighty and will conquer the whole kingdom of Nimrod. He will dethrone all the princes and take their possessions, which will be inherited by the son of Terah and his offspring. His children will one day inherit the worlds below and above." [1] Thus spoke the courtiers, councillors, and soothsayers of Nimrod on that memorable night at Chur in Mesopotamia. On the following morning the councillors of King Nimrod, who had been the guests of Terah on the previous evening, hastened to the King and informed him of the events of last night and what they had read in the stars.

" And what am I to do?" asked the King, greatly perplexed. " Mighty King," replied the astrologers, " we advise thee to buy the newly born boy of Terah, and to kill the child immediately. Thus wilt thou have peace and continue to reign."

Nimrod listened to their advice, and at once sent for Terah to appear in his presence. And when Terah appeared in the presence of King Nimrod, the latter thus addressed the commander of his armies:

" I hear that thy wife Emtelai has borne a son unto thee. Now I will offer thee much gold and silver and vast treasures, if thou wilt hand over thy son unto me to do as I please."

" Great King," replied Terah, " thy word is law, and it is not for me, thy humble servant, to oppose thy royal wish, but may thy servant speak into thine royal ear?" [2]

" Speak," said Nimrod.

" Yesterday," said Terah, " a friend came to me offering a high price for the horse which thou hast once given me as a gift. I crave, therefore, thy permission to sell this horse to my friend."

When the King heard the request of Terah, the commander

---

[1] Jellinek, *Beth-Hamidrash*, II, 118.   [2] *Sepher Hajashar*.

of his armies, he waxed very wroth and exclaimed: " Art
thou then in such sore need of gold and silver that thou
wouldst fain sell this precious horse, a token of my
royal favour?"

" Great King," replied Terah, " be not angry with thy
servant. Even such a request thou makest now. Thou didst
offer me great treasures for my son who is a gift from Heaven.
What will the treasures avail me if I have no son to leave them
to? I would be like the man in the fable who allowed his horse
to be killed in exchange for a house full of oats." Thus spoke
Terah, greatly daring. On hearing such words from the
mouth of the commander of his armies, the King waxed mightily
wroth, and he commanded Terah to bring his son immediately.
The unhappy father agreed to do the bidding of the King,
but craved three days grace so as to prepare his wife for the
sad tidings. When three days had passed, the King sent his
servants to fetch the son of Terah. " If the boy is not delivered
unto our hands," the messengers informed the unhappy
father, " King Nimrod will wreak terrible vengeance and
destroy thy whole house and family." [1]

Thus threatened and yet unwilling to hand over his own
son, Terah took the newly born child of one of his slaves and
handed it over to the King's servants. Faithful to his royal
promise, King Nimrod bestowed upon Terah much wealth,
and bade his servants to slay the boy who had been brought
to him. Fearing, however, that one day Nimrod might learn
of the substitution, Terah sent his wife and her baby away
from home and concealed them in a cave.

Another version of this legend runs as follows:

Nimrod, the great King of Babylon, was a great astrologer
himself, and in the stars, which he constantly consulted, he
had read that a boy would be born in Mesopotamia who
would one day declare war unto the King and his religion

[1] *Sepher Hajashar.* Cf. Jellinek, *Beth-Hamidrash*, Vol. II, pp. 118–119.

and in the end come forth victorious.[1] Greatly troubled in his mind, Nimrod asked his councillors for advice. At the advice of the latter, he built a big house eighty yards in length and sixty in breadth, wherein all the women about to give birth to a child were kept and closely watched. The midwives and nurses were commanded to kill unhesitatingly every new born boy, but to bestow rich presents upon those women who would give birth to a girl. Thus 70,000 boys were massacred by order of the King Nimrod. Thereupon the angels in Heaven implored the Lord of the Universe, the God of Justice, to wreak vengeance upon Nimrod and to punish him for this massacre of the innocent babies. And the Lord of the Universe replied:

" I slumber not, neither do I sleep; in good time the cruel murderer will be punished and his deeds avenged."

Soon Emtelai, the wife of Terah, was about to give birth to a child, and was brought into custody by order of the King. But lo! a miracle happened and all the outward signs of her pregnancy disappeared, so that she was set free. And when the day of her delivery approached, she secretly left the town and concealed herself in a cave. Here she bore a son, Abraham, the radiance of whose countenance shed a brilliant light in the dark cave.[2] Wrapping the child in one of her garments, she left it there, relying upon the mercy of God Almighty. And when the Lord of the Universe heard the wailing of the boy, He sent His angel Gabriel into the cave to feed the baby. The angel Gabriel offered one finger of his right hand to the crying babe to suck, and lo! from the angelic finger milk flowed abundantly.[3]

When Abraham was thirteen[4] years, or, according to some,

---

[1] *Maasse Abraham*, Jellinek, *Beth-Hamidrash*, I, pp. 25–34; Weil, *Biblische Legenden der Muselmänner*, p. 68; Herbelot, *Bibliothèque Orientale*, s.v. *Abraham*.

[2] See *Exodus Rabba*, 1, and *Sotah*, 12a, where this incident is told of Moses.

[3] See also Weil, *loc. cit.*; and Herbelot, *loc. cit.*

[4] *Pirke de Rabbi Eliezer*, Ch. 26. See also *Sepher Hajashar*; and *Maasse Abraham*, Jellinek, *Beth-Hamidrash*, I, where it is said that Abraham was either three or ten years old, when he left the cave.

only ten days old, he left the cave. Perceiving the wide expanse
of the firmaments he began to wonder where the firmaments
and earth had come from and who was their Creator. It was
soon after dawn, and at that moment the sun arose upon the
horizon in its morning splendour; it tinted with orient hues
the morning sky. This, thought the boy, must be the Creator
of the Universe, and Abraham knelt and worshipped the sun.
Thus he remained the whole day, when lo! the sun set in
the west and twilight came. " This radiant orb," thought the
boy, "which is changeable, cannot be the All-Father, the Creator
of the Universe," and lifting up his eyes he perceived the
moon in its pale glory, surrounded by myriads of stars twink-
ling in the firmaments. " This pale and radiant orb," thought
the boy, "must be the Creator of the Universe, and the myriads
of minor lights his servants." He prostrated himself before
the moon and worshipped. But lo! the night passed and
once more the sun rose in the east, the light of the moon
having waned and disappeared.

" Neither the big nor the smaller heavenly lights," thought
Abraham, " can be the Creators of the Universe. They both
come and go and must be obeying an invisible ruler who
alone is the Creator of all the Universe. Him alone will I
henceforth worship and adore." [1]

Proceeding on his way, the boy met his mother, Emtelai.
She had come to visit the cave where she had left her baby,
and not finding it was greatly grieved. She wandered along
the bank of the river, trying to discover where her child might
be. Thus she met Abraham, but she knew him not, for he
had already grown up and appeared to her as a boy.

" Knowest thou anything about a baby which I left in
yonder cave?" she inquired.

" I am thy child whom thou seekest, Mother," replied
Abraham.

---

[1] *Sepher Hajashar*; *Maasse Abraham*, Jellinek, *Beth-Hamidrash*, Vol. I.

His mother wondered greatly and would scarcely believe it.

" How is it possible," she exclaimed, " that thou shouldst speak and walk about, only ten days old?"

" Yes, Mother," replied the boy, " everything is possible for the living, eternal, and omnipotent God, the Creator of the world, the Ruler of the Universe. He dwelleth above in the heavens, but His glory filleth the whole earth. He sees and hears everything and nothing is hidden from him."

" Is there another God besides Nimrod?" queried Emtelai, Abraham's mother.

" Yes, Mother," replied Abraham. " He is the God of Heaven and earth, the God of the Universe, who is also the God of Nimrod. Go and tell Nimrod so." [1]

Emtelai, the wife of Terah, went and told her husband all that had happened unto their son and how miraculously he had been saved. And when Nimrod heard all about this wonder child, a great terror seized him and he summoned all his councillors, magicians, and soothsayers and asked them their opinion. " Great King," spoke the councillors and astrologers, " verily, a great and mighty king like Nimrod need not fear an infant, like the son of Terah. It will be easy for the King to bid one of his smallest army commanders to capture the boy and put him to death." But Satan, arrayed in the silken garments of one of the royal councillors, and mingling with them, opened his mouth and thus he spoke:

" Great King! I advise thee to summon thy best officers and to arm thy best regiments, and send them out to capture this boy who is a real danger unto thee and unto thy kingdom." And Nimrod did as Satan, arrayed in the garb of one of his councillors, had advised him. Thus a mighty legion of warriors was sent out in pursuit of Abraham. [2]

---

[1] *Sepher Hajashar*; see also Jellinek, *loc. cit.*
[2] *Maasse Abraham*, Jellinek, *Beth-Hamidrash*, Vol. I.

When the son of Terah heard what had happened and
knew that many legions had been dispatched to capture him,
and that a mighty host was drawn up in battle array, he prayed
unto God in this hour of his need to save and protect him
from the wrath and vengeance of Nimrod. And the Lord
of the Universe commanded His angel Gabriel to protect the
son of Terah. Gabriel thereupon sent clouds and thick mists
to envelop Abraham and render him invisible to the eyes of
his pursuers. The mists and clouds were so dense, and the
darkness so great, that the soldiers of Nimrod were greatly
frightened, gave up their pursuit, and returned to Babylon.
Carried on the shoulders of Gabriel, Abraham followed them,
reaching the gates of Babylon at the same time as the royal
soldiers.[1]

And opening his mouth Abraham cried to the inhabitants
of the city and thus he spoke:

" The Eternal is the true and only God, and there is no
one like Him. Worship God, the Lord of the Universe, all
ye men and women of Babylon, as I, Abraham, His servant,
am worshipping Him."

Abraham then went to his parents and admonished them
to worship the only and true God. But Terah, now greatly
frightened, hastened to Nimrod and informed him of all that
had occurred; how his son Abraham, whom the royal soldiers
had set out to capture, had travelled in such a short time over
a long distance, a journey of forty days. Hearing these words,
Nimrod was greatly frightened, and once more summoned his
councillors into his presence. The astrologers and magicians
thereupon advised the King to order a seven days festival, and
to command all his subjects to appear in the royal palace and
worship the king. But Nimrod, being anxious to behold the
wonder child Abraham, bade Terah to come before him
accompanied by his son.[2] Abraham now appeared in the pre-

---

[1] *Maasse Abraham*, Jellinek, *Beth-Hamidrash*, Vol. I; *Sepher Hajashar*.   [2] *Ibid*.

sence of Nimrod. He entered the vast throne room, thronged
with all the mighty princes, magicians, and astrologers. Without fear or hesitation the boy approached the throne, seized
it with his hand so that it shook and trembled, and called
aloud:

" Woe unto Nimrod, the abominable blasphemer! Tremble,
O Nimrod, before the living, only God, the Ruler of the Universe, who liveth for ever, who neither slumbereth nor sleepeth.
Worship Him, Nimrod, even as I worship Him, for it is He
who hath created the whole world, the heavens and the earth."
Thus spake Abraham, and all the idols were immediately
thrown to the ground by an invisible hand, so that Nimrod
and his court were greatly frightened. Nimrod himself fell
into a swoon which lasted two hours. When he recovered
consciousness, the King asked Abraham:

" Was this thy voice, or the voice of thy God?"

" It was the voice of one of His humblest servants," replied
Abraham.

" Then," said Nimrod, " thy God must verily be great
and mighty and King of all the kings."

Nimrod allowed Terah and his son to depart unmolested,
and they left his presence unharmed. Abraham, no longer
fearing the wrath of Nimrod, dwelt for thirty-nine years
with Noah and Shem, and studied the law and the wonders
of the Creator.[1]

[1] *Maasse Abraham*, Jellinek, *Beth-Hamidrash*, Vol. I.

CHAPTER XX

The Mighty Tower of Babel, and the Iconoclast

Nimrod, the son of Kush—His garment—It was made for Adam—Stolen by Ham in the ark—The power of the garment—Esau covets the garment of Nimrod—Nimrod is worshipped as a god—The arrogance of the King—The mighty tower—Abraham preaches to the builders of the tower—The confusion of languages—The seventy nations—The relics of the tower—Terah, the seller of idols—Abraham smashes the idols of his father—The story of the poor woman who came to buy a nice god—Abraham before Nimrod—Another story relating how Abraham smashed the idols of his father—The story of the idols who refused to partake of the savoury meat—The Patriarch denounces idolatry—The illness of Terah—His son Haran sells a few idols—The story of the woman whose gods had been stolen—The conversion of the old woman.

AND in those days it came to pass that men still feared a recurrence of the flood which had visited the earth in the days of Noah.[1] Afraid, lest they would be destroyed and wiped out from the face of the earth, all men left the pleasant country of Palestine,[2] where Noah had dwelt and sacrificed unto the Lord,[3] and came to dwell in the valley of Shinnar. Here they no longer submitted to the wise rule of the God-fearing Shem,[4] the son of Noah, but paid homage unto Nimrod, the son of Kush,[5] the son of Ham, and Nimrod became very mighty indeed. He had been the darling of his father Kush, and the latter had bestowed upon him the garment which Adam had worn when he was expelled from the Garden of Eden. This garment Adam had left to Enoch, Enoch to Methuselah, and

[1] Josephus, *Antiquities*, I, 4, 1; *Pirke de Rabbi Eliezer*, Ch. 11.
[2] *Pirke de Rabbi Eliezer*, Ch. 24. [3] *Targum Jerushalmi, Genesis*, 7, 20.
[4] *Targum Jerushalmi, Genesis*, 10, 9. [5] *Pirke de Rabbi Eliezer*, Ch. 11 and Ch. 24

Methuselah to Noah who took it with him into the ark. Here
Ham stole it and left it to his son Kush. It was in this garment
that Nimrod arrayed himself, thus becoming invulnerable
and invincible. He easily conquered all his enemies and
slew all the hostile armies. Arrayed in the clothes which
God had made for Adam and Eve, Nimrod was possessed of
great power. When he put on these garments all the animals,
the beasts in the fields and the animals in the air came at once
and prostrated themselves before him.[1] The sons of men,
thinking that this submission of the animals, beasts, and birds,
was due to Nimrod's power and might, made him king
over themselves. These coats of Nimrod were, however, in
the end the cause of his violent death. Esau, the son of Isaac,
who was also a mighty hunter, saw the coats which the Almighty
had once made for Adam and Eve, and he coveted them in
his heart. He was very anxious to make himself possessed of
this precious raiment, hoping thus to become a mighty and
powerful hunter and hero by means of these clothes. Esau,
therefore, slew Nimrod and took the raiment from him, and
was thus enabled to catch the animals and become a cunning
hunter.[2] The clothes were subsequently concealed in the earth
by Jacob, who said that none was worthy to wear them.[3]

Thus Nimrod had triumphed over the King of Babylon,
and he became a mighty ruler. And soon the whole earth and
all its inhabitants recognized his rule and became his humble
subjects:[4] they worshipped him as a ruler and as a god, for
Nimrod made men forget the love and worship of the true
God, the Creator of the Universe, and led them on the path
of sin and transgression. The longer Nimrod sat upon his
throne, the more arrogant he grew. And yet he was uneasy
in his mind, and in constant fear of losing his throne. He

[1] *Sepher Hajashar*; *Pirke de Rabbi Eliezer*, Ch. 24.
[2] *Genesis Rabba*, 65; *Targum Jerushalmi, Genesis*, 25, 27
[3] *Pirke de Rabbi Eliezer*, Ch. 24.
[4] *Targum Jerushalmi, Genesis*, 10, 9; *Pirke de Rabbi Eliezer*, Ch. 11.

had read in the stars that one day a man would arise who would teach the world the knowledge of the true God, the Ruler of the Universe, to whom alone belongs all power and greatness. In order to prevent such an occurrence and to turn men away entirely from the worship of the true God,[1] Nimrod gathered his people and thus addressed them: " Come, let us build a big city, where we can dwell so that we may not be scattered all over the face of the earth. Let us further erect in the midst of this city a high tower which will reach into Heaven, so lofty that a flood may not reach its summit, and so firm that a fire-flood will not destroy it. Let us then ascend upon the summit of this tower and climb up to Heaven.[2] With our axes we will cut open the firmament and let it empty itself of all the waters contained therein, so that it may never be a danger unto us. Thus will we also avenge our ancestors who perished by water, the only weapon of our enemy. Let us then wage war against the ruler who dwelleth upon the firmament above our heads and hurl spears and arrows against him. Never will he be able to resist our mighty hosts and our spears and arrows. And upon the summit of the high tower we will place an idol with a sword in his hand that he may fight our battles and protect us. Thus our fame will be great from one end of the earth to the other, and we will rule over the whole world." [3]

Thus spoke Nimrod in his pride and arrogance, and although not all his subjects had faith in him and believed him that he would truly conquer Heaven and establish his rule there, yet they all gathered round him, determined to help him carry out his design. Some of Nimrod's subjects believed that a high and mighty tower in the valley of Shinnar would indeed protect them against another deluge, whilst others

[1] *Pesachim*, 94b; *Hagigah*,13a; Josephus, *Antiquities*, I, 42; Herbelot, *Bibliothèque Orientale, s.v. Nimrod*; Weil, *Biblische Legenden der Muselmänner*. p. 77.

[2] *Sepher Hajashar*; *Pirke de Rabbi Eliezer*, Ch. 24; *Sanhedrin*, 109a. See also Josephus, *Antiquities*, I, 4, 1-2; Jellinek, *Beth-Hamidrash*, Vol. III, 46.

[3] *Sepher Hajashar*; *Sanhedrin*, 109a; *Genesis Rabba*, 38, *Targum Jerushalmi. Genesis*, 11, 4.

hoped thus to glorify their idols, the idols which they worshipped.[1] Thereupon 600,000 [2] men gathered round Nimrod
and among them were 1000 princes. They started to build
the mighty tower and never rested until the structure had
reached a height of seven mils.[3] As there were no stones
wherewith to build the tower, they made bricks, and built up
the tower to a height of fourteen thousand cubits, or seven mils,
making ascents for the labourers on the east and the west side.
Those who carried up the bricks went up on the eastern side,
whilst those who descended had to go down on the western
side. The work and completion of the tower they valued
very highly, but to the lives of the labourers they attached
no importance. If a workman fell down and died, they paid
but little heed to it, but when a brick fell down and broke,
they were grieved, and even shed tears.[4] They now began to
send their arrows against the firmament, and when the arrows
fell down upon earth covered with blood, they shouted: " We
have killed all those who dwell in Heaven." [5]

And it came to pass that Abraham, who was then in his
48th year, heard [6] of the mighty tower which was being built
in the valley of Shinnar. He travelled to the valley and endeavoured to make the builders desist from their sinful undertaking, but they refused to listen unto him. Abraham thereupon
prayed to the Lord of the Universe: " God Almighty," he
prayed, " confuse their language and scatter them over the
face of the earth."[7]

And the Lord called seventy of His ministering angels and
bade them go and confuse the speech of the builders, so that
one did no longer understand the speech of the other. The
Creator of the Universe called to the seventy ministering

---

[1] *Midrash Tanchuma, Genesis,* 1, 11; *Midrash Shokher Tob, Ps.* 1.   [2] *Sepher Hajashar.*
[3] *Pirke de Rabbi Eliezer,* Ch. 24.
[4] *Sepher Hajashar; Pirke de Rabbi Eliezer,* Ch. 24.
[5] *Sepher Hajashar.* See also Weil, *Biblische Legenden der Muselmänner,* p. 78.
[6] *Seder Olam,* Ch. 1.
[7] *Pirke de Rabbi Eliezer,* Ch. 24; *Genesis Rabba,* 61; *Midrash Shokher Tob, Ps.* 1;
Yalkut, 2, § 703.

angels surrounding the Throne of Glory, and thus He said:
" Let us go down and confuse their languages." The Lord
then confused their languages, so that when the builders of
the tower wished to speak one to another none understood the
language of his fellow man. Thereupon they all seized their
swords and fought one another, so that half the world fell
by the sword, and the other half was scattered from the valley
of Shinnar upon the face of the earth.[1]

They were thus compelled to give up the construction
of the tower by means of which they had hoped in their arrogance to ascend to Heaven. And they were divided into seventy
nations, each speaking a different tongue. Instead of being
destroyed, even as the generation of the flood had been
destroyed, the builders of the mighty tower were only scattered
over the face of the earth. God had mercy upon them because,
although they worshipped idols, they nevertheless lived peacefully among themselves and never robbed one another, whilst
the generation of the flood had been addicted to robbery and
discord.[2] As for the tower itself, one third, the uppermost,
was destroyed by fire, one third by an earthquake, whilst one
third remained.[3] But the worship of idols spread among men
in those days. Not only Nimrod and his court, his councillors
and magicians, but also Terah, the father of Abraham, worshipped idols. Terah had twelve idols, one for every month,
whom he worshipped and to whom he sacrificed. He even
manufactured many idols which he sold to strangers.

And it came to pass that Abraham, who had long studied in
the school of Shem and Eber and was now fifty years old, returned to his parental home.[4] He was now intent upon showing
how void and false this worship of the idols was, so as to make
his father give it up and acknowledge the true God instead. And
thus it happened one day, when he was alone in the shop

---

[1] *Sepher Hajashar.*   [2] *Genesis Rabba,* 38.
[3] *Sanhedrin,* 109a. See also Josephus, *Antiquities,* I, 4, 3. See also Beer, *Das Leben Abrahams,* p. 109, note 84.   [4] *Sepher Hajashar.*

where his father had left him to sell the idols to those who might ask for some, that he seized the opportunity to carry out his design. There were numbers of idols of various sizes. A strong and powerfully built man now came and asked for an idol, one that would be as strong as himself. Abraham took up an idol and handed it to him, but the purchaser expressed some doubt as to the strength of the idol.[1]

"If this idol did not possess great strength it would not have been placed above all the others and occupied the place of honour," said Abraham. "If thou wilt pay the price, thou canst carry away thy god and he himself will then speak unto thee."

The purchaser paid the price and was about to leave, when Abraham called him back: "And how old art thou?" he queried.

"I am seventy years old," replied the purchaser of the strong idol.

"And wilt thou prostrate thyself before the image or dost thou expect the idol to bow to thee?" further queried Abraham.[2]

"How canst thou ask?" said the stranger by way of a reply. "He is my god and I will prostrate myself before him and worship him."

"Then," rejoined Abraham, "thou art much older than the god thou hast just acquired, for he was only manufactured to-day." The disappointed purchaser threw away the idol he had just bought and asked his money back, which Abraham at once returned to him.

Thereupon a poor and scantily clad woman came and asked for a god who was as poor as she was herself. Abraham took up an idol which was very small in size and placed on the lowest shelf. "Here is a god as thou wouldst have."

"And will he not be exacting?" queried the poor woman. "I am a lonely and poor widow, and my poverty is very great,

---

[1] *Tana debe Eliahu*, 2, 25.   [2] *Ibid.*

so that I cannot satisfy gods who claim too much from their worshippers and whose claims only rich folk can satisfy."

" Dost thou not see," rejoined Abraham, " that this is a very modest god who will have compassion with thy poverty and not trouble thee overmuch?"

Well satisfied, the poor widow paid the price for her idol and was about to leave, when Abraham called her back. He pointed out to her that, however modest the god she had just acquired was, he was still inferior to herself, because he had only been manufactured this very morning. Greatly disappointed, the woman threw away the idol and went her way.[1]

Thereupon another woman brought a dishful of meal. " Place this dish," she said, " before the gods, so that they may eat and be satisfied." Thus she spoke and went her way.

Thereupon Abraham took up a stick and smashed all the idols with the exception of the biggest, into whose hands he placed the stick.[2] Now, when Terah, the father of Abraham, returned and saw how all the idols had been broken, his anger was great and he asked his son who it was that had wrought such havoc among the gods.

" Why should I withhold the truth from thee, O Father mine?" replied Abraham. " A woman came this morning bringing a dish full of fine meal to feed the gods with. I accordingly placed the dish before them to partake of it. But they began to quarrel among themselves, each wanting to have the entire dish for himself. Then the biggest among them took up yonder stick and broke them all." [3]

Thus spake Abraham. But Terah replied: " Dost thou mock me, boy? Have the idols power of speech and are they able to move and act?"

" O Father," said Abraham, " doth not thine ear hear what thy mouth is saying?"

---

[1] *Tana debe Eliahu*, 2, 25. See also *Genesis Rabba*, 38. Cf. Abulfeda, *Historia Ante-Islamica.*   [2] *Genesis Rabba*, 38.   [3] *Ibid.*

Terah, very angry on hearing these words, straightway went to report to Nimrod the conduct of his son. He moreover handed Abraham over to the King that he might punish him.

" If," said Nimrod to Abraham, " thou wilt not worship the gods of thy father, then worship at least fire!"

" Why," said Abraham, " should we worship fire rather than water? Is not water stronger than fire which it has the power to quench?"

" Well then," replied Nimrod, " prostrate thyself before water and worship it."

" But clouds," said Abraham, " are greater than water, for they contain in themselves this element."

" Well then, adore the clouds," said Nimrod.

" The wind," again said Abraham, " is more powerful than the clouds, for it disperses them. Why should we not worship the wind?"

" Well then, worship the wind," said Nimrod, growing impatient.

" Man," said Abraham, imperturbably, " is even stronger than wind, for he can fight against it. Why should we not worship man?"

Nimrod's patience, however, was at an end and he thus spoke unto Abraham: " Thou speakest idle words; fire is my god and I will throw thee into the fire and let thy God save thee if He can." [1]

Another version of this interview between Abraham and Nimrod runs as follows: One day, Abraham begged his father to show him the god who had created Heaven and earth and the whole Universe. Thereupon Terah led his son into an inner chamber where he showed him twelve big idols and a number of smaller ones, prostrated himself before them and went off.

Abraham at once ran to his mother Emtelai and thus

[1] *Genesis Rabba*, 38.

he spoke: "Mother dear, my father hath just shown unto me the gods who have created Heaven and earth and all the Universe. Now prithee, take a young kid from the goats and make it savoury meat for the gods, and let me bring it to them that they may eat and bless me." [1]

And Emtelai, the mother of Abraham, went and did as her son had asked her to. She fetched a young kid from the goats, made it savoury meat and placed it before the idols. As the idols neither moved nor did stir, Abraham said mockingly: " Perchance the meat is not savoury enough for the gods and the quantity too small. To-morrow they shall have a larger dish and meat that is even more savoury."

And indeed, on the following morning, Emtelai fetched from the flocks three of the best kids of the goats, made them savoury meat and placed the dish before the idols of Terah. But still the idols remained dumb and motionless. They never spoke, neither did they stir.

Thereupon Abraham exclaimed: "Woe unto those who worship idols, for they are vain and foolish." Straightway he seized an axe, smashed all the idols, with the exception of the biggest, and placed his axe in the hands of the latter.

Terah was just returning home, when he heard the noise of the smashing of his idols.[2] He hastened into the inner chamber and was amazed to see what had happened. All the idols, except the biggest, were no more; there was only a heap of splinters and stone.

"And who hath dared to do this?" called Terah in angry tones. In vain did Abraham try to make his father believe that the big idol had done this and had smashed all the smaller ones. " No," cried Terah, " this cannot be; the image could not have done such a deed, for he is only stone and wood, the result of mine own handiwork."

Thereupon Abraham told his father the truth and admon-

[1] *Sepher Hajashar.*   [2] *Ibid.*

ished him to give up his idolatry and acknowledge the true and only God, the Eternal and the Creator of the Universe.[1] As Terah, however, would not listen to his son's admonitions, Abraham seized the axe and cut the biggest idol too. And when Terah saw what Abraham had done, he grew very angry, hastened to Nimrod and related unto him what his own son had done to his gods.

Nimrod bade the daring god-smasher appear in his royal presence. Abraham repeated to the King what he had already said to his own father. He pointed out the stupidity of worshipping idols made by man, manufactured out of stone and wood. He reminded Nimrod of the flood of waters which the Eternal, the only God and Creator of the Universe, had brought upon the earth and destroyed all flesh because of the wickedness of man, and because all flesh had corrupted His way and the earth was filled with violence. He admonished Nimrod in fiery words to repent and to acknowledge the true God, the living Ruler of the Universe, lest he and his house should be destroyed, even as the generation of the flood had been destroyed from under Heaven. But Nimrod replied:

" I am a god myself; dost thou not know that I have created Heaven and earth with mine own hands?" [2]

" If thou art a god," replied Abraham, " then change the course of the sun, cause it to rise in the west and to set in the east. If thou canst do this I will worship and acknowledge thee as my god, but if thou art unable to accomplish this, I will refuse to obey thy commands. The God who lent me strength to destroy the idols will give me strength to fight against thee, O Nimrod."

" Do not be surprised," he continued, " to hear me speak thus unto thee. Thou art not the ruler of the Universe, but only a mortal man, the son of Kush. Hadst thou been a god

[1] *Sepher Hajashar*; Koran, *Sura*, 19, 43.
[2] *Tana debe Eliahu*; see also Herbelot, *Bibliothèque Orientale, s.v. Abraham.*

thine own father would not have died even like other men. And thou, too, wilt not escape death which will soon claim thee." [1]

Another version of the legend relating the scene between Abraham and Nimrod runs as follows: One day Terah fell ill and bade his sons Abraham and Haran to sell a few images so as to have the wherewithal to live upon. Haran at once did as his father had bidden him, sold the idols and brought his father the money he had received. Thereupon Abraham took a rope and dragging two of the idols into the streets offered them for sale, and thus he spake:

" For sale, two images, utterly useless; each idol hath a mouth but doth not speak; it hath eyes but cannot see; it hath feet but cannot stand; it hath ears but cannot hear." [2]

The people were amazed when they heard his words. Now an old woman came along and asked Abraham to sell her a fine beautiful image which she could cherish and worship properly. " Didst thou not buy an idol from my brother Haran?" asked Abraham.

" So I did," replied the old woman, " but thieves came and stole it while I was in the bath!"

" And how canst thou worship an idol which cannot protect itself from thieves?" queried Abraham. " Such an idol," he continued, " cannot protect thee."

" But whom shall I worship then?" asked the woman, " for I must have a god to worship in my old age, a god who will bless me."

" Worship the living God," said Abraham, " the God who is the Lord of the Universe, and who hath created Heaven and earth, the sea and all that is therein." [3]

" But what will it avail me," persisted the old woman, " if I worship thy God?"

---

[1] Beer, *Das Leben Abrahams*, p. 12, and note 102, p. 110.
[2] *Maasse Abraham*, Jellinek, *Beth-Hamidrash*, Vol. I. See also Weil, *Biblische Legenden* p. 70.
[3] Jellinek, *Beth-Hamidrash*, Vol. I.

" Thou wilt recover thy lost property," replied Abraham; " and, moreover, thy soul will be saved from perdition."

And the old woman followed Abraham's advice and acknowledged the only living God, the Lord of the Universe. Soon afterwards the woman found the thieves and recovered her property. Then she dragged the idol she had once bought from Haran through the town and called aloud so that all the people could hear her:

" Woe unto the idols and woe unto those folks who worship stone and wood. Let all those who wish to save their souls acknowledge the God of Abraham who will give them protection and bless their handiwork."

Thus spoke the old woman, and the people listened unto her voice, and many among them abandoned their idols and acknowledged the God of Abraham.

When Nimrod heard of the doings of this old woman, he bade her appear in his presence, and commanded her to worship the idols and acknowledge himself as a god. This the woman refused to do, and she was beheaded at the command of Nimrod.[1]

[1] *Ibid.*

CHAPTER XXI

The Fiery Furnace and the Garden of Roses

The distinguished prisoner—He is fed by the angel Gabriel—The fiery furnace—The conversion of the jailer—Abraham in the fiery furnace—The prayer of the martyr—The whispering of Sammael—Emtelai implores her son to give in—The terrible death of Haran—The garden of roses—The Patriarch teaches men the knowledge of God—The marriage of Abraham—Nimrod's strange dream—The man with the naked sword— The egg that changed into a river—Anuko, one of Nimrod's astrologers, interprets the dream of the King—Eliezer saves Abraham—Terah and his family leave Mesopotamia.

WHEN Nimrod saw that Abraham had so many followers among the people who were beginning to listen to his voice, fear and terror seized him. At the advice of his councillors and magicians he, therefore, commanded that a seven days feast be held in the royal palace. All the idols, richly arrayed, were brought to the palace, and the people were bidden to assemble and witness the great splendour of the gods and worship them. A great banquet was given in honour of the gods, and Nimrod bade Terah bring his son Abraham, so that he, too, might witness the splendour and power of the gods and of Nimrod himself.[1] But Abraham refused to come to court, and remained alone in his father's house, where he broke all the idols, cutting them to pieces.

Nimrod thereupon bade his servants throw Abraham into prison, where he was to remain without food and drink. The servants of Nimrod did the bidding of their master, and

[1] Jellinek, *Beth-Hamidrash*, Vol. I, 25–34.

Abraham was thrown into a dungeon, where he remained a whole year. The walls of his prison opened, however, and a source of clear water issued forth, enabling Abraham to quench his thirst, whilst the angel Gabriel daily brought him food.[1]

Nimrod now assembled his councillors and magicians, and asked them to decide what was to be done with Abraham who had dared to declare war unto the gods of Nimrod.

" He is a blasphemer," said the councillors in one voice, " and deserves to be burned upon the stake." Accordingly Nimrod gave orders that after forty days Abraham should be thrown into a fiery furnace and burnt alive.[2] All the inhabitants were commanded to gather fuel for the furnace in which Abraham was to be burned.[3] An immense pile was lit, and the flames were so great that they reached up to the skies, sending fear and terror into the hearts of the people. All the people, rich and poor, high and low, men, women, and children, flocked to the place of execution in order to witness the burning of Abraham who had overthrown the idols. Multitudes of people thronged the roofs and towers, all waiting to see how the son of Terah would perish in the flames.

Nimrod now bade the jailer to lead Abraham forth from prison. " Mighty King," said the jailer, " how canst thou expect Abraham to be still alive, he who hath remained in prison for over a year without food or drink?"

Angrily Nimrod replied: " I command thee to bring forth Abraham, living or dead, so that his body may be thrown into the flames and the people witness the power of my gods." Thus spake Nimrod, and the prison-keeper went forth to fetch Abraham. Approaching the pit into which Abraham had been thrown a year ago he called aloud:

" Abraham, Abraham, art thou still alive?"

[1] Jellinek, *Beth-Hamidrash*, Vol. I, 25–34; see also *Pirke de Rabbi Eliezer*, Ch. 26; *Baba Batra*, 91a.

[2] *Sepher Hajashar*; Jellinek, *Beth-Hamidrash*, Vol. I, 25–34.

[3] *Ibid*; see also Weil, *Biblische Legenden der Muselmänner*, p. 72.

" Verily, I am still alive," [1] replied Abraham.

" But how can that be," asked the jailer, " who gave thee food and drink?"

" The Almighty," replied Abraham, " the God of the Universe, the Lord of Hosts who works miracles, He who is the God of Nimrod, of Terah, and of the whole world, He who feeds every living creature sent me meat and drink. He sees everything but is invisible Himself. He dwelleth in the Heavens above, but His majesty filleth the world." [2]

Thus spake Abraham, and the jailer was mightily impressed. He abandoned the worship of the idols and acknowledged the God of Abraham who had wrought such a miracle. Loudly he declared that the gods of Nimrod were useless idols and should be overthrown.

When the King heard what had happened, he bade his servants seize the prison-keeper and have him beheaded. But the sword, when it touched him, was blunted and broke in twain, so that he went unharmed. Now Nimrod's wrath knew no bounds; he commanded that Abraham be at once thrown into the flames, and the prisoner was led into the presence of the King.

When the soothsayers saw Abraham, they at once exclaimed: " This is the man of whose doings we read in the stars on the night of his birth. Terah, his father, hath deceived thee, O King.[3] It is he of whom it was written in the stars that he will be a great nation which will inherit the world."

" Who gave thee the advice to hand over to my messengers the son of thy slave in the place of thine own son?" asked Nimrod, addressing himself to Terah.

" It was Haran, my other son," said Terah. " It was he indeed who advised me to deceive the King."

Terah said so because he well knew that Haran was inclined to follow the teachings of his brother Abraham. He

[1] *Maasse Abraham*, Jellinek, *loc. cit.*   [2] *Ibid.*   [3] *Sepher Hajashar*.

had moreover read in the stars that Haran was destined to be burnt alive.[1]

" Well then," replied Nimrod, " Haran, too, shall die together with thy son Abraham." And the servants of Nimrod seized both Abraham and his brother Haran, and made ready to divest them of their garments, bind them with ropes and throw them into the flames. But lo! no sooner did they approach Abraham when they were themselves devoured by the flames.

And now Satan, in the shape of man, appeared before Nimrod and thus he spake:

" Great King, bid thy servants take a long spear and by means of it throw Abraham into the furnace, so that no one need approach him." And the King gave orders that it should be done so.[2]

Now Abraham raised his eyes to Heaven and prayed to God Almighty to save him from such a terrible death. Satan thereupon approached Abraham and whispered into his ear: " Verily, Abraham, thou art doomed to perish in the flames, and no one can save thee. Listen to my advice and acknowledge the god of Nimrod, thus wilt thou be saved." But Abraham knew the voice of the tempter and exclaimed: " Get thee hence, Satan, I will not listen unto thee."

Abraham's mother, Emtelai, fearing lest her beloved son perish in the flames, now fell upon his neck and with tears streaming down her face implored him to obey the command of the King and thus be saved from a terrible death.

But Abraham, firm in his faith, replied: " No, Mother dear, I cannot deny my God and forsake my faith. Water will extinguish the fire lit by Nimrod's servants, but the fires of the Lord burn everlastingly. Woe unto those who forsake the Lord." [3]

[1] *Midrash Shokhor Tob*, Ps. 118; *Sepher Hajashar*.
[2] *Maasse Abraham*, Jellinek, *Beth-Hamidrash*, Vol. I, 25–34; see also Weil, *loc. cit.*, p. 74.
[3] *Maasse Abraham*, Jellinek, *loc. cit.*

Encouraged by his fortitude, Emtelai herself began to hope that the God of Abraham would save her son from the flames.

Now, Haran was waiting to see whether the flames would devour his brother or not. " If Abraham is saved," he thought in his heart, " I will worship the God of my brother, but if he perisheth, then I will acknowledge the gods of Nimrod."

Haran, however, was seized first and thrown into the flames where his entrails were burnt at once.[1] He wailed and cried aloud that he was ready to prostrate himself before the gods of Nimrod, but it was too late. An angel appeared and threw his burnt body at the feet of Terah.[2]

When Abraham was thrown into the flames, they never touched him. The ropes with which he had been bound were burnt to ashes, but Abraham himself walked about in the midst of the flames for three days and three nights. All the slaves who had lit the fire and all those who approached the furnace became at once a prey to the flames and they died, suffering great torture.[3]

When Nimrod saw that the fire had no power over Abraham, he called out:

" Abraham, thou faithful servant of the God who dwelleth in Heaven, come out of the flames and appear before me." Abraham, accordingly, left the flames and stood before the King.

" Tell me," asked Nimrod, " how didst thou manage to escape the flames which none of my servants were able to withstand?"

" The Lord of the Universe, of the heavens and of the earth, who rules the world and in whom I had faith, he alone saved me from a terrible death and did not let his servant perish in the flames." [4]

---

[1] *Sepher Hajashar*; see also *Targum Jerushalmi*; *Genesis*, 11, 28.
[2] *Midrash Shokhor Tob*, Ps. 118. See also *Book of Jubilees*, 12, 12–14, and Josephus, *Antiquities*, I, 6, 5, who says that the tomb of Haran was to be seen at Ur, in Chaldea.
[3] *Sepher Hajashar*; see also Weil, *loc. cit.* p. 76.
[4] *Sepher Hajashar*; *Maasse Abraham*, Jellinek, *Beth-Hamidrash*, Vol. I, 25–34.

Thus spake Abraham. And lo! suddenly the flames were extinguished, and in the place where they had been a while ago a beautiful and lovely garden appeared. There were fruit bearing trees, lovely to behold, and angels were wandering about who received Abraham in their midst.[1]

When Nimrod beheld the scene, he exclaimed:

" This is only magic, and now I understand how Abraham was saved from the flames. He is a great magician and he knew well enough that the flames would not touch him."

But the magicians at Nimrod's court replied: " No, great King, the power of magic doth not go so far, and it is only the living God who hath saved Abraham from the flames."

Thereupon the people came and wanted to prostrate themselves before Abraham and pay him homage, but he rebuked them, saying: " Do not prostrate yourselves before me, but worship the true God, the Lord of the Universe. It is He who hath saved me from the flames, and He will save all those who have faith in Him." [2]

The King now bestowed many presents upon Abraham, and also made him a gift of two slaves whose names were Oni and Eliezer.[3] And the great ones of the realm also came, praised Abraham and bestowed gifts upon him, so that he grew very rich and went away in peace. Many of the people, seeing how his God had saved Abraham from the flames, brought their children to him and asked him to teach them the ways of the Lord.[4] Thus over 300 gathered round Abraham, and among them were many of the royal servants, who followed him to his father's house, listening unto his words. Thereupon Abraham took to wife the daughter of his brother Haran, whose name was Sarai (or Sarah) and also Jiska, that is the seeress, because she was so beautiful that everyone turned round to look at her.[5]

[1] *Maasse Abraham*, Jellinek, *Beth-Hamidrash*, Vol. I, 29–34. See also Weil, *loc. cit.*, p. 76.
[2] *Sepher Hajashar.*   [3] *Ibid.*   [4] *Ibid.*
[5] *Sepher Hajashar; Megilla,* 14a; *Sanhedrin,* 69b.

And it came to pass that at the end of two full years, Nimrod had a dream. And behold, in his dream he stood with his army on the very spot where once the fire had been kindled, and the furnace stood, into the flames of which Abraham had been cast. And behold, a man greatly resembling Abraham issued forth from the flames. In his hand he held a naked sword and thus advanced upon the King. When Nimrod recoiled, the man with the naked sword threw an egg at him; and behold, the egg was soon changed into a large river which drowned all the King's army. The King alone and three of his companions escaped with their lives. Nimrod now looked into the countenances of his companions, and he saw that they were all arrayed in royal garments and resembled himself. And behold, the stream suddenly became an egg once more, and out of it came a hen which sat upon the King's head and picked out one of his eyes.[1]

And it came to pass that when Nimrod awoke in the morning his spirit was greatly troubled. He sent and called for all the magicians and soothsayers of his land and the wise men thereof; and he told them his dream. Then rose up one of the magicians and interpreters of dreams, Anuko by name, and thus he spake:

" Know, O King, that thy dream can be interpreted only in one way. It foretells thee the misfortune which Abraham and his offspring will one day bring upon thee and thy house. A day will come when he will wage war against thee and destroy thine army. Thou alone wilt escape with three of thy companions, but one of Abraham's offspring will put thee to death. Well do I remember, O King, that fifty-two years ago, when Abraham was born, we read his destiny in the stars and we warned the King. As long as Abraham liveth, there will be no peace for Nimrod." [2]

Thus spake Anuko. And when Nimrod heard his words

---

[1] *Sepher Hajashar.*   [2] *Ibid.*

and the interpretation of the dream, he secretly sent out his servants, commanding them to seize Abraham and to kill him. But Eliezer, one of the servants whom Nimrod had given as a gift to Abraham, happened to be at court and knew of the danger threatening his new master.

He hied himself to Abraham, and even before the servants of Nimrod had arrived, Abraham knew of the danger awaiting him. He accordingly fled to the house of Noah and Shem, where he remained hidden for one month.

Now it came to pass that Terah came in secret to see his son, and Abraham thus addressed his father: " My father, Nimrod is once more threatening me with death, and who knows what he hath in mind against thee. Misfortune may await thee at any moment, and thine own life is not safe as long as thou dost remain in Nimrod's service. To-day he bestoweth gifts upon thee, but to-morrow he may take thy life. Listen unto my voice, O Father mine, and leave the service of Nimrod. Let us be off and journey to Canaan, where we shall be able to live in peace and serve the only living God."

Thus spoke Abraham, and both Noah and Shem approved his words. And Terah did listen unto the words of Abraham, because he now hated Chaldaea (or Mesopotamia) since the terrible death of his son Haran.[1] Terah, accordingly, took his son Abraham, and Sarah, his daughter-in-law, the wife of his son Abraham, and Lot, the son of Haran, his son's son, and all his household, and he went forth with them from Ur of the Chaldees, to go into the land of Canaan. But when they came to Haran and saw the land which was very fruitful and large, they dwelt there. And the inhabitants of Haran loved Abraham and listened to his words, because he walked in the path of God and of virtue, and he was beloved by God and men.[2]

[1] Josephus, *Antiquities*, I, 6, 5.
[2] *Sepher Hajashar.* See also *Abodah Zarah*, 9a; *Targum Jerushalmi, Genesis*, 12, 5.

CHAPTER XXII

The Journey to Egypt and the Battle of the Kings

The journey to Canaan—The visit to Haran—The return to Canaan—
The great famine—The journey to Egypt—On the banks of the river Wadi-
el-Arish—Sarah, the beautiful—At the Egyptian frontier—The mysterious
chest and the custom-officers—The divine beauty of Sarah—She is brought
before the Pharaoh of Egypt—The prayer of Sarah—The punishment of
the King—The jealousy of the princes of Canaan—The attack upon Sodom
—The news brought by Og, the giant—Og's love for Sarah, the beautiful
—Abraham's instructions to his servants—The midnight battle—The
spears which turned to earth, and the arrows which turned to straw—In
the Kings' dale—The homage of the Kings—The modesty of the Patriarch
—The venerable Shem—Melchizedek.

FOR three years Abraham remained in Haran, together with
his family. And then the Lord commanded him to get out of
his country and from his kindred, and from his father's house
and to journey to Canaan. Abraham obeyed the command
of the Lord and journeyed with his wife Sarah to Canaan,
whilst Terah and Lot remained in Haran. When Abraham
arrived in Canaan, he pitched his tent amidst the inhabitants
of the land. He built an altar and proclaimed the name of the
Lord. Fifteen years Abraham dwelt in the country, and
when he reached his 70th year, he returned to Haran on a
visit to his father and kindred.[1] He remained five years in
Haran, but he disliked the idle and luxurious life of the inhabitants and yearned for the country of Canaan, the inhabitants of which were leading an agricultural and industrious
life.[2]

[1] *Sepher Hajashar.*   [2] *Genesis Rabba,* 39.

And it came to pass that at the end of five years, the Lord once more spoke unto Abraham and thus He said:

"Twenty years ago I commanded thee to leave Haran and to go to Canaan; and now I again tell thee get thee out of this country, thou and thy wife and thy kindred. Take all thy substance and all the souls which thou hast gotten and all who have accepted thy faith. Fear not the troubles and hardships of thy journey, for I will strengthen thee and thy fame will be great. And I will make of thee a great nation,[1] and I will bless thee, and make thy name great. And I will bless all those who will bless thee, and I will turn into a blessing the curses of thine enemies."[2]

Thus spake the Lord, and Abraham replied: "O God Almighty! What will the folks say when they see me leave my old father alone?"

"Thy father," said the Lord, "is a worshipper of idols, but the mission with which thou art entrusted is sacred; thy duty to mankind is greater than that which thou owest to thy father."[3]

And Abraham did as the Lord had bidden him. He journeyed as far as Sichem, and as far as the plains between the mountains of Gerisim and Ebal. Here he builded altars and pitched his tents. He first made a tent for his wife Sarah and then one for himself.[4]

And it now came to pass that a famine came upon the land of Canaan. It was the third famine since the world had been created, and it was sent to try Abraham.[5] Abraham, without a murmur, left Canaan, accompanied by his wife and his servants, and went out to Egypt. When he reached Wadi-el-Arish, the river of Egypt, he rested a few days.

Here Abraham and Sarah walked along on the river's bank, and for the first time the Patriarch saw reflected in the

[1] *Genesis Rabba*, 39; *Midrash Tanchuma, Genesis*, 12, 2.   [2] *Genesis Rabba*, 39.
[3] *Ibid.* See also *Rashi* to *Genesis*, 11, 32.   [4] *Genesis Rabba, ibid.*   [5] *Genesis Rabba*, 25

water the extraordinary beauty of his wife.[1] Never before
had he, in his great modesty, lifted up his eyes to her face,
and he knew not what she was like, until he saw her face
reflected in the water.[2] He was now aware of the fact that
she was very beautiful indeed, and he therefore asked her to
pass as his sister in Egypt, for fear lest he should be slain.
When they approached the frontiers of Egypt, Abraham,
however, as a further precaution, shut up his wife in a chest.
The frontiers of Egypt were reached, and the custom officers
made the Patriarch pay heavy duty on all his goods. They
insisted on his opening the chest wherein he had shut up
his wife.

" I will pay the customs due for the box," said Abraham,
" as if it contained not only silk or silver, but gold and costly
gems."

The custom-house officers, however, required that the
box should be opened, and Abraham's refusal to do so availed
him not. The chest was violently broken open, and lo! in
it was seated one of the most beautiful women ever seen.[3]
The custom-house officers were struck by her divine beauty,
for her countenance illumined all the land of Egypt. Speedily
they informed Pharaoh of the event.[4] Abraham and Sarah
were thereupon taken before the ruler of Egypt.[5] They were
sorely troubled and prayed to the Lord to protect them, and
an angel came down from Heaven to protect the Patriarch
and his beautiful wife.

" Fear not," said the angel to Sarah, " and be comforted,
for God has heard thy petitions."

" Who is the man," asked Pharaoh, when Sarah was
before him, " who accompanied thee to Egypt?"

" He is my brother," replied Sarah.

---

[1] *Sepher Hajashar*; *Midrash Tanchuma*, ed. Buber, pp. 65–66.
[2] *Targum Jerushalmi*, Genesis, 12, 11; *Baba Batra*, 16a.
[3] *Sepher Hajashar*; *Genesis Rabba*, 40; *Midrash Tanchuma*, ibid, p. 66; *Megilla* 15a.
See also Weil, *Biblische Legenden der Muselmänner*, p. 81.   [4] *Genesis Rabba, loc. cit.*
[5] *Sepher Hajashar*; see also Josephus, *De bello Judaico*, V, 9, 4.

"Who is this woman?" he asked Abraham.

"She is my sister," replied the latter. This lie of Abraham is called in legendary lore a justifiable falsehood.

Now Pharaoh's heart was filled with great love for Sarah, and he asked for her hand.

"I will give thee," he pleaded, "as my royal present for thy hand, all the gold and silver and slaves which I possess, and also the fair land of Goshen."

Sarah would not listen to his pleadings, and Pharaoh pressed his suit in an impetuous and vehement manner.[1] In her great trouble she cried to God and prayed for protection. Pharaoh was thereupon smitten with paralysis, and plagues afflicted all his servants.[2] And when he heard that Sarah was already married to Abraham, he sent for the latter and not only returned to him his wife but also dismissed him with many costly gifts. To Sarah, too, he gave many presents,[3] and also presented to her his daughter Hagar, by one of his concubines, to be the servant of Sarah.

"My daughter," said Pharaoh, "it is better to be a servant in a house which enjoys the special protection of God, than to command elsewhere."[4]

And it now came to pass that the fame of Abraham spread all over the land, and he was a blessing to the people. But the kings and rulers of men were jealous of him and said in their hearts:

"Let us kill Abraham and wipe out his name from the earth, so that our people will no longer talk of him and forget him." But one of the kings said:

"If we attack Abraham, his many friends will gather round him and protect him. Let us therefore go to Sodom and take captive his brother's son Lot and take all his sub-

[1] *Pirke de Rabbi Eliezer*, Ch. 26; *Sepher Hajashar*; *Midrash Tanchuma*, ibid.; *Genesis Rabba*, 41.   [2] *Pirke de Rabbi Eliezer*, Ch. 26; *Sepher Hajashar*; *Genesis Rabbi*, 41.
[3] *Pirke de Rabbi Eliezer*, Ch. 26.
[4] *Sepher Hajashar*; *Pirke de Rabbi Eliezer*, Ch. 26. See also Weil, *loc. cit.*, p. 82.

stance. When Abraham will learn that his kinsman is
in our hands he will pursue us. It will then be easy for us
to get him into our hands and do with him as we please."
Thus spake one of the kings, and his words pleased his con-
federates. They accordingly went to Sodom and made captive
many men, women, and children, and among them Lot, the
son of Haran, the brother of Abraham.

Now Og the giant, one of whose descendants afterwards
became king of Bashan, had long ago cast his eyes upon
Sarah, the wife of Abraham, and coveted her for her great
beauty. Og had been saved from perdition during the flood
in the days of Noah and had been fighting in the ranks of
the giants vanquished by King Amraphel, who was no other
than Nimrod. Og escaped and hastened to Abraham, who
at that time dwelt in the plain of Mamre the Amorite,
and brought him the news of the captivity of Lot.
"Abraham," thought Og in his heart, "is a mighty
hunter and a great warrior, and if he hears that his brother's
son has been taken captive, he will surely arm his trained
servants and go out against the enemy to set Lot free. He
will be killed in battle, and Sarah will no longer resist me and
be mine." [1] Thus thought Og the giant.

When Abraham heard that his brother's son had been
taken captive, he indeed grew angry. He gathered all his
followers whom he was teaching the ways of the Lord, and
asked them to follow and support him in his fight. But as
few only would listen unto him, Abraham went out accompanied only by his faithful servant Eliezer and his trained
servants.[2]

Then Abraham said unto his armed servants: "I know
full well that ye will only think of booty and the goods to be
taken in battle, but will pay little heed to the captives and
make no effort to save them. I will therefore give everyone

[1] *Genesis Rabba*, 42; *Yalkut*, 1, § 42.   [2] *Genesis Rabba*, 43.

of you much silver and gold and precious stones, if ye will swear to me not to turn your attention to the booty, but only seek to deliver the captives, and above all the women and children, and try to save them from the hands of their captors." [1]

The armed servants of Abraham swore to do as they were bidden. Towards midnight, Abraham met the enemy. The angels hastened to Abraham's assistance, and the stars in Heaven fought for him. [2] When the enemy beheld Abraham and his armed servants from far, he prepared for battle. The kings threw their sharp spears at Abraham and his followers, but behold, the spears were turned to earth and did not harm the gallant Patriarch. [3] The kings then sent their arrows against Abraham, but the arrows turned to straw and fell to the ground, without causing any harm to either Abraham or his faithful followers. Greatly marvelling at this, the kings said: " Let us rush up and seize him quickly, for the angels in Heaven and the stars are fighting on his side." But no sooner did they make a step forward, when Abraham seized the earth and the straw, which had fallen at his feet, and threw both at the enemy. And behold, earth and straw turned again to spears and arrows and hit the advancing enemy. [4]

When the kings saw what had happened, they said: " Verily, Abraham is the beloved of God in Heaven." The Patriarch then smote the enemy, scattered the pursuers, and they hastily fled, leaving all the booty and captives behind. Abraham took all the goods and the captives and turned homewards. [5]

The kings, whom he had smitten and whose armies he had dispersed, met him in a valley called afterwards the Kings' dale. Here they had hastily constructed a throne, and when Abraham and his men approached, they thus addressed him: " We have seen thy strength and witnessed the wonders thou hast done; now we know that thou art in-

---

[1] Cf. *Midrash Tanchuma, ibid.*, p. 73.   [2] *Sanhedrin.* 96a.
[3] *Sanhedrin*, 108b; *Genesis Rabba*, 43; *Midrash Tanchuma*, ed. Buber, p. 76; *Midrash Shokhor Tob, Ps.* 110.   [4] *Ibid.*   [5] *Genesis Rabba*, 43.

deed the beloved of God. We, therefore, prostrate ourselves before thee and proclaim thee our king, our ruler, and our God." Thus spoke the kings in the dale of Kings.[1]

Thereupon Abraham replied:

" Far be it from me to be your king, much less your God! Know ye not that I am only a mortal man, like other men. It is not I, but the God in Heaven who has worked the wonders. If, however, I have found grace in your eyes, then go your ways, live peacefully together, wage no more wars, but be merciful and meek, and walk humbly before your God. Open your doors to the poor, the widow, the stranger, and the wanderer, and acknowledge the true God in Heaven and serve Him with all your heart." [2]

Thus spake Abraham, and taking leave of the kings he returned home. And yet Abraham was troubled in his mind, for he was thinking of that venerable old man, Shem, the son of Noah, in whose school he had studied for years and learnt to fear God and love men. " What will Shem think," thought Abraham, " will he not rebuke me for having drawn my sword against the sons of Elam, his grandchildren?" [3]

And behold, Shem, who was now priest of the most high God and ruled at Salem under the name of Melchizedek,[4] came to meet him, bringing forth bread and wine.

" What must Abraham have thought of me," said Shem in his heart, " when he learned that my own grandchildren with their wicked armies had invaded the peaceful valleys of the Jordan, plundered the inhabitants, and taken captives even the nearest kinsfolk of Abraham." Thus thought Shem, and aloud he spake thus:

" Blessed be thou, Abraham, and blessed be the most high God who hath delivered thine enemies into thy hands. It is indeed noble of thee to have delivered the captives and

---

[1] Genesis Rabba, 43.   [2] Ibid.   [3] Genesis Rabba, 44.
[4] Genesis Rabba, 44; Midrash Shokhor Tob, Ps. 76, 3; Sanhedrin, 108b.

restored unto them their goods, taking nought unto thyself, from a thread even to a shoe-latchet."

And Abraham gave thanks to the Lord, and thus he prayed:

" Lord of the Universe, it is not by the strength of my arm but by Thy power that I have been able to smite mine enemy and deliver the women and the children. Thou hast protected me and been my shield." Thus prayed the Patriarch and the angels in Heaven replied: " Blessed be the name of the Lord, the shield of Abraham." [1]

[1] *Midrash Shokhor Tob, Ps.* 106. See for the entire chapter, Jellinek, *Beth-Hamidrash*, Vol. I, pp. 25–34; Vol. II, pp. 118–119; Lewner, *Kol Agadoth*, Vol. I, pp. 63–65.

CHAPTER XXIII

The Sin of Sodom

The three travellers—The visit of the angels: Michael, Raphael, and Gabriel—The mission of the angels—The prosperity of Sodom—The cruelty of the people of Sodom—Charity is a crime—The thieves and the pitchers full of balsam—The perverted laws—The story of the poor boy who killed the cattle of the townspeople—The story of the stranger who had crossed the river—The claim of the inhabitants—The verdict of the judges—Eliezer visits the town—The bleeding judge—The banquet, and the flight of the guests—The empty house—The two beds—The story of the stranger, the ass, the carpet, and the greedy landlord—The strange dream—The interpretation of the dream—The hungry maiden—The story of Peletith and the starving beggar—The cry of the poor girl that ascended to Heaven—The girl dipped in honey, and the bees—The worshippers of the sun, and the worshippers of the moon—The news of the terrible destruction—The Patriarch travels to the land of the Philistines.

It was noon of the 15th of Nisan,[1] on the third day after Abraham's operation, and he was sitting in front of his tent. The heat was intense, for Hell had been let loose, so that the world might feel its heat, and also because the Lord wanted to test Abraham once more.[2] Abraham never thought of his suffering, for he was troubled in his mind on account of his inability on such a day to find an opportunity to practise his hospitality. No wanderer was to be seen on the dusty road. At first Abraham sent out his servant Eliezer to watch for any stranger that might happen to pass along, and invite him to his hospitable tent. Soon Eliezer returned and informed his master that, look as he might, no wanderer was to be seen. Abraham now raised his eyes, and behold, there were three

[1] *Midrash Tanchuma, Exodus,* 12, 41.
[2] *Baba Mezia,* 86b; *Midrash Tanchuma, Genesis,* 18.

strangers.[1] They seemed to be Arabs, Saracens or Naba-
thaeans, but in reality they were the angels Michael, Raphael,
and Gabriel, each entrusted with a separate message.[2] And
after Abraham had offered the three strangers his hospitality,
Michael informed him that his wife Sarai, or Sarah, would
bear a son. His mission accomplished, he spread out his
wings and returned to the celestial regions.

But Raphael and Gabriel had another mission. Gabriel
had been sent to overturn Sodom and Gomorrah, whilst
Raphael had been entrusted with the mission of saving Lot.
They both therefore wended their way towards Sodom, but
even after having accomplished their mission they remained
138 years upon earth, having no permission to return to the
celestial regions. This was their punishment for having
dared to announce to Lot that *they* would destroy the city,
thus speaking in their own name as if it was their own free
action and not a command they had received from the Most
High.

And in those days the sin of the men of Sodom was very
grevious.[3] The men of Sodom were very wealthy and prosperous, because their land was very rich and yielded good
harvests and plenty of fruit. There were moreover in Sodom
mines of gold, of silver, and of precious stones which the
inhabitants exploited. It often happened that when a master
said unto his servant: " Go and weed out the herbs in the
garden," the servant, in weeding out the herbs, would suddenly
discover a mine of gold.[4] Thus the men of Sodom waxed
rich, but forgot the name of the Lord who had sent them all
their wealth and made them prosperous and happy. They
worshipped the sun and the moon and all the stars in heaven,
and served them. Moreover, the inhabitants of Sodom never

---

[1] *Genesis Rabba*, 48.
[2] *Midrash Agadah*, ed. Buber, p. 39; *Yoma*, 37a; *Genesis Rabba*, 50; *Baba Mezia*, 86b.
[3] *Sepher Hajashar*; *Pirke de Rabbi Eliezer*, Ch. 25; *Sanhedrin*, 109b.
[4] *Pirke de Rabbi Eliezer*, Ch. 25; *Yalkut, Job*, § 915.

gave of their substance to the poor and the alien who came to their city. They passed a law according to which all aliens were to be expelled, and poor men seeking food never to receive a piece of bread. Charity was a crime punished heavily within the walls of the city of Sodom.[1] The men of Sodom elected as their judges and rulers men of falsehood and wickedness, who mocked justice and equity, and committed evil deeds.[2] Whenever a stranger happened to enter the city of Sodom, the inhabitants at once took away his goods and substance, divested him of his clothes, and sent him away poor and naked. There was no use to appeal to the laws of the city, for the judges themselves approved such deeds.

Thus the inhabitants of Sodom, who knew neither charity nor human kindness, waxed rich and exceedingly prosperous, and lived in peace. They even passed a law that whoever was guilty of a charitable action, were it only the gift of a piece of bread to a starving beggar, was to die.

Earthquakes and storms had several times disturbed the peaceful lives of the inhabitants of Sodom, but they never attributed such visitation to the wrath of the Lord and never mended their ways, but continued to persevere in their deeds of wickedness. When a wealthy man came to the city, they placed him underneath a rickety structure or wall, and when the wall fell down and killed him, they pretended that it was an accident and took away all his possessions. They frequently robbed one another too.

As the rich men jealously guarded their wealth in secret vaults and chambers, men, seeking to rob them, acted as follows: they would take pitchers full of balsam, and approaching the rich thus speak unto them: " Take these pitchers full of precious oil and place them in your treasury, keeping them for us." The rich man complied, took the pitchers full

---

[1] *Targum Jerushalmi, Genesis*, 17.
[2] *Sepher Hajashar; Sanhedrin*, 109ab; *Pirke de Rabbi Eliezer*, Ch. 25; *Genesis Rabba*, 50; See also Homer, *Iliad*, 16, 386–389.

of balsam and placed them in his treasury. At night these hunters for gold and treasure went about, and like dogs smelt out the hiding-place, and made away with all the gold and silver hoarded up in the secret chambers.[1]

The judges who ruled in Sodom passed also the following laws. Whoever was the possessor of one ox was compelled to find pasture during one day for all the cattle of the town; but he who was poor and had none was compelled to find pasture for the cattle of the town for five days. All those who passed the river had to pay one *suz* (silver coin); but if anyone, to escape payment, chose to take a longer way without crossing the river, he was obliged to pay two *suz*. Whenever a man cut off the ear of another man's donkey, he was compelled to keep and feed the animal until the ear had healed.[2] Whenever one man 'n a quarrel with his neighbour, hurt the latter and caused him a wound, the judges made the wounded man pay a certain sum to his assailant for the service he had rendered him by bleeding him, which, they maintained, was a medical operation. Whenever one of the inhabitants of Sodom dared to invite a stranger to some festivity, he was immediately divested of his garments and thrown into the streets.

And it came to pass that one day the guardians of the town came to the son of a poor widow and thus they spoke: " Thou hast no ox and therefore we command thee to go and find pasture for two days for all the cattle of the town." The son of the widow seemingly complied with the request of the guardians, but when he was in the fields he rose up and slaughtered all the cattle. And when the men of Sodom, on hearing what had occurred, hastened to the fields, the boy said:

" Everyone who possessed one ox let him take one hide, but he who had none, because he was poor, let him take two hides." [3]

---

[1] *Sanhedrin*, 109b; *Sepher Hajashar.*
[2] See Beer, *Das Leben Abrahams*, p. 162, note 441.   [3] *Sanhedrin*, 109a.

" Thou art talking foolishly," said the men of Sodom;
" didst thou not slaughter all our cattle, and now thou wouldst
distribute their hides among the numerous poor beggars.
This is not justice!"

" Talk ye of justice?" asked the boy. " Am I not acting
even according to your own laws? Have not your judges
decreed that he who was the possessor of one ox was to pasture
the cattle of the town for one day, but he who possessed none
shall be obliged to find pasture for all the cattle for two days?"

The men of Sodom had the good grace to feel confounded
and ashamed, but they vented their wrath by spitting into
the face of the boy, knowing that by their own perverted laws
which they had passed he would go unscathed if brought before
the judges.[1]

The peculiarity of Sodom was the fact that there was a
semblance of order and justice, and that the men claimed
always to be in the right and law-abiding, never doing any
wrong. But their laws were perverted.

One day a stranger came to Sodom, having crossed the
river. The men of the town at once gathered round him and
said: " Pay four *suz* to the owner of the ferry."

" I never availed myself of the ferry," said the stranger,
" but waded through the river." [2]

" If this be the case," replied the Sodomites, " then pay
him eight *suz* for having tried to defraud him of four." And
when the stranger refused to pay, saying that indeed he had
no money and had therefore waded through the river, they
fell upon him and beat him until blood oozed from his face.
The stranger, unacquainted with the laws of Sodom, hastened
before the judges and related how he had been beaten, and
what treatment he had met with at the hands of the wicked
inhabitants. But the judges severely replied:

" Stranger! thou art indeed unacquainted, as we see,

---

[1] *Sepher Hajashar.*   [2] *Sanhedrin,* 109b.

with the laws of Sodom. This, however, is no excuse, for every stranger who cometh to our town must abide by our excellent laws. Know then, O ignorant stranger, that the claims of the men of Sodom are justified. The men of our town never can do wrong, especially where a stranger is concerned. By the laws of our country, we condemn thee, therefore, to pay eight *suz* to the owner of the ferry, because wantonly thou didst try to defraud him of four. Moreover, thou wilt pay some money unto those men who have beaten thee and caused blood to issue from thy body, as we well perceive from thy bleeding countenance. Thou must pay them for their trouble in performing a medical operation upon thee." [1]

Thus spoke the judges with an air of severity and self complacency, for were they not the guardians of the law?

And it came to pass that Eliezer, the faithful servant of Abraham, one day came to Sodom, bringing a message to Lot from his uncle Abraham. Passing through the town, he perceived one of the inhabitants wrestling with a stranger and beating him. Eliezer—accustomed in the house of his new master Abraham to treat men with loving kindness, to practise charity and to espouse the cause of justice—interfered between the two combatants. " What wrong hath this man done unto thee, and why art thou ill-treating him?" asked Eliezer, addressing the man of Sodom.

" Because," replied the latter, " he is not law-abiding and refuseth to obey me. I did ask him according to the laws of our town, to divest himself of his clothes and hand them over to me, but he refuseth." [2]

" The laws of thy country are perverted indeed," replied Eliezer, " leave therefore this man alone and do him no harm."

But the man of Sodom, hearing such words from Eliezer, waxed wroth, and seizing a stone threw it at him, causing him a grievous wound. When he saw the blood on Eliezer's

[1] *Sanhedrin*, 109.　　[2] *Sepher Hajashar*.

countenance, he took hold of him, saying: " Now thou wilt
have to pay me money, for I have bled thee. Such indeed
are the laws of our land."

" What," exclaimed Eliezer, " thou art talking foolishly;
thou hast caused me a wound and now thou dost ask for
money for having caused it."

" I see," replied the man of Sodom, " that thou art a
stranger indeed and unacquainted with our excellent laws;
let us betake ourselves before the judge."

And so before the judge they went. To Eliezer's great
amazement, the judge spoke as follows:

" This man hath indeed bled thee, and by the laws of our
country he who wounds another and causeth him a grievous
wound must pay damages, for it is the weakest, the loser,
who payeth. Besides, he had some trouble to draw thy
blood."

Eliezer, amazed and angry, seized a stone and hurled it
at the judge's head. " Now," he said, " I have a claim on
thee, pay me and I will pay this man, or thou canst pay him
thyself in my stead." [1] Thereupon Eliezer left the judge and
betook himself to the river where he washed his face. He
then entered a house and asked the inmates to sell him some
food. But instead of food he received insults and harsh words;
he fared not better at several other houses, where he repeated
his request. No man of Sodom ever sold food to a stranger.
Such were the laws of the land. And when Eliezer severely
felt the pangs of hunger he entered a house where a banquet
was being offered to the townspeople by one of the inhabitants,
and calmly sat down at the end of the table. Some of the
guests, perceiving that he was a stranger, asked him: " Who
called thee hither?"

" The man by whose side I am sitting invited me hither."
But when the latter heard such words, terror seized him.

[1] See *Sepher Hajashar.*

THE WAYFARER IN SODOM IS STRETCHED TO FIT HIS BED

He knew full well what awaited him, for his fellow citizens
would soon divest him of his clothes for having dared to
invite a stranger to a feast. They would, moreover, not believe
his words, if he tried to deny Eliezer's statement. He, therefore, hastily rose up and fled. Eliezer thereupon sat down by
the side of the next guest.

" Blessed be thou," he said, " for having invited me hither
to partake of food, for I am hungry indeed." Hearing such
words the guest was greatly frightened and he, too, hastily
left the house. Eliezer now continued his stratagem by thus
addressing all the guests, one after another. After a while
they had all left the house whither they had been invited,
and Eliezer, remaining alone, partook of food, left money
behind in payment of what he had partaken, blessed the Lord,
and left the house and the town of Sodom.[1]

In an open square of the town there were four beds for
strangers to sleep in. Two of the beds were long ones and
two very short ones. And when a stranger, unacquainted
with the customs and doings of the town, came to Sodom,
the inhabitants pretended to offer him hospitality.

" Choose any of these beds you prefer and sleep in peace,"
they spoke quite pleasantly. And when the unsuspecting
stranger laid himself down upon one of the short beds, they
cut off his feet, saying that the bed was too short for him
and they would make it fit him properly. When, on the other
hand, he laid himself down upon one of the long beds, six
strong men immediately took hold of his head and feet, began
to pull his head and limbs one way and the other, so as to
stretch his body out and make it fit the long bed.[2] Now Eliezer,
on leaving the house where he had managed to find food, passed
the open square. The men of Sodom invited him to pass the
night in one of the beds. Eliezer, however, very wary and not

[1] Lewner, *Kol Agadoth*, Vol. I, p. 75.
[2] *Sanhedrin*, 109a; *Sepher Hajashar*. Cf. The Story of the Bed of Procrustes; see also
Introduction.

trusting the men of Sodom, replied to them: " I am greatly beholden unto you for your hospitality, but ever since the death of my mother I have vowed never in my life to sleep in a bed, but to pass the night on the ground."

And one day it came to pass that a stranger happened to visit Sodom, for many strangers, unacquainted with the customs and manners of the country and the wicked deeds of the inhabitants, frequently came thither. The stranger had an ass which he was leading by a long rope, and a costly carpet. He sat in the road, and no one invited him into the house. Thereupon a man, named Heydad, came along. Beholding the stranger, his ass and carpet, he went up to him and thus addressed him:

" Come, blessed of the Lord, why dost thou remain in the road? Follow me to my house and there thou wilt find food and shelter."

The stranger thanked the kindly host and followed him to his house. He passed the night under the seemingly hospitable roof of Heydad, and in the morning, thanking his host for his hospitality, made up his mind to continue his journey.

" Tarry awhile," said the host, " I will not let thee go until thou hast refreshed thyself." And he insisted so much that the man yielded.

Thereupon the stranger said: " Blessed be thou, mine host, for having taken me in and given me food and shelter, but now I must really be off."

" Nay," said the host; " why this hurry? The day is exceedingly hot; the heat of the sun is unbearable, and the roads are dusty. Wait until the sun sets and then thou wilt go thy way in the coolness of the night."

He begged and insisted so much that the stranger once more yielded to his entreaties and remained until after sunset. But when the night had come down and sent her shadows, Heydad once more refused to let him go.

"Dost thou not see that it is a very dark night, and no pale moon sends its rays of light to show thee the way. I am afraid lest something happen unto thee on the road and thou mayest meet with an accident." Thereupon he once more insisted upon the guest remaining under his roof another night. On the following morning, however, the stranger was firmly decided to leave the town, although Heydad still pressed him to remain a little longer.

"Nay," said he, "I have tarried too long and must really be off now."

Thereupon the wife of Heydad said unto her husband: "This man has remained in our house two nights, he has had food and drink and shelter, but has never paid us anything. Why art thou such a fool to throw away thy substance upon strangers?"

Thus spoke the wife of Heydad, but her husband bade her be quiet.

"Do not worry," he said, "I will make him pay."

Thereupon the stranger asked Heydad to hand him the rope by which he was leading his ass and also the costly carpet which he had given him on his arrival, so as to put it in a safe place.

"Rope and carpet!" said the host, in assumed amazement, "verily, thou hast had a strange dream, for thou hast only dreamed of the rope and of the beautiful carpet. I will, however, interpret the dream for thee. The rope means long years, whilst the carpet is surely a beautiful garden. The Lord loveth thee surely and hath shown thee in this dream that thou wilt live many years and possess a beautiful garden wherein thou wilt plant many trees, beautiful to behold."

"Why dost thou speak foolishly?" replied the stranger. "It is no dream I am speaking about, but of a real rope and carpet I handed over to thee. Hand it back to me that I may go my way." But Heydad imperturbably repeated that it was a dream.

" And now," he added, " pay me my fee for the interpretation of this dream." The stranger protested loudly and betook himself to the judge. Heydad went with him and once more claimed his fee for the interpretation of the dream.

" Pay him his fee," decided the judge. And when the stranger indignantly cried that the host had stolen his property, the judge added: " Throw this man out of the town."

The inhabitants came, insulted him and threw him out of the town.[1]

Now it also happened that two maidens of Sodom came to draw water at the well, and one of the maidens said to her friend:

" Why dost thou look so ill to-day?"

" Because," replied her friend, " I have had no food for two days, there is not a crust of bread in the house."

Taking pity upon her friend, the first maiden said:

" Tarry thou a moment here and await my return." She came back after a while and thus spoke to her friend:

" Take my pitcher and give me thine."

The hungry maiden did as her friend had bidden her, but when she came home she found that her friend had filled her pitcher with meal. She quickly kneaded a dough and made cakes. But when the deed of the first maiden became known to the people of the town, they took her and burned her on the stake, for charity was a great crime at Sodom.

Now it came to pass that one of Lot's daughters, Peletith[2] by name, was wedded to one of the great and mighty men of Sodom. One day she noticed in the street of the city a very poor man who was starving, and the sight of him touched her

---

[1] Sepher Hajashar.
[2] Sanhedrin, 109a; Targum Jerushalmi, Genesis, 18, 21; Sepher Hajashar; Pirke de Rabbi Eliezer, Ch. 25; cf. Midrash Agadah, ed. Buber, Vol. I, p. 42, where the name of the maiden is Kalah.

kind heart so that she was grieved on his account. Afraid openly to strengthen his hand with a loaf of bread, she put into her pitcher all sorts of provisions, and whenever she went out to the well to draw water she handed the provisions to the poor man and thus fed him daily.

The wicked men of Sodom, who would not themselves strengthen the hand of this poor man with a loaf of bread, wondered greatly and said: " How does this poor man manage to live?"

They watched, ascertained the facts and at last knew that it was Peletith, the daughter of Lot, who fed the hungry man. They brought her out, according to their perverse laws, and burnt her.

She cried unto the Lord and prayed: " Sovereign of all the worlds, maker of the Universe, maintain my right and my cause." Her cry ascended to Heaven, right to the Throne of Glory. And the Lord said: " I will descend and see whether the wicked men of Sodom have done according to the cry of this woman." [1]

One day a maiden of Sodom met a stranger in the street. " Whence hast thou come?" she asked him.

" I have come a long way from here, but the sun hath set and I thought I would pass the night in this town and await the dawn." He then asked the maiden for a piece of bread and a drink of water, for he was very hungry and thirsty.

She gave him bread and water, and he ate and drank and blessed her. But when her deed became known, the judges of the town were very angry. They condemned her to be divested of her clothes, be dipped in a cask of honey and placed near a beehive. The bees gathered round her to suck the honey, and the poor maiden, suffering greatly, cried unto the Lord.[2]

It was to such a town that the angels Gabriel and Raphael,

---

[1] *Pirke de Rabbi Eliezer*, Ch. 25; *Targum Jerushalmi, Genesis*, 18, 20.
[2] *Sanhedrin*, 109b. See also *Genesis Rabba*, 49–50; *Sepher Hajashar*.

upon leaving Abraham, wended their way, for they had been commanded by the Most High to destroy the town and its wicked inhabitants. And when at last the men of Sodom heard that the town would soon be destroyed, the worshippers of the sun said:

" If only the morning would come and the sun rise, the sun which we are worshipping will surely save us from perdition."

But the men who worshipped the moon said: " Let the sun never rise but the moon continue to cast its light, for it is the moon we are worshipping which will save us from any calamity." [1]

The Lord Almighty, however, destroyed their town when both the moon and the sun were visible upon the firmament. At the very moment He rained upon Sodom and Gomorrah brimstone and fire from Heaven, and the cities were overthrown, and all the plain and all the inhabitants perished, and all that which grew upon the ground. What had been prosperous towns and laughing verdant valleys were now a heap of ruins, and the smoke of the country which went up as the smoke of a furnace was seen far and wide.

The news of the destruction of the cities of Sodom and Gomorrah spread to distant lands, whilst the smoke was visible in the neighbouring towns. Fear and trembling seized the people, and no wanderer now wended his way to the places where once had stood prosperous cities. And as no strangers now passed the plain of Mamre, where Abraham had pitched his tent, the Patriarch no longer had an opportunity to offer hospitality as he had been accustomed to for some time. When many days passed and no one appeared at the door of his tent, Abraham was very troubled in his mind, and at last, in sheer despair, he left the lonely and desolate region and, travelling towards the south, he settled at Gerar, in the land of the Philistines. [2]

[1] *Genesis Rabba*, 50.
[2] *Genesis Rabba*, 52. See also for the entire chapter, Beer, *Das Leben Abrahams*; Bin Gorion, *Die Sagen der Juden*, Vol. II, pp. 209–237; Lewner, *loc. cit.*, pp. 72–79.

CHAPTER XXIV

The Hospitable Emir

Shem-Melchizedek, and the generous Patriarch—The feeding of the animals in the ark—Hospitality on a large scale—The palace with many doors—The tree that either spread out or raised its branches—The fame of the Patriarch—The charitable lady—Thank my master—The short blessing —The Patriarch as judge and arbitrator—The story of the two associates— Muddled accounts—The story of the obstinate old man—The anger of the host—The rebuke of God—The apology of Abraham.

"TELL me," said Abraham one day to Shem-Melchizedek, "what were the merits of thy father and of thy brothers in virtue of which you were all saved in the ark?"

"Our merit," replied Shem-Melchizedek, "consisted in our having practised charity and fed the needy."

"The needy?" queried Abraham, "but there were no needy in the ark, the inmates of which were only thy father and his household."

"There were also the dumb animals," replied Shem-Melchizedek, "the dumb animals whom we fed, giving them their daily food whenever they needed it. We never forgot to give them their daily ration, and even in the night we attended to their needs." [1]

Thus spake Shem-Melchizedek, and Abraham thought in his heart:

"If it was counted as a righteous deed to Noah and to his sons to feed the dumb animals, how much greater must be the merit of him who feeds man who is needy and hungry, man who has been created in the image of God!" [2]

[1] *Midrash Tanchuma, Genesis, 8, 16.*   [2] *Midrash Shokhor Tob, Ps. 37.*

And Abraham decided to practise hospitality on a very
large scale, and to feed the needy and hungry wanderer and
the tired traveller. Thereupon he planted a garden with
vine, fig trees and other fruit-bearing trees, built a sumptuous
palace, the doors of which were open to east, west, north, and
south.[1] Here food and drink were offered in abundance to all
passers-by, to all needy wanderers and tired travellers. And
when a traveller, suffering from the heat of the sun, tired,
hungry and thirsty passed by, he was invited to enter the
hospitable place. Here he found food and shelter. He rested
his weary limbs upon one of the couches, slaked his thirst and
appeased his hunger. Beneath the shady trees he found protection against the burning sun of the east. And it came to
pass that when a good man, believing in the God of Heaven,
sat down under one of the trees, the tree immediately spread
out its branches giving him protection. But when a worshipper
of idols came, the tree raised its branches and he was exposed
to the intense heat and the burning rays of the sun. Thus
Abraham knew at once whether his guest was a believer in
the God in Heaven or an idolater. And when Abraham
knew that his guest was a worshipper of idols, he hastened to
welcome him and to offer him refreshment.[2]

" Eat and drink, my friend," he said, " and bless the Lord
who feeds the needy." He waited upon him as a servant waits
upon his master, and spoke to him about the loving kindness
of the Lord, of Him who had created Heaven and earth, and
all its creatures. And he never left the worshipper of idols
until the latter had opened his eyes and begun to understand
the power and love of the Lord of the Universe.[3]

And the fame of Abraham the Hebrew spread far and wide,
so that from all the corners of the earth men, women, and
children, all the lowly and oppressed, the needy and miserable,

---

[1] *Sepher Hajashar; Midrash Shokhor Tob*, Ps. 37; *Abot de Rabbi Nathan*, Ch. 7.
[2] *Abot de Rabbi Nathan*, Ch. 7; *Sotah*, 10.   [3] Cf. *Pirke de Rabbi Eliezer*, Ch. 25.

the suffering and the downtrodden, the hungry and the naked, came to him to seek solace and help. All of them Abraham received with open arms. He fed and clothed them, comforted and consoled them and wiped away their tears.

And Sarah, his wife, was sharing in the charitable work of her aged husband. Indefatigably she worked day and night. During the day she assisted her husband and waited upon the travellers, offering them food and drink; and during the night she worked assiduously and industriously, weaving, with her own hands, garments to cover the naked. Girding her loins with strength, she strengthened her arms; she laid her hand to the spindle, and her hands held the distaff. She sought wool and flax and worked willingly with her hands, she, the aged mate of the wealthy and prosperous oriental Emir, who owned fields and vineyards, slaves and cattle, and who was the friend and companion of potentates and princes. Her candle never went out at night, from Saturday to Saturday.

And the more Abraham and his wife Sarah worked and laboured for the benefit and in the interests of the poor and needy, the miserable, afflicted and suffering, the greater grew their fame, and the Lord blessed their work, and they became a blessing.

And it came to pass that when the guests who had found such hospitable treatment in the house of Abraham and his wife, such comfort and consolation, kissed his hands and thanked him for his help, Abraham used to reply:

"Nay, do not thank me, but my master who sendeth food to the hungry and help to the needy."

"And where is thy master?" asked the ignorant; "show him unto us that we may thank him and bless him."

"The Master, mine and yours, my friends," replied Abraham, "is the Lord of the Universe whose glory fills the whole world; it is He who feedeth all creatures in His great loving kindness and mercy." [1]

And Abraham's listeners wondered greatly, saying: " Verily, great and glorious is this master, the Lord of the Universe, but He is invisible and we know not how to thank and bless Him for His loving kindness; teach us how to thank Him daily for His mercies."

" My friends," replied Abraham, and his heart was full of joy, " say only a few words: ' Blessed be the Eternal, our Lord, from eternity to eternity.' It is a short blessing, but coming from the heart it is agreeable to God Almighty." [2]

But men came to Abraham not solely to ask his charity. They also came to seek his advice and judgment. Those who had some dispute, knocked at the gate of the famous hospitable Emir of Canaan saying: " We bring our difference before thee and ask thee to be our judge." Abraham, as a rule, patiently heard their claims and always endeavoured to bring about a reconciliation, so that the parties left his house not as enemies but as friends.

And it came to pass that one day two men came to Abraham laying their case before him. " For a long time," said the first of the disputants, " we traded together as associates, and now, having separated, I find that my former associate oweth me one hundred shekels, but he refuseth to pay me this sum."

Thereupon Abraham took out one hundred shekels from his own purse and, giving it to the claimant, said: " Here is thy money, but let us listen now to what thy former associate hath to say."

" My Lord," said the other, " he is mistaken, for instead of owing him such a sum, it is he who oweth me money." Thereupon the claimant brought witnesses to prove that he

---

[1] *Midrash Tanchuma, Genesis,* 15, 1.
[2] *Ibid.; Genesis Rabba,* 43 and 54; *Abot de Rabbi Nathan,* Ch. 7.

was right. Yet both associates persevered in their statement.

Abraham, therefore, sat down and examined all their business transactions, and found that they had both erred and that none owed the other anything. He proved their error unto them, and they were reconciled, blessed Abraham, and praised his wisdom.

" My brothers," said Abraham, " keep the hundred shekels I have given you and divide the sum between you. As my sole reward, I beg you to love one another, to live in peace, and never to quarrel." [1]

Sometimes, however, it happened that Abraham lost his patience, trying in vain to open the eyes of an obstinate worshipper of idols who persistently refused to acknowledge the God in Heaven, the Lord of the Universe. Thus one day an old man, tired and hungry, approached his gate. Abraham rose at once to meet him and invited him into his house.

" Come into my tent," said Abraham, " refresh thyself, and rest thy weary limbs upon a couch; pass the night in my tent, and when the sun riseth in the east thou wilt continue thy way." The old man at first refused, preferring to pass the night under one of the trees in the open, but Abraham insisted and begged him to accept his hospitality, until the old man yielded.

Abraham hastened to wait upon the old man, placing butter and milk and cakes before the traveller, who ate and was satisfied.

" Render thanks, my friend," said Abraham, " to God Almighty, and bless His name, for it is He who sendeth their food to all His creatures." But the traveller replied:

" I know not thy God, the God thou speakest of; I know my idols which I have made with my own hands, them do I worship and to them do I render thanks."

All Abraham's persuasions and pleadings were of no avail,

[1] *Abot de Rabbi Nathan*, Ch. 4.

for the old man obstinately persisted in his error, and angrily exclaimed: " Why dost thou endeavour to make me abandon my gods? Leave me alone that I may continue to worship the gods of my youth until I die." Hearing such words, Abraham waxed wroth and called to his guest:

" Woe unto thee, thou sinful and wicked old man; leave my house immediately, for I never wish to see thee again." Thus spake Abraham in his righteous indignation, and the old man left Abraham's house in the night and went out into the desert. But the Lord rebuked Abraham for his rashness and his treatment of the old man, whom he had driven out of his tent in the darkness of the night.

" Where is the weary wanderer," asked the Lord, " who came into thy tent?"

" I have sent him away," replied Abraham, " for he was very obstinate and would persist in his evil ways."

But the Lord replied:

" I have borne the sin of this old man for many years and have not waxed angry. In spite of his errors, I have given him food and clothes, magnanimously waiting until he had mended his ways. He came to thee and thou didst not bear with him even for one short night, but didst drive him out of thy tent, sending him away in the darkness of the night into the desert. Now, hasten and run after thy guest and beg his forgiveness."

Abraham repented of his rash act, and hastened out in search of the old man whom he had so inhospitably sent away from beneath his roof. He found him at last, and falling upon his knees he begged the old man's forgiveness. He implored him to return to his tent and there to pass the night.[1]

---

[1] Lewner, *Kol Agadoth*, Vol. I, pp. 90–91; see for the entire chapter, Beer, *Das Leben Abrahams*; Weil, *Biblische Legenden der Muselmänner*. Lewner, *Kol Agadoth*, Vol. I, pp. 86–91.

CHAPTER XXV

The Sacrifice of a Father

The sumptuous banquet—The royal guests—Sammael appears in the guise of a beggar—The accusation of Sammael—His challenge—The visit of the father—The angry wife—The message of the father—The threshold of the tent—The second visit of Abraham to Ishmael—Fatima, the good wife—The two sons—The virtuous Isaac—The tempter before the Throne of Glory—The accusing angels—Shaftiel, the accuser—The speech of Sammael—The sacrifice of the beloved son—The ruse of the Patriarch—The joyous meal—The preparations for the journey—A mother's sorrow—Another version of the story of the journey—The saddling of the ass—The hopes of Eliezer and of Ishmael—The anger of Sammael—The whisperings of the tempter—Sammael appears as a youth and tempts Isaac—The stream barring the way—The prayer of the father—Sammael's new effort—The holy mountain—Abraham addresses his son—The dutiful boy—A son's message to his mother—Isaac's vision of the heavens—The weeping angels—Their prayer—The ram that was created before sunset on the sixth day of Creation—Sammael, and the ram—The voice from the Throne of Glory—God's promise to the Patriarch.

IT was at Gerar that Abraham's son Isaac was born, and all the folks marvelled at the miracle God had wrought. When Isaac was weaned, Abraham made a great feast, " the same day that the child was weaned ". [1] And many were the guests invited to that splendid feast at which Abraham was happy to display his usual hospitality. Kings and princes and the great ones of the land gathered at the house of Abraham. There was Abi-Melech, the King of Gerar, and his suite, Og, the giant, envious in his heart and still brooding mischief, and all the princes of Canaan, with the commanders of their armies, sixty-two in all. And Og's friends mocked him and said:

[1] Cf. *Pirke de Rabbi Eliezer*, Ch. 29; *Midrash Shokhor Tob*, Ps. 112.

281

" Didst thou not laugh at Abraham, saying that he was even like a mule which hath no offspring? What sayest thou now?" But Og replied: " I could squash this imp of his with the little finger of my hand." [1]

At the feast arranged by Abraham on the day when his son was weaned, there were also present the venerable Shem and Eber, as well as Abraham's old father Terah and his brother Nahor.[2] They had all hastened to come and rejoice with Abraham in his great happiness. But Sammael, he who is also called Satan, was exceedingly jealous of the happy father, and black were his thoughts. He thereupon appeared at the feast in the guise of a beggar standing in the door. Abraham, too busy waiting upon his distinguished guests, never noticed the beggar standing in the door and did not invite him to sit down at the table. Satan, who had only come in search of some incident which he could bring up against the old man, was rejoiced at this neglect. Straightway he spread his wings and appeared before the Throne of Glory and thus he spoke:

" Lord of the Universe! Thou hast given unto Abraham all that his heart desireth; Thou hast heaped upon him wealth and prosperity, and, in his old age, Thou hast even given him a son. Now his heart is swelled with pride and his head is lifted high. No longer doth he care for the poor and the needy. To-day I did test him, standing at his once hospitable door in the guise of a beggar, but he never paid the slightest attention to me and never invited me to break bread at his table. Such is the frailty of man, and even the best and most God-fearing become arrogant in their days of happiness and prosperity." Thus spoke Satan, accusing Abraham before the Throne of Glory. But a voice from the Throne of Glory replied:

" There is no one so charitable as Abraham, and there

---

[1] *Sepher Hajashar*; *Yalkut*, 2, § 973; *Genesis Rabba*, 53; *Baba Mezia*, 86a.
[2] *Sepher Hajashar*.

is none so pious and so God-fearing. Thou wilt see, Satan, accuser of men, that when I command Abraham to sacrifice his only son, born unto him in his old age, he will gladly and unhesitatingly obey My command."

But Satan only grinned and shook his head:

" Never," said he, " will a father, not even Abraham, obey such a command." [1]

Now it came to pass that after a while Abraham, urged by his wife Sarah, sent away from home his bondwoman Hagar, a daughter of the Pharaoh, or king, of Egypt, who had borne unto him a son named Ishmael. Mother and son left the house of Abraham and dwelt in the desert of Paran, where Ishmael became an archer and a mighty hunter.

His mother then took him a wife out of Egypt. Three years had thus passed, when Abraham felt a yearning for his son Ishmael and greatly wished to see him. He thereupon spoke to his wife Sarah and thus he said: " Three years have now passed since Ishmael hath left my house and settled in the desert. I will therefore go and visit him and see if he fareth well." [2] Sarah agreed to this; and Abraham bade his servant saddle his camel, and he went off into the desert.

He arrived at noon before the tent of his son. Neither Ishmael nor his mother Hagar were present, for they had gone to fetch dates and pomegranates. Abraham saw his son's wife and her children, and gave them his greeting; but the woman never replied, nor even turned her head to take notice of him.

" Where is thy husband?" asked Abraham.

The woman, without even turning her head, replied in an angry tone: " My husband is away."

" My daughter," again spoke Abraham, " prithee, give me a drink of water, for I am very thirsty."

---

[1] *Sepher Hajashar.*
[2] *Sepher Hajashar; Pirke de Rabbi Eliezer*, Ch. 30; *Yalkut, Genesis*, § 95. See also Weil, *Biblische Legenden der Muselmänner*, p. 90.

" I have neither drink nor food for thee," cried the woman, " go thy way."

Thereupon she entered the inner tent, and Abraham heard her curse and beat her children and also curse her husband.

Kindly and patiently Abraham called again to the wife of his son:

" My daughter, if I have found grace in thine eyes, hearken for a moment to what I have to say to thee."

The woman came out of the tent and with bad grace replied:

" Speak, old man, I am listening unto thee."

" When Ishmael, thy husband, returneth home, tell him this: an old man from the land of Canaan was here and inquired after thee; he also bade thee change the threshold of thy tent, for it is a bad one, and to put a better one in its place." [1]

Thus spoke Abraham and departed. When Ishmael came home, his wife told him what had happened and what message the old man from Canaan had left. Ishmael at once knew that his father had been to see him and that his wife had not found favour in the old man's eyes. He therefore bestowed gifts upon her, sent her back to her own people, and took unto himself another wife, Fatima by name, out of Egypt.

Again three years passed, and Abraham once more felt an urgent desire to visit his son Ishmael and to know how he fared. With the permission of his wife Sarah he once more travelled to the desert of Paran where his son dwelt. When he reached the tent of his son, Ishmael's wife came out and gave him friendly greeting.

" Where is thy husband, my daughter?" queried Abraham.

" He is away from home, hunting; but prithee, my Lord,

[1] *Pirke de Rabbi Eliezer*, Ch. 30.

come down from thy camel and honour me with thy presence
in our humble tent. Rest awhile from the fatigue of thy journey
and refresh thyself with food and drink. Thou wilt thus
bestow a great favour upon thy servant."

Abraham at first declined, for he was in a hurry to return
home before the sun set. But Fatima [1] insisted so much that
he gave in. Dismounting his camel, he entered the tent and
partook of refreshment which the woman had placed before
him. He blessed her and prayed unto the Lord to send happiness and prosperity into this tent. Turning to Fatima he thus
spoke:

" When thy husband, Ishmael, returns from his hunting,
tell him this, my daughter: an old man from the land of the
Philistines hath been here and inquired after thee. He also
bade me say that he found the new threshold of thy tent a
very good one. He bade thee keep it and cherish it."

Thereupon he took his departure.

And when Ishmael returned and heard what had happened,
he knew that his father had been to visit him, and that he had
approved of his new wife who had found grace in his eyes. [2]

Although he loved his son Ishmael, Abraham cherished his
son Isaac, the son Sarah had borne unto him, much more.
Isaac indeed deserved the love of his fond old father, for
he was a God-fearing lad and walked in the ways of the Lord.
He followed in the path of his pious parents, and his good
deeds were many. His charity and generosity were boundless.
If Abraham loved his son Isaac given to him in his old age,
the boy endeared himself to his parents even more on account
of his many virtues and his sweet disposition. He did more
than his duty to his parents, and was zealous in the worship
of God. But the Lord wanted to test Abraham. He decided
to test the religious disposition of the Patriarch, and thus

[1] *Targum Jerushalmi, Genesis,* 21, 21; *Pirke de Rabbi Eliezer,* Ch. 30.
[2] *Pirke de Rabbi Eliezer,* Ch. 30; *Sepher Hajashar;* see also Weil, *Biblische Legenden
der Muselmänner,* pp. 90–93.

show to the world to what an extent a pious man was able not only to fear but also to love his God.

Now there was a day when the sons of God came to present themselves before the Lord,[1] and among them were also Satan, he who is called Sammael, the tempter and accuser of men, and all the other accusing angels. And the Lord said unto them:

" Whence come ye?" And they answered and said: " From going to and fro in the earth, and from walking up and down in it." And the Lord said unto them: " What have ye to say concerning the actions of man?" And the accusing angels answered the Lord and said:

" Verily, we find that men only worship and serve Thee when they are in need of Thy help and have a favour to ask from Thee. Once Thou hast granted them this favour they at once forsake Thee."

The Lord then said unto the accusing angels:

" Have ye considered My servant Abraham, that there is none like him on earth, a perfect and an upright man, one that feareth God and loveth Him and escheweth evil, and still he holdeth fast his integrity. Ye moved Me against man, saying, when I once decided to create him in My image, that I would repent having done so. Now ye behold the righteousness of Abraham and the number of men he has converted to the knowledge of Me, teaching them to bless and glorify My name."

Thereupon Shaftiel, one of the accusing angels, came and stood before the Lord and thus he spake: " Verily, the good deeds of Thy servant Abraham are many, and there is none like him in the earth. But even Abraham will not obey Thee, O Lord, if Thou shouldst command him to sacrifice his own dear and beloved son."

---

[1] *Sepher Hajashar; Sanhedrin;* 89*b*; *Tana debe Eliahu,* Ch. 7. See also *The Book of Jubilees,* 3, 13.

Then Satan, he who is called Sammael, the accuser of man and the tempter, came and stood before the Lord, and thus he spoke: " Verily, it is not astonishing that Abraham worshipped Thee as long as he was childless. He builded altars, praised Thy name and spread Thy worship among men. But now, since Thou hast vouchsafed unto him Thy loving kindness, granted him his heart's desire and given him in his old age a son, he is already beginning to forsake Thee. He prepared a feast on the day when Isaac, his son, was weaned, but he paid no heed to a poor beggar who stood upon his threshold." [1]

But the Lord said unto Satan, who is called Sammael: " I know that there is none like Abraham in the earth, a perfect and an upright man, and even if I were to command him to take his son, his only son Isaac, whom he loveth, and offer him for a burnt offering upon one of the mountains, he would obey My command with a glad heart."

And Sammael said: " Do this, O Lord, and if Abraham obeys Thy command and offers his beloved son Isaac for a burnt offering upon one of the mountains, then I will know that indeed there is none like him on the earth."

Thereupon the Lord decided to test his servant Abraham and to show to Sammael that there was none so perfect as Abraham. The Lord therefore called unto Abraham and said: " I have a favour to ask of thee. I have bestowed many blessings upon thee and made thee superior to thine enemies. I have given thee a son in thy old age, thy son Isaac who is the cause of thy happiness, but now I require of thee to offer this son of thine as a sacrifice and a holy oblation." And the Lord accordingly commanded Abraham to carry his son to the mountain Moriah, to the country where mountains rise in the midst of dales, where once light and law and the fear of God were destined to dwell, and whence the light of wisdom and of the knowledge

---

[1] *Tana debe Eliahu*, Ch. 7; *Sepher Hajashar*.

of the true God will issue forth and cast its rays upon the world at large. He commanded Abraham to build an altar there and to offer Isaac as a burnt offering upon it.[1] " For thus," said the Lord, " thou wilt best manifest thy religious disposition towards Me, if thou wilt prefer what is pleasing to Me before the preservation even of thine own son."

Abraham listened to the voice of the Lord and thought in his heart that it was not right to disobey God in anything, and that he was indeed obliged to serve Him in every circumstance of life without asking any questions. " For do not," so thought Abraham, " all creatures that live enjoy life by divine providence and the kindness God bestoweth on them." He was, however, troubled in his mind about one thing and thought how he could best conceal this command of God from his dear wife Sarah.[2] " If I tell my wife of this command of the Lord," thought Abraham in his heart, " she will take the matter to heart and the loss of her beloved son will be such a blow to her in her old age that she will surely die of a broken heart. If again I take Isaac unbeknown to my wife, she will seek for him everywhere and not finding him will grieve greatly, and her sorrow and grief will bring her to the grave. I will, therefore, employ a ruse, so as to spare my dear wife and keep her in ignorance of what is about to happen." Thereupon Abraham, with joyous mien, although his own heart was very heavy in his breast, approached his wife and thus he spake:

" My dear one, prepare a special repast to-day that we may enjoy ourselves and make merry in our old age." Thus spoke Abraham, and Sarah asked in astonishment: " Why, dear husband mine, to-day of all days, and why this festivity?"

" To-day like every other day is a day of rejoicing for us when we remember the great loving kindness the Lord has

---

[1] *Sanhedrin*, 89b; *Midrash Tanchuma*, Section *Wayera*; *Genesis Rabba*, 39; *Pirke de Rabbi Eliezer*, Ch. 31.

[2] Josephus, *Antiquities*, I, 13, 2; *Sepher Hajashar*; *Yalkut*, 1, § 98.

vouchsafed unto us, when He gave us such a precious gift in our old age; when He bestowed upon us our beloved son Isaac, who is indeed a blessing to his old and aged parents." Sarah went and did as Abraham, her dear husband, had bidden her, and prepared a festive meal.

When they were at table, Abraham said unto his wife: " Hearken unto my words, wife of mine. Thou knowest well that I was only three years old when I already acknowledged the true, living and only God, the Creator of the Universe, and learned both to fear and to love Him. Now our son Isaac is growing up and it is high time that he, too, should learn the knowledge of God and the wonders He is working; it is time to instruct Isaac and to educate him in the fear of the Lord. I have therefore decided to take him to-day and bring him to the school established by our near relatives Shem and Eber.[1] There he will learn wisdom and knowledge and the fear of the Lord."

Thus spoke Abraham, and his wife, always accustomed to obey her husband, approved of his plan, although her heart ached at the thought of being separated for a long time from her beloved child. " Do this, husband mine," she said, " although thou knowest well that the boy is dearer unto me than life itself." And she kissed and embraced her son and prepared his festive garments and a headgear, but the tears were running down her face when she thought of the separation.

The whole night Sarah was busy with the preparations for the journey, and when dawn broke and the first rays of the sun tinted with orient hues the sombre sky, she arrayed her dear son in a costly garment, one of those garments which Abi-Melech, King of Gerar, had once made a present unto her, and placed upon his head a headgear ornamented with pearls and precious stones. She fell upon the neck of her only son and shed tears copiously. " Farewell, my beloved son," she

---

[1] *Sepher Hajashar*; *Midrash Tanchuma*, section *Wayera*.

said, " the Lord knoweth whether and when I shall behold thy dear countenance again in this world, for I am old and my years are numbered." [1]

In the meantime Abraham went out and with his own hands, although he was a wealthy and slave-owning Emir, saddled his ass, quite contrary to custom. Sarah prepared food for the journey and accompanied by her maids escorted her husband and her son part of the way. She once more begged her husband to take care of her boy during the journey and to minister to all his needs. Thereupon, she returned home, and Abraham and his son Isaac continued their journey.

According to another version,[2] Sarah did not accompany her husband and child. When Abraham saw her so greatly upset and weeping so bitterly, he said unto her: " Hearken unto my words, my dear, and lie down for a while and snatch some sleep. Isaac, too, needs rest for our weary journey, for we intend to leave with sunrise." Sarah listened to the advice of her husband and lay down upon her couch, but she could find no sleep, and cried all night; at dawn only she fell into a troubled sleep. When Abraham saw her asleep, he seized this opportunity to leave as speedily as possible before his wife awoke, so that she might not hinder him in his enterprise at the last moment.

Abraham thus rose up early in the morning, took with him Ishmael, Eliezer, and Isaac, his son, and saddled his ass. It was the offspring of that ass which had been created during the twilight on the eve of the first Sabbath, in the week of creation. The same ass was afterwards ridden by Moses when he came to Egypt, and will be ridden upon in the future by the son of David.[3]

On the way, a dispute arose between Eliezer and Ishmael.

" Abraham, my father," said Ishmael, " will now offer my

---

[1] *Sepher Hajashar.*   [2] *Midrash Tanchuma*, section *Wayera.*
[3] *Pirke de Rabbi Eliezer*, Ch. 31.

brother Isaac for a burnt offering, and I, his first born, will now inherit all his possessions."

" Thy father hath already once driven thee out and sent thee away into the wilderness. I, on the other hand, am his faithful servant, serving him by day and night, and I shall be his heir," [1] replied Eliezer.

Now Sammael waxed angry, when he realized how upright and God-fearing Abraham was and how he did not refuse to sacrifice and offer as a burnt offering his only begotten son, when God bade him do so. Sammael's whole aim now was to find means and ways how to prevent Abraham from accomplishing his journey and fulfilling the command of the Lord. He thereupon assumed the shape of an aged and broken man, bent with years, and in such disguise met Abraham and his companions: " Whither art thou going, venerable old man?" he queried.[2]

" To say my prayers to the Lord upon the mountains yonder," replied Abraham.

" But I see thee carrying fire and a knife in thine hand, and wood upon thy shoulders," said Satan, who is also called Sammael.

" I have provided myself," replied Abraham, " with all that we shall require on our journey. Should we be compelled to remain a few days, we can light a fire, kill an animal, and bake bread."

" Thou canst not deceive me, old man," cried Sammael, throwing off his disguise. " Was I not present when the Lord commanded thee to take thy beloved son and bring him for a burnt offering upon one of the mountains yonder? Verily, thou art a fool, and there is no fool like an old fool. Dost thou imagine that if thou dost bring for a burnt offering thy only begotten son, born unto thee at the age of a hundred

[1] Sepher Hajashar;. Genesis Rabba, 56; Pirke de Rabbi Eliezer, Ch. 31; Midrash Haggadol, col. 320.
[2] Genesis Rabba, 56; Midrash Tanchuma, section Wayera, Sepher Hajashar.

years, thou wilt ever have another son? Besides, thou never didst hear the voice of the Lord who commanded thee to sacrifice thine own son. It was the voice of the tempter thou didst hear, the tempter who is endeavouring to lead thee to perdition. To-morrow the Lord will take thee to account for this wicked deed thou art about to perform. He will accuse thee of manslaughter, of the slaughter of thine own son whose blood thou didst not hesitate to shed, misled by the voice of the tempter. Could the Lord, who loveth thee so much, ever have asked thee to bring such a sacrifice and bid thee kill thine own son with thine own hands? [1] Verily, thy piety is exaggerated, and thou wilt soon have occasion to repent of it." [2]

Thus spake Sammael, trying to beguile Abraham and to make him waver. But Abraham held fast to his integrity.

" It was not the voice of the tempter I heard," said Abraham, " but the voice of the Lord, the Creator of Heaven and earth.[3] It is He who, indeed, commanded me to bring my son for a burnt offering, and it is not for man to question the ways of the Lord. His intentions are hidden from mortals, and we only have to obey and to have faith in Him who rules from eternity to eternity."

When Sammael saw that he could not move Abraham and make him waver in his purpose for even a fleeting moment, he tried to tempt Isaac and make him hearken to his words. Disguised as a youth, he suddenly appeared to the travellers,[4] and approaching the boy who was being led to the slaughter he thus addressed him:

" And whither mayest thou be travelling, young man?"

" To the school established by Shem and Eber, there to study wisdom and the fear of the Lord," replied Isaac.

" Art thou going to study this wisdom and the fear of the

[1] Sanhedrin, 89b.   [2] Jellinek, Beth-Hamidrash, Midrash Wayosha, Vol. I, p. 36.
[3] Sanhedrin, 89b.   [4] Sepher Hajashar; Midrash Tanchuma, ed. Buber, p. 114.

Lord," asked Sammael mockingly, " whilst thou art still among the living or after thy death?"

" Thou speakest foolishly," replied Isaac, " is there any study after death?"

Thereupon Sammael said: " Son of an unhappy sorrowing mother! Dost thou not know that thine own foolish father is leading thee like a lamb to the slaughter? Is it for this end that thy mother has wept and prayed and fasted and begged the Lord to send her a son in her old age? And now thou art going to die, and she will remain alone and desolate. Is not thy mother dear to thee?"

" She is dear to me, dearer than life itself," replied Isaac, " but I must obey the command of the Creator and that of my father." [1]

But in spite of his firmness Isaac was troubled in his mind, and related to his father what he had just heard from the youth who was none other than Sammael in disguise.[2]

" Hearken not unto him, my son," replied Abraham, " he is speaking with the voice of the tempter, who is trying to make us waver in our obedience to the commands of our Maker, our Father in Heaven."

They continued their way, and behold, there was a stream barring their way. They decided to wade through it and thus reach the opposite bank. The water soon reached to their knees, and when they were midways, it soon rose to their necks. Abraham, who knew the country well, was quite certain that he had never seen either stream or river in this region, and guessed right enough that it was the work of Satan. Lifting up his eyes to Heaven, he thus prayed unto his Maker:

" Lord of the Universe, thou didst manifest Thy glory unto me and didst say that none was like me in piety. Thou didst command me to bring my son Isaac as a burnt offering, and I never questioned Thy words, but whole-heartedly I

---

[1] Jellinek, *ibid.*   [2] *Tanchuma*, ed. Buber, p. 114.

obeyed Thy command, for through me Thy name shall be sanctified. But now, if we perish in these waters, how shall I be able to do Thy bidding and sanctify Thy name?" [1]

Thus prayed Abraham in his anguish, and behold, the stream suddenly disappeared, and Abraham and his companions were standing upon dry land.

Sammael, however, did not yet consider himself beaten. He tried again to prevent Abraham from doing the bidding of the Lord and to make him turn back. He once more appeared before the old man, and thus he spoke to him:

" Abraham, in vain dost thou continue this weary journey. A thing was secretly brought to me, and mine ear received a little thereof. I have heard it proclaimed in Heaven that the Almighty really desires a lamb as burnt offering, but not thy son."

" Even if it were so," said Abraham, " I would not believe thee now, for thou hast proved a liar too often." [2] And Abraham continued his way. Then, on the third day, Abraham lifted up his eyes and saw the place afar off. There was a wide valley before him surrounded by lofty mountains. And behold, all the mountains suddenly moved and, gathering together, became one immense mountain, and a pillar of fire came down from Heaven and hovered over the mountain and it reached up to Heaven. A cloud rose up and enveloped the mountain, and the glory of the Lord was visible unto Abraham. [3]

" What seest thou, my son?" asked Abraham, turning to Isaac.

" My Father," said Isaac, " I see a pillar of fire and a cloud."

" What do ye see?" asked Abraham of Ishmael and Eliezer who were accompanying them.

" We see mountains," replied both Eliezer and Ishmael.

---

[1] Jellinek, *ibid.*, pp. 36–37; see also *Midrash Tanchuma*, section *Wayera*.
[2] *Sanhedrin*, 109.   [3] *Pirke de Rabbi Eliezer*, Ch. 31; *Genesis Rabba*, 56.

And Abraham knew that it was not given to them to see the Glory of the Lord. He thereupon left them behind and proceeded on his way with his son Isaac.[1]

Isaac now understood that he was destined to be brought as a burnt offering, but he gladly and willingly accepted his lot. Abraham then opened his mouth and thus addressed his son:

" O my son! A vast number of prayers have I poured out that I might have thee for my son; when thou didst come into the world, there was nothing that could contribute to thy support for which I was not greatly solicitous, nor anything wherein I thought myself happier than to see thee grown up to a man's estate and that I might have thee at my death the successor of my dominions; but since it was by God's will that I became thy father, and it is now His will that I relinquish thee, bear this consecration to God with a generous mind, for I resign thee up to God who hath thought fit now to require this testimony of honour to Himself, on account of the favours He hath conferred on me in being to me a supporter and a defender. Accordingly, thou my son, wilt now die, not in any common way of going out of the world, but sent to God, the Father of all men, beforehand, by thy own father, in the nature of a sacrifice. I suppose He thinks thee worthy to get clear of this world, neither by disease, neither by war, nor by any other severe way, by which death usually comes upon men, but so that He will receive thy soul with prayers and holy offices of religion, and will place thee near to Himself, and thou wilt there be to me a succourer and supporter in my old age." Thus spoke Abraham to his son Isaac before bringing him as a burnt offering according to the will of God.[2] Now Isaac was of a very generous disposition, as indeed became the son of such a father, and he was pleased with his father's discourse.

[1] *Sepher Hajashar*; *Genesis Rabba*, 56. See also *Midrash Haggadol*, col. 320.
[2] Josephus, *Antiquities*, I, 13, 3.

"My Father," he said, "I was not worthy to be born at first, if I should reject the determination of God and of my father, and should not resign myself up readily to both your pleasures, since it would have been unjust if I had not obeyed, even if my father alone had so resolved." [1]

Thereupon Abraham builded an altar, laid the wood in order, bound Isaac his son, and laid him on the altar upon the wood. Well might Abraham's hand have shook a little, when he stretched it out to take the knife to slay his son. But Isaac, ready to be sacrificed, because such had been the will of his Maker, encouraged his father.

"My Father," said Isaac, "take heart, bare thy hand, bind my hands and feet, for I am a lad in all the strength of my youth, whilst thou art an old man. When I see the knife in thine hand, I may, against my own will, lose heart, seize thy arm to save myself. The instinct of self-preservation is deeply implanted in man and may prompt me to disobey thee. I implore thee, Father mine, fulfil as speedily as possible the will of the Lord. And when my body will have been burnt to ashes, take these ashes and place them in an urn in my mother's room that she may remember her son whenever she enters her room. But I tremble when I think what a hard task thou wilt have to break the news to my mother, and to inform her that her beloved son is no more, but has been brought as a burnt offering upon the altar of the Lord and of duty." [2]

Thus spoke Isaac and bared his throat. Tears were streaming down from Abraham's eyes, his hand trembled and shook, and the knife fell from his hand, for Satan was making a last desperate effort to make the old man waver in his purpose. The Patriarch pulled himself together and once more

[1] Josephus, *Antiquities*, I, 13, 3.
[2] *Pirke de Rabbi Eliezer*, Ch. 31; *Sepher Hajashar*; *Targum Jerushalmi*, Genesis, 22, 10; *Genesis Rabba*, 56; *Midrash Tanchuma*, ed. Buber, p. 114; Jellinek, *Beth-Hamidrash*, Vol. I, p. 37; cf. also Grünbaum, *loc. cit.*, pp. 112, 115-116.

seized the knife, his eyes looking deeply into the eyes of his beloved son, as if to drink in remembrance. Isaac's eyes were directed heavenwards, and he beheld the heavenly hosts hastening to surround the Throne of Glory.[1] For, in this supreme moment, nature was hushed, the radiance of the sun was obscured, and fear and admiration seized the heavenly hosts who were witnessing the old father ready to slaughter his only son, and the son willing to accept his lot, because the Lord had so ordained. The mighty spirits, the beings of fire and flame, loudly lamented and cried:

" Behold! an extraordinary deed is being committed, a father is sacrificing his son upon the altar of the Lord and of duty." Bitterly wept the mild angels of peace[2], of love and mercy, and their tears fell down upon the eyes of Isaac, so that in old age his sight grew dim. And the heavenly hosts, the fiery spirits, and the angels of mercy, of love and of peace, prostrated themselves before the Throne of Glory and prayed to the Creator of the Universe, and thus they said:

" Sovereign of all the worlds, Creator of the Universe, merciful and compassionate art Thou called, Thy mercy being upon all Thy works, have now mercy upon Isaac, who is bound before Thee like an animal, he who is a human being and the son of a human being. O Lord! Thy righteousness is like the mighty mountains, and Thy judgments are like a great deep. O Lord, Thou preservest man and beasts." [3]

Thus prayed the ministering angels, and the Most High replied: " Now ye see, how man, whose creation ye once opposed, can glorify and sanctify My name and how perfect he can be." Thereupon He commanded the angel Michael to call unto the pious old man, the loving father who would not spare his own son, not to lay his hand upon the lad. Michael immediately obeyed the command of his Master,

---

[1] *Genesis Rabba*, 56; *Pirke de Rabbi Eliezer*, Ch. 32.   [2] *Genesis Rabba*, 56.
[3] *Pirke de Rabbi Eliezer*, Ch. 31; *Sepher Hajashar.*

but Abraham would not listen to the voice of the arch-angel.[1]

"God alone," he replied, "commanded me to bring my son as a burnt offering, and Him alone will I obey but not his messengers." Thereupon the cloud dispersed, the mist lifted, and the heavenly spheres became visible to Abraham, and the voice from the Throne of Glory repeated the words of the archangel.[2]

And Abraham lifted up his eyes, and behold, behind him a ram was caught in a thicket by his horns. It was the ram which had been created before sunset on the sixth day of creation. It had dwelt in Paradise, under the tree of life, and had drunk the waters of the rivers of Paradise. One of the ministering angels had brought the ram down to be ready to take the place of Isaac.[3]

Now Sammael, black with envy and anger on seeing that all his efforts had been frustrated, tried to hide the ram from Abraham's sight,[4] but Abraham pursued it, and discovering it at last, he offered it as a burnt offering in the stead of his son. Abraham then prostrated himself before the Eternal and thus he prayed:

"Lord Almighty! Thou who knowest the innermost thoughts of man hast seen how ready I was to obey Thy com-mands. I did not withhold my only son, when Thou didst command me to bring him as a burnt offering. Remember my intentions, O Lord, and when one day the children of Isaac will sin against Thee and transgress Thy commands, let Thy mercy prevail against Thy just wrath. Have mercy upon them and forgive them their errors."[5]

And a voice from the Throne of Glory replied: "It was not out of a desire for human blood that thou wast commanded

---

[1] Jellinek, *loc. cit.*, p. 38.
[2] *Midrash Tanchuma*, ed. Buber, p. 115. Cf. Grünbaum, *loc. cit.*, p. 116; Weil, *loc. cit.*, pp. 86–89: see also *Pirke de Rabbi Eliezer*, Ch. 31.
[3] Beer, *Das Leben Abrahams*, p. 70.
[4] *Sepher Hajashar*; *Pirke de Rabbi Eliezer*, Ch. 31.   [5] Beer, *loc. cit.* p. 70.

SAMMAEL TRIES TO HIDE THE RAM FROM ABRAHAM'S SIGHT

Facing page 298, Vol. 1

to slay thy son, nor was I willing that thy son should be taken away from thee, for I am merciful. It was only to try the temper of thy mind, and to confound the tempter and accuser of man, whom I have created in My image. Since I am now satisfied as to thy alacrity and obedience even to such a command as the immolation of thy son, and the surprising readiness thou hast shown in this, thy piety, I will bestow blessings upon thee. Thou wilt leave an everlasting name, and thy family will increase into many nations." [1]

And now Abraham left the mount Moriah, and journeyed with Isaac to the schools once established by Shem and Eber, where the lad was to remain three years.[2]

ABRAHAM'S SACRIFICE

Angelus. Abraham, how! Abraham,
  Lyst and herke weylle onto me.
Abraham. Al redy, sere, here I am;
  Telle me your wylle what that it be.
Angelus. Almyghty God thus doth bydde the,—
  Ysaac this sone anon thou take,
And loke hym thou sclee anoon, lete se,
  And sacrifice to God hym make.

Thy welbelovyd childe thou must now kylle,
  To God thou offyr him, as I say,
Evyn upon yon hey hylle,
  That I the shewe here in the way,
Tarye not be nyght nor day,
  But smertly thi gate thou goo;
Upon yon hille thou knele and pray
  To God, and kylle the childe ther and scloo.

[1] *Pirke de Rabbi Eliezer*, Ch. 31.
[2] Cf. for this chapter also: Wünsche, *Aus Israels Lehrhallen*, Vol. I, pp. 49–58; Bin Gorion, *loc. cit.*, Vol. II, pp. 274—285; Lewner, *loc. cit.*, pp. 93–101; Beer, *Das Leben Abrahams.*

Abraham. Now Goddys commaundement must nedys
    be done,
  Alle his wyl is wourthy to be wrought;
But yitt the fadyr to sclee the sone,
  Grett care it causyth in my thought,
In byttyr bale now am I brought
  My swete childe with knyf to kylle;
But yit my sorwe avaylith ryght nowth,
  For nedys I must werke Goddys wylle.

With evy hert I walke and wende,
  My childys deth now for to be,
Now must the fadyr his swete sone schende
  Alas! for ruthe it is peté!
My swete sone, come hedyr to me:
  How, Isaac, my sone dere,
Com to thi ffadyr, my childe so fre,
  ffor we must wende to-gedyr in fere.

Isaac. Alle redy fadyr, evyn at your wylle,
  And at your byddyng I am yow by,
With zow to walk ovyr dale and hille,
  At youre callyng I am redy,
To the fadyr evyr mast comly,
  It ovyth the childe evyr batom to be;
I wyl obey, ful hertyly,
  To alle thyng that ye bydde me.

Abraham. Now, son, in thi necke this faget thou take,
  And this fyre here in thinne honde,
ffor we must now sacrefyse go make,
  Evyn aftyr the wylle of Goddys sonde.
Take this brennyng bronde,
  My swete childe, and lete us go;
Ther may no man that levyth in londe,
  Have more sorwe than I have wo.

Isaac. ffayr fadyr, ze go ryght stylle,
  I pray zow, ffadyr, speke onto me.

Abraham. Mi gode childe, what is thi wylle?
    Telle me thyn hert, I pray to the.

Isaac. ffadyr, fyre and wood here is plenté,
    But I kan se no sacryfice;
What ye xulde offre fayn wold I se,
    That it were don at the best anyse.

Abraham. God xal that ordeyn that sytt in hevynne,
    My swete sone, ffor this offryng,
A derrere sacryfice may no man nempne,
    Than this xal be, ny dere derlyng.

> *Ludus Coventriæ.* A collection of mysteries, formerly repre-
> sented at Coventry on the Feast of Corpus Christi;
> edited by J. O. Halliwell, London, 1841; pp. 51–53.

CHAPTER XXVI

A Mother's Broken Heart, or the Death of Sarah

Sammael and Sarah—A mother's fright—The tempter and the weeping mother—The terrible news—Another version of Sammael's efforts —The heartbroken mother seeks her son—The pity of Sammael—Joy kills the mother—The grief of husband and son—Their lamentations—The friend of the poor—The double cave—Ephron, the commoner, elected chief by the sons of Heth—The transfer of the land—The covenant with the sons of Heth—The engraving upon the pillars of brass—The city of Jebus—The funeral of Sarah—The protest of Adam and Eve—They return to their resting place—The fame of Isaac—His generosity—Abraham thanks the Lord—The old age of the Patriarch—His daughter Bakila— The Patriarch and the magicians of Egypt—He teaches them arithmetic and astronomy.

Now Sammael, when he saw that all his efforts and endeavours to make either Abraham or Isaac waver in their determination had been of no avail, grew black with anger. Neither father nor son would hearken unto his voice, his promptings and whisperings. In vain had he appeared to the pious pair in many disguises, in the shape of a man bent with age or in that of a youth. Even his sudden change into a mighty stream, barring Abraham's way, had not succeeded to prevent the latter from continuing his way. Sammael, therefore, even before Abraham had reached the mount Moriah, decided to turn to Sarah. "Woman," he thought, "is weaker than man, as I know from experience, when I once tempted Eve in the Garden of Eden and succeeded. Woman is always inclined to lend an ear to the whisperings of the tempter."

Straightaway Sammael spread out his wings and flew to Beer-Sheba. There he found Sarah who, after accompanying her husband and son for a distance, had returned to her tent, her heart full of grief and forebodings. Suddenly an old man, who was none other than Sammael in disguise, appeared before Sarah.

" Where is thy son?" queried the old man.

" He has left," replied the mother sadly, " for his father took him to the school once established by Shem and Eber, there to study wisdom and the fear of the Lord."

" Thou poor deceived mother," spoke the tempter, " my heart aches for thee, for thou wilt never see thy son alive, never wilt thou behold his countenance and feast thine eyes upon it. Thy foolish old husband hath indeed deceived thee, for not to the school of Shem and Eber hath he taken thy beloved son, but to the mount of Moriah, there to bring him as a burnt offering to his God."

When she heard this, Sarah was so frightened that a tremor seized her. She laid her head on the bosom of a slave and fainted.[1] Soon, however, she regained consciousness and thus replied to Sammael, disguised as an old man who seemed to pity her in her grief: " May the will of the Lord be done. What my dear husband doeth in obedience to the command of our Maker is well done."

Greatly disappointed, Sammael left the heroic mother. But when he knew that Abraham and Isaac had left mount Moriah where God had commanded the old man not to lay a hand upon the lad, he grew desperate, for all his efforts had been in vain.[2] Once more he appeared before the weeping mother and said: " Woe unto thee, bereaved mother, hast thou not yet heard what hath happened? I bring thee sad tidings indeed; my heart aches for thee, and mine eyes shed tears of grief and sorrow."

[1] *Yalkut*, I, § 98.   [2] *Pirke de Rabbi Eliezer*, Ch. 32.

" What has happened?" cried Sarah piteously.

" The deed is done," said Sammael sadly. " Thy foolish husband, in his mistaken piety, hath indeed sacrificed thy son and brought him up as a burnt offering. Isaac is no more, and his ashes will be placed in an urn in thy room, so that thou mayest weep and mourn when thou wilt remember him who is no more. Greatly did thy poor son suffer. He wept and begged his hard-hearted father to have pity and spare him, but thy mistaken old husband lent not his ear to the prayers of thy son. He took his knife and slew him. It is a pity though that Abraham was so precipitate, for a voice from Heaven did indeed bid him stay his hand and not to lay it upon the lad, but it was too late. The deed had already been accomplished, that cruel deed which leaves thee a bereaved and sorrowing mother." [1]

Thus spoke Sammael. And when Sarah heard these words spoken by the tempter in a voice broken by sobbing, although there was no pity but rage in his black heart, the poor mother wept aloud. Bitterly she cried, until she fell down dead. Sammael cast a look of triumph upon her and went off.

Another version of this legend runs as follows:[2]

Whilst Abraham was busy sacrificing the ram, that ram which had been created for the purpose before sunset on the sixth day of creation, Sammael, disguised as an old man, came to Sarah and pretended to be greatly concerned in her sorrow. He told her in detail all that had occurred. " Abraham," he said, " had builded an altar upon mount Moriah, had bound his son, bared his throat and slain him with cruel hand. In vain did the lad wail and lament, begging his cruel father to spare him for the sake of his mother. His tears had been of no avail, and Isaac was now dead and burnt to ashes."

Sarah, who thought that the kindly, pitying old man was an acquaintance of her husband or of her son and to whom they

---

[1] *Midrash Tanchuma*, section *Wayera*.   [2] *Sepher Hajashar*.

had perhaps once rendered a service, never doubted the words of Sammael. Convinced that what had been told her was true, she broke out into loud wailing, crying piteously: " O my son, my beloved son, could I have died in thy stead to-day. I have prayed for thee and wept over thee, and blessed the Lord when He sent me such a precious gift. I was ninety years of age when thou wast given unto me, but now thou hast been burnt to ashes. My only consolation is that thou, my son, didst obey the will of the Lord, and who durst question the commands of our Maker in whose hands are all living creatures. Just art Thou, O Lord of the Universe, and inscrutable are Thy ways. If my eyes weep for my beloved son, for I am only flesh and blood, my heart is grateful for the honour done unto my son."

Wearily Sarah laid her head upon the knees of her favourite maid and fainted. She awoke soon, however, and still clinging to the hope that her fears had perhaps been groundless and that the old man who had brought her the terrible news had been mistaken, she hurried with her servants to find out the truth. Accompanied by her faithful maids, she set off towards Hebron, there to find out where her husband and son were and whether the sad tidings about her beloved son's fate were true or false. In vain, however, did she question the inhabitants of Hebron, no one could answer her. Too weak and weary to proceed any farther, Sarah herself remained at Hebron, dispatching her slaves to go and make further inquiry. They went as far as the school of Shem and Eber, but none could inform them of the whereabouts of the well-known and highly respected Emir Abraham. Disappointed, the messengers returned to their mistress lying ill and exhausted at Hebron. And suddenly a spark of pity entered the heart of Sammael himself, when he heard the wailing and heart-rending cries of the weeping mother, sorely cast down and broken in spirit, and saw her agony. He decided to make an end to her suspense. He suddenly appeared to her, disguised as her beloved son Isaac,[1] rushing to embrace his mother. But the shock was too great for Sarah. She rose up, uttered a cry, fell down, and was dead. Joy had killed her.[2] The joy at the sight of her beloved son had been too great for the exhausted old woman, and uttering a loud cry she fell dead.

Sammael's efforts to prevent Abraham from doing the bidding of the Lord had been frustrated, but even when he tried to do a good action, it only had disastrous results.

Abraham was in the meantime hastening home to inform his wife of what had occurred. Great, however, was his astonishment when, on his arrival at Beer-Sheba, he found the doors of his tent locked and no one to welcome him. His heart told him that a misfortune had befallen him. He inquired of his neighbours whether they knew anything about his wife and her maids, and learned that Sarah had journeyed to Hebron.

"News," said the neighbours, "had been brought to thy wife that thy son Isaac had been brought up as a burnt offering, and in great distress she went off to Hebron to find out the truth."[3]

Hastily, therefore, Abraham went off to Hebron, where he found his wife whom he had only left a few days ago lying dead. Bitterly he cried and lamented the death of his dear wife, the companion of his youth and of his old age. "Closed," he cried, "are the eyes which shed such a light, casting looks of love upon all whom she met; stiff are the hands which were busy in distributing help to the poor and the needy and in wiping the tears from the countenances of the afflicted. Not I alone and our dear son will miss thee, my wife, but all the orphans and widows, whose friend and supporter thou hast always been."

[1] *Leviticus Rabba*, 20; *Ecclesiasticus Rabba*, 9, 1; cf. *Midrash Haggadol*.
[2] Beer, *Das Leben Abrahams*, p. 74.   [3] Beer, *loc. cit.*, p. 74.

The neighbours and townsfolk also wept at the death of Sarah, the generous and charitable lady they had known so well.

Abraham at once sent a messenger to his son Isaac to inform him of their sad bereavement. The son hastened to Hebron, there to pay the last respects to his beloved mother. He fell upon the dead and wept bitterly.

" Alas," he cried, " Mother dear, why hast thou forsaken me so suddenly? Why hast thou gone away? I had hoped to keep thee still for a long time and feast mine eyes upon thy countenance which was as radiant as the sun in its splendour. I was looking forward to hearing thy sweet voice and hoped to listen to thy words which were music in mine ears. But, alas, the sun of my life is now darkened, and my joy is gone." And Isaac wept bitterly, and all who were present joined in his lamentations.

All the people of Hebron, men, women, and children came to the house where the dead body of Sarah was lying. The townspeople had ceased work on that day in honour of the memory of the deceased lady, whose charity, generosity and good deeds were so well known.[1]

" The friend of the poor, of the suffering and of the afflicted is now dead," they said, " and we must be ready to pay her the last respects and accompany her in great numbers to her last resting-place."

As Abraham was bowing over the body of his dear wife, he heard the loud laugh of the angel of death who is none other than Sammael.[2] " Wherefore dost thou weep," mocked the angel of death. " The blame of her death is thine. For hadst thou not taken her son from her, she would certainly be alive now."

Abraham now rose from the body of his wife and set out to find a burying place for the dead. He approached the sons of Heth, the Hittites, and asked them to grant him a sepulchre

---

[1] *Midrash Tanchuma*, section *Hayé-Sarah*.   [2] *Genesis Rabba*, 58.

so that he might bury his dead. Thereupon the sons of Heth replied: " My Lord, take the choice of our sepulchres." Abraham bowed to the sons of Heth and said:

" If I have found grace in your eyes, then obtain for me the cave of Machpelah, the double cave which is in possession of Ephron, the son of Zohar, for it is this sepulchre that I have chosen there to bury my dead."

Now Abraham was rather anxious to buy this cave in possession of Ephron for the following reason. When he had gone out, sometime ago, after the calf which he slew for the three angels who came to him just before the destruction of Sodom, that calf had fled from him and entered the double cave. And when Abraham entered the cave, he found in an inner recess the bodies of Adam and Eve laid out. There were burning tapers round them, and there was the fragrance of incense in the air.[1]

When the sons of Heth heard Abraham's request, they said one to another: " Ephron is only a common person, let us hasten and elect him as our chief and prince, so that such a mighty and distinguished Emir like Abraham be not compelled to have dealings with an inferior, ordinary person." [2]

They therefore approached Ephron, the son of Zohar, saying unto him: " Wilt thou be our chief?" Greatly wondering at this unexpected honour, Ephron inquired after the reason, and was informed of the request of Abraham.

Thereupon Ephron hastened to meet the distinguished stranger, on whose account such great honour had been thrust upon him, and begged him to accept the field and the double cave as a gift. But Abraham refused to accept the place as a gift, and Ephron agreed to take four hundred shekels of silver from Abraham, which the latter weighed out in the current money of the land. A deed of sale was thereupon drawn up, duly signed and witnessed, and the field and cave became the

---

[1] *Pirke de Rabbi Eliezer*, Ch. 36.　　[2] *Sepher Hajashar.*

property of Abraham. The transfer of the land and cave was signed by Amigal, son of Abishna, the Hittite, Elichoran, son of Essunass, the Hittite, Abdon son of Ahirah, the Gamorrhite, and Akdil, son of Abdis, the Sidonian.[1] The cave was called Machpelah, or the double cave, because it contained two chambers, or because Abraham paid double value for it. Some also say that it was so called, because it was doubly holy, or because Adam's body had to be doubled up so as to get it into the cave.[2]

Now the sons of Heth said one to another: " Days will come when the children and children's children of Abraham will take possession of the entire land and will inherit it. They will also conquer and take possession of our city of Jebus. Let us therefore make a covenant with Abraham that his offspring will never take possession by force of the town of Jebus and of the country and possessions of the Jebusites." The sons of Heth thereupon turned unto Abraham and thus addressed him:

" Thou shalt not bury thy dead before making a covenant with us that thy children and their children shall never take by force the possessions of the Jebusites." Abraham agreed to grant their request, and they brought their idols, engraved upon them the conditions of the covenant and placed them in the market-place of the town. There they remained until the days of David. When the Israelites conquered Canaan, they respected the covenant and left the Jebusites unmolested, so that they continued to dwell with them. And when David sought to take the stronghold of Jebus, the inhabitants said unto him: " Thou canst not storm our city, because of the covenant of Abraham which is engraven on the pillars of brass." David removed the pillars, but respecting the covenant, he *purchased* the city of Jebus.[3]

[1] *Sepher Hajashar.*   [2] *Erubin,* 53a; *Genesis Rabba,* 58.
[3] *Pirke de Rabbi Eliezer,* Ch. 26; *Midrash Haggadol,* Col. 350.

Thereupon Abraham buried his wife Sarah, and multitudes of people came to pay her the last respects. Shem and his son Eber came, and also Abi-Melech, King of Gerar, and all the great ones of the land. It was indeed a very great company which went to bury Sarah, the wife of Abraham, and all the people who followed the bier wailed and lamented. Abraham caused a great mourning to be made for seven days.

When he went into the cave to take off the stone which he had placed upon the grave he had digged for Sarah, Adam and Eve both arose and thus they spake unto him:

" How can we lie at rest in the same cave where thy wife Sarah will be buried? We have never ceased to repent and to be ashamed of our sin, the sin we committed and on account of which we have been expelled from the Garden of Eden. And now this perfect and righteous woman has come here, and we feel our shame even more." Thus spoke our first parents. But Abraham replied:

" Return to your resting place and sleep in peace, for I will pray on your behalf and ye will no longer need be ashamed of your transgression." Adam at once returned to his resting place, but Eve still protested, and her spirit would not be appeased. Abraham, however, begged her to return to her resting place and sleep in peace until she yielded to his entreaties. After the funeral Abraham sent his son Isaac to the school of Shem and Eber there to continue his studies.[1]

Isaac remained three years in the school of Shem and Eber, and there he learned wisdom and increased his knowledge greatly. He became learned and wise and God-fearing. He loved the poor and the needy and was their friend on every occasion, consoling the suffering, and wiping away the tears of the unhappy. He was beloved by all who came into contact with him, and he became a blessing to all who knew him. When Abraham heard how the fame of his beloved son was

[1] Cf. Lewner, *Kol Agadoth*, Vol. I, p. 106.

spreading far and wide, he was happy indeed. He thanked the Lord of the Universe for the favours he had bestowed on him.

"Almighty God!" he said, "great indeed is Thy loving kindness, for after many trials and afflictions, Thou hast blessed my old age and poured prosperity, wealth and fame upon me. I am honoured more than I indeed deserve, for kings and potentates come daily to inquire after my welfare. Thou knowest well, O Lord of the Universe, that my heart is not swelled with pride, for I am only like all the other mortals. But behold, Thou hast even sent me a blessing which is more than wealth, and fame, and life to me. Thou hast granted me the greatest joy of my life and a consolation in my old age, for Isaac, my beloved son, is as perfect as mortal man can be, and Thou hast given him a golden heart, full of pity for suffering humanity, and his deeds of kindness and generosity are numerous. This, O Lord, is the greatest blessing that Thou couldst have bestowed upon an aged father."[1]

Abraham's old age was indeed a happy one, for the Lord had blessed him in all things. Some say that Hagar, whom he had taken back, bore him a daughter named Bakila,[2] whilst others maintain that, on the contrary, his blessing was great and consisted in this that he had no daughters.[3] It would have caused the old man great worry to have a daughter in the midst of the dissolute and idol-worshipping inhabitants of Canaan, where he could not have found for her a fitting husband.

Abraham's fame as a reader of the stars was also very great, and the princes of both the East and the West constantly came to consult him. He conferred with the wise men of the land and always confuted the reasonings they made use of, when they refused to believe in the God whom Abraham taught them to love. But Abraham demonstrated

---

[1] *Ibid.*, pp. 107–108. [2] *Baba Batra*, 16b, 141a; *Genesis Rabba*. [3] *Genesis Rabba*, 59.

to them that their reasonings were vain and void of truth. He was therefore admired even by the readers of the stars and the magicians of Egypt and of Babylonia as a very wise man and one of great sagacity when he discoursed on any subject he undertook, and this not only in understanding it, but in persuading other men also to assent to him. It is said that Abraham communicated to the wise men of Egypt arithmetic, and delivered to them the science of astronomy. His presence was very magnetic, and it is said that the sick who approached him were at once healed.[1] Upon his breast he wore a precious stone, and the patient who gazed at it was at once cured from his disease. Thus Abraham's old age was indeed a happy one. He had only one desire left, and that was to see his son Isaac happily married, married to a mate worthy of him. This desire, too, was soon to be fulfilled.

ISAAC

Mon Dieu et mon souverain maistre, 10983
En quelle place ne quel estre
Est maintenant ma povre mère?
Hellas! j'ay aidé à la mettre
En terre! Qui pourra congnoistre
Que j'en ay eu douleur amère?

O misère
Fière, austère,
A porter
Impropère,
Qui propère
Me advorter
Sans doubter!
Supporter

[1] Josephus, *Antiquities*, I, 8, 2. See also *Rashi*, *Yoma*, 28*b*.

A peine puis, c'est chose clère,
Tel douleur, qui desconforter
M'a fait si fort et tormenter
Que regarder n'ose mon père.

Aux champs m'en voys sçavoir se aucun confort
Me viendra point contre ce desconfort
Pour rapaiser mon pleur, qui est si fort,
Et repulser l'accez de mon mesaise,
Non obstant ce que je cuyde avoir tort,
Car arriver ne puis en aucun port
Ou il y ayt voix doulce ne accort
Armonieulx qui nullement me plaise.

Pleurs et souspirs sont mes gieux et mon ayse;
Au monde n'est rien qui ne me desplaise,
Considerant qu'il fauldra que je voyse,
Comme ma mère, par ung assault de mort,
Et ne sçay quant. O mort sure et mauvaise,
Tant ton fardeau pesant à porter poyse!
Nul ne le sçayt fors celuy qui le poyse.
Cruelle mort, tu as mauvais raport!

Le Mistère du Viel Testament. Edited by J. de Rothschild,
Paris, 1877, Tome II, pp. 95-96.

CHAPTER XXVII

A Rose among Thorns, or the Marriage of Isaac

The mission of Eliezer—The journey to Haran—The guardian angels—
Eliezer's prayer—A rose among thorns—The beautiful and virtuous maiden
—The generosity of Rebekah—The damsel at the well—The royal present
—The greedy brother—The poisoned bowl—The death of the father—
The speedy departure—A blessing but no dowry—The meeting of bride
and bridegroom—The fall from the camel—The vision of Rebekah—The
wife fills the place of the mother.

FOR three years Isaac had mourned the death of his mother,[1]
but when this time had elapsed, Abraham called his faithful
servant Eliezer and sent him to Mesopotamia, his own country,
and to his own kindred there to take a wife for his son Isaac.
Eliezer ventured to suggest his own daughter as a suitable
mate for the son of his master, " For," said he, " peradventure
the woman in thy own country and of thy own kindred will
not be willing to accompany me unto this land of Canaan."
Eliezer, however, being of the race of Ham, Abraham was not
willing to allow his son to marry a daughter of Eliezer. Eliezer
now did as his master had bidden him. Abraham signed
a deed [2] wherein he declared that he left all his worldly possessions to his son Isaac and handing over this deed to Eliezer
thus said to him:

" This deed thou wilt show to the father of the maiden
thou wilt have chosen as a wife for my son."

[1] *Pirke de Rabbi Eliezer*, Ch. 32; *Midrash Haggadol*, col. 388.
[2] *Genesis Rabba*, 59; cf. *Baba Batra*, 130a.

And Eliezer, taking ten camels from the camels of his master, departed to Mesopotamia. The distance from Kirjath Arba or Hebron to Haran was a seventeen-days journey, but Eliezer and his suite reached Haran, their destination, in three hours, for the earth fled under the feet of his camels.[1] God called two of His ministering angels and commanded them to accompany Eliezer, the servant of Abraham, on his delicate errand.[2] One of the angels received as his mission to protect Eliezer on his way, whilst the other's mission was to cause Rebekah to be present at the well just at the moment when Eliezer arrived.

Eliezer had journeyed some distance when behold, he found himself already at the well in Haran. To have travelled such a long distance in such a short time was wonderful indeed, and Eliezer marvelled greatly and understood that the Lord had shortened the distance and wrought this miracle on his behalf. Thereupon he prayed unto the Lord, saying: " Lord of the Universe, show kindness unto my master Abraham and let me meet a damsel who is righteous and perfect, endowed with a kind and noble heart, who will thus be a suitable companion and mate for Isaac, the son of my master." [3] Thus spake Eliezer, and at that moment the second ministering angel arrived and caused Rebekah to leave her father's house and to go out to the well to draw water.

Rebekah, the daughter of Bethuel, the son of Nahor of Mesopotamia, was indeed like a rose among thorns. She had witnessed the sinful life and the wicked deeds of her father and brother, and had made up her mind not to follow in their ways. She was kind and generous and never missed an opportunity to practise charity. The poor who called at Bethuel's house found a kind helper in Rebekah, the beautiful and noble-hearted daughter of the house, who never allowed them to go away empty-handed. And

[1] *Ibid.*   [2] *Ibid.*   [3] Josephus, *Antiquities*, I, 16, 1.

although she had been brought up as it behoved the daughter of a great, wealthy and influential man of the land, although she had many slaves to serve her, she was never idle, indulging in frivolous pursuits, but diligently looked after the household. She was one of those women who eat not the bread of idleness. She stretched out her hand to the poor, yea, she reached forth her hand to the needy, not only in her father's house but also in the town, going out among the poor in search of opportunities to do good. Often, when Rebekah saw the wicked deeds and the sinful conduct of the men of her town, and the idle frivolous life led by those oriental women-folk, she said in her heart: " I wish I could leave this town and its wicked, idle, and frivolous life, useless and purposeless!" [1]

All who knew Rebekah called her a rose among thorns. But still, she was the daughter of a noble and distinguished house, and was not in the habit of taking up the pitcher and going out to the well to draw water.[2] But it was the angel this time who prompted her to undertake this task to-day, as it might give her an opportunity to do some kindness on her way where she would meet the poorer classes of her towns-folk.

When Rebekah approached the well, carrying her pitcher, the waters in the well rose by themselves,[3] and Eliezer, noticing this, marvelled greatly. " I must watch this damsel," said Eliezer, " and see her conduct, for methinks that she is the one appointed by the Lord to be the wife of the son of my master. She is very fair to look upon, and if she showeth a kind heart, I will speak unto her."

And Eliezer watched Rebekah for some time. He saw her approach a child that was crying bitterly by the side of the

---

[1] Cf. Lewner, *loc. cit.*, p. 107.

[2] *Pirke de Rabbi Eliezer*, Ch. 16; *Midrash Haggadol, Genesis,* col. 367; *Yalkut, Genesis,* § 109. In *Pirke de Rabbi Eliezer* we read: " A daughter of kings, who had never gone out to draw water ". [3] *Genesis Rabba,* 60.

well, and ask it to tell her the cause of its trouble. " I have
hurt my foot," said the child, " and it is bleeding." Rebekah
at once bathed and dressed the wound of the child and comforted it, sending it home to its mother. Thereupon, not far
from the well, she met an old woman whose sight was dim.
Rebekah took pity upon the aged woman and smilingly inquired: " Canst thou find thy way, Mother?"

" Sometimes," replied the old woman, " it happens that
I lose my way home and am compelled to pass the night in
the open." Rebekah asked her where she dwelt and accompanied the woman home. Thereupon she returned to the
well, pitcher in hand, but being evidently tired she sat down
upon a log to rest awhile. No sooner had she done so, than
an old man, tired and travel stained, came along. She hastened
up and offered him her seat to rest his weary limbs.[1]

When Eliezer saw her conduct and behaviour he said to
himself: " This damsel hath a noble heart and a kind nature,
and is, moreover, very fair to look upon. She will be a fitting
companion and helpmate for my master's son." Thereupon
he approached and asked her to give him some water to
drink. He had previously addressed to all the other maidens
a similar request, but one and all had refused, on pretence
that they wanted it all at home and could spare none for him,
and that the drawing of water was not an easy task. " We may
not tarry," they replied, " for we must take the water home." [2]
Rebekah complied with Eliezer's request with a kindness and
grace which charmed him greatly.

Eliezer now began to hope that his journey would not have
been in vain, and that his enterprise would succeed. But
he still desired to know the truth and to learn the name of the
damsel's father and the social position of her parents. He, therefore, commended her for her generosity and good nature, saying

---

[1] *Genesis Rabba*, 59, and 60; *Sanhedrin*, 110; *Yoma*, 28b: see also Lewner, *loc. cit.*, p. 107.
[2] Josephus, *Antiquities*, I, 16, 2.

that she did not hesitate to offer a sufficiency of water to those who wanted it, though it cost her some pains to draw it.[1] He then asked her who were her parents, and wished them joy of such a daughter. " And mayest thou be espoused," said he, " to their satisfaction, into the family of an agreeable husband, and bring him good children."

Rebekah did not disdain to satisfy Eliezer's inquiries, but told him her family. When he heard who she was, he was very glad at what had happened, and at what she told him, for he perceived that God had thus plainly directed his journey and crowned his efforts with success. Producing some bracelets and some other ornaments which it was esteemed in that country decent for virgins to wear, Eliezer gave them to the damsel by way of acknowledgment, and as a reward for her kindness in giving him water to drink; saying it was but just that she should have them, because she was so much more obliging than any of the rest. Rebekah thanked him gracefully and said that she desired that he would come and lodge with them, since the approach of the night gave him no time to proceed farther.[2] Eliezer replied that he might guess at the hospitality of her people from the virtue he found in her. Moreover, he would not be burdensome, for he was willing to pay the hire for his entertainment, and spend his own money. To which the maiden replied that he guessed quite right as to the hospitality of her parents, but complained that he should think them so parsimonious as to take money from him. She further said that she would run and inform her brother Laban, and would then conduct him in.[3]

Rebekah thereupon quickly ran home and informed her parents of all that had occurred. When her brother Laban, a greedy youth, who was so called from the paleness of his face,[4] or from the cowardice of his breast which made him

---

[1] Josephus, *Antiquities*, I, 16, 2.   [2] *Genesis Rabba*, 60.
[3] Josephus, *Antiquities*, I, 16, 2; cf. *Pirke de Rabbi Eliezer*, Ch. 16; *Genesis Rabba*, 59–60; *Sanhedrin*, 110; *Yoma*, 286.   [4] *Genesis Rabba*, 60.

pale, saw the bracelets and other presents the stranger had made to his fair sister, he thought in his heart that the generous stranger must be a very wealthy man indeed, and decided to take his money from him by fair or foul means.[1] When Eliezer saw Laban coming, he at once knew that the youth was capable of any bad action. He, therefore, gave him proof of his strength. He lifted up the two camels as if they were toys, and Laban wondered and was greatly impressed.

" Come into the house," said Laban, very gracefully, " thou blessed of the Lord, for I have prepared the house and removed all the idols from within." [2]

Suddenly Eliezer heard the noise of running feet. He lifted up his eyes and saw men running to the well. Some of the inhabitants had already heard of the wealthy stranger and of his generosity, and had made up their minds to rob him. But when they came nearer and saw Eliezer lifting up the camels as if they were toys, they drew back duly impressed.[3] Eliezer thereupon followed the maiden and her brother into the house.

He was met by Bethuel and his wife who bade him welcome. Refreshments were placed upon the table, but the bowl of meat placed before Eliezer was poisoned, for Bethuel and Laban could not resist their innate greed and were intent upon robbing the wealthy stranger and taking possession of his money and valuables. But although there was meat before him, Eliezer said: " I will not eat until I have told my errand." He proceeded to do so, not touching the meat, and informed them who he was and what was his business in Mesopotamia. At that moment, one of the ministering angels who accompanied Eliezer and was there to protect him from any mishap, turned the table so that the poisoned bowl placed before Eliezer fell to the portion of Bethuel. And it came to pass that after he had finished his speech, Eliezer gave jewels of silver, and jewels of

---

[1] *Midrash Abkhir* quoted in *Yalkut*, 1, § 109.
[2] *Abot di Rabbi Nathan*, Ch. 8. [3] *Sanhedrin*, 105a.

gold, and raiment to Rebekah and also to her brother and to
her mother, and then they did eat and drink and make merry.
But no sooner had Bethuel partaken of the poisoned meat
which he had intended for Eliezer, than he felt great pains
and died in agony that same night.[1]

When they rose in the morning, Eliezer urged Rebekah's
mother and brother to give him their answer. Eliezer now
insisted upon a speedy decision.

" I must know at once," he said, " whether you agree to let
your daughter go with me or not, otherwise I shall have to
look for a wife for the son of my master among the daughters
of Ishmael or Lot." [2]   Rebekah's mother and brother, however, asked Eliezer to allow the maiden not only to abide
with them the seven days of mourning for her father, but
also to tarry another year or at least ten months, according
to the usual custom, so that she could prepare her raiment.
But Eliezer would brook no delay, and urged for a speedy
departure. Thereupon they called the damsel and asked her
opinion.

" Art thou willing," they said, " to go with this man to
the house of Abraham, the uncle of thy father, and marry
his son Isaac?"

Rebekah had already heard of Abraham, the mighty and
generous Emir of Canaan who was so famed for his wisdom,
his fear of the Lord and his many generous deeds and kind
actions, and she declared her willingness to accompany Eliezer
at once. But her mother still objected to such a speedy
departure.

" How wilt thou go and thou hast not yet prepared thy
raiment as is fitting for the daughter of our house?" But
Rebekah replied: " Let not such trifles detain me." [3]

And when the mother of Rebekah and her brother Laban

[1] *Yalkut*, i, § 109; *Genesis Rabba*, 59; *Pirke de Rabbi Eliezer*, Ch. 16; cf. Lewner, *loc. cit.*,
p. 112.   [2] *Genesis Rabba*, 60.   [3] *Genesis Rabba*, 60; *Sanhedrin*, 110.

THE PUNISHMENT OF TREACHERY: BETHUEL FALLS A VICTIM TO
THE POISONED BOWL

Facing page 320, Vol. I

saw that she was in such a hurry to leave them, they said unto themselves: " Well then, let her go, we will not give her any dowry but only our blessing."

Thus at noon of that day Eliezer and Rebekah, accompanied by her faithful and loving nurse Deborah, left Haran for Hebron. It was a long and weary journey from Mesopotamia to Canaan, but once more the journey was completed in three hours, for the earth fled under the feet of the camels.[1]

And it came to pass that at the same time Isaac was returning home from the school of Shem and Eber.[2] Rebekah saw him and was struck by his beauty and his noble appearance. She also saw that a guardian angel was accompanying him, and she wondered in her mind whether this distinguished stranger was the husband destined for her:

" Who is this man yonder," she asked Eliezer, " whose countenance is so radiant and whose bearing so noble?" " This is my master Isaac," said Eliezer, and in her confusion Rebekah fell off from the camel.[3] Some say that with prophetic vision Rebekah saw at that moment that she would become the mother of Esau, and that, therefore, she trembled and fell off the camel.[4] Eliezer related unto Isaac all that had occurred and all the wonders which the Lord had wrought.

Rebekah was duly married to Isaac, and once more the house of Abraham had a noble and generous mistress who took the place vacated by the noble-minded Sarah. The bride filled the vacated place with distinction, and once more the doors were opened to all the poor and the needy who flocked to the house to find help, comfort, and consolation.[5] The perpetual lamp was kindled again, and to Isaac it seemed that all the happiness —that had gone from his life when his mother died—had returned again with Rebekah. Isaac loved his wife dearly,

---

[1] *Targum Jerushalmi, Genesis,* 24, 61.
[2] He went out to say the afternoon prayer, say some Midrashim. See *Pirke de Rabbi Eliezer,* Ch. 16; *Midrash Haggadol,* col. 370.
[3] *Genesis Rabba,* 60; *Sanhedrin,* 110; see Lewner, *loc. cit.,* pp. 113-114.
[4] *Yalkut,* 1, § 109.   [5] *Genesis Rabba,* 60.

and he cherished her the more when he saw that she continued the traditions of his dear, never-to-be-forgotten mother.[1]

Abraham thanked Eliezer for his faithful services and the intelligence with which he had accomplished his delicate mission. In recognition of his services he set him entirely free, and it is said that he afterwards became King of Bashan.[2] Some say that Eliezer was one of the few who were taken into Paradise without having tasted death.[3]

[1] *Pirke de Rabbi Eliezer*, Ch. 32.   [2] *Ibid.*, Ch. 16.   [3] *Derekh Erez Sutta*, Ch. 1.

CHAPTER XXVIII

The Death of the Patriarch

Abraham's second wife—Keturah, the bondwoman—Ophren, the grandson of Keturah—The city with iron walls—Artificial lighting—Abraham exhorts his son Isaac—The archangel comes to prepare the Patriarch for the last journey—The sun-like splendour of the stranger—The tears that change into pearls—The pleading of the angel—Isaac's dream—The sun, the moon, and the stars—Abraham's request to be allowed to witness the wonders of creation, while yet in the body—The ride in the heavenly chariot—The wickedness of man—The Patriarch's indignation—A voice from heaven calls: Stop the ride—The visit to Paradise—The two roads and the two gates—Adam seated on a golden throne—His tears and his joy—The court of justice—The scales of justice—Abraham intercedes for a soul in distress—Michael refuses to take the soul of Abraham—The sixty-three thousand eight hundred and seventy-five days of Abraham's life bear witness to the perfection of the Patriarch—Abraham's vision of bliss in Paradise—Abraham's soul departs heavenwards—The funeral—Princes and potentates express their grief at the funeral of the Patriarch.

AND it came to pass that after having married his son Isaac, Abraham also took a wife named Keturah. Some say that Keturah was Hagar,[1] as the word signifies the Bondwoman, she having regarded herself as bound to Abraham.[2] To the sons of Keturah Abraham gave many gifts, and he also instructed them in the art of magic.[3] He settled them in colonies, and they afterwards took possession of Troglodytis and of the country of Arabia the Happy, as far as it reaches the Red Sea. One of the grandchildren of Keturah, named Ophren, made war against Libya and took it, and his grandchildren,

---

[1] *Baba Kama*, 92b; *Genesis Rabba*, 50; *Midrash Tanchuma*. See also Josephus, *Antiquities*, I, 15–16.
[2] *Targum Jerushalmi*; *Yalkut*, 1, § 109; 2, 1073. Another explanation is that her name was Keturah, because she was perfumed with all kinds of scents.
[3] *Sanhedrin*, 91a; *Pirke de Rabbi Eliezer*, Ch. 30.

when they inhabited it, called the land from his name Africa. Abraham also built for the sons of Keturah and for her grandchildren a city surrounded by iron walls, and as the walls were so high that the rays of the sun could not penetrate into the town, Abraham installed artificial lighting by means of disks made of pearls and precious stones, which shed a pale light upon the city.[1] Abraham was now one hundred and seventy-five years of age, and he felt his end approaching. He, therefore, called his son Isaac and thus spake unto him:

" Thou knowest, my son, that the Eternal is the only God, the Creator of Heaven and earth and of the Universe. He took me from my native land and from the house of my father, and brought me to this country of Canaan. In His loving kindness, which He vouchsafed unto me, He saved me from the furnace into which Nimrod had cast me, and wrought many wonders on my behalf, for great is His power. When I was cast into the fire by Nimrod's order, the flame turned into a bed of roses, on which I went to sleep. I therefore command thee, my son, to remain faithful to thy God and to serve Him with all thy heart all the days of thy life upon earth. Hearken unto His voice and have faith in His loving kindness and mercy. Be kind and charitable and generous to all thy fellowmen. Be a protector to the needy and comfort the afflicted. Never turn away a poor man from thy gate, but be ready to give food and shelter to those who require it and raiment to the naked. Comfort and console and wipe away the tears of the unhappy. The Lord will bless thee, and thou wilt be a blessing. Teach also thy children and thy children's children to love peace and mercy and to walk humbly before their God." [2] Thus spake Abraham, and Isaac promised faithfully to do as his beloved father had bidden him.

Now Abraham, not only the friend of God and the beloved

---

[1] *Tractate Sopherim*, Ch. 21; Josephus, *Antiquities*, I, 15.
[2] *Sepher Hajashar*; see also *The Book of Jubilees*.

of the Eternal, but also the friend of strangers, the hospitable and beneficent Emir, had reached the full measure of years allotted to him, and his time to die had arrived. God now sent His archangel Michael to prepare the Patriarch for the last journey.[1]

Disguised as a common traveller, seeking hospitality, the archangel appeared before the tent which Abraham had pitched in the plain of Mamre, that tent which was open to the four high-roads, and where all were welcomed as guests: rich and poor, beggars and kings. Abraham was not at home at that moment, for he was superintending his ploughing in the fields. Here the traveller met the old man who invited him home.[2] Abraham was struck by the radiance and the sun-like splendour of the stranger, and with his customary politeness and hospitality offered the guest one of his horses to ride home. The angel, however, refused the offer, and they walked home together. On their way home Abraham heard a huge tamarisk tree with its three hundred and thirty-one branches singing a song and whispering to him that God was about to summon him to himself.[3]

On their arrival home, Isaac hastened to bring water for his father to wash the feet of the guest as was customary. Abraham now had the presentiment that he was to perform the pious act for the last time, and tears came to his eyes. Isaac, too, cried. The archangel, knowing the nature of the tidings he was the bearer of, also shed tears which quickly changed into pearls. Now the archangel, before sitting down at a sumptuously prepared table, absented himself for a little while. Spreading out his wings, he rose speedily to Heaven there to join the choir of ministering angels who daily assemble before the Throne of Glory at sunset to sing the praises of the Eternal.[4] The archangel prostrated himself before the Throne of Glory and thus he spake:

---

[1] *Midrash Agadah*, Ed. Buber, p. 162.
[2] M. R. James, *The Testament of Abraham* in Robinson's Texts and Studies, II, 2, Cambridge, 1892, pp. 76–119. [3] See *Succa*, 28a. [4] *Yalkut, Genesis*, § 133.

" Lord of the Universe! how can I bring the sad message to the pious and generous old man, who has no equal in the world for goodness of heart? And how can I sit down at the sumptuous table prepared for me, unable as I am, being a celestial, to partake of food?"

Thus spake Michael, and the voice from the Throne of Glory replied: " Go thou and do My bidding. A dream will come upon Isaac, a prophetic dream which will announce to him the approaching death of his father. Thou wilt interpret the dream to him. I will furthermore send a spirit who will devour all that is placed upon the table for thee."

Michael thereupon descended upon earth and entering Abraham's tent, sat down at the table prepared for him.

After midnight, Isaac had a dream, seeing the death of Abraham. Greatly disturbed, he hastened to his father and roused the household.

" Tell me thy dream, O son," said Abraham, " that I may hear."

And Isaac thus spake: " In my dream, I saw the sun and the moon and the stars upon my head, giving me light. Thereupon a shining man, who was brighter than seven suns, came down from Heaven and prepared to take the sun from my head. I cried bitterly and asked him not to take the sun. And the moon and the stars also begged him not to take the sun away. The sun, too, implored him to give her a little time so that she might collect all her rays and leave none behind. But although I beseeched the shining man to leave the sun behind, he would not yield to my request. He only said: ' Grieve not, Isaac, for I am taking the sun from thee to carry it to the heavenly Father who is asking for it. I am taking it from sorrow to eternal joy and bliss.' Thus spake the shining one, and I awoke, greatly disturbed."

When Abraham heard what dream Isaac had dreamt, he wept

bitterly. Thereupon Michael, whose radiance was like the splendour of the sun, appeared before his hosts and, addressing Abraham, said: " The dream of thy son, Isaac, will come true. I am the shining man who hath come down from Heaven, and thou, Abraham, art the sun. I have come down to take thy soul and carry it up to the Father in Heaven, for thy time to die hath come. I am the prince of the Presence, the archangel Michael, who visited thee in the plain of Mamre, before the birth of thy son. I was one of the three strangers whom thou didst so hospitably invite to thy house." [1]

And when Abraham heard what message the angel had brought, he refused to give up his soul. Thereupon the archangel Michael spread out his wings and rose to Heaven to report the refusal of the perfect servant of God to give up his soul. But the Lord bade him go back to Abraham and tell him that all the offspring of Adam are doomed to die, and that none could escape.

Then the voice of the Lord spoke to Abraham and said: " My ministering angel Michael, the prince of the Presence, will lead thee from earth to the heavenly Paradise, and the angel of death will have no power to strike thee with his sword. Thou wilt be transferred from earth to a better world without suffering the pangs and agony of death."

Abraham now yielded, but asked yet a favour of God. " May I be allowed," he prayed, " while yet in the body, to witness the wonders of Thy creation, to see the world which Thou hast created by the word of Thy mouth; may I be allowed to see the world and all its inhabitants, and the heavenly order, that I may thereafter depart in peace."

Thus prayed Abraham, and Michael interceded for him before the Throne of Glory. The request of the old man, the perfect servant of the Lord, was granted.[2]

Thereupon Michael, at the bidding of the Lord, placed

---

[1] M. R. James, *The Testament of Abraham*, § VII.   [2] *Ibid*, § IX

Abraham in the heavenly chariot of the Cherubim, sixty ministering angels surrounding it, and upon a cloud of light carried him high above to Heaven, there to show him the inhabited world and the wonders of creation. And thus the Patriarch was allowed to see the whole world and to witness the scenes of earthly existence, of human life and labour, human joys and sorrows, human weal and woe, gladness and grief, all the vicissitudes of man's life. He was also allowed to see the actions of man, good and evil, beautiful and ugly, and rejoice at the good deeds of man. A wave of righteous indignation swept over the old man, when he saw the crimes committed by men in every station of life. And he saw murderous swords raised by man against his brother, and by nation against nation, and acts of violence committed everywhere. Beholding such evil-doers with swords in their hands, ready to fall upon and slaughter their brethren, he called out in agony, and prayed unto the Lord: " O Lord! Let Thy wild beasts out of the forest come speedily forth and devour these evil-doers who are about to commit murder." And behold, at his prayer, wild beasts came out of the forest and devoured the evil-doers about to commit murder.

Thereupon Abraham saw men and women who were guilty of adultery, and once more in his righteous indignation he prayed: " O Lord, may the earth open her mouth and swallow them that they may not contaminate others." And behold, the earth opened her mouth and swallowed up the adulterers. Riding farther in the heavenly chariot, and upon the cloud of light, surveying the world, Abraham beheld thieves digging holes in houses and preparing to rob their fellowmen and to carry off their possessions. " O Lord," he prayed, " let a fire come down from Heaven and consume these thieves who are about to carry away the earnings of hard-working men." And lo! a fire fell down from Heaven and consumed the thieves. The archangel Michael had been ordered to do whatever Abraham told him to do. And he thus smote with instant death all the malefactors whom Abraham, who had never sinned, condemned to death.[1]

But a voice from the Throne of Glory resounded and said: " Stop thy ride, Michael, and turn back the chariot, lest Abraham destroy all My creatures in his wrath and righteous indignation, for *all* live in wickedness. He hath no pity on sinners, for he hath never sinned. But I am the Maker of the Universe, and take no delight in destroying My creatures. I defer the death of the sinner, so that he may repent and live. Go thou now and direct the chariot to the eastern gate of Heaven, towards Paradise, and there show him the judgments and retributions.[2] He will then learn to have compassion upon the souls of the sinners he killed in his pious wrath." Thus spake the voice from the Throne of Glory. And Michael, doing the bidding of the Lord, turned the heavenly chariot and took Abraham to the first gate of Heaven.

And behold, there were two roads, one broad and one narrow, stretched out and leading to two gates or doors, a large door and a small door. Between the two doors there sat one upon a golden throne, a man of wondrous figure, whose appearance was terrible, like that of the Lord. Abraham beheld this wondrous figure upon the golden throne alternately weep and laugh, but his weeping was much more than his laughing, indeed his weeping was seven times as much as his laughing. Abraham then asked the angel Michael to explain unto him the meaning of the two doors, the large door and the small door, and to tell him who the wondrous figure was upon the golden throne.

Michael answered and thus he said: " The small door, the narrow one, leads to the path of life and to eternal bliss, but the large door, the wide one, leads to perdition and to

[1] M. R. James, *The Testament of Abraham*, § X.   [2] Cf. Charles, *The Book of Enoch*, 32.

destruction. The man who is seated upon the golden throne, and whose appearance is terrible like that of the Lord, is Adam, man's first parent. He is allowed by the Eternal to sit here and watch the procession of the souls which depart from their bodies and enter either by the narrow or by the wide gate. But he weepeth and grieveth when he witnesses the multitudes that go through the wide gate, and rejoiceth when a soul passeth through the narrow gate. But behold, his weeping is more than his laughing, for whilst multitudes of souls which go forth from their bodies and pass him enter by the wide gate, only few are allowed to enter through the narrow gate into eternal life. Against seven thousand walking on the wide road and entering by the wide gate, leading to perdition, very few walk on the narrow path of righteousness and thus enter through the narrow gate into bliss and life eternal. And because of this, Adam's weeping greatly exceeds his laughing." [1]

Thus spake the angel Michael, and Abraham looked and watched the procession of souls and witnessed the judgments awaiting them. And behold, he saw myriads of souls to whom the angel refused admittance through the narrow gate, so that they were compelled to enter through the wide gate which leads to destruction. Abraham also beheld two fiery angels driving with fiery thongs ten thousand souls through the wide gate to perdition and destruction, whilst one angel was leading a single soul. Then Abraham and Michael followed the multitudes through the gate, to see whether any would be saved.

There they beheld a man, whose countenance was as radiant as the sun, before a crystal table, upon which was spread out a book six cubits in thickness and ten cubits in breadth, whilst two angels were standing at his sides and officiating as recorders. The actions of man were weighed in

[1] *The Testament of Abraham*, § XI. The same legend is also found in Moslem tradition. See W. St. Clair Tisdall, *The Original Sources of the Quran*, 1905, pp. 206–207.

a balance by a fiery angel. The soul which Abraham had seen carried by one angel was now brought in. It asked for mercy, but its good actions and sins were looked out in the book, and it was found that its meritorious acts were outbalanced by its evil doings. The archangel Dokiel was holding the scales of justice, and Purael was holding the probing fire. Abel, the son of Adam, who was the judge, ordered the scrolls to be unrolled, and Enoch, the writer of righteousness, and the teacher of Heaven and earth, read out the account.[1] The soul was that of a woman who had murdered her own daughter, and although it protested of its innocence and pleaded not guilty, its crimes were proved and found recorded in the scrolls.

Loud did the soul lament: "Woe to me," cried the soul, "I have forgotten all my sins and crimes, but they are not forgotten here."

Another soul was then brought in, and her sins and good actions were weighed on the scales [2] and lo! it was found that her sins and righteous acts were exactly alike. It needed but one good deed to outweigh her sins, and the judge would neither condemn the soul for her sins nor grant her salvation, but decided that she must remain there until God, the judge of all, had decided her fate. Abraham had compassion upon that soul, which needed only one good deed to be saved. "What can we do for this poor soul?" he asked, and Michael replied that if she had one more meritorious deed she would be saved. Pitying that soul, Abraham interceded for her and prayed to the Lord of the Universe.[3] He was joined in his supplications by the angels themselves, by the judge and the recorder. And lo, the Lord of the Universe heard the righteous prayer of Abraham, and the soul was carried into Paradise by a shining angel.

[1] *Ibid.*, § XII–XIII. See also *Erubin*, 21a; *Hagigah*, 16a; *Targum Jerushalmi, Genesis*, 5, 24.
[2] *Ibid.*, § XIV. See also *Erubin*, 19a; *Hagigah*, 27a; *Rosh Hashana*, 17a. See also Koran, *Sura*, 7, 21.   [3] *Sotah*, 10b.

Thereupon Abraham saw the souls of those who had been destroyed by his prayer for their wickedness. Taking compassion upon them, he prayed to the Almighty to forgive them: " O Lord!" said Abraham, " I have been too precipitate in my wrath and have caused the death of the sinners, before they had time to repent. Forgive them now their sins or restore them to life again, so that they may be able to mend their ways and repent." And a voice from the Throne of Glory replied that the souls were forgiven, for they had suffered an uncommon mode of death.[1] Having witnessed the judgment in Heaven, Abraham was now taken back by the angel Michael to his home upon earth.[2]

" It is time," Michael said to the venerable old man, " to yield thy soul. Put thy house in order, and make thy will, for thou must now die."

But still the Patriarch refused to give up his soul.

And thereupon the archangel ascended to Heaven, and prostrating himself before the Throne of Glory thus he spoke: " O Lord of the Universe! I cannot lay hands upon Abraham and take his soul, for he was Thy friend, and there is none like him on earth."

And now the sixty-three thousand eight hundred and seventy-five days, during which Abraham had walked upon the face of the earth, appeared before the Throne of Glory and thus they spake: " We have come before Thee, O Lord of the Universe! to bear witness to the perfection and righteousness of Thy servant Abraham, that there is none so righteous and perfect in the land. On none of us," said the days of Abraham's life, " hath he done wrong or forgotten his duty, but hath always wrought good deeds, practised charity, and glorified Thy name." [3]

And suddenly Abraham felt himself carried upon wings

---

[1] *Sanhedrin*, 43b.   [2] M. R. James, *The Testament of Abraham*, § XV.
[3] Lewner, *Kol Agadoth*, p. 119.

high up to the celestial regions. Higher and higher he was carried, into regions of radiance and of splendour. And behold, he came to a place where there was a great light, and he could perceive the whole world from end to end. Thereupon two gates made of precious stones were thrust open before him, and he entered the city of the just. Myriads of ministering angels, whose countenances were as radiant as the splendour of Heaven, hurried to his encounter and bade him welcome. Divesting him of his raiment, they clothed him in clouds of glory and he could smell the perfumes of the Garden of Eden which sent a never-experienced feeling of bliss and delight through his whole being. And the ministering angels took crowns made of precious stones and pearls and placed them upon his head. And eight branches of myrtle they put into his hands, and their perfume filled the world. They brought Abraham to shores of lovely rivers, such as he had never seen in his life, and there he saw roses and myrtles, whose perfume filled his being with delight. Thereupon the angels brought him to a canopy prepared for him, and he beheld four rivers, flowing from underneath it, and they were rivers of honey, wine, oil, and balsam.[1]

Lifting up his eyes, he saw that his canopy was set in with pearls, and precious stones sent out a dazzling light. Beneath the canopy, he beheld a table of pure gold, set in with precious stones; and ministering angels were standing around ready to wait on him. Whilst he was still wondering at the splendour and radiance and delights surrounding him, behold, he felt himself quite a young child, happy and careless. He saw a number of other children, of his own age, coming to meet him and to play with him. Happily he joined his little playmates, and together they ran off to listen to the music of the spheres and of the angels, gambolled and danced among the lovely

[1] Lewner, *loc. cit.* See also Gaster, *The Chronicles of Jerahmeel*, 18, 4; Jellinek, *Beth-Hamidrash*, II, 52–53.

smelling trees, and rested under the shade of the tree of life.

And behold, the days of his childhood had passed, and Abraham felt himself a youth, full of life and the joy of life. The children, his playmates, had disappeared, but in their stead, happy and joyous and resplendent with health and beauty, youths, as young as himself, came to meet him, and he shared their joys and their pleasures. He beheld wonders without end and found delights innumerable. Youth and middle age passed swiftly away, and once more Abraham felt himself a venerable old man. He met other venerable and handsome old men, who came out to bid him welcome, and he enjoyed their talk and their company. They talked of justice, mercy and charity, and of the duties of man towards his Maker and towards his fellowmen. They talked of human life, of human suffering, and of the destiny of man.[1] The old and venerable men thereupon brought Abraham to the canopy prepared for him, and there he noticed a curtain made of lightning. He looked behind the curtain, and beheld three hundred and ten worlds spreading out before his gaze, wonderful worlds extending into infinity. The clouds of glory invaded the garden, and Abraham felt an indescribable delight, and he heard a voice calling to him and saying: " This is only a part of the delight and happiness which awaits thee in the next world."[2]

And then the Lord took the soul of Abraham from his body, never allowing the angel of death to touch his perfect and faithful servant.[3] The soul departed heavenwards to dwell in the celestial regions, among the angels and perfect souls. And at that moment the stone, which was hanging upon a chain on Abraham's breast, rose up, was carried heavenwards and placed in the sun.[4]

---

[1] Lewner, loc. cit. See also Gaster, The Chronicles of Jerahmeel, 18, 4; Jellinek, Beth-Hamidrash, II, 52–53.   [2] Ibid. See also Lewner, loc. cit., pp. 119–121.
[3] Baba Batra, 17a; see Weil, loc. cit., p. 98. See, however, James, loc. cit., § XX, where it is said that Abraham died because he had been induced to kiss the hand of the Angel of Death.   [4] Baba Batra, 16b.

No sooner had the news of the death of the famous and generous Emir Abraham, the son of Terah, spread at Beer-Sheba, than loud lamentations and wailing filled the town. The news was carried to the neighbouring towns, and at once crowds of men, women, and children, flocked to Beer-Sheba, weeping and lamenting. They all came to bewail the death of the man who had been a friend of the poor and an adviser of the rich.

From distant Mesopotamia, from Haran and other places, men came to pay their last respects to the pious, generous, and famous Emir, to lament his death, in truly oriental fashion,[1] and to accompany to his last resting place this wise man of the East.

Abraham's son Isaac was greatly astonished, when he noticed among those who came to follow the procession many of the old and venerable men who had come to the funeral of his mother Sarah, thirty-eight years ago. " Were you not present, my friends," Isaac asked some of these old men, " at the funeral of my never-to-be-forgotten mother Sarah?"

" That is so," replied the old and venerable men, " but since that day the Creator of the Universe gave us a new lease of life and lent us strength, allowing us to live to this day, so that we might be able to accompany thy father to his resting place and pay him the last respects. Now we know that it is agreeable to the Lord that men pay the last respects to the dead."[2]

And Isaac placed his father upon a bier which was carried upon the shoulders of friends to the place of burial. Isaac and Ishmael, and the venerable relatives of the deceased, Shem and Eber, walked in front,[3] and men called out: " Make way for the bier of Abraham." When the people beheld the bier, they broke out into loud wailing, saying: " Woe unto

[1] Sepher Hajashar.   [2] Sepher Hajashar; Cf. Genesis Rabba, 62.   [3] Genesis Rabba, 64.

us, now that our father Abraham, the generous, our benefactor is dead and gone."

And the princes and potentates of Canaan, who had hastened to Beer-Sheba to follow the procession, asked the bearers
of the bier to wait a moment, so that they might give expression to their grief in suitable words. In a voice broken by
sobs, amidst the awed silence of the crowd, they cried:

" Woe unto the land which hath lost its leader, woe unto
mankind which hath lost the friend of peace, and woe also
unto us, the rulers of men, who have lost such an adviser and
a friend. Men have lost an instructor and a teacher, and the
poor their benefactor. We are all like a vessel which hath lost
its pilot, and like children whose father hath left them." [1]

Thus lamented the princes and potentates of Canaan, and
all the people wept loudly and shed copious tears. Thereupon
Ishmael and Isaac, and Shem and Eber, entered the cave of
Machpelah and laid Abraham to rest by the side of his wife
Sarah.[2]

[1] *Baba Batra*, 91a.   [2] Cf. Lewner, *loc. cit.*, pp. 121–122; Bin Gorion, *loc. cit.*, pp. 358–362.

CHAPTER XXIX

The Way of Life and the Way of Death, or the Twin Brothers

The prayers of Isaac and Rebekah—The struggle of the twins—They divide the two worlds—The contention of the angels—Michael and Sammael —The way of life and the way of death—Esau deceives his father— Rebekah's love for Jacob—Grandfather and grandson—Abraham's blessing —The death of Nimrod—The precious garment—The pottage of lentils The sword that had slain a thousand devils—A father's blessing—Wine from Paradise—The vision of Hell—Thoughts of revenge—The exile— Eliphaz, the robber—The quick journey—The quarrel of the stones.

AFTER his marriage, Isaac continued to live with his father Abraham in the land of Canaan. Rebekah was barren for twenty years and she said to her husband: " I have heard that thy mother, too, was barren and that thy father prayed unto the Lord and He sent her a son. Pray thou now on my behalf, and the Lord will listen to thy prayers." Thereupon Isaac took his wife Rebekah, and they went to mount Moriah, to the place where Isaac had been bound and offered as a burnt offering to the Lord. Isaac entreated the Lord and prayed on behalf of his wife, whilst Rebekah, too, prayed and implored the Sovereign of all the Worlds to bless her and to give her children. And God hearkened unto their prayer, and Rebekah conceived twins.[1]

Now the children were contending with one another in their mother's womb, like mighty warriors. When Rebekah

[1] *Jebamoth*, 64a; *Targum Jerushalmi, Genesis*, 25, 21; *Pirke de Rabbi Eliezer*, Ch. 32.

passed before an idol temple Esau made violent efforts to come forth, whilst whenever she went before a house of learning or a synagogue Jacob struggled and desired to escape into the world, so that he might attend the house of God. Rebekah suffered great agony, so that her soul was nigh unto death, on account of the pains.[1]   It is also related that Jacob said unto Esau: " My brother, two worlds are before us, the world below and a world above, or a world to come. If it pleases thee, take thou this world, and I will take the other." Esau, however, denied the existence of a world to come and the resurrection of the dead.   He, therefore, made a compact with his brother Jacob, giving over to him the right to the next world, whilst he himself took the right to this world.[2]   Not only the children, but also the angels in Heaven contended one with another. Sammael, who is also the tutelary angel of Esau, wanted to kill Jacob already in his mother's womb, but Michael protected him.   Some of the angels were on Sammael's side, whilst others supported Michael.   But the Lord rebuked Sammael and his followers.[3]

Now when Rebekah was suffering great pains, she questioned all the other women whether anything similar had happened unto them, but they said that never had such a thing happened unto them.   " Why should it only happen to me," said Rebekah, and she went to consult Shem and Eber, and begged them to intercede on her behalf before the Lord.   She also asked Abraham to pray on her account to the Lord.   And through Shem and Eber the Lord answered Rebekah that there were two nations in her womb. When the lads were born one was called Esau and the other Jacob.

The elder brother was called Esau, because he was hairy, having red hair all over his body, covering him like a garment. He was also called Edom, or Red, because before his birth he

---

[1] *Genesis Rabba,* 63; *Sepher Hajashar.*
[2] Bin Gorion, *Die Sagen der Juden,* Vol. II, p. 353.
[3] *Midrash Abkhir,* quoted in *Yalkut Shimeoni, Genesis,* § 110.

already sucked his mother's blood, and during his life he frequently shed blood.[1]

The lads grew up, and Esau went the way of death, being a cunning hunter, catching birds and beasts, and deceiving and cheating men, whilst Jacob went the way of life, dwelling in academies and in houses of learning, where he studied the law all his days. He studied in the schools of Shem and Eber, continuing to seek instruction and acquiring the knowledge of God.[2]

Esau knew that his father was a holy man and that he whom he would bless would be blessed indeed. He, therefore, endeavoured to find favour in the eyes of Isaac and never omitted an opportunity to please him. Whenever he visited his father, he came arrayed in his best garments and brought him the best meat and wine, saying unto himself: " My father will see how I honour him and will bless me." As Isaac, however, paid but little attention to these things, the wily Esau changed his tactics and decided to pretend to his father that he was a man of justice and piety. One day Esau came to see his father and thus he spoke:

" Father dear, I have been to listen to the words of God in the house of learning, and I am now giving a tithe to the poor from all that I earn. I have now come to ask thee how to give tithe from salt and straw."

When Isaac heard these words he was very pleased with the piety of the lad, and made up his mind to bless him before he died. But the Lord decreed that the eyes of Isaac should grow dim so that Jacob would be enabled to obtain the blessing.[3]

But Isaac loved Esau, in whose mouth were words of deceit, whilst both Abraham and Rebekah loved Jacob. Abraham, indeed, saw the deeds of Esau and knew that

---

[1] See Eisenmenger, *Endecktes Judentum*, Vol. I, p. 646.
[2] *Pirke de Rabbi Eliezer*, Ch. 32; *Yalkut, Genesis*, § 110.
[3] See Lewner, *loc. cit.*, pp. 117–118.

they were wicked. He therefore called his daughter-in-law and thus he spoke unto her: " My daughter, watch over the boy Jacob, for it is he who will be in my stead on earth and a blessing among men. It is him whom the Lord will choose to be a people for possession unto Himself. It grieveth me to see that Isaac loveth Esau, but I am glad to notice that thou dost love Jacob. Therefore, my daughter, watch over the lad, for all the blessings wherewith the Lord hath blessed me and my seed shall belong to Jacob." And Abraham called Jacob and blessed him, and thus he said: " May the Lord give thee, my son, all the blessings wherewith He blessed Adam, and Enoch, Noah, and Shem, and may the spirits of Mastema never have any power over thee or over thy seed to turn thee from the Lord, who is thy God." [1]

Now it happened that on the day when Abraham died, Esau, as was his habit, went out to hunt. Nimrod, King of Babel, who was called Amraphel, also went out to hunt on that day. Being very jealous of Nimrod, Esau constantly sought for an opportunity to slay the King. Meeting Nimrod alone far away from his royal suite, he fell upon him, killed him and took away the coats of Nimrod, which the Holy One had once made for Adam and Eve.[2] On these garments the forms of all the wild beasts and birds which are on the face of the earth were embroidered in their proper colours. Suddenly Esau saw Nimrod's men approaching and he took to flight, carrying off the precious raiment, hurrying to conceal it in his father's house. Very weak and exhausted, he met Jacob and was surprised to see traces of tears upon his brother's countenance. " Why art thou crying, my brother," he asked, " and why hast thou dressed pottage of lentils to-day, which is food only fit for the poor?"

" Alas, dear brother," replied Jacob, " didst thou not know

[1] Charles, *Book of Jubilees*, 19, 15-29.
[2] *Targum Jerushalmi, Genesis*, 25, 27; *Midrash Agadah, Genesis*, 28, 13; *Midrash Lekach Tob, Genesis*; *Yalkut, Genesis*, § 115; *Pirke de Rabbi Eliezer*, Ch. 24; *Sepher Hajashar*.

that our dear grandfather Abraham died to-day? Lentil food
is a sign of mourning and sorrow." [1] " If this pious old man,"
said Esau, " hath died like any other mortal, why should I
believe in God and in punishment and reward? Now, my
brother," he continued, " I am very faint, therefore let me
taste some of thy red pottage."

Thereupon Jacob said: " Sell me to-day thy birthright."
And Esau said: " I am going to die and I do not believe
in another world; this birthright, therefore, hath no value
in mine eyes." Jacob then wrote a deed of transfer upon a
leaf, and Esau signed it, selling his birthright for a mess
of lentils.

Esau thereupon laughed at Jacob, and mocked him, saying: " Thou fool, thou hast bought to-day something which
is worthless." Esau indeed thought that he had had the better
of Jacob, who, in addition to bread and pottage of lentils,
had given him also the sword of Methuselah, wherewith the
latter had slain a thousand devils.[2] And Esau went forth and
told his friends of what had occurred, and they all laughed
and mocked at Jacob.[3]

On the nightfall of the festive day of Passover, Isaac
called Esau, his first born, and thus he spoke unto him: " To-
night the treasuries of dew and blessing are opened, and the
angels in Heaven utter songs and implore the Creator to
bestow the blessing of dew upon the world. As it is a time
of blessing, go thou, catch venison and make me savoury meat,
that I may bless thee, whilst I am still alive. Take care, however,
not to bring me anything stolen or robbed."

Esau went forth to catch venison but thought in his mind:
" If I am not successful I will steal a lamb or a kid from my
neighbours and make savoury meat for my father." Esau,
however, had forgotten to take the garment of Nimrod and,

---

[1] *Pirke de Rabbi Eliezer*, Ch. 35.   [2] See Eisenmenger, *loc. cit.*, Vol. I, p. 651.
[3] For the entire passage see *Pirke de Rabbi Eliezer*, Ch. 35; *Targum Jerushalmi, Genesis*, 25,
29; *Genesis Rabba*, 63; *Baba Batra*, 16b; *Sepher Hajashar*.

not being successful in hunting as usually, was delayed.[1]

Now Rebekah had heard the words of her husband, and made up her mind to deprive Esau of his father's promised blessing for the benefit of Jacob. She called her younger son and thus she spoke to him:

" My son, on this night, the treasuries of the dew will be opened, and on this night, in the future, thy children will be redeemed from bondage and will utter a song.[2] Make thou, therefore, savoury meat for thy father that he may bless thee." But Jacob's heart dreaded the deceit, and he cried bitterly and said:

" O Mother dear, I cannot do such a thing." But his mother insisted, saying: " If it be a blessing may it come upon thee and upon thy seed, and if it be a curse, let it be upon me and upon my soul." [3] And Jacob did as his mother bade him, but wept copiously.

Rebekah dressed Jacob in the coats of Esau and sent him off to his father. When Jacob appeared before the latter, the room was suddenly filled with a fragrant smell, like the smell from Paradise. And Isaac ate of the meat his son had brought him, but he was thirsty, and an angel brought him from Paradise the juice of the grapes growing on the vine there.[4] Isaac blessed his son Jacob with ten blessings concerning the dews of Heaven and the corn of the earth, and Jacob left the presence of his father crowned like a bridegroom, on account of the blessing he had received. The dew which is destined to revive the dead came down from Heaven and descended upon him, and his bones were refreshed and became stronger, and he himself became a mighty man.[5]

But scarcely had Jacob left his father's presence, when Esau

---

[1] Lewner, *Kol Agadoth*, Vol. I, p. 128; *Pirke de Rabbi Eliezer*, Ch. 32; *Genesis Rabba*, 66; *Midrash Tanchuma*, section *Toledoth*. [2] *Pirke de Rabbi Eliezer*, ibid.; *Sotah*, 12b.

[3] *Genesis Rabba*, 65, 66; *Midrash Tanchuma*, section *Toledoth*; *Targum Jerushalmi*; *Genesis*, 27, 13; see also Lewner, *loc. cit.*, pp. 128–130.

[4] *Genesis Rabba*, 66; *Midrash Tanchuma*, section *Toledoth*; Lewner, *loc. cit.*, p. 129. See also Eisenmenger, *loc. cit.*, Vol. II, p. 879, where Eisenmenger gives a wrong translation.

[5] *Pirke de Rabbi Eliezer*, Ch. 32.

returned. He entered Isaac's room with vehemence, and called aloud: " Arise, Father, and bless me." At that moment Isaac had a terrible vision. He saw Hell opened to him beneath his feet,[1] he saw an abyss of fire, and his son Esau standing over it and throwing fuel into it. Trembling at the sight, he asked in terror: " Who art thou?" And when he heard what had happened and that Jacob had bought the birthright from Esau he thought: " Now it is right that he should have my blessing." [2] But when he heard Esau crying, he blessed him too.

Esau now hated his brother and said unto himself: " If I kill my brother, I will be punished and my father will curse me. I will therefore go to my uncle Ishmael and marry one of his daughters. Then I will induce him to seek quarrel with Jacob, on account of my birthright; he will fight my brother and kill him. Then I will pretend to avenge the death of my brother, kill Ishmael and inherit the possessions of both my father and my uncle." Such were the wicked thoughts of Esau, but the Lord frustrated them.[3]

According to others, Esau said in his heart: " Cain made a mistake in killing his brother Abel whilst his parents were still alive, for his father afterwards begat Seth. I will wait until my father dies, then I will kill Jacob, and will thus be sole heir to all his possessions."

Afraid to meet his brother, Jacob went out only at night, hiding in the day. Jacob then fled and went to the school of Shem and Eber, where he remained for fourteen years, studying the law. After fourteen years he returned home, but found that his brother was still harbouring the thought of killing him. It was then that his mother advised him to go to Padan-Aram.

" Go thou to thy Uncle Laban," said Rebekah, " to my brother, the son of Bethuel. He is old and very wealthy.

[1] *Genesis Rabba*, 65 and 67.
[2] *Genesis Rabba*, 67; *Midrash Tanchuma*, section *Toledoth*: see also Lewner, *loc. cit.*, pp. 130–131.   [3] *Sotah*, 13; *Genesis Rabba*, 67.

Ask him to give thee one of his daughters as wife, and abide with him until the day when thy brother's anger will have abated."

And when Isaac heard what Esau was meditating, he called his son Jacob, and enjoined him not to marry any of the daughters of Canaan, but take to wife one of the daughters of Laban. He blessed his son and gave him gold and silver, as much as he could carry, to take with him.[1]

Now it happened that when Jacob set out on his way, Esau called Eliphaz, his first born, and thus spoke to him: "Take up thy sword, and hasten after Jacob who has just left and is carrying much wealth with him. Kill him and take away all his possessions."

Eliphaz, a nimble youth, clever in handling both the sword and the bow, hastened to comply with his father's request. He took ten of his followers with him, pursued his uncle Jacob and met him at the frontier of Canaan, near Sochem.

When Jacob saw Eliphaz and his men pursuing him, he stood still and awaited them.

"My father," said Eliphaz, when he came near, "has sent me to kill thee and to take away all thy possessions. Now prepare to die, for I must obey my father's command."

But Jacob begged his nephew to spare his life and not to commit such a sin before the Lord. "Take all the gold and silver I have," said he, "and leave me my life, so that the Lord will count it as a generous deed and bless thee." And God touched the heart of Eliphaz, so that he had pity with his uncle. He took, however, all the latter's possessions, leaving him quite poor, and returned to his father to Beer-Sheba. When Esau heard what had happened, he was very angry with his son for having allowed Jacob to escape. He nevertheless took all the gold and silver which Eliphaz and his men had brought.[2]

---

[1] *Sepher Hajashar*; *Yalkut*, § 115.
[2] *Genesis Rabba*, 68; *Sepher Hajashar*; see Lewner, *loc. cit.*, p. 134.

Now when Eliphaz had left him, Jacob prayed to the
Lord to help him in his misery: " When Eliezer, the steward
of my grandfather Abraham, came to Haran, he showed all
the signs of wealth and prosperity, whilst I am now poor and
no one will take any notice of me." And then he lifted up his
eyes and saw twelve stars shining brightly upon the firmament,
and he marvelled greatly. " How is it," thought Jacob, " that
I see stars shining during the day? No doubt, the Lord of the
Universe, of whom my father and grandfather have told me,
is beginning to show me His wonders." But this was not the
only event which caused the Patriarch to wonder. Many
miracles were wrought for him on that journey, when he
went forth from Beer-Sheba. From Beer-Sheba to mount
Moriah is a journey of two days, and yet in a few hours Jacob
was there, arriving at midday. He therefore decided to continue his journey, but suddenly the hours of the day were
shortened, and the sun went down before its time, because
the Lord desired to speak to him and to reveal unto him the
future.[1] And when Jacob saw that the sun had set in the west,
he took twelve stones, of the stones of that altar on which his
father had been bound, and placed them as a rampart against
the prowling beasts, and the other stones he set as a pillow
and went to sleep.

With regard to the stones, some say that Jacob took twelve
stones, corresponding to the twelve tribes, whilst others relate
that he took only three stones.[2] It is also related that the stones
had been set up by Adam as an altar, and that on it Abel
offered his sacrifice. After the deluge, Noah collected the
scattered stones and offered his sacrifice upon the altar. Abraham once more reared the altar which had been overthrown,
when he came to bind Isaac and to offer him as a burnt offering.[3]

[1] *Genesis Rabba*, 68; *Pirke de Rabbi Eliezer*, Ch. 35.
[2] *Pirke de Rabbi Eliezer*, Ch. 35; *Genesis Rabba*, 68; *Hullin*, 91a; *Sanhedrin*, 95b· see
also *Midrash Shokher Tob*, Ps. 91.   [3] *Pirke de Rabbi Eliezer, ibid.*

But the stones began to quarrel among themselves, for each one said: " It is upon me that this pious man will lay his head." And the Lord said: " For many years Jacob did not sleep at nights, but studied the law, and now he has set stones for his pillow and they, too, quarrel." He therefore commanded the stones to merge into one stone and to be as soft as a cushion.[1]

THE STRUGGLE OF THE CHILDREN

Fra biginning o þe werld
O suilk a strijf o childir tuin
Þat lai þer moder wamb wit-in;
Þair strut it was vu-stern stith,
Wit wrathli wrestes aiþer writh,
Bituix vu-born a batel blind,
Suilk an was ferli to find.
He þat on þe right side lai
Þe toþer him wraisted oft away;
And he þat lay a-pon þe left
Þe toþer oft his sted him reft.
Þe leuedi was ful ferli drad,
Als womman þat ful hard was stad.
Bot oure lauerd o suthfastnes
Had don hir in to sikernes,
Thoru his werrai prophecie,
Quat suld be paa childer vie,
O þair weird and o þair lijf,
And quat for besening bar þe strijf.

Cursor Mundi, Edited by Richard Morris. Early English
Text Society, 1874–92. Part I, p. 206, ll. 3457–3476.

[1] *Genesis Rabba*, 68; *Midrash Tanchuma*, section *Wayeze*; *Hullin*, 91; *Pirke de Rabbi Eliezer*, Ch. 35.

CHAPTER XXX

Love, Hate, and Strife, or the Troubles of a Father

The wonderful dream—The four kingdoms—The vision of the future—The stone of foundation—Love at the well—The beautiful cousin—The greedy uncle—The patient shepherd—The deceit of Laban—The promise of the neighbours—The banquet and the pawned valuables—The Teraphim—Laban's message to Esau—The protecting angels—The consecration of Levi—The embarrassment of the angel—The heavenly songs—The High-Priest in Heaven—Sammael, the tutelary angel of Esau—A brotherly kiss and bite—The troubles of a father—The abandoned baby—The death of a mother—The hatred of a brother.

SLEEPING with his head on the pillow of stones, Jacob saw in his dream a ladder fixed in the earth, its summit reaching to the height of Heaven. And he beheld the angels who had accompanied him ascending to make known to the angels on high that Jacob, the pious, whose likeness was on the Throne of Glory, had arrived.

And in that night the Lord showed Jacob the four kingdoms, their dominion and subsequent destruction. He showed him the prince of the kingdom of Babylon ascending seventy rungs, and descending, and He also showed him the prince of the kingdom of Media ascending fifty-two rungs and descending. He then showed him the prince of the kingdom of Greece who ascended 180 rungs of the ladder and then descended. Jacob thereupon saw the prince of the kingdom of Edom ascending, but not descending, for he was saying to himself: " I will ascend above the heights of the clouds, and be like the Most High."

But the Glory of the Lord stood above Jacob, the seven heavens were opened, the world was filled with dazzling light, and the Lord spoke to Jacob: " Fear not the prince of Edom, for the land thou art lying upon I will give to thy children, who will be as many as the dust of the earth." And in that moment the whole land of Palestine folded up and placed itself under Jacob's head, so that in later days his children would have a right to conquer it. Thereupon Jacob had a vision of the future. He saw Mount Sinai surrounded by flames, and Moses receiving the Law. He saw the Temple in its glory, and Israel living in a land flowing with milk and honey. Suddenly the vision changed, and he saw Jerusalem burning, and the sack of the Temple. And once more he saw, gathering from the four corners of the earth, Israel returning from exile to rebuild the Temple and re-establish its glory.[1]

Jacob rose up early in the morning in great fear and said: " The House of the Lord is in this place." Thereupon he went to gather the stones, but found that they had turned into one stone. The Lord then planted His right foot on the stone and sank it to the bottom of the depths, making it the keystone of the earth. It is therefore called the foundation stone, for from it all the earth was evolved and upon it the Sanctuary of the Lord stands.[2]

Jacob now left Bethel and in a short time he was at Haran. There he saw a well in a field, and a great stone laid upon the mouth of the well; three flocks were lying near it. Jacob asked the shepherds whether they knew Laban, the son of Bethuel, at Haran, and they said: " We know him well. A plague had broken out among his sheep and only a few had been left, and he had therefore dismissed his shepherds, entrusting the remainder of the flock to his daughter Rachel who is tending them.[3] Behold," they added, " here the young

[1] Genesis Rabba, 68, 69; Hullin, 91a; Pirke de Rabbi Eliezer, Ch. 35; Midrash Tanchuma, section Wayeze. [2] Pirke de Eliezer, Ch. 35; Midrash Tanchuma, ibid.
[3] Pirke de Rabbi Eliezer, Ch. 36: see also Lewner, loc. cit. pp. 140–141.

THE MEETING OF JACOB AND RACHEL

shepherdess cometh." Jacob hastened to roll away the stone
from the mouth of the well, and the water came up and spread
outside.[1] Jacob, when he saw Rachel coming, was glad indeed,
for she was beautiful. But he was also glad, because he knew
that he would now be prosperous. For whenever a man enters
a city and maidens come forth before him, his way is prosperous.
Thus it happened to Eliezer, the steward of Abraham; thus
it happened to Moses, when he came to Midian; thus it happened to Saul, when he acquired the sovereignty, and thus it
happened to Jacob.[2] And when Jacob had watered the sheep
of Laban, his uncle, he kissed Rachel and lifted up his voice
and wept. At that moment a prophetic vision came over him
and he knew that Rachel would die young, on the road, and
would not be buried in the double cave by his side.[3]

He thereupon told his cousin who he was, and that he had
come to stay with her father, and to marry one of his daughters.
" Thou canst not stay with my father," said Rachel, " for he
is cunning and deceitful." But Jacob assured her that the
Lord would be on his side and protect him against Laban.
The maiden thereupon went to inform her father of the arrival
of her cousin.

And when Laban heard the tidings of Jacob, how the
Lord had revealed Himself to him at Bethel, and what
power he had displayed at the well, rolling away the stone,
and how the water had risen and the well had overflowed,
he ran out, kissed and embraced him and led him into the
house.

Laban had also other reasons to rush out, embrace and
kiss his nephew. He said unto himself: " When Eliezer,
the steward of Abraham, came, he brought with him gold and
silver, pearls and precious stones, and now my nephew Jacob,
who is the favourite son of Rebekah, has come and no doubt

---

[1] *Tergum Jerushalmi Genesis*, 69, 10; *Genesis Rabba*, 70.
[2] *Pirke de Rabbi Eliezer*, Ch. 36.   [3] *Genesis Rabba*, 70.

he does not come empty-handed." When he noticed that Jacob had arrived on foot and had neither camels nor servants with him, Laban thought that perhaps all his wealth consisted in precious stones concealed on his person. He therefore hugged him, thus having an opportunity of feeling his pockets. But again he was disappointed. At last he kissed his nephew, thinking that perchance he had pearls and gems concealed under his tongue. Once more he was disappointed. And when, at last, Laban heard that Jacob had been robbed on his way by his nephew Eliphaz and that he was poor indeed, his enthusiasm abated, and he said to his nephew: " Stay with me a few days." [1]

Now Jacob loved Rachel, because she was beautiful, whilst the eyes of her elder sister Leah were weak and moist. And Jacob was informed by the neighbours that Leah's eyes were running because she had wept and prayed before the Lord that He would not destine her to be the wife of Esau the wicked. Jacob began to serve Laban seven years for his daughter Rachel. When seven years had passed, Laban gathered together all his neighbours, and thus he spoke to them: " My friends, well do you know that the Lord has blessed us all on account of Jacob. Now his seven years are at end; he will marry my daughter Rachel and leave this town, and then the blessing of the Lord, which we enjoyed on his account, will no longer be bestowed upon us and we will no longer prosper." Thus spoke Laban, and his neighbours grew sad, and asked anxiously:

" What shall we do, so as to prevent Jacob from leaving our city?" " I will tell you," said Laban; " I will deceive Jacob, for in the place of Rachel I will give him Leah, so that he will be obliged to serve me another seven years for Rachel." When Laban's friends heard these words, they greatly rejoiced, and approved his plan.

---

[1] *Genesis Rabba*, 70; *Pirke de Rabba Eliezer*, Ch. 36.

" Thou speakest well," they said.

" If such is your conviction," replied Laban, " then promise me that you will not reveal the secret to Jacob."

" We promise," said the men of the place.

But Laban, not content with their promise, asked them as a guarantee of their good faith to bring him valuables of gold and silver as a pledge that they would keep the secret until the morrow. The men of the town, not suspecting Laban's good faith, hastened to bring him their valuables as a pledge.

Laban at once pawned the things, bought wine and meat, and invited all the men of the town to a banquet and rejoicing. They ate and drank and rejoiced, making merry, singing songs, and shouting Ha-Lia-Ha-Lia (this is Lia), although Jacob never paid any attention to their allusions. When the neighbours came the next day to claim their valuables, Laban laughingly told them that they had enjoyed themselves last night at the banquet he had offered " on their account." The men of the town were compelled to redeem their possessions which Laban had pawned at the butcher's and the wine merchants and thus pay for the banquet. Henceforth, they called Laban no longer the son of Bethuel, but Laban the Deceiver.[1]

Jacob served another seven years for Rachel and six years for cattle which his father-in-law gave him, and then he fled to get away from Laban. On this occasion, his wife Rachel stole the image which Laban worshipped. This image, called Teraphim, was really the head of a man, a first born, which the worshipper had slain, pinched off his head and salted it with salt and balsam. The name of an unclean spirit and incantations were then written upon a plate of gold and placed under the tongue of this head. The head was then placed in the wall, lamps were lit in front of it, and the worshipper, bowing down before the head, asked it to tell him oracles.[2]

[1] *Genesis Rabba*, 70, 71.
[2] *Pirke de Rabbi Eliezer*, Ch. 36; *Sepher Hajashar*; *Yalkut, Genesis*, § 130; *Midrash Tanchuma*, section *Wayeze*; see also *Targum Jerushalmi, Genesis*, 31, 19.

As Laban had not been able to discover his Teraphim, he kissed his daughters and grandchildren and returned home. He was, however, far from reconciled, and still brooded mischief. On his arrival at Padan-Aram, he immediately dispatched his son Beor, accompanied by ten men, to his nephew Esau, with the following message: " Twenty years ago thy brother Jacob came to me naked and poor. I took him in, treated him well and gave him my two daughters as wives. He prospered exceedingly, thanks to my kindness and generosity, and he now possesses gold and silver, camels, asses, sheep, and oxen. But now he has left my house secretly, stealing my gods and never allowing me even to kiss my daughters and grandchildren before their departure. I advise thee, therefore, to go out with thy men against Jacob and slay him."

When Esau received this message, he remembered how Jacob had obtained his father's blessing, and his anger was very violent. He armed his followers and servants, and went out against Jacob at the head of an army of three hundred and forty men. But the messengers of Laban, upon leaving Esau, proceeded to Canaan and informed Rebekah of what had occurred. In haste the fond mother sent out seventy-two men to stand by Jacob in case of need.

They met Jacob and delivered to him the following message from his mother: " When thou wilt meet Esau, instead of waging war, offer him presents and beg him to make peace with thee. Perchance, he will be moved by thy prayers and presents." Jacob promised to listen to the words of his mother and to follow her advice. When he reached the ford of Jabbok, he saw 120,000 angels coming to meet him, and he sent out as many as he judged necessary to go to Esau's encounter.[1]

The nearer, however, Jacob came to Seir, the land of Esau, the greater became his fear that his brother's enmity and

[1] *Genesis Rabba*, 74; *Sepher Hajashar*.

anger had not yet abated. He prayed therefore to the Lord
to protect him, and the Most High granted his prayer. The
Creator of the Universe sent four angels to protect the Patriarch.
At the head of one thousand horsemen each angel, in turn,
met Esau and his men. Shouting aloud: " We are the servants
of Jacob," they swept along, fell upon the troop that accompanied
Esau, and dispersed it. Fear and trembling seized Esau, and
he exclaimed:

" I am the brother of Jacob, and am hastening to meet
my brother whom I have not seen for twenty years. Why
are you thus treating me and my men?"

" Hadst thou not been the brother of Jacob, we would
have destroyed thee long ago," replied the angels.[1]

In the meantime, Jacob, who was unaware of the help
rendered to him by the celestials, prepared rich presents
which he sent to his brother Esau, to appease his anger. Jacob
was indeed like a man who had fled from a lion and was about
to meet a bear.[2] The lion was Laban, and the bear was Esau.
But Jacob prayed to the Lord and thus he said: " Sovereign
of all the worlds! Thou didst say unto me ' Return unto the
land of thy fathers, and I will be with thee.' And now my
brother Esau has come ready to slay me and my house."

But the Lord sent down the angel Michael to protect and
deliver Jacob, and he appeared to the Patriarch like a man.
It happened at the ford of Jabbok. " Hast thou not promised
once," said the angel to Jacob, " to give a tenth of all that thou
dost possess to the Lord?" " I did," replied the Patriarch,
and at once took all the cattle which he had brought from
Padan-Aram and gave a tithe of them, amounting to 550
animals. Having done this, Jacob wished to cross the ford of
Jabbok, but once more the angel Michael detained him, and
thus he spoke: " Thou hast ten sons, but thou hast not given
a tithe of them to the Lord." Again the Patriarch agreed.

---

[1] *Sepher Hajashar.*   [2] *Amos,* 5, 19.

He immediately set aside the four first born of the four mothers, and there remained eight children.[1] He thereupon counted from Simeon, finishing with Benjamin who was still in his mother's womb, and then started again to count from the beginning, so that Levi was the tenth. He accordingly set Levi aside as the tithe and consecrated him to the Lord.[2]

The angel Michael thereupon took up Levi and brought him up before the Lord and the Throne of Glory.[3] " Sovereign of all the worlds," said Michael, " this is Thy lot."

Thereupon the Lord of the Universe stretched out His right hand and blessed Levi, and thus He said: " Thy sons shall minister on earth before me, just as the angels are ministering in Heaven."

Michael then further spake and said: " Sovereign of all the worlds, Thou hast blessed Levi and his sons, but those who serve the king have no time to cultivate their fields and earn their sustenance."

And the Lord replied: " The sons of Levi will possess no land in the country which I shall give to the children of Israel, but provision of their food will be given to them, for they shall eat the offerings of the Lord, and all the tithes will be given to them." [4]

The angel was no longer able to hurt Jacob, but he wrestled with him until dawn broke, and the first rays of the sun tinted with orient hues the eastern sky.

Now Michael had been commanded not to leave Jacob until the latter had given him permission to do so. When day broke, the angel therefore asked Jacob to let him go, for the time had arrived when angels offer praise to the Most High and he must be there to lead the chant. As Jacob refused to grant his permission, Michael began to sing the praises from

---

[1] See Bechoroth, 53b, where it is said that the first born is excluded from the law of tithe.
[2] *Pirke de Rabbi Eliezer*, Ch. 37; *Genesis Rabba*, 70; *Book of Jubilees*, 32, 3.
[3] See *Testament of Twelve Patriarchs, Testament of Levi*, 2, 6.
[4] *Pirke de Rabbi Eliezer*, Ch. 37.

the earth. Thereupon the angels from on high came down
and bade Michael rise up to the Throne of Glory and chant the
morning hymn, but Michael could not leave before Jacob had
given him permission. He blessed Jacob and changed his
name from Jacob to Israel.[1] But the Lord rebuked his ministering angel for having touched the hollow of Jacob's thigh.

"Why didst thou hurt my ministering priest Jacob?"
asked the Lord. "Sovereign of all the worlds," replied the
angel, "am I not Thy High-Priest, ministering unto Thee?"
"Thou art my High-Priest in Heaven," replied the Lord,
"but Jacob is my High-Priest on earth." Thereupon Michael
begged his colleague Raphael to heal Jacob, and Raphael
complied with the request.[2] Although he had blessed him,
the angel Michael refused to reveal unto the Patriarch the
future. "If I do this," he said, "I shall be expelled from
Heaven for 138 years, even as the angels who announced
the destruction of Sodom had been expelled."[3]

Another version of this legend runs as follows: Sammael,
he who is Satan, and not Michael, wrestled with Jacob at the
ford of Jabbok. Sammael is the guardian angel of Esau and
Edom, and he made up his mind to destroy Jacob on that
night at the ford of Jabbok. He strove and contended with
him, but could do the Patriarch no harm. The Patriarch had
ferried over his wives and children and all his cattle, when
he remembered that he had left behind some of his possessions.
His servants had worked hard and were tired, and the Patriarch
made up his mind to go over himself and fetch his possessions.
Here he met the tutelary angel of Esau who appeared to him
in the guise of a shepherd, and who tried to harm Jacob. The
angel touched the hollow of his thigh, so that he halted afterwards. When dawn broke, Sammael begged the Patriarch to
let him go, but Jacob refused until he had blessed him. "When

---

[1] *Pirke de Rabbi Eliezer*, Ch. 37. Cf. *Genesis Rabba*, 78. See Friedlaender's remark in
his edition of *Pirke de Rabbi Eliezer*, p. 282.
[2] *Midrash Abkhir*, quoted in *Yalkut Shimeoni*.   [3] *Yalkut Rubeni*; *Genesis Rabba*, 78.

the angels came to visit my grandfather," said Jacob, "they never left him until they had blessed him." "Those angels," replied the tutelary angel of Edom, "were specially sent to bless thy grandfather, but I did not come to bless thee." [1]

Lifting up his eyes, Jacob saw his brother approaching with four hundred men of war. He divided his children and wives and went out before them, praying to the Lord, and bowing to the earth seven times, but it was to the Lord that he bowed.

Now when Esau perceived Jacob, his anger again rose up. Remembering, however, the defeat and humiliation inflicted upon him by the horsemen led by the angels, who proclaimed themselves the servants of Jacob, he said in his heart: "I will not try to slay Jacob with bow and arrows, but will bite him with my teeth, suck his blood and thus slay him." And then he ran up, embraced Jacob, and falling upon his neck, tried to bite him. Jacob's neck, however, became like marble, and as soon as Esau tried to bite Jacob, he broke his teeth. And he wept on the neck of Jacob, because of the pain of his teeth.[2] Esau pretended now to make peace with his brother, and the latter proceeded to Shechem.

Jacob never met Esau until the death of Isaac, when the sons came to bury the father. On this occasion, Jacob bought from Esau for a considerable sum his right to a burial place in the double cave of Machpelah, which Esau once more claimed at the funeral of his brother.[3]

Jacob and his family now settled at Shechem, where they prospered exceedingly. The Patriarch possessed over a million heads of cattle, and thousands of sheep-dogs. Some say that he had innumerable sheep and 600,000 sheep-dogs. He was not allowed, however, to end his days in peace at Shechem.

[1] *Midrash Abkhir*, quoted in *Yalkut Shimeoni*; *Genesis Rabba*, 78; *Hullin*, 91a.
[2] *Sabbath*, 30a; *Genesis Rabba*, 78; *Midrash Tanchuma*, section *Wayishlach*; cf. *Midrash Haggadol*, col. 517; *Pirke de Rabbi Eliezer*, Ch. 37.
[3] *Sepher Hajashar*; *Tractate Sopherim*, 21, 8.

His daughter Dinah was dishonoured by Shechem, the son of Hamor, and subsequently gave birth to a daughter who received the name of Asenath.

Jacob was greatly worried on account of this illegitimate child. Seeing that his sons hated her and wished to kill her, he wrote her name and the name of his family upon a gold plate, placed it on her neck and sent her away. Thereupon the angel Michael came down and led her to the frontier of Egypt. Potiphar, the captain of Pharaoh's guard, found her. As his wife Zuleika was barren, he adopted the baby and brought her up.[1] She subsequently married Joseph.

Sometime afterwards news was brought to Jacob that his mother Rebekah had died. Rebekah, at her own request, was buried very quietly at night, so that no one was present at her funeral. The reason of her request was that Jacob was away and only Esau near. People, thought the dying mother, would point to her son and say: " Here is the bier of the woman who bore the wicked Esau." [2] The clouds alone shed tears upon the mother's grave, and the night wind sighed and sobbed.

Jacob now decided to go and visit his old father Isaac at Hebron. On the road to Ephrath, Rachel died and was buried there. A prophetic vision had come over the Patriarch, and he knew that one day his descendants would be driven into captivity along that road. " When my children will pass this way," thought the Patriarch, " crying and lamenting, they will need Rachel's intercession. In her tomb she will hear their cries, implore the Lord's mercy and plead for the restoration of Israel."[3]

When he returned from Hebron, and again settled in Shechem, Jacob once more had to wage a long and terrible war against the princes of Canaan who were jealous of his

---

[1] *Midrash Abkhir*, quoted in *Yalkut Shimeoni*, § 146: see also *Sepher Rasiel*, p. 7a; *Pirke de Rabbi Eliezer*, Ch. 38.
[2] *Genesis Rabba*, 81: see Lewner, *loc. cit.*, pp. 166–167.
[3] *Yalkut Shimeoni*; *Genesis Rabba*, 82; *Midrash Agadah* to *Genesis*, 35, 19; *Midrash Threni*, § 25: see Lewner, *loc. cit.*, pp. 167–168.

power and prosperity. A long and weary war it was, wherein the sons of Jacob, and particularly Judah, gave proofs of their courage, bravery, and strength. Esau, too, was still brooding mischief and waiting for an opportunity to fall upon his brother. When he heard that Leah had died and that his brother and his sons were mourning their loss, he thought the moment propitious to carry out his plan. He came with a great army and attacked Jacob. In vain did the latter plead from the wall of his fortress, and not until Judah had hit Esau in his right loin with an arrow, did the latter's followers draw back. The greatest blow, however, came to the fond father when he suddenly lost his beloved son Joseph.[1]

[1] Cf. also for the entire chapter, Bin Gorion, *Die Sagen der Juden*, Vol. II, notes on pp. 430–432, sections XXXV–XLIV.

BIBLIOGRAPHY

I. WORKS IN HEBREW

Abot di Rabbi Nathan, ed. Schechter, Vienna, 1887.
Agadath Bereshith, ed. Buber, Cracow, 1903.
Alphabetum Siracidis, ed. Steinschneider, Berlin, 1858.
Bachja ben Asher, *Commentary to the Pentateuch*, Venice, 1549.
Ein Jacob, by Jacob Ibn Habib, Vilna.
Emek Hamelekh, Amsterdam, 1653.
Gedullath Moshe, Amsterdam, 1754.
Horovitz, Ch. M., *Agada Agadoth*, Berlin, 1881.
Jellinek, A., *Beth-Hamidrash*, 6 vols., Leipzig and Vienna, 1853–77.
Josippon (Josephus Gorionides), ed. Breithaupt, Halle, 1707; ed. Amsterdam, 1771.
Kalonymos ben Kalonymos, *Iggeret Baale Hayyim*, transl. by Julius Landsberger, 1882.
Kol Bo (*Sepher Halikkutim*), Venice, 1547.
Levita, Elia, *Tishbi*, Isny, 1541.
Luria, Isaac, *Sepher Hagilgulim*, Frankfurt a/M., 1684.
Menachem Recanati, *Commentary to the Pentateuch*, Venice 1545.
Menorath ha-Maor, Mantua, 1563.
Midrash Agada, ed. Buber, Vienna, 1894.
Midrash Bamidbar Rabba (*Numbers Rabba*).
Midrash Bereshith Rabba (*Genesis Rabba*).
Midrash Debarim Rabba (*Deuteronomy Rabba*).
Midrash Haggadol, ed. Schechter, Cambridge, 1902.
Midrash Koheleth Rabba (*Eccles. Rabba*).
Midrash Lekach Tob, ed. Buber, Vilna, 1884.
Midrash Shemuel (Samuel), ed. Buber, Cracow, 1893.
Midrash Shemoth Rabba (*Exodus Rabba*).
Midrash Shir Hashirim (*Song of Songs*).
Midrash Tanchuma (also called *Jelamdenu*), 1865.
Midrash Tanchuma, ed. Buber, 1865.
Midrash Tehillim, or *Shokher Tob*, ed. Buber, Vilna, 1891.
Nachmanides, *Commentary to the Pentateuch*, 1831.
Othioth de Rabbi Akiba, Venice, 1546.
Pirke de Rabbi Eliezer, Venice, 1544; and Lemberg, 1867.

359

Seder Olam Rabba, Vilna, 1897.
Sepher Hajashar, Prague, 1840. (French translation in Migne, *Dictionnaire des Apocryphes*, vol. 2.)
Sepher Rasiel, Amsterdam, 1700.
Shalsheleth Hakabbalah, by Gedalja Ibn Jachia, ed. Amsterdam, 1697.
Talmud Babli (Babylonian Talmud).

The Babylonian Talmud is classified under six orders or series:

    I. *Seder Zeraim* (Seeds).
    II. *Seder Moed* (Festivals).
    III. *Seder Nashim* (Women).
    IV. *Seder Nezikin* (Injuries).
    V. *Seder Kodashin* (Holy Things).
    VI. *Seder Taharot* (Purifications).

These sections, or *sedarim*, are divided into treatises or tractates (Massictot) of which there are seventy-one in all, including the minor treatises. Their order is as follows:

I. *Seder Zeraim.*

    1. *Berachoth* (Blessings).
    2. *Peah* (Corner).
    3. *Demai* (Doubtful).
    4. *Kilaiyim* (Heterogeneous).
    5. *Shebiith* (Sabbatical Year).
    6. *Terumot* (Offerings).
    7. *Maaserot* (Tithes).
    8. *Maaser Sheni* (Second Tithe).
    9. *Hallah* (Cake).
    10. *Orlah* (Foreskin of the trees).
    11. *Bikkurim* (First Fruits).

II. *Moed.*

    1. *Shabbat* (Sabbath).
    2. *Erubin* (Mingling).
    3. *Pesachim* (Passover Festivals).
    4. *Bezah* (Egg).
    5. *Hagigah* (Feasting).
    6. *Moed Katan* (Half Feasts).
    7. *Rosh-ha-Shanah* (New Year).
    8. *Taanit* (Fasting).
    9. *Yoma* (Day).
    10. *Succah* (Booth).
    11. *Shekalim* (Shekels).
    12. *Megillah* (Esther Scroll).

III. *Nashim.*

    1. *Yebamot* (Widows who are obliged to contract a Levirate marriage.)
    2. *Ketubot* (Marriage Contracts).

3. *Kiddushin* (Betrothal).
4. *Gittin* (Documents).
5. *Nedarim* (Vows).
6. *Nazir* (Nazarite).
7. *Sotah* (Woman suspected of adultery).

IV. *Nezikin*.

1. *Baba Kamma* (First Gate).
2. *Baba Mezia* (Middle Gate).
3. *Baba Batra* (Last Gate).
4. *Abodah Zarah* (Idolatrous Worship).
5. *Sanhedrin* (Court of Law).
6. *Makkot* (Blows).
7. *Shebuot* (Oaths).
8. *Horayot* (Decisions).
9. *Eduyot* (Evidence).
10. *Abot*, or *Pirke Abot* (Sayings of the Fathers).

V. *Kodashin*.

1. *Zebahim* (Sacrifice).
2. *Menahot* (Meat Offerings).
3. *Bekorot* (First Born).
4. *Hullin* (Profane slaughtering of non-consecrated animals).
5. *Arakin* (Estimations).
6. *Temurah* (Exchange).
7. *Keritot* (Extirpations).
8. *Meilah* (Trespass).
9. *Kinnim* (Birds' Nests).
10. *Tamid* (Daily morning and evening burnt offering).
11. *Middot* (Measures).

VI. *Taharot*.

1. *Niddah* (Menstruous woman).
2. *Kelim* (Utensils).
3. *Oholot* (Tents).
4. *Negaïm* (Leprosy).
5. *Parah* (Red Heifer).
6. *Taharot* (Purities).
7. *Mikvaot* (Ritual Baths).
8. *Makshirin* (Predisposings).
9. *Zabim* (Sufferers from discharges).
10. *Tebulyom* (Ablutions of the day).
11. *Yadayim* (Hands).
12. *Okatzin* (Stalks).

In the editions of the Talmud after Abot usually follow Abot de Rabbi Nathan and the other minor treatises: *Sopherim* (Scribes); *Ebel Rabbati* (Great Mourning); also called *Semakhot* (Joy); *Kallah* (The Bride);

Derekh Eretz (The Way of the World); *Perek Hashalom* (A chapter on Peace); *Gerim* (Proselytes); *Cuthim* (Cuthites); *Abadim* (Slaves).

Talmud Jerushalmi (Palestinian Talmud) Jitomir, 1860–1867 (Schwab's transl., Paris, 1883–1889.)
Tana debe Eliahu, also called *Seder Eliahu Rabba,* ed. Friedmann, 1902.
Targum Jerushalmi (Palestinian Targum).
Wertheimer, S. A., *Bathe Midrashot,* Jerusalem, 1893.
Yalkut, also called *Yalkut Shimeoni,* Vilna, 1898.
Yalkut Reubeni, 1680.

II. OTHER WORKS

Abulfeda, *Historia Ante-Islamica,* ed. Fleischer, Leipzig, 1831.
Bacher, W., *Die Agada der Palestinensischen Amoräer,* 3 vols., 1892-1899.
——*Die Agada der Tanaiten,* 2 vols., 1884–1899.
Bartolocci, *Bibliotheca Magna Rabbinica,* 4 vols., Romae, 1675–1693.
Basnage, J., *Histoire des Juifs,* 15 vols., La Haye, 1716.
Beer, *Das Leben Abrahams,* Leipzig, 1859.
Bergel, J., *Mythologie der alten Hebräer,* 2 vols., Leipzig, 1882.
Bezold, C., *Die Schatzhöhle (The Cave of Treasures),* 1885.
Bin Gorion, *Die Sagen der Juden,* Vol. I, 1919.
Bischoff, E., *Babylonisch-Astrales, Ein Weltbild des Talmud und Midrash,* Leipzig, 1907.
——*Die Elemente der Kabbalah,* 2 vols., Berlin, 1913.
Braun, J., *Naturgeschichte der Sage,* 2 vols., Leipzig, 1864–1865.
Bundehesh, The, transl. by West (Sacred Books of the East, Vol. V.).
Buxtorf, J., *Synagoga Judaica,* 1604.
Calmet, Dom Augustin, *Dictionary of the Holy Bible,* 5 vols., London, 1830.
Cassel, P., *Der Phœnix u. seine Aera,* Berlin.
Cedrenus, G., (in *Byzantinæ Hist. Scriptores,* ed. Paris, 1645–1711).
Charles, R. H., *The Book of Enoch,* Oxford, 1893.
—— *The Book of Jubilees,* Oxford, 1895, London, 1917.
—— *The Testaments of the Twelve Patriarchs,* Oxford, 1908. (See Translations of Early Documents, I, 5, London, 1917).
Charles and Morfill, *The Secrets of Enoch.*
Collin de Plancy, *Légendes de l'Ancien Testament,* Paris, 1861.
Edersheim, A., *The Life and Times of Jesus the Messiah,* 2 vols., London, 1883.
Eisenmenger, J. A., *Entdecktes Judentum,* 2 vols., 1700.
Eutychius, *Annales* (Chaplet of Pearls), Oxford, 1658.
Expository Times, The, 1895.
Fabricius, J. A., *Codex Pseudoepigraphicus, Vet. Test.,* 1722–1723.
Fleck, F. F., *Wissenschaftliche Reise durch d. südl. Deutschland,* Leipzig 1835–1838.
Frank, A., *La Kabbale,* Paris, 1843.
Frankels' Zeitschrift, 1846.
Friedlaender, G., *Pirke de Rabbi Eliezer,* London, 1916.
Fuchs, *Das Leben Adams und Evas* (in Kautzsch, *Apokryphen und Pseudoepigraphen* Vol. II.)

Gaster, M., *The Chronicles of Jerahmeel*, London, 1899.
—— *Roumanian Bird and Beast Stories*, London, 1915.
Gesta Romanorum, ed. Oesterley, Berlin, 1882.
Geiger, A., *Was hat Mohammed aus dem Judentum genommen*, Bonn, 1833.
Ginzberg, L., *Die Haggada bei den Kirchenvätern*, Berlin, 1900.
Görres, J., *Mythen-geschichte der asiatischen Welt*, 1810.
Graesse, J. G. T., *Gesta Romanorum*, Leipzig, 1905.
Grünbaum, M., *Gesammelte Aufsätze zur Sprache und Sagenkunde*, Berlin,
    1901. (See also *Zeitschrift der Deutsch-Morgenländischen Gesell-
    schaft*, Vol. 31).
—— *Neue Beiträge zur semistischen Sagenkunde*, Berlin, 1893.
Gunter, H., *Die Christliche Legende des Abendlandes*, 1910.
Hamburger, J., *Real-encyclopädie für Bibel und Talmud*, 5 vols., 1870–1892.
Hastings, *Dictionary of the Bible*, 5 vols., Edinburgh, 1898.
Herbelot de Molainville, *Bibliothèque Orientale*, 6 vols., Paris, 1781–1783.
Hershon, P. I., *Treasures of the Talmud*, London, 1882.
—— *A Talmudic Miscellany*, London, 1880.
James, M. R., *The Testament of Abraham* (in Robinson's *Texts and Studies*,
    Cambridge, 1892).
Jastrow, M., *Dictionary of the Targumim*, 2 vols., 1895.
Jeremias, A., *Das alte Testament im Lichte des alten Orients*, 1904.
Jewish Quarterly Review, Tomes VII, XI.
Journal of the Royal Asiatic Society, 1893.
Josephus, *Antiquities* (Whiston's).
Kautzsch, E., *Die Apokryphen und Pseudoepigraphen d. A. T.*, 2 vols, 1900.
Kazwini, *Cosmography* (Ethés' transl.).
Kohut, A., *Zur jüdischen Angelologie und Demonologie* (*Abhandlungen der
    D. M. G.*, 1886).
Koran, The.
Landesberger, J., *Iggeret Baale Hayyim*, 1882.
Lenormant, F., *Les Origines de l'Histoire*, 2 vols., Paris, 1882.
Mackenzie, D. A., *Indian Myth and Legend*, London.
Mahabharata, The (Roy's transl.).
Malan, S. C., *The Book of Adam and Eve*, London, 1882.
Meyer, W., *Vita Adae et Evae* (in *Abhandlungen der bayrischen Akademe
    der Wissenschaften*, Phil.-philosoph. Classe, XIV, 3, 1878).
Monatsschrift für Literatur und Wissenschaft des Judentums, vol. 43.
Proceedings of the Society of Biblical Archæology, Vol. 9.
Raymondus Martinus, *Pugio Fidei*, ed. Leipzig.
Robinson, *Texts and Studies*, Cambridge, 1892.
Rothschild, J. de (ed.), *Le Mistère du Viel Testament*, 6 vols., Paris, 1877.
Suidas, *Lexicon*, ed. 1854.
Tabari, *Chronique de*, by H. Zotenberg, Paris, 1867–1874.
Tischendorff, *Apocalypses Apocryphae*, 1866.
Tisdall, W. St. Clair, *The Original Sources of the Quran*, London, 1905.
Weil, G., *Biblische Legenden der Muselmänner*, Frankfurt a/M., 1845.
Zeitschrift der Deutsch-Morgenländischen Gesellschaft, Vols. 25 and 31.
Zeitschrift für Historische Theologie.